# Human Evolution

# Human Evolution

## A Guide to the Debates

*Brian Regal*

Santa Barbara, California    Denver, Colorado    Oxford, England

Regal, Brian.
    Human evolution : a guide to the debates / Brian Regal.
        p. cm. — (Controversies in science)
    Includes bibliographical references and index.
    ISBN 1-85109-418-0 (hardback : alk. paper.) — ISBN 1-85109-423-7 (e-book)
    1. Human evolution—Philosophy.  2. Human evolution—Religious aspects.
    3. Human beings—Origin.  4. Human beings—Migrations.  I. Title.  II. Series.


    GN281.R412313  2004
    599.93'8–dc22                                                    2004022585


08   07   06   05   04        10  9  8  7  6  5  4  3  2  1

This book is also available on the World Wide Web as an eBook. Visit abc-clio.com for details.

ABC-CLIO, Inc.
130 Cremona Drive, P.O. Box 1911
Santa Barbara, California 93116-1911

3 3131 00083 8916

This book is printed on acid-free paper ∞.

Manufactured in the United States of America

*To my mother, Elizabeth,*
*My sister, Celeste,*
*And my father, Henry,*
*Who was my hero*

# Contents

IIwrote most of this book at the New York Public Library in the two years following the terror attacks of 2001. I had just begun a new teaching position (September 11 was my first day). On the commuter train into Manhattan I and my fellow passengers watched in horror as the towers burned. That day started me thinking about human evolution in a new light. How, I asked myself, could humans have evolved to the point where we were capable of performing such acts upon one another? The story of human evolution shows that we descended from the same place. We are all one big family, not alien forms to one another. Yet we can justify unspeakable horrors in the name of different religions, politics, revenge, self-defense, patriotism, national security, and ethnic hatred—a whole laundry list of reasons. How could our highly cognitive brains, the products of millions of years of evolution, accept the murder of thousands as a legitimate way of achieving our ends? Could a study of how we learned where we came from and how we evolved explain any of this?

As I watched the towers come down (towers I had watched go up as a kid across the river in New Jersey), I wondered whether the study of the history of human evolution was a waste of time. I thought how monogenesis versus polygenesis, creationism versus evolution, the age of the KBS Tuff, and the relationship between the Neanderthals and Cro-Magnons suddenly seemed incredibly inconsequential arguments. In the end, however, I have to think that they are not inconsequential, that the study of our origins and the various debates and arguments that have raged over them can help tell us something useful about ourselves. Watching my fellow New Yorkers and fellow Americans, and my fellow humans around the world, react to that day, I was comforted by the notion that evolution had created heroes as well as villains and that whatever our story turns out to be, we used that advanced cognitive power, grasping hands, and upright posture to make it a worthwhile one.

I have several people to thank in putting this project together. The content of this book was inspired in part by my participation in the 2001 International Summer Academy on Human Origins I was invited to attend at the Max Planck Institute for the History of Science in Berlin, Germany.

During those two weeks in August I was privileged to spend time talking about human origins with professionals in the field as well as many up-and-coming young scholars from across North America and Europe. Robert Proctor, Pat Shipman, Ian Tattersall, Martin Rudwick, and others, as well as new scholars like Anna Märker, Olof Ljungström, Jeremy Vetter, and Anne Katrine Gjerloff, debated many of the same questions discussed in this book. Some of them—Grace Yen Shen, Juliet Burba, and Holly Dunsworth—were kind enough to comment on different parts of the manuscript and guide me in the right direction when I got lost (though I take full responsibility for any factual mistakes). I would also like to thank Kevin Downing for helping to get the whole project rolling. At ABC-CLIO, Art Stickney and his staff were invaluable in keeping the project together and having it turn out as well as it did. Thanks to Jason Brunson for helping with some research and for doing the transcriptions of many of the original texts. Also thanks to fellow travelers Velma Dinkely and Daria Morgandorffer.

And always, finally, Lisa Nocks. I have long since run out of words to describe how important she is to me.

# Introduction: Difficult Ancestry

All families have them, those relatives and ancestors whose antics, predilections, or appearance make them difficult for us to accept: Uncle Harry who always told the off-color jokes, Aunt Agnes who drank, your great-grandfather whose photo showed that he just looked weird. They are the relatives others talk about in whispers and prefer to forget that they were relatives at all. The greater human family has its strange relatives as well—beings whose looks or behavior have made us uncomfortable or whose history we could not quite explain. The study of the evolution and origins of the human race is one long story of trying to make sense of, and come to terms with, this difficult ancestry. No matter how much we may not like them, our difficult ancestors will always be ours. No matter how much Aunt Agnes drinks, she is still our aunt.

While in the 1700s Western philosophers began to question the Genesis story of the Bible, the modern search for the human race's origins began in the 1830s and 1840s. Bones and artifacts were being discovered that seemed to suggest humans had been around much longer than anyone suspected. Almost immediately, controversies and arguments broke out over the validity of these relics and what they meant: Were they really human? How old were they? And how would these discoveries affect our spiritual selves? These arguments continue to this day. There is no aspect of paleoanthropology—the study of ancient humans—that is not controversial. This book is the story of the search for our ancestors and the fights that have arisen from that search.

The question then becomes, why all the controversy? The study of human origins reaches down into the heart of who we are and who we think we are; it questions our very identity, our very existence. The origins of horses, quasars, radio waves, or mountain ranges are argued over, but the origin of ourselves strikes a much deeper and more personal chord. There may be no real answer to why we get so worked up over human evolution, but it may have to do with the relation between science and religion. All cultures around the world from the beginning of time have had beliefs and legends about where we came from. They are stories based primarily upon supernatural belief and notions handed down from past generations. These stories soothed people's feelings, made them feel good about themselves, made them feel special, made them feel that in a world of chaos, danger, and dread, a greater being, a creator, a god or gods, was looking out for us and seeing to our welfare. These beliefs gave much-needed comfort. The rise of modern science, however, began chipping away at that comfort. In the Western tradition, the sticking point came because of the idea that God put humans in a special, exalted place close to him at the top of the cosmic pile. For Christians in particular, but also for Jews, Muslims, and others, evolution forced this question: Was man an angel or an ape? Answers put forward by some troubled many—and deeply.

Taken in the aggregate, the search for the origins of humanity is in part a philosophical endeavor along with being an empirical and rationally scientific one. Even the fossil hunter's discoveries and radiometric dating ultimately beg such questions. Are we the products of the random throw of cosmic dice, left to fend for ourselves in a universe vast and cool and unsympathetic, or are we the offspring of the warm breath of life exhaled by a grand creator who placed us in a garden? Or is it a combination of both? Or neither? All these questions are attempts to find the ultimate answer to the question of who we are and what our place in the universe is. T. H. Huxley, the British author of the 1863 book *Man's Place in Nature,* understood perhaps better than anyone what was at stake, argued that if humans really were the products of a materialist process, if there was no higher power looking after us (and he was not entirely convinced that there was not one), this might not be so bad. If there was no God, nothing to give meaning to our lives, nothing to give us purpose, then it was our moral responsibility to give ourselves meaning and purpose, and the ability to do such a thing or even contemplate doing it was what made us human.

It must be remembered, however, that science was not originally in such an antagonistic position to religious belief. Indeed, most early naturalists were deeply religious people who sought to use science to support and bolster religious belief. By the end of the 1800s, this position was growing more and more difficult to hold. Science was everywhere undermining religion by the very nature of its discoveries about how the universe worked. Religion and spirituality were growing quaint and old-fashioned or even dangerous to the modern way of thinking, with its notions of progress and scientific authority.

There were several elements that contributed to the resistance to the idea of human evolution in Western circles in particular. First and foremost was the Genesis story of the Bible. For many, this account was all that was needed to explain the origin of humans, so why bother with anything else? That God created Adam and Eve as the first humans was a concept that stood firm for more than two thousand years. Another obstacle was our relationship to the primates. Few were comfortable with the idea that we were at best cousins to and at worst children of chattering monkeys and grunting apes. It is interesting to speculate how people would have reacted to evolution if the apes had not been so, well, apish. The apparent stability of the human form was another stumbling block for transmutationists. The oldest civilizations on earth, from the Babylonians to the Egyptians, left pictorial representations of themselves. They were no different anatomically from people of the modern era. If evolution really worked, why was there no visible change even after thousands of years? Finally, in the early days of human antiquity studies, there was very little physical evidence to base theories on. There was nothing proevolutionists could point to conclusively to say, this proves it.

That said, arguments over human evolution were never solely between the religious and the secular. There was much contention between scientists over the analysis of fossils, genetics, rock strata, and related areas. The mainstream world of biology and paleoanthropology accepted that humans evolved from other forms but quarreled over some of the details of that process. In addition to the normal give and take of intellectual inquiry there have been misinterpretations of material, rushes to judgment, animosity between personalities, and outright fraud in the search for humankind's family history. Most of the disagreements in this book were and are between scientists and have nothing to do with religion or metaphysics.

This book will discuss the questions of human evolution, both broadly defined and sharply focused. It is split into ten chapters that run in rough chronological order (from the eighteenth century to the present), each with a basic theme. It will cover the topic from a Western point of view, since much of the work done on the subject of human evolution has come from the West. Also, this is not a science book; it is a work of history. I am not attempting to prove evolution (though I admit I support the evolutionary point of view). I have tried not to favor one school of thought over another. The purpose of this book is to discuss the various controversies involved in charting the evolutionary past of our species and the history of paleoanthropology.

The term *human evolution* refers here to both the mechanics of how humans descended from different species and their protohuman and primate ancestors as well as the course of those changes over time. The term *human* is far more complex. One argument in paleo-anthropology is how one determines what "human" is. Modern *Homo sapiens* were called human, but there was much debate over just where the demarcation line between human and nonhuman existed (this debate begins in chapter 5). The differences in terms here are subtle but important to the overall discussion.

Much of this book is written in narrative form, but a word should be mentioned about the pitfalls of such an approach. The concept of narrative has fallen in and out of favor with historians over time. From the 1960s through the 1980s, it was seen as passé, unscholarly, and unscientific. Indeed, although the narrative form has regained popularity in the late twentieth and early twenty-first centuries, it is still looked down upon by some purists. As this book deals with scientific discovery, a reliance on chronology is important. Also, as it is written for a nonspecialist audience, the narrative form gives readers a point of reference for the action taking place and the ideas being formed. This book covers a wide range of people, places, and ideas over four hundred years or so. Therefore, some structure is needed to maintain a level of continuity. The first three chapters follow events roughly from the late 1600s through the early twentieth century. They are followed by an alternating series of chapters dealing with conceptual ideas rather than a simple chronology with more strictly chronological chapters to bring the narrative to some kind of conclusion. I have separated these broader issues from the body of the narrative simply so that closer attention can be paid, not as an indication of genuine separateness. Issues such as what our ancestors looked or behaved like or how they acquired intelligence were deeply woven into the fabric of human evolution studies from the start. My narrative structure, by necessity, is therefore artificial, an arrangement I the storyteller have imposed upon the actual chronology of events so that I might tell the story more clearly.

But narrative can give a false sense of connection between various people, actions, and ideas that may not actually exist. Simply because something occurred in 1830, for example, does not mean it led to what happened in 1840. Scholars have learned that history is not a simple linear sequence of events leading from *A* to *Z*. Sometimes *A* can lead to *G*, or *K* to *B*, or *A* can lead nowhere. The past is a jumble of events and ideas that do not always follow a logical pattern. We as humans impose order upon chaos in order to make sense of it. The story told here should not be seen as a definitive account, only a starting point for further study and contemplation. I make no allusion to having covered every controversy or debate in detail, nor should the book be taken as encyclopedic.

To assist the student, there is a chronology at the end of the book. There is also a list of further readings at the end of each chapter. The titles listed in the further reading give only the authors, titles, and dates. Complete bibliographic information can be found for these and other related works in the bibliography at the end of the book. Finally, there are selections of original texts at the end of the book. These selections will give the reader a chance to hear the words of some of the protagonists in this story firsthand.

# 1

## The Rock of Ages and the Age of Rocks

By now the story has reached mythic proportions and has several versions. It turned out to be a landmark public debate over evolution. The crowd that gathered for the annual meeting of the British Association for the Advancement of Science (BAAS) at Oxford University that hot August day in 1860—students, theologians, politicians, and a large number of average working people—sat uncomfortably yet attentively in the sweltering conditions. The Reverend Samuel Wilberforce (1805–1873), a powerful voice of the Anglican Church, was just finishing a confident-sounding refutation of the theory of evolution. Wilberforce had been coached by Professor Richard Owen (1804–1892), England's leading naturalist and antievolutionist, on how to demolish the growing interest in the idea proposed in Charles Darwin's book *On the Origin of Species,* which had been published only a year before. Darwin (1809–1882) argued that the vast diversity of life on earth was the result of organisms evolving from one form to another over vast periods of time through a process he called natural selection. Wilberforce disagreed and argued that life had no explanation except that it had been designed by God. The idea (only implied in Darwin's book) that humans too evolved from lower animals was a blasphemy that went against everything Wilberforce and many Christians held dear. Worse still, it was now being thought in some circles that men and apes might share a common ancestor.

Emboldened by his performance, the reverend could not resist one last dig. Smiling broadly, he turned to a slim, dark-haired man sitting in the audience. Wilberforce smugly asked Thomas Henry Huxley (1825–1895), a proevolutionist who had been fighting with Owen over the similarities between human and primate anatomy for two years, if he had descended from a monkey on his grandmother's or his grandfather's side. The question raised a storm of applause and laughter from the crowd—books and papers were waved, hats tossed in the air, feet stomped. The Reverend Wilberforce thought he had won the day. Huxley calmly rose to his feet amid the din, smoothed his vest and jacket, and spoke. He said that he would rather be related to a monkey than to an educated man like Wilberforce who introduced ridicule and personal attack into a discussion of science and who would use his gifts and talents in the service of prejudice. The audience exploded again, only this time in support of Huxley. He allowed himself a little smile of triumph. The controversy over human evolution had just begun in earnest.

### Religion and Geology

The Victorian Age—roughly the 1830s through 1900, named after Britain's Queen Victoria—was to a large degree the ground zero for the technological and intellectual advances of the era. At the height of the Industrial Revolution, much discovery about the natural world took place: developments in physics, chemistry, astronomy, and biology cast doubts on scriptural explanations for how the universe came to be. As European empires—particularly the British Empire—grew, governments as well as numerous private learned societies and clubs sponsored expeditions around the globe that generated large amounts of new data. Information about the world's plant and animal life, geology, and weather would be a major asset in the struggle to rule the planet and its inhabitants. In this rush to knowledge much was discovered, but not all that information was welcome. People of the ruling and middle classes had traditionally seen themselves at the top of the ladder of life. They sensed themselves superior physically, morally, and culturally, not only to the plants and animals but to other humans as well. It was a position they liked and one they wanted to keep. In a flurry of discontent the Victorians began to learn things that many of them would rather have not learned. The most troubling of all concerned the fundamental nature of humanity itself.

Beginning with the fall of the Roman Empire and Christian ascendancy in the fifth century, questions of science were expected to conform to a biblical framework. For Christians around the world the paradigm for the creation of the universe was the story of Genesis. God, it said, had created the universe and everything in it in six days and had placed Adam and Eve in the Garden of Eden to enjoy his bounty. But Genesis is vague on actual dates, so in 1658 Archbishop James Ussher (1581–1656) of the Church of Ireland took on the task of calculating the date of Creation. By tallying the genealogies and biographies in the Bible and other Middle Eastern texts, he determined that God had created the universe on Sunday, October 23, 4004 B.C. This chronology became the standard throughout Christendom, but it was called into question both by accident and by design. Natural historians began asking questions about what they were seeing in the ground, and Archbishop Ussher's date was not answering them. To some, the rock-solid Genesis story, which had held sway for so long, began to show cracks.

Ironically, the first stage in the debate on human evolution dealt not with humans at all but with the age of the earth. As Archbishop Ussher was putting together the date of Creation, rock and fossil hunting was becoming a popular pastime in Britain and Europe. As amateurs fanned out across the landscape collecting and cataloging, strange creatures and strange geologic formations seemed to be everywhere. One of the first things the fossil hunters noticed was that the earth was made up of various layers of rocks and gravels. In 1669 Nicolaus Steno (1638–1686), a Dane living in Italy, first argued that the fossils found in the layers were the remains of dead animals. Others argued that these layers had formed in a sequence, with the youngest at the top and the oldest at the bottom. This layering process is known as superposition, and the layers themselves are strata (the study of the strata is called stratigraphy). Later, Englishman William Smith (1769–1839), a surveyor and engineer, determined that the key to differentiating between the levels was the fossils. Stratigraphy had economic importance, as the Industrial Revolution needed vast amounts of coal. Geologists like Smith could find it. Fossils found in the layers also seemed to conform to a sequence, with the simplest forms at the bottom and the more complex toward the top.

As more was learned about the anatomy of the earth, ideas were presented to explain it. In France, Georges-Louis Leclerc de Buffon (1707–1788), one of the philosophers of the period of intellectual growth known as the Enlightenment, saw the earth as a dynamic machine. For him, geologic change was slow, deliberate, and never-ending. He believed that the universe worked according to divine laws that could be figured out by the human intellect. He argued that although God had made the laws by which the universe operated, He then stepped back and let it work on its own without direct intervention. For Buffon, Scripture was not necessary to understand how the world was made. Unlike Steno, Buffon quoted numbers, saying he thought the earth was around 120,000 years old, and he was chastised by the Catholic Church for doing so.

The most powerful scientist in France had no such problems. Georges Cuvier (1769–1832) was a gifted naturalist who pioneered the concept of comparative anatomy. He opposed the idea that living things changed from one form into another over time yet developed the concept of extinction. He compared modern elephants with fossil ones and hypothesized that the fossil versions were like, but not exactly like, the living forms. Therefore, he concluded, the earlier variant must have gone extinct to be replaced by the newer model. Cuvier believed that all new species were the products of divine Creation. However, he generally did not bring theology into the discussion, preferring to base his assertions on scientific evidence. As the head of the French scientific community in the early part of the nineteenth century, Cuvier quashed the rudimentary evolutionary theories of other French naturalists such as Buffon and Jean-Baptiste Lamarck (1744–1829). He also argued that the face of the earth was the result of periods of catastrophic upheaval in the distant past. It was at the end of each catastrophic period that old species became extinct and new ones were created. He believed that modern geologic activity was too slow to produce the surface of the earth in only 6,000 years. Localized volcanic eruptions, floods, and apocalyptic earthquakes, he said, were the acts God used to create the earth.

Although "catastrophism" became popular, not everyone accepted it. The most influential British geologist of the period was Charles Lyell (1797–1875). A lawyer by training, Lyell abandoned the law to pursue his interest in the earth. Lyell was unsatisfied with catastrophism and looked for a new explanation. His study of the earth led him to a conclusion very different from that of Cuvier. Although Lyell was a Christian, he was bothered by attempts to support Scripture by geological evidence. He considered it too easy to simply put everything down to violent geological activity, especially when he could see no evidence for it in the rocks. In 1830 he published *Principles of Geology,* in which he championed uniformitarianism, an idea suggested by Buffon and the Scottish geologist James Hutton in the 1700s. This view held that a slow, predictable, and unending process of geologic change created the face of the earth. These changes, Lyell said, had been going on since the beginning of time and would continue to go on in the same way. He could see no evidence for the sudden, abrupt, and catastrophic change Cuvier suggested. This "steady-state" approach could easily account for the fossils and strata as well as many of the problems of geologic formation. Also, uniformitarianism meant that the earth must be immensely old: slow change needed vast amounts of time to work. Like Buffon, Lyell thought the earth at least more than 100,000 years old.

Catastrophism and uniformitarianism were not the only theories available. "Day-age" theorists held that each day of Genesis was much longer than twenty-four hours; "gap" theorists held that although the Genesis description of the creation of the world was literally true, it was followed by a gap of indeterminate length, which in turn was followed by the historical ages of man. Neptunism argued that the world had been totally covered with water and that land formations appeared when the water levels dropped. Plutonism argued that the strata were the results of volcanic activity alone.

*Portrait of Charles Lyell (Library of Congress)*

How the surface of the earth was produced was a point of great contention. Both biblical literalists and nonliteralists believed geology could give the answer. Geology was the central interest for many of the first scientific communities in Britain. They believed each layer of strata could be read like the chapter in a book. The deeper you went, however, the more difficult the chapters were to read. From this grew the Devonian controversy of the early nineteenth century. The individual layers of strata were often named for the place they were first discovered. The layer that proved to be crucial to understanding the age of the earth was first identified near Devon, England. By studying this layer—and what lay just above and below—geologists saw that the strata system was a worldwide, not local, phenomenon. It was seen that the strata were the same as in Europe, Russia, North America, and indeed everywhere. This seemingly mundane discovery showed a commonality to the earth's structure that gave a fixed reference point for dating the formations.

Although this kind of geological knowledge solved some problems, it could cause others. Frenchman Jean André Deluc (1727–1817) believed in Noah's Flood and a catastrophic past. Deluc said the evidence of the strata showed that a great flood had occurred around 6,000 years before, a flood he equated with the biblical story of Noah. Cuvier thought this flooding was linked to the extinction of the mammoths and other large mammals and used it as a marker for humans (if the strata that contained the mammoths did not contain humans, then humans must have appeared only after that point). Deluc called the flood-level strata diluvium. Historian Donald Grayson argues that in their attempt to discern the age of the earth, naturalists opened up the possibility that man had appeared well before the Bible said he was supposed to. That in turn threw doubt on the belief that the Scriptures were to be taken literally. In other words, if a fundamental biblical "fact" (man had appeared on earth recently, at the end of the six days) was suspect because of the evidence in rocks, what else was? Deluc, seeing the danger in this thinking, argued that belief in an old earth promoted atheism because it undermined biblical literalism.

Archaeologists and antiquarians look for human remains and artifacts. The early natural historians mentioned so far were not archaeologists but geologists who studied rock formations and paleontologists who studied the fossils contained in them. A way to reconcile knowledge of the geologic past with biblical accounts was to separate time into two periods. The "ancient world" was the first era, in which God molded the primordial earth and prepared it for the appearance of his great creation, man. This would allow for the existence of a furiously unstable geological past as well as a place for the wild fossil beasts to roam. Only after the ancient world was complete did God introduce man and did it become the "modern world." Naturalists and theologians could literally have the best of both worlds: geologists could study the rocks and fossils of the ancient world, whereas archaeologists could study the modern world of man without offending biblical sensibilities. This nonconfrontational compartmentalizing of knowledge kept contradictions to a minimum. It was not until the 1840s and 1850s, when archaeologists and geologists began to work together and consider each other's positions, that serious contradictions began to show.

## Early Clues

While all this study of rocks and strata was going on there had been some tantalizing discoveries of human artifacts, but the recent-earth model kept most people from thinking of the possibility of ancient humans. Briton Robert Plot (1640–1696) discussed archaic stone tools in his *Natural History of Stratford-Shire* (1686). Plot saw the artifacts as man-made but said they belonged to the early modern world, not the ancient world. In the summer of 1797 an amateur archaeologist named John Frere (1740–1807) was traveling through Suffolk,

England, near the town of Hoxne, and stopped to watch the digging at a brick quarry. He noticed that the workmen were pulling unusual triangular-shaped flints from the pit. Upon examining them Frere realized that they were undoubtedly man-made. Previously, local people had written them off as the products of elves or pixies or other mythological beings. Frere concluded that since they looked like weapons and were discovered under several layers of strata that looked as if they had once constituted a river, the flints were not only human products but also of great antiquity. He promptly sent a letter describing his theory to the secretary of the Royal Society of Antiquaries, who published it in the society's journal in 1800, where it was just as promptly forgotten.

British naturalists during this period were for the most part deeply religious men. In fact, many of them were Anglican ministers who studied the natural history of Britain as a hobby. It was all very middle-class, with the ranks filled out by lawyers and doctors who pottered about the countryside digging for fossils and other relics. Through these activities fossil hunters like Gideon Mantell, Thomas Hawkins, the working-class woman Mary Anning, and others discovered an entire menagerie of weird beasts: the marine plesiosaurs and ichthyosaurs, strange shellfish, elephantlike mammoths, and unusual plant life. Another of these fossil hunters was the Reverend William Buckland (1784–1856). A doctor by training, Buckland wanted to study geology and fossils as a way of supporting the biblical view of Creation. He saw science as perfectly compatible with religion and believed nature was proof that God had created the world for man's benefit. Buckland, who eventually became professor of geology at the University of Oxford, believed, as many did, that there was a long line—a great chain of being—of animals, from simple to complex, whose very existence showed that God had designed them and that the laws of nature were the laws of God. This concept was known as natural theology. An idea that went back to the eighteenth century, natural theology came into vogue in 1802 with the publication of William Paley's book *Natural Theology*. He argued that knowledge of God could be drawn from evidence in nature. Paley used the example of the pocket watch. A pocket watch is a complex machine made of many parts. You would assume from its complexity that it had been designed and built purposefully. Applying this model, Paley argued that the unending complexity of the natural world was itself proof that God had created it and that any laws governing the operation of nature must, therefore, also be of divine origin.

Along with the strange tools, strange bones were being discovered. The Reverend Buckland found bones in 1822 when he was led to Paviland Cave on the coast of Wales near Swansea. There he encountered bones of an extinct woolly mammoth and a woman. The bones were stained red, leading to the woman being called the Red Lady of Paviland. He surmised that the human bones had been placed near the mammoth long after the animal had died and that the red staining was done as a burial ritual. He never suspected that the lady could have died at the same time as the mammoth and that the bones were stained red due to absorption of minerals in the cave. Buckland assumed that she was associated with a nearby archaeological site thought to date back to the time of the Romans. "From all these circumstance," he said, "there is reason to conclude that these human bones are coeval with that of the . . . occupation on the adjacent summit" (Gordon 68). He thought her at most a few thousand years old (modern radiocarbon dating showed the skeleton to be 18,000 years old and that of a male).

The strangest bones discovered during this period were fossil reptiles found first by physician Gideon Mantell in Sussex in 1822. Mantell had found fossil bones and teeth of an obviously huge creature. A London medical student, Samuel Stutchbury, noticed that the teeth resembled those of the living iguana, except that they were much larger. Mantell called the creature an iguanodon (iguana tooth) and another that he found a megalosaur (giant reptile). In 1841 an up-and-coming naturalist, Richard Owen, named them, collectively, dinosaurs.

The idea that geology supported Scripture, that the works of the earth paralleled the works of the Bible, was widespread in Britain. When Cuvier's work was translated into English in 1813, the British saw it as an example of natural theology. There were British naturalists who explicitly connected Cuvier's localized flooding and catastrophic activity with Noah, as Jean André Deluc did. William Buckland too believed that God took a direct part in the running of the earth and guided it toward a good end with a specific purpose. He was pleased that geology supported the scriptural account of Creation.

There was an inherent problem with associating Cuvier's late-period flooding with Noah, however. The Bible says that there were people before the Flood. Where were their remains? If you did find remains from before the Flood, then how far back could you go? Conceivably, if there were pre-Flood people, then there could be *extremely* pre-Flood people. Some, like geologist Adam Sedgwick (1785–1873), argued that to solve this problem, just drop the Flood connection. That way you would lose the obstacle of early man and still retain scriptural integrity.

In the early 1830s Buckland did just that. He accepted that there was an unspecified period of time in the creation of the earth during which great change took place. These geological changes, however, were in no way connected to the appearance of man, who he believed was a recent addition to the landscape. Though Buckland did not believe in ancient humans or transmutation, his work at Paviland Cave and other sites helped bring about interest in the topic and spur discussion. By the middle part of the nineteenth century, the question of the age of the earth and the two worlds was no longer strictly a religion versus science issue. Many clerics had come to exchange Bishop Ussher's chronology for a more naturalistic explanation, though not always one as extreme as Lyell's or Buffon's.

It was in 1859 that John Evans, an archaeologist interested in the question of human antiquity, realized that the Hoxne finds were similar to artifacts that had been discovered in France. Jacques Boucher de Crèvecoeur de Perthes (1788–1868) was a French customs official fascinated by natural history who in the 1840s began discovering man-made artifacts along the Somme River near Abbeville. He was convinced the hand axes he found were from before Noah's Flood (the deluge), so he used the word *antediluvian* (before the deluge) to describe the period he thought they came from and created an entire story of the lives of the toolmakers. Since the church of Saint Acheul was nearby, later archaeologists dubbed the artifacts from this strata Acheulian. No one really accepted Boucher's assertions until John Evans and Joseph Prestwich came to see him. They immediately recognized the similarity between the Acheulian finds and those from Hoxne. The pieces began to come together: the great age of the earth and the obviously ancient tools. Human beings were far older than anyone had thought.

Artifacts like the Hoxne finds had been discovered on and off for years in both Britain and Europe, but they were few in number and often not human. Whenever human bones were discovered they were put down to early civilizations or even as examples of people killed off during Noah's Flood. Johann Jacob Scheuchzer (1672–1733), a Swiss researcher, coined the term *Homo diluvinii testis* to describe them. When Georges Cuvier examined these supposed human remains in 1809, his anatomist's eye saw that the *Homo diluvinii* were

Homo diluvinii
testis. *Was it an
ancient human or a
salamander? (Mid-
nineteenth-century
print of fossils)*

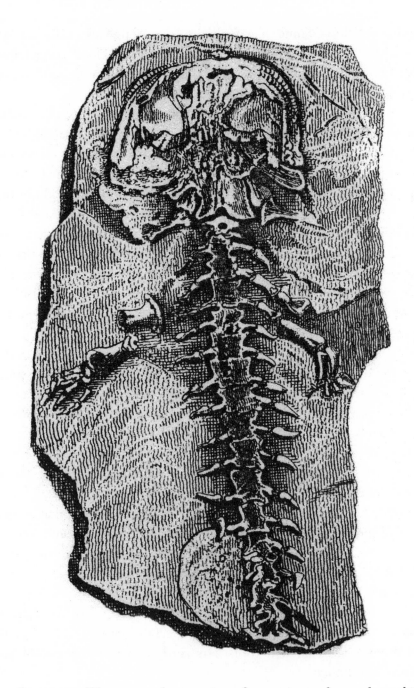

not human at all but were the remains of an extinct salamander, which in just the right light could appear humanlike.

Another possible candidate for human antiquity was the "Guade-loupe" skeleton found in 1805. This was the first obviously human skeleton encased in a rock matrix (a condition that suggested great age). Again, Cuvier weighed in and pointed out that the matrix was a type of sand known to exist in a liquid form, but it could harden quickly. His interpretation was that the skeleton was a modern one whose unfortunate owner had either fallen into or been buried by the sand recently. Most archaeologists of the day were too interested in the grand remains of classical Greece and Rome to concern themselves with the rude and insignificant relics of a supposed early human period. To make things worse, Boucher had fudged some of his material to fit his theories. He was himself, in turn, fooled by some of his collectors who had manufactured artifacts to sell him. Regardless, the circumstantial evidence was growing into a body that could not be easily dismissed. Questions pondering the possibility that man had lived in the ancient past were being added to those concerning other aspects of human biology.

### The Question of Race

An important element in the debate on human evolution was, and for many still is, the question of race. Intellectuals searched for something to account for the wide range of human diversity. As a biological idea, race can be traced back to attempts to classify and order all living things begun in the eighteenth century. European travelers

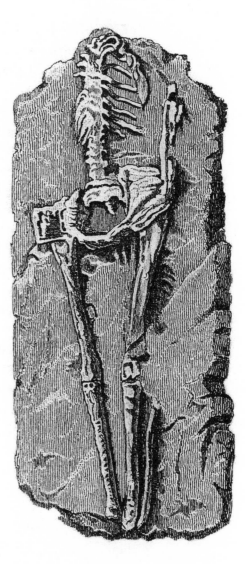

*The Guadeloupe skeleton. Some thought it ancient, but George Cuvier thought not. (Mid-nineteenth-century print of fossils)*

went to the ends of the earth in search of exotic flora and fauna and encountered people as unusual and exotic to them as the plants and animals. They began arranging the different kinds of humans into a hierarchical order. The technique of biological classification was pioneered by Carolus Linnaeus (1707–1778) in his *Systema Naturae* (1735). He arranged plant life into groups based upon common appearance.

German naturalist Johann Friedrich Blumenbach (1752–1840) hypothesized that the first people must have been light-skinned inhabitants of the Caucasus region of Asia and that racial variation was a result of the original light pigment turning dark. Blumenbach created the term *Caucasian* and was the first to attach the concept of "race" to humans. In 1775, he classified the five races of man as Caucasoid, Negroid, Mongoloid, Polynesian, and American. This system of classifying organisms soon turned to one suggesting relative superiority and inferiority. Comparisons were made among the various races and the recently discovered primates. Most in Europe took it for granted that dark-skinned people were fundamentally different from light-skinned ones. Charles White's *Regular Gradations of Man* (1799) argued that the lighter one's skin, the higher on the chain of being toward God. Racial hierarchies may have given Europeans an exaggerated sense of their place in the world, but they did nothing to address the question of how the races had appeared.

According to Scripture, Noah and his family fanned out over the earth with the order to "be fruitful and multiply." Each of Noah's sons was held responsible for creating the various races. As it had for the age of the earth, the Bible was growing increasingly unable to explain the issue of racial diversity. When the species concept was attached to humans, disagreement immediately arose as to whether the races were distinct species and whether they had separate origins. In 1665 Isaac de la Peyrere (1594–1676) asked uncomfortable questions and gave uncomfortable answers in his controversial book, *Men before Adam*. He argued that "pre-Adamites" had appeared on Earth very early and that Adam was not the first man, only the first Jewish man. The heathens, that is, people of color, he said, were descendants of the pre-Adamites and were created along with the beasts by God. He also suggested that the Bible was really the history of the Jews, not all people. *Men before Adam* was not popular with church officials, and de la Peyrere was jailed and forced to recant his position.

To better address the problem of human variation, two lines of thinking developed. The first—the single-creation, or monogenetic, school—argued that all humans descended from the same stock. In opposition to this notion was the multiple-creation, or polygenetic, school whose adherents held that each race had somehow appeared separately. Whereas the monogenists thought all men nominally equal, the polygenists argued that the races were inherently different and separate.

Initially, monogenesis was based upon scriptural authority. During the second decade of the nineteenth century a pair of Britons laid the groundwork for the scientific approach to monogenesis. William Lawrence (1783–1869), a professor of anatomy at the Royal College of Surgeons, gave a series of lectures, later published as *Physiology, Zoology, and the Natural History of Man* (1828), comparing human and primate morphologies. (Morphology is the study of the physical structure of an organism.) Most people held that humans were so special and different that they deserved to be a class by themselves, apart from and above all other animals. Lawrence was interested in showing not how humans descended from primates but that humans were so much like other animals that it was nonsense to separate them from the rest of the animal world. He also argued that human diversity was not the result of miracles or special creations but that the races were derived from a common origin.

Initially, Lawrence was hesitant to give environment any role in human diversity. He pointed out that modern-day Egyptians were no different from those depicted in classical Egyptian artwork that was several thousand years old. He added that though Africans had lived in large numbers in the Americas for centuries, they too had not changed in response to their new environment. He claimed that there were examples of African families that had produced white children while Arab and European parents had produced black children. He was not sure what caused such sudden changes but believed it was probably due to some aspect of human domestication, which was vaguely defined as the effects of civilization and close living and breeding among people. If domestication in animals caused varieties, he argued, why not in man as well? Later, Lawrence did give in to the environment, asserting that "external or adventitious causes such as climate, situation, food [or] way of life have considerable effect in altering the constitution of man and animals" (1838, 469). The idea of domestication was also part of the work of the central figure in the monogenetic school.

In his *Researches into the Physical History of Man* (1813), James Cowles Prichard (1786–1848) argued that humans were not as diverse as claimed by polygenists and that they were a single species. Basing his work on science, not Scripture, Prichard said that there were no examples of other species appearing in different parts of the world separately, so humans could not have either. He did not accept that the environment caused variation, preferring to put it down to domestication. As an abolitionist, he separated the apes from the human lineage because he feared racists would claim blacks as the missing link between monkeys and humans and therefore unworthy of equal and just treatment. (Well into the twentieth century, Christian polygenists were still arguing that both science and Scripture "proved" blacks were not human but beasts given the power of speech by God in order to better serve their white masters.) Eventually, like Lawrence, Prichard came around to accepting the role of environment in human variation and racial diversity.

Though a deeply religious man, Prichard saw the inherent drawback in trying to force science and empirical evidence into a biblical framework. He insisted that race and human diversity be studied scientifically.

Polygenetic belief in Britain had its supporters in the Anthropological Society of London. Formed in 1863, the society was the brainchild of Dr. James Hunt, who linked race, science, and politics to give empirical backing to racial discrimination. He was inspired to prove that blacks were inferior by the American Civil War. Hunt was a student of anatomist Robert Knox, whose *Races of Man: A Fragment* (1850) held that race was the primary agent of human character and promoted the ineffectiveness of environment on human development. Some argued that if humans were all of the same group, then how could they be so different? Whereas the monogenetic school argued that diversity proved single origin, the polygenetic school argued the exact opposite. The Native Americans, they said, surely must represent a separate creation. How could they have arrived in the Americas any other way?

The answer to the unity or plurality of origin question, as well as transmutation, had particular political import in the United States. The abolition movement forced the question of the ethical treatment of the slave population whose very presence undermined the American ideals of freedom, justice, and equality. Polygenesis could bolster those who supported slavery and thus aid the South in the looming Civil War, whereas monogenesis would assist the antislavery movement.

The unity school in the United States was typified by the work of Samuel Stanhope Smith (1751–1819) and his *Essays on the Causes of the Variety of Complexion and Figure in the Human Species* (1789). Smith argued that natural causes were responsible for the different races. He said that though God may have created the first people, environment produced the diversity.

Support for the slave cause came in the form of Samuel George Morton's *Crania Americana* (1839). Morton filled his home with an enormous collection of human skulls that chattered away silently to him and his visitors. He bragged that he had specimens of every race on earth in his living room. The unsettling collection was used to research skull shape and determine whether the races could be ranked by intelligence based on brain size. Wanting to show that brains of whites were larger than brains of blacks, he used different materials, from steel balls to seeds, to measure the volume of the skulls. Frustrated that black skulls often showed greater brain size than whites, he gave up and said blacks were less intelligent regardless of the size of their brains. Morton argued that slavery was as ancient as man himself and that blacks were good for little else. Using the argument pioneered by William Lawrence, Morton pointed to the apparent lack of change among Egyptians measured by ancient art, arguing that multiple creations were necessary to account for racial diversity.

Swiss comparative anatomist Louis Agassiz (1807–1873) entered the fray on the side of the plurality men in 1846 after taking a teaching position in the United States. Agassiz could not accept unity because it suggested that humans evolved, an idea he repudiated. In 1855 he said the physical differences in the races were permanent and found single origin morally repugnant because it suggested that mankind was the result of incest.

Morton's student Josiah Clarke Nott (1804–1873) and Nott's friend George Gliddon used Morton's and Agassiz's theories as the "scientific" support for their racist agendas. As pro-Southern slavery supporters, Nott and Gliddon argued in *Types of Mankind* (1854) that science clearly showed blacks were of separate origin and inferior, that slavery was not against the natural order of things, and that environment had no effect upon human variation.

With all the discussions of unity and plurality, racial variation, and the origins of the races, there was still little evidence that humans were very old, let alone that they evolved. It should be remembered that the ancient-man idea was originally stumbled upon in the course of the study of the age of the earth. This was not a simplistic "religion doesn't like it" scenario, either. Although many refused to accept any idea that went contrary to Scripture, the evidence for human antiquity and the arguments for it were, though suggestive, not compelling. The arguments could be reasoned away with other explanations. For example, if a tool was found alone, it could simply be a stone that looked like a tool; just because a human skeleton was found near an extinct animal skeleton did not mean they had died at the same time. Human material had so far been discovered at the topmost layers of strata only, not below the diluvium. Many ancient-earth proponents opposed transmutation, not only in France (including Cuvier and even Boucher) but in Britain as well. There was no general consensus. Antiquity, diversity, and transmutation were largely separate issues until the middle of the nineteenth century. What pulled all these areas of concern into sharp focus was not the discovery of a tool or bone but the publication of a book. In 1859 Charles Darwin published *On the Origin of Species*.

Though Charles Darwin studied first to be a doctor and then to be a minister, his real love was natural history. In the 1830s he was given the chance to sail aboard the British survey ship HMS *Beagle* as a naturalist. The *Beagle*'s mission was to map the coast of South America for the British government. During the voyage Darwin, who had brought along a copy of Lyell's *Principles of Geology,* amassed a collection of specimens and made firsthand observations of nature that would change the world. When he returned home and began to study his specimens and notes, an idea occurred to him. What he had seen, particularly on the Galapagos Islands off Chile, suggested that living things did transmute, or evolve, into other things. He argued that living things struggled to survive and that they were all born slightly different from each other. Sometimes these differences amounted to advantages. Individuals and groups who built up tiny variations that allowed them to survive their environments produced offspring who had the same advantages. Those who did not have the right variation of traits died off and produced no offspring. Included in this process were changes in environment, population pressure, and food supply. Natural selection, he speculated, went on for vast periods of time until so many new traits built up in a particular population that a completely new species would appear. The concept of natural selection is at the heart of *The Origin of Species.* Darwin used evidence, not only from his voyage on the *Beagle* but also from animal breeders, to prove his point. Humans had been altering animals and creating new strains of cats, dogs, and horses for centuries by crossing selected individuals to produce offspring with specific traits. If artificial selection worked, Darwin thought, why not natural selection?

There had been theories of evolution before. As far back as the Greeks at least, there had been some rudimentary notion that living things changed. The French naturalist Jean-Baptiste Lamarck in 1802 put forth the most significant pre-Darwinian theory of evolution. Lamarck, whose full name was Jean-Baptiste-Pierre-Antoine de Monet, Chevalier de Lamarck, was a former officer who took up botany after leaving the French army. In 1779 he went to work at the Jardin des Plantes (a large botanical garden), where he did extensive work in biology as well as botany, coining the term *invertebrate* to label animals without backbones. He turned to evolution and created a theory of organic change that stressed the "use and disuse" of parts. Lamarck believed that personal willpower could cause an organism to

change. The classic example of this idea is the giraffe. Originally, giraffes had short necks, but individuals stretched their necks to reach leaves higher up on trees. Longer necks were then passed down to the offspring of these creatures, who in turn stretched their necks. By repeating this procedure over and over, long-necked giraffes appeared. This concept was known as the law of acquired characters and seemed a plausible explanation for transmutation. Interestingly, Lamarck did not believe in extinction. He thought organisms transformed themselves into other organisms. The reason there were no ancient mammoths left, the theory suggested, was because they had transformed themselves into modern elephants in response to their environment.

The other significant book on evolution prior to Darwin's was *The Vestiges of the Natural History of Creation* (1844). Published anonymously but written by Robert Chambers (1802–1871), *Vestiges* argued that God's divine plan could be better understood if people accepted that living things gave rise to other living things. As a popularization of transmutation, it supported the Lamarckian mechanism and said that evolution was perfectly respectable. Basing his work on the works of Blumenbach, Prichard, and others, Chambers argued that humans had developed from lower orders and that there was evidence of it in the great level of human diversity, all of which was brought on by environment and lifestyle. The book caused a scandal for its modern position (though Chambers's understanding and explanation of transmutation, and science in general, were at best shaky) and produced much debate—or, more accurately, name-calling and arguing. T. H. Huxley, for example, wrote a stinging review, referring to *Vestiges* as a work of fiction and sloppy logic, and antitransmutationist books were written specifically to counter it.

Darwin's book also created a furor when it was published. What was supposed to be a quiet scientific tome became a best-seller and arguably the most influential book in Western history, second only to the Bible itself. Darwin was hailed as a hero by some and reviled as a devil by others. He had permanently thrown a wrench into the machinery of Judeo-Christian society. Darwin was accused of being an atheist and of purposefully trying to undermine belief in God. Although *The Origin of Species* has been forever linked to human evolution in the public eye, it is only at the very end that Darwin refers to man. Readers made the connection for themselves: if living things evolved, then humans did as well. Darwin was not up to the public storm his book created. He was a shy, retiring, sickly man, and he generally left defending his position up to others. The man who defended him most doggedly was his young friend Thomas Henry Huxley.

T. H. Huxley grew up a lower-middle-class child with little formal education who taught himself science by reading voraciously. In 1845 he won a scholarship to London's Charing Cross Hospital, where he learned medicine and anatomy. He then joined the Royal Navy and shipped out on HMS *Rattlesnake,* as a ship's surgeon, on a survey mission to Australia. Much like Darwin's voyage on the *Beagle,* Huxley's time on the *Rattlesnake* changed his life. In 1854 he was appointed professor of natural history at the Royal School of Mines. He was a great believer in education and gave public science lectures in which he spread knowledge of science, evolution, and other biological issues to Britain's working-class population.

Huxley, though full of praise for Darwin and ready to defend him at any time, did harbor some initial doubts about natural selection. He argued that natural selection had to be proven empirically, preferably through a repeatable experiment. He argued that one had to show that two forms produced from one species could not breed with each other (the essential definition of a species is a group of organisms that can breed only with similar organisms). He also thought evolution could be jumpy from time to time, not always slow and steady the way Darwin said. Darwin, though greatly admiring Huxley, thought that the sterility question was inappropriate for proving natural selection because artificial breeding did something (and Darwin did not know what) to upset the sterility that would occur during natural speciation. Huxley was perceptive enough to see that the sterilization issue, the issue of producing experimental proof of evolution, would be essential to gaining wide acceptance. He did not disagree with Darwin, as some have claimed, but wanted better proof of the idea.

A common critique of evolution, then and now, was that no transitional forms between species existed. However, when Huxley visited the United States in the 1870s he met with Yale University paleontologist Othniel Charles Marsh (1831–1899) and found what he was looking for. Marsh had assembled an impressive collection of horse fossils from the American West. The collection showed what appeared to be an unbroken line of descent from ancient horses to modern ones. This was the proof Huxley needed, and he dropped any reservations about natural selection once and for all. His big disagreement was with Richard Owen.

Huxley's great rival, Richard Owen, did not support transmutation. He became fascinated by comparative anatomy after taking classes with Georges Cuvier and cataloging the huge specimen collection at the Royal College of Surgeons. By 1831 he was the Hunterian Lecturer of comparative anatomy at the college. His reputation, power, and influence grew steadily, and he even became tutor to the children of Queen Victoria. In 1856 he became superintendent of natural history at the British Museum. A prolific worker, he coined the term *homology* to describe the phenomenon in which different organisms have similar structures but use them for different purposes. For example, the human arm, the bat's wing, and the seal's flipper are essentially the same mechanism but with different uses.

Owen speculated that if there are common structures throughout the animal world, there must be one basic model for all vertebrates. He called this hypothetical, generalized creature the archetype. He insisted, however, that the archetype was not an ancestor that gave rise to other forms. Owen explained the archetype as being an idea in the Divine mind, that it was the basic template God used to create all other organisms in a group. Owen never really explained this concept clearly, or at least as clearly as some thought he should have.

As a leader of the British scientific establishment, Owen was a natural candidate for Darwin to send a copy of his book to before it was published. Owen read Darwin's manuscript and told him that although he did not agree with natural selection, he thought it the best explanation of transmutation up to that point. This nod of approval made Darwin doubly upset when, shortly after it appeared, Owen wrote a scathing review of *The Origin of Species.* Owen feared that natural selection would become the basis of some grand atheistic worldview, abused by those who would bring about a godless universe. For Owen, transmutation or evolution, or whatever Darwin called it, debased humans by lowering them to the level of animals and removing them from their special place at the feet of God. Owen originally thought Darwin's work implied a form of natural theology, the argument that the Almighty designed the universe. It was a major miscommunication between the two and led to bitter rivalries and warring camps. It would be only the first example of people misunderstanding, oversimplifying, and popularizing the evolution concept to the point that few understood the basic mechanics of it and therefore opposed what they *thought* evolution meant.

In his position as head of museums, collections, and even a zoo, Richard Owen dissected and studied many exotic creatures and learned their anatomy firsthand. He was probably the first Briton to dissect a gorilla. This strange creature had been "discovered" by Europeans only in 1847. French American adventurer Paul Du Chaillu (1831–1903) brought the first gorilla bodies to England from Africa and put them on display with a collection of other primates. Du Chaillu told harrowing tales of the beastly ways of the gorilla, which he said was savage, violent, and even kidnapped and assaulted human women. Into the seventeenth century, Europeans were only vaguely aware of the primates. Pioneering early works, like William Jardine's *Natural History of Monkeys* (1833), argued against primates being the same species as humans, as some thought they might be. Edward Tyson (1650–1708) did the first description of a chimpanzee in England in 1698. He called it a pygmy and also an ape. The word *chimpanzee* was not yet in common usage; the word *ape* was a generic word used for any of the large tailless primates. Tyson also used the terms *Orang-Outang* and *Homo sylvestris* (man of the woods). By the mid–nineteenth century, apes, monkeys, and orangutans were sorted out and given their modern labels. Tyson thought the chimpanzee was an intermediate link between humans and monkeys. His work showed for the first time the considerable similarity of primate and human morphologies. He said, "Man is part brute, part angel; and is that link in Creation, that joyns them together" (1699, 55). Since the anatomies of the two groups were so similar, Tyson felt the only distinction was that God had given humans a higher order of intelligence and powers of reason.

Richard Owen's study of the primates led him to state in 1854 that there were enough anatomical differences between them and humans to prove they were not related. He based his scientific opinion in part on his discovery that an organ in the human brain, known as the hippocampus minor, was not present in primates. Owen and T. H. Huxley began fighting over this point in private two years before their famous public encounter at Oxford in 1860. Huxley, whose feelings for Owen had gone from admiration and respect to dislike and contempt, did some dissections of his own and showed that Owen was wrong. Huxley showed that primates did indeed have a hippocampus minor and that the basis for Owen's rejection of man's primate ancestry had no validity. It was a major blow to Owen's reputation. To compound the humiliation, British author (and Huxley friend) Charles Kingsley later parodied the battle over the hippocampus in his best-selling children's book, *The Water Babies* (1863). In the story, a scientist patterned after Owen is made to look pompous, vain, and just plain wrong in his pronouncements.

Huxley showed that Owen had been wrong about the hippocampus and, to ram home the point about how similar humans and primates were, listed the anatomical structure of hands and feet as further

*Paul Du Chaillu dressed for action in Africa in the 1860s (Du Chaillu's* Story's of the Gorilla Country *[New York: Harper and Brothers, 1867])*

This illustration from Du Chaillu's book on equatorial Africa helped establish the gorilla as a menace in Western popular culture. (Du Chaillu's Equatorial Africa and the Country of the Dwarfs [London: John Murray, 1892])

evidence of the fact. He said that primates were two-handed like humans, not four-footed as Owen believed. Johann Friedrich Blumenbach had originally separated humans from the primates by calling humans *bimana* (two-handed) and the primates *quadrumana* (four-footed). Cuvier and Owen agreed, whereas Geoffroy Saint-Hilaire and Huxley did not. Saying primates had four feet instead of two hands clearly set them apart. Owen said the primate "hand" was identical to its foot. Therefore, the ape was manifestly different from humans. Huxley said that although apes and monkeys had hands that looked like feet, they were in fact proper hands. Huxley said a human's hands and feet are different in their structure based upon the arrangement of the tarsal bones. Primate hands and feet were similarly different.

One of the problems between Owen and Huxley was that Owen wanted humans to be angels, and he accused Huxley of wanting them to be apes. Huxley said they were neither and saw the issue as more complex. The two engaged in an airing of grievances in the media and in private. Huxley's grand airing of grievances came with his controversial 1863 book, *Man's Place in Nature.* He had been developing his ideas by giving a whirlwind series of public lectures, particularly at the Working Men's College. Begun by Frederick Denison Maurice in 1854, the Working Men's College was a unique experiment. It was meant to bring higher education to the working-class men of England who could not afford or were not allowed to receive a college education through the normal channels. Huxley thought he could bring his work to the public and get a favorable reception: he was right. Night after night he lectured to a packed house of working-class people. He gave bravura performances and explained that humans had arisen from base origins.

The idea reverberated among the "lower orders" of England's rigid and oppressive class system. They saw the political content as well as the biological. If lowly primates could grow into sophisticated humans, then they too could break the bonds of their lower-class status and move up. Growth and attainment were possible, not only physically but also intellectually, not only biologically but also economically. The idea of evolution was growing beyond the bounds of natural history

*William Jardine's book of the 1830s helped increase the Western fascination with "apes." (From Jardine's* Natural History of Monkeys, *Edinburgh edition, 1833)*

and playing a role in wider society. Radical writers and politicians saw biblical Creation as the establishment's way of keeping the masses in their place. Ape ancestry gave them a way to rise up, and they loved Huxley for it. The mainstream press and those in the corridors of power were aghast at his assertions. His human/primate relations idea was called "the vilest and beastliest paradox ever vented in ancient or modern times" (Desmond 1997, 301). The British political and religious establishment saw the concept of primate ancestry as degrading to the noble human spirit and threatening to their privileged status. The hordes of British workers who slaved away in the "dark satanic mills" of the Industrial Revolution saw the harsh conditions they lived in as even more so. Ironically, with all the shouting about morality, Huxley said that the question of human evolution was indeed one of morality, but for a different reason. Man may have had primate ancestors, he argued, but he was not an ape himself. Man had risen from humble origins to achieve spiritual and evolutionary success.

Huxley refused to be subtle; he named names and did so loudly and clearly. Since humans and the other primates were closely related and shared a common ancestor, they had to be thought of as part of nature, not separate from it. *Man's Place in Nature* brought the human-ape

The biologist Thomas Henry Huxley (1825–1895), ca. 1870. It was Huxley, not Darwin, who brought the human/monkey connection into the discussion of evolution. (Hulton-Deutsch Collection/Corbis)

question out into the light of day. Darwin called it the "monkey book" and could barely contain his glee. Huxley also introduced the icon of human evolution. He included a drawing that placed the skeletons of a human and several primates in a sort of macabre police lineup. The picture gave the impression that the skeletons formed a line of descent leading to man. This image said more than the book itself. One glance and the idea seemed clear that humans and apes were similar in structure and closely related. More than any other visual in the debate, the skeleton lineup became the shorthand for human evolution. It has been copied, ridiculed, misunderstood, and parodied since the day it appeared. But neither Huxley nor Darwin ever said that humans descended from apes. They said that humans and apes, as well as all primates, shared a common ancestor.

It was an uphill battle. The proevolution newspaper the *National Reformer* on March 28, 1863, reported the forces ranging against Huxley, his colleagues, and their ideas. "The origin of man has been considered hitherto the theologian's strongest ground. . . . Darwin will never be forgiven for propounding so ably his theory; neither will Sir Charles Lyell add to his reputation by the publicity of his last volume; and above all, will Professor Huxley be unsparingly condemned for proving to the working-classes that man is not a distinct creation, but that he originated by a process of development."

Huxley was interested in more than simply jousting with Owen over the excruciating minutiae of primate and human anatomy. As much as he was fighting for the acceptance of evolutionary thinking, he was fighting for a place for himself in the British scientific hierarchy. He was also not the atheist people made him out to be. His insistence upon factual evidence to support theory led him to coin the term *agnostic* to describe those like him who wanted to believe in God but saw no direct physical evidence of Him. He was much less anti-God than he was anti-dogmatism. The American writer and journalist H. L. Mencken (1880–1956) saw that Huxley fought for the right to think his own thoughts without a religious or political authority telling him how.

In addition to Huxley's work, 1863 saw the publication of Charles Lyell's foray into human evolution, *The Antiquity of Man.* Lyell took a comprehensive look at the available material that suggested great human antiquity. He collated bones and artifacts from Britain, Denmark, Germany, Egypt, and the Americas, concentrating on burial mounds, rubbish heaps, and cave deposits. Lyell was convinced that in the aggregate, this material proved humans were ancient, not recent. He left the discussion of whether they evolved until the end. Though he grudgingly accepted evolution, he allowed that it was not incompatible with natural theology. Hedging his bet, he said, "they who maintain that the . . . origin of species . . . can be explained only by the direct action of the creative cause, may retain their favorite theory compatible with the doctrine of transmutation" (505–506).

Though Lyell's work had been embraced by Darwin, the reverse was not so at first. Lyell was slow to come around to transmutation. He was always a bit murky in his understanding and support. Lyell, like many who initially had reservations about evolution for humans, was reluctant to give up man's special place in the universe—something that was implicit in Darwinian theory. Both Lyell's *Antiquity of Man* and Huxley's *Man's Place in Nature* impacted Darwin's species theory and his thinking on human origins. Darwin worried about how the public perceived his work. He approved of Huxley's argument for the close association of humans and primates but was not so pleased with Lyell's book. Darwin thought Lyell had been too timid in his acceptance of natural selection and that he should have championed it louder and more forcefully. Darwin lamented that, on the one hand, Lyell seemed to say he did not believe in human-primate ancestry but, on the other hand, then argued that human intelligence had suddenly appeared out of some more primitive creature. This drove Darwin crazy, and he snapped at Lyell to come out and say definitively that he believed humans had descended from some other species and that in fact all life evolved. Darwin was especially disappointed in his old friend because he believed that, of all the naturalists in the world, Lyell would be able to bring people around to belief in transmutation, but because he hedged he had lost his chance to do so. Lyell replied that he took the softer road because he was afraid he would create a backlash if he was too forceful.

Indeed, some staunch evolution supporters felt the same way. They wanted to bring people around slowly to the idea of human evolution. The American Asa Gray (1810–1888) agreed. He was nervous about Huxley's take-no-prisoners attitude. Gray had been corresponding with Darwin for some years before *The Origin of Species* was released and was the first major scientist in North America to embrace Darwin's work. He feared that Huxley's approach would make more enemies than friends.

Charles Darwin finally had his say on human evolution with *The Descent of Man* (1871). Whereas Huxley had concentrated on the physical similarities of humans and animals, Darwin looked at less tangible characteristics. He argued that human behavior was just as much a product of natural selection as physical stature. He compared human social behavior to that of the animal kingdom and found them roughly the same. To him, human sexual selection (how humans choose mates) was in large part a biological function. People might not realize they were following instinctive and evolutionary movements, but they were. There was little difference between a bird strutting and showing off brightly colored plumage to attract the right mate and a human at a party courting a prospective spouse. Intellect, consciousness, sympathy for others, the appreciation of beauty, ethical behavior—even religious predilection—were biologically structured and the results of ages of evolutionary change. Darwin stretched the human evolution argument to include traits of "humanness" as well as simple morphology. He was taking humans further from divine intervention and putting them squarely in the animal world. He said that anyone looking at the evidence in nature "cannot any longer believe that man is a work of a separate act of creation" (1898, 602).

*Conclusion*

There were theologians who accepted evolution and scientists who did not. By the end of the nineteenth century several primary strains of opposition to human evolution had solidified into basic arguments, not all of which fell along altogether theological or scientific lines. William Paley's proof from design proved to be one of the most popular. In his *Reign of Law* (1867), George Douglas Campbell, the duke of Argyll, said that humans instinctively see purpose and design when it exists and recognize them in nature's complexity. Darwin, he said, had taken that purpose away. The perceptive American philosopher William James (1842–1910) saw that the fundamental hook of evolution was whether life was the result of chance or design. The Scottish geologist and theologian Hugh Miller (1802–1856) covered many of the basic arguments against human evolution years before Darwin's book appeared. Miller was speaking to Robert Chambers and Jean-Baptiste Lamarck when he said that transmutation (or development, as it was also sometimes known) was dangerous because it would "transfer the work of the creation from the department of miracles to the province of natural law, and would strike down . . . all the old landmarks, ethical and religious" (Miller 1859, 36). In other words, without ethical and religious landmarks, society would have no governance, no mechanism to keep it under control, and as such would self-destruct. Transmutation would render Christianity useless and would reduce people to savagery. It would take away the immortality of the soul and man's responsibility to and fear of God.

There were more than just theological complaints. Sir John William Dawson argued that human evolution had no real proof of its efficacy and had been put together from random bits of inferences and ideas. The fossil record had too many gaps in it to show progression from one species to another. Adding religion to his science, the Canadian geologist argued that evolution debased humans, made them evil, and removed the final cause of man's existence as well as his connection to the Almighty. Evolution would cause unrest among the masses, which would lead to riots, anarchy, and social upheaval.

William Thomson, Lord Kelvin (1824–1907), calculated the age of the earth based upon what he thought was its rate of internal cooling. Lord Kelvin believed the earth had once been a molten mass, which over time became progressively cooler as heat radiated away. Applying the second law of thermodynamics (heat always travels from a warm to a cool body), he argued that the earth was cooling at a fixed rate, which showed the earth to be too young for Lyell's uniformitarianism or Darwinian evolution.

There were many theologians and scientists who wanted to accept human evolution but not Darwin's thesis completely. Many sought conciliation between science and religion and looked for a graceful way out. St. George Jackson Mivart (1827–1900), an English Catholic convert, for example, formed a sort of loyal opposition to human evolution. His *Man and Apes* (1876) argued that sudden change was reasonable in evolution but that nature showed there was a Creator. Taking a popular middle road, he said all development and adaptation was a product of God's laws. Mivart opposed natural selection because he failed to see how a half-formed characteristic or adaptation could help an organism before it was complete: how could half a heart or part of an eye be useful? He also had problems with primate ancestry. The apes and monkeys were similar to humans, but that did not prove a direct relationship. The American George Frederick Wright (1838–1921) supported catastrophism and transmutation. He also accepted primate descent but argued that although the human body was the result of evolution, the human mind was the product of divine creation. Alfred Russel Wallace (1823–1913), the man who discovered natural selection independent of Darwin, also argued that man's higher mental faculties had to be the product of special creation because he could not account for them by selection alone. Most of these arguments are still in use today in one form or another.

The theories and ideas about human evolution discussed in this chapter were just that—theories. They were based on inferences taken from Scripture, from the anatomy and behavior of modern animals, from geology, and from wishful thinking. There was little physical evidence to support any idea. The few fossil bones and tools discovered were at worst misidentifications and at best inconclusive. What was needed was unambiguous evidence in the form of fossils. Theories by themselves could always be reasoned away, but grasping fossil hands and staring fossil eyes were more difficult to deny or look away from. With *Man's Place in Nature,* Thomas Henry Huxley gave his response to Richard Owen and the Reverend Wilberforce at the BAAS meeting in 1860 and the question about his family: not only was the ape Huxley's grandparent but he was Owen's and Wilberforce's as well. Huxley's biographer, Adrian Desmond, has likened him to Copernicus. Whereas the Polish astronomer took the earth out of the center of the universe and placed it among the stars, Huxley took humans out of the Garden of Eden and put them out among the rest of the animals. A slight modification to this apt analogy would be to say that Huxley was to Darwin what Galileo was to Copernicus. The authorities wanted to burn Galileo for his blasphemy; they wanted to burn Huxley, too. Unfortunately for the authorities, the blasphemy was only growing stronger.

*Further Reading*

There is a large and growing body of scholarship on the Victorian-era debates on geology, human evolution, and related areas. Two very good examples are Donald Grayson's *Establishment of Human Antiquity* (1983) and A. Bowdoin Van Riper's *Men among the Mammoths: Victorian Science and the Discovery of Human Prehistory* (1993). Both discuss the intellectual dilemmas brought about by researches into the age of the earth, the discovery of artifacts and tools, and the implications for human antiquity. Christopher McGowan's *Dragon Seekers* (2001) deals with some of the same characters but with more emphasis on the discovery of ancient beasts rather than humans. For the geology, see Martin Rudwick's *Great Devonian Controversy* (1985). There are also many works dealing with early concepts of race. For example, see Pat Shipman, *The Evolution of Racism: Human Differences and the Use and Abuse of Science* (1994) and George W. Stocking, ed., *Race, Culture, and Evolution* (1982). For the life of T. H. Huxley, see Adrian Desmond's *Huxley: From Devil's Disciple to Evolution's High Priest* (1997) and *Archetypes and Ancestors: Paleontology in Victorian London, 1850–1875* (1984).

When studying the past, scholars always try to go to the original writings of the people involved. For human evolution, Charles Darwin's *On the Origin of Species* (1859) and *The Descent of Man and the Selection in Relation to Sex* (1871) are good places to start, and also see T. H. Huxley's *Man's Place in Nature and Other Anthropological Essays* and Charles Lyell's *The Geological Evidence of the Antiquity of Man*, both of 1863; all of them are available as modern reprints. Some early pivotal original works on the human/primate connection are William Lawrence's *Physiology, Zoology, and the Natural History of Man* (1828) and Edward Tyson's *Anatomy of the Pygmie Compared with That of the Monkey, Ape, and a Man* (1699).

Finally, there are several versions of the infamous Oxford showdown between Huxley and Wilberforce. Not all are the same. The one I recounted is admittedly a more romantic one. A good place to start is the versions contained in volume 1 of *The Life and Letters of Thomas Henry Huxley* (1901), edited by his son Leonard Huxley.

# 2
## *The First Fossils*

He was old. He was tired. His arthritis made every step painful. He climbed into the small cave located high above the little stream at the base of the densely wooded valley and lay down. He was dying. We will never know more than a few details of this man's life, not even his name. As he closed his eyes for the last time he may have thought of his family, he may have thought of his life, he may even have thought of what awaited him after death. He could never have thought that forty thousand years later his remains would be discovered and held up as a great treasure. He would become not only the most famous human fossil but also our single most difficult ancestor: Neanderthal man.

The nineteenth century was a golden age of human evolution theory. Theory can be discussed, argued over, constructed and reconstructed, extrapolated wildly, but never proved or disproved if there is no hard evidence to go with it. With ideas alone thinkers were safe from reality. Once genuine fossils began to turn up, the theorizing took on a new flavor. The rope of theory was tied to fossils, and the tug-of-war began. Whereas all human fossils are controversial, none has caused debate quite like the very first ones found. The Neanderthals seem to have a special hold over our imaginations. They are so like us yet so different. The later Cro-Magnons are virtually indistinguishable from us, and the earlier australopithecines and *Homo erectus* are so very different from us that we do not take them personally. It is the Neanderthals who make us uncomfortable. The common, but erroneous, view of the Neanderthals as savage, dim-witted cavemen haunts us like a gunshot that just misses our heads; half a step either way, and it would have been us. At various times they have come to represent everything ugly, evil, and violent in human nature. It is they whom we fear seeing when we look in the mirror.

## The Neanderthal Man

In the summer of 1856 workers quarrying for lime dug out bones from under several feet of mud in the darkness of a tunnel known as Feldhofer Cave in southern Germany, near Düsseldorf. The Neanderthal (meaning "Neander valley" and pronounced nee-ander-tall) was named in honor of the seventeenth-century theologian and songwriter Joachim Neuman, who would stroll through the wooded, narrow valley dreamily composing hymns. By the middle of the nineteenth century the area had become a source of limestone, blasted and hacked out of the cliffs. Initially, the men who found the bones thought they were those of some forest animal, a bear perhaps. As they were searching for lime, not fossils, they tossed the bones out the mouth of the cave to be lost forever in the piles of debris below. When more bones turned up they were given to a natural historian and teacher at the nearby Elberfield School, Johann Karl Fuhlrott (1804–1877). Whether there were any artifacts to go with the bones is unclear. The workers were not particular in their recovery, and Fuhlrott did not visit the site himself until later. After examining the bones, Fuhlrott, who was a transmutationist, came to believe that they represented an ancient human.

Fuhlrott took plaster casts of his treasure to professor of natural history Hermann Schaaffhausen (1816–1893) of the University of Bonn. Later receiving the originals, Schaaffhausen, who favored transmutation and opposed catastrophism, accepted Fuhlrott's assessment of antiquity. Excited by what they had, the two men arranged to present their findings at the next meeting of the Natural History Society of Prussian Rhineland and Westphalia, at Kassel, on February 4, 1857. The meeting was attended by many of the leading natural historians, physicians, and anatomists of Europe. Both Fuhlrott and Schaaffhausen had high hopes for their presentations. Fuhlrott, the lowly schoolteacher, was the first presenter. He discussed how and where the bones had been recovered and pointed out that the bones were etched with dendritic deposits (minerals that attach themselves to fossils and grow into branching patterns). These deposits routinely appeared on fossils whose extreme age was taken for granted. When finished, Fuhlrott respectfully stepped aside to allow Schaaffhausen to take over.

Hermann Schaaffhausen was a respected university professor who with the assuredness of his position started by saying he thought the creature an ancient human. He said it "belonged to a period antecedent to the time of the Celts and Germans and probably derived from one of the wild races of Northwestern Europe" (1861, 171). Since the medieval period there had been a tradition in Europe of belief in the existence of strange, oddly built, and bizarre people who had inhabited remote regions in the past. They included wild people, people with one giant foot, or people whose faces were in their chests. Looking at the bones within the context of the belief in these "monstrous races," Schaaffhausen believed the creature predated even these ancients. He then went on to describe the bones themselves. There were leg bones that were unusually heavy in their build and bowed outward, a piece of a pelvis, some ribs, both upper arms, a misshapen lower arm, and a skullcap with noticeably heavy brow ridges. It seemed obvious that, despite a withered arm that had been broken in life and healed badly, the individual was robust and powerful in stature. The muscle scars on the long bones, for example, were considerable. Muscles on a human, or any mammal, are not simply glued on; they grow out of bones. Because of this fact, muscles leave telltale marks known as muscle scars at their attachment points: the larger the scar, the larger the muscle. Big muscle scars were not the only anomalies of the specimen. Schaaffhausen, like almost every subsequent commentator, remarked on the unusual shape of the skull and the protruding brow ridges. Based on these oddities, Schaaffhausen conjectured that the individual must have been a savage brute. What is important about Schaaffhausen's description is that he insisted the skeleton was ancient and that the strangeness of the bones was normal. He had previously written an article titled "The Stability and Transformation of Species" (1853), so even though Darwin's *Origin of Species* was not published until several years later, Schaaffhausen had no trouble with an evolutionary approach. Unfortunately, few in the room thought the same way.

The response to their presentation was not exactly what Fuhlrott and Schaaffhausen had had in mind. Professor Von Mayer, a colleague of Schaaffhausen's at Bonn, dismissed the skeleton as that of a modern individual who must have been an Asiatic who suffered from the disease of rickets or possibly arthritis, which accounted for the bowed legs. He suggested that the skeleton could have been that of a soldier in the Russian army who had died in the recent invasion. He pointed out that a Cossack detachment had camped in the Neanderthal area in 1814. He also argued that if the skeleton was a human ancestor leading from the primate line, then why did it not have at least some vestige of a sagittal crest down the skull? Many of the great apes have this crest running from the front of their skulls to the back for the attachment of jaw muscles. Von Mayer assumed that if humans were related to primates, an idea he did not support, then their ancestors would surely have had this feature.

The other major dissenting voice at the meeting was that of the distinguished physician, anatomist, and pathologist Rudolf Virchow (1821–1902). Virchow's work on cell structure and its relation to gross pathology helped revolutionize medicine. Pathology is the study of the causes and spread of disease and how it alters the structure of an organism. As a teacher Virchow was troubled by the lack of knowledge, even among medical students, about the origins of disease. Most people did not understand how deformities or illness came about. Virchow intended to correct this condition by studying disease and deformity firsthand. To this end he amassed a considerable collection of specimens as teaching aids, including diseased skin samples, hydro- and microcephalic skulls, misshapen skeletons of all kinds, two-headed babies and other monstrous births, dissected brains, skin lesions, and others all carefully preserved for study. With these aids he could show his students the prosaic medical causes of disease and thus learn how to treat, cure, and prevent it.

While a pioneering medical teacher, Virchow was not a transmutationist. He believed that one kind of creature could give rise only to the same kind. This was a biological order that kept the universe from slipping into chaos. He was a polygenist who believed that all the human races had different origins. Years later, Virchow ran head-on into his countryman Ernst Haeckel (1834–1919) and his strongly evolutionist leanings. Haeckel supported evolution as well as German biological and cultural superiority. Where Haeckel embraced *The Origin of Species,* Virchow wrote an uncompromising critique of it. Virchow opposed Haeckel because he saw the younger man as a supporter of everything Virchow hated in both science and society. Virchow was politically active and vigorously opposed the growing militarism of the now unified German state. He ran for and was elected to office so he could more effectively resist the power of German prime minister Otto von Bismarck.

When Virchow encountered the Neanderthal specimen, he looked at it with the critical eye of a pathologist and antitransmutationist. This background led him to what seemed the only logical explanation for the bones: the Neanderthal man was a modern human who suffered from several conditions that left his body in a pitiful state. Virchow was both right and wrong in his assessment. The skeleton was pathological, but the pathology itself was ancient. The Neanderthal had a stooped, disease-racked body, but it was a Neanderthal nonetheless. Intellectual traditions led the professors to different conclusions: Schaaffhausen was thinking ancient monstrous races, while Virchow and the others were thinking modern monstrous births. The general conclusion of the learned men was that the Neanderthal specimen represented some poor wretch who had suffered from various diseases that twisted his body and deformed his mind. It was certainly not an evolutionary human forerunner. Schaaffhausen was going up against a powerful and entrenched elite who held sway over all matters scientific in Germany. Fuhlrott and Schaaffhausen left the meeting deeply disappointed.

After the dismal reception the Neanderthal specimen received at the Kassel meeting, it disappeared from view. Virchow and the other German *Doktors* had passed judgment, and that was that. Schaaffhausen published his findings, as did Fuhlrott, but the accounts were relegated to obscurity for the time being. The situation remained that way until April 1861, when George Busk (1807–1886), professor of anatomy at the Royal College of Surgeons in London, translated Schaaffhausen's paper into English for the *Natural History Review*. Now the British anthropological community took up the Neanderthal debate. Busk attached some notes of his own to his translation, speculating that the shape of the skull was indicative of savagery. The naturalist C. Carter Blake argued that it looked like a modern African or Mongol of Asia. The Neanderthal skull began to remind some of a pair of skulls that had been found years before but relegated to freak status and forgotten. In 1830 an odd skull had been found in a cave at Engis, Belgium. In 1848, on the island of Gibraltar, another skull had been found and put away in a museum to collect dust. Busk tracked down the Gibraltar skull and, realizing it was much like the Neanderthal one, brought it to light.

Charles Lyell also thought the Neanderthal and Gibraltar skulls were similar. Lyell's student William King began referring to the German skull as Neanderthal man and gave it an official label of *Homo sapiens neanderthalensis* in order to set it off as a distinct species. This two-part name system is known as binomial nomenclature, the first part being the genus (a group of closely related species) and the second the species name. The suggestion here is that although the Neanderthal man was related to humans (*Homo*), it was a separate species. (All modern humans are of the same species, *Homo sapiens*—the smart people.) King argued that the flatness of the Neanderthal skull rendered it incapable of higher intellectual function. He added that the creature could not possibly have been able to believe in God or understand morality and was therefore not on the same level as modern people. To him it was a degenerate ancestor no more intelligent than a chimp. King's conception of Neanderthal man as a separate species did not catch on at first. Many referred to the Neanderthal as an ape-man. Historian Frank Spencer points out that when terms such as *ape-man* were used to describe human fossils, they were not always meant to imply an evolutionary relationship. The terms often meant that the human fossils looked like apes or monkeys or that they must have behaved like them. *Ape-man* or *apelike* could mean culture as well as biology.

Charles Lyell was able to procure plaster casts of the Neanderthal and Engis material and showed them to T. H. Huxley. Although Huxley was unsure if Neanderthal man was an intermediate step between apes and humans, he knew it was not a dead Cossack or a modern idiot ravaged by rickets. He argued that the Neanderthal helped prove the primate lineage of humans, contending further that Neanderthal man was not a separate species but part of the human line. This find fed right into Huxley's argument for *Man's Place in Nature*. He carefully measured all the skulls and had meticulous drawings and casts made and photos taken. He compared the skulls directly to one another and to modern ones as a point of reference and compared specific anatomical locations to chart their similarities and differences. Along the way he helped define the fledgling methodology of physical anthropology and the rigorous standards that had to be maintained in order to get useful data and make the field a respected one. Based on this assessment, Huxley said that the skull, though apelike, was still human. It simply represented an earlier version of the human race. He said that it was, "in reality, the extreme term of a series leading gradually from it to the highest and best developed of human crania" (1863, 206). In other words, Neanderthal man was at the earlier end of a continuous line of evolution toward modern humans. He added that the Neanderthal confirmed not only the antiquity of man and that humans evolved, but also that human antiquity must be pushed back even further.

Huxley's interpretation became part of the larger discussion of what Neanderthals were. There were basically three schools of thought. The first was that it was not ancient, just a deformed modern human (Virchow). The second was that it was an ancient human but a different species (King). The third was that it is an ancient ancestor but not a different species (Huxley). Generally, the camps for and against whatever Neanderthal man was were drawn along evolutionary lines. Those who supported its antiquity and ancestry were proevolutionists, whereas those who denied it also denied evolution. This makes sense, as the whole controversy initially related to whether Neanderthal man was an ancient or a modern person. One had to accept or deny Neanderthals as direct human ancestors before much more could be said. The past was becoming more and more complicated.

In 1865 British archaeologist John Lubbock (1834–1913) published *Prehistoric Times* as a way to get the growing mess of fossils and artifacts under some kind of control. The idea of "ages" of man was already in use by the 1830s, based upon tool technology. The Iron and older Bronze and Stone Ages were established as points of reference for cultural antiquity. The use of metals for artifact manufacture became an indicator of the sophistication of past societies. Lubbock modified the Stone Age by dividing it into the Neolithic (new stone) and the earlier Paleolithic (old stone) periods. The Paleolithic was characterized by flaked stone tools, whereas the Neolithic was characterized by more sophisticated ground and polished tools. Organizing the past in this fashion implied a certain linear progression. The organization suggested that history as well as human biological development went from simple to complex in an ever ascending line to the present. Lubbock worked backward, applying modern ideas and cultural norms to the past. It was believed by many Europeans that modern "savage" or "primitive" people—Australian Aborigines, for example—were living lives much as our ancient ancestors did. By observing these modern primitives one could get a good idea of how ancient primitives lived. In this way the Neanderthals could be viewed as just very old Aborigines. This model argued that ancient people clawed their way from the darkness and crudeness of the past to the light and sophistication of the present. There were other more subtle ideas about interpreting the past being employed as well.

Reactions and arguments over Neanderthal man in France also appeared. I. F. Pruner-Bey suggested it was a mentally defective, idiotic Irishman or an early Celt. Paul Broca (1824–1880) dismissed that assertion. The skull, he said, though unusual, did not exhibit any of the signs of microcephaly (abnormally small skull and brain) that would indicate idiocy. Broca was a leading member of the recently formed Société d'Anthropologie of Paris. Members of this organization were in general opposition to the older, more established, and conservative Musée National d'Histoire Naturelle that Georges Cuvier had established and over which his ghost still hovered. Broca and his colleagues were evolutionists, though not classic Darwinians (they were more inclined to the Lamarckian system). In the 1870s Broca began studying the anatomy of the human brain and saw that lesions or other damage might affect only one aspect of a person's mind. His work led to the discovery that speech abilities reside in a specific spot on the left side of the brain (now known as Broca's area). In his studies of the brain, however, Broca fell into the trap of equating brain size with intelligence. He originally believed that whites were smarter than blacks because they had larger brains. But his careful examinations of a wide range of human brains showed that physical size had almost no correlation to intelligence. His position was not popular with the denizens of the Musée National, and so he left to form the Société d'Anthropologie. In an odd twist of governmental interference in science, Broca had to ask permission from the French government to form his new organization. They balked at first, as he was considered a political radical because of his evolutionary beliefs. In the end the government relented but made a stipulation that a police officer had to attend every meeting of the society in order to ensure that no radical or dangerous ideas were discussed that might corrupt French society.

One of Broca's students was Gabriel de Mortillet (1821–1898). Like Broca, Mortillet was a political liberal, even a radical, in his thinking. Mortillet distrusted the church, the state, and the middle class from which he came. He studied geology in France until the revolution of 1848 forced him out when the left-wing forces he had joined were put down. He went to Italy and became interested in anthropology after studying some ancient sites there. After returning to France in 1864, Mortillet attacked the scientific establishment with as much zeal as he had the government. He naturally gravitated to Paul Broca and the Société d'Anthropologie. The Société opened a school in 1876 called the École d'Anthropologie. The two merged in 1878 as the Institut d'Anthropologie. Mortillet soon became a professor there and began blending politics with science, arguing that society and human evolution were closely linked. The ancients, he said, had been ruined by the appearance of religious and political oppression. The same, he contended, was happening in the present. Mortillet soon had many followers of his own, like André Lefevre, who became known as the "combat anthropologists" for their articles and lectures that used the story of humanity's past to critique the present, especially institutions of religion and superstition. Though initially philosophically close, Broca and Mortillet grew apart. In 1880 Paul Broca died, and Mortillet and his combat men gained control over the institute.

After the Feldhofer Cave find, it was a few years before another Neanderthal skeleton came to light. In 1866 Edouard Dupont discovered jaw parts of a Neanderthal in La Naulette Cave, Belgium. The bones helped established that the Neanderthal was not a freak but a representative of a genuinely different form of human. Looking at the La Naulette material, Mortillet proposed modifying Lubbock's prehistoric ages to equate biological advance with cultural advance. He began his ladder of progression with fossils and artifacts that dated from the earliest humans and worked up to the most recent forms. He broke up the Paleolithic age into yet smaller periods: the older Neanderthal cultures of the Mousterian to the Acheulian, the Aurignacian (to about 34,000–18,000 years ago), the Solutrean (15,000 to 18,000 years ago), and the Magdalenian, the most recent (10,000 to 15,000 years ago). As did Lubbock's, this system suggested a linear evolutionary pattern, not a jumping catastrophic progression as in the old Cuvierian model. Earlier human forms, like the Neanderthals, it was suggested, were biologically inferior to moderns, but they represented an earlier stop on the path to the present. Consequently, their culture was also at an inferior stage. As you came forward in time, you would see a cultural development that paralleled the biological improvement. This logic helped when sites were found with only fossils or only artifacts. Since they were believed to go hand in hand chronologically, you could tell what fossils should be there if only artifacts were found and vice versa. It was all very linear: older rude ancestors grew slowly more biologically advanced and culturally sophisticated as they worked their way to modernity.

Mortillet eventually saw a connection between the development of humans, their cultures, and the environment, particularly during the ice ages. During these periods vast parts of Europe, North America, and Asia were covered by thick layers of ice that advanced and retreated as the temperature rose and fell worldwide. The discovery of the ice ages was largely a Swiss accomplishment. The existing glaciers of the Swiss Alps suggested to men like Louis Agassiz (1807–1873) and Johann von Charpentier (1786–1855) that enormous ice packs had been moving about the earth in the past. The ice ages lasted from a little less than 2 million years ago up to about 10,000 years ago. These periodic invasions of ice drastically altered the weather and environment and thus human behavior and evolution. Being able to roughly date the ice ages, anthropologists could get a fix on the age of the human fossils and artifacts found in the strata. This technique gave several ways to date a human fossil: by the age of the strata they were found in, by the sophistication of their artifacts, and by associated fossil animals. The glacial period was originally called the Pleistocene Age by Charles Lyell in the 1830s. The French called the same period the Quaternary Age. Today the ice age period is still called the Pleistocene, whereas Quaternary covers both the Pleistocene glacial era and the postglacial Recent Age.

## Skulls

All the people who looked at the Neanderthal specimen zeroed in on the skull for special notice. Although all the bones had peculiar aspects, it was the skull that seemed especially otherworldly: the flatness of the head and the bulging brow ridges. Researchers seemed to conclude that these characteristics meant that Neanderthal man was a dim-witted brute. But why would they think that? Why did they not think Neanderthal man was a genius? The question can be partly answered by understanding that the nineteenth century saw a growth in the discipline of physical anthropology. Wrapped up in this new study of the anatomical structure of different groups of people was the belief that the shape of a person's head said much about their personality.

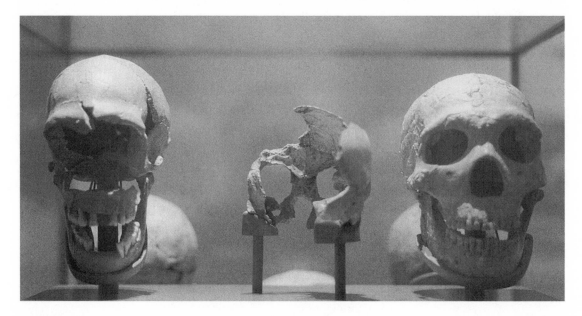

*Fossils tracing the evolution of man from a cat-sized, tree-dwelling ape to an upright, big-brained toolmaker. A Neanderthal skull and some of the Mousterian tools used by Neanderthals are shown in this display from the "Ancestors" exhibit at the American Museum of Natural History, New York, April 12, 1984. (Bettmann / Corbis)*

The Viennese physician Franz Joseph Gall (1758–1828) was convinced that a scientific study of a person's skull and facial features could give deep insight into his nature. An early advocate of the scientific study of brain function, Gall saw the brain as the physical manifestation of the "mind." The mind, he argued, had many parts that governed behavior and intellectual capability. In the 1790s Gall began studies on the relationship among skull shape, the proportions of the face, and the intellect. He believed these elements were related and could be studied with unambiguous technical precision. Until the 1810s, Gall's work was restricted to German-speaking regions. After several articles were published in English in 1815, his work caught on in Britain and the United States and led to offshoot studies, including the less scientific craniometry and the even more dubious, but popular, phrenology.

Phrenology, as much of this skull-related work was known, was generally looked down upon by the scientific establishment. Advocates of phrenology asserted that the geography of the skull and the way ridges and bumps appeared in specific spots denoted such personal characteristics as bravery, cowardice, combativeness, benevolence, self-esteem, and so on. Gall himself did not like the word *phrenology,* which he considered a bastardized Anglo-American hybrid. In the United States phrenology was popularized by Lorenzo Niles Fowler and his brother. They did head readings and lectures throughout North America and the British Isles. Reading the bumps on someone's head became a fun party game. The Fowlers turned their work into a merchandising enterprise by publishing books and study aids, including porcelain heads with areas of human cognition painted on the sides.

Though of doubtful scientific utility, the idea that skull shape gave insightful information about an individual was absorbed into mainstream anthropology. The preoccupation with human skulls was widespread. The American Samuel George Morton used his macabre collection to research skull shape and determine whether the races could be ranked by intelligence based on brain size and shape. Morton's physician friend from Philadelphia, J. Aitken Meigs, supported the collection and study of skulls because, he said, the skull "exhibits race-characters more striking and distinguishing than those presented by any other part of the bony system" (1858, 1). It was common in the literature of the day to see illustrations comparing the skulls of various human races, primates, and Neanderthals. Though the connection between phrenology and Neanderthal man is not often mentioned today,

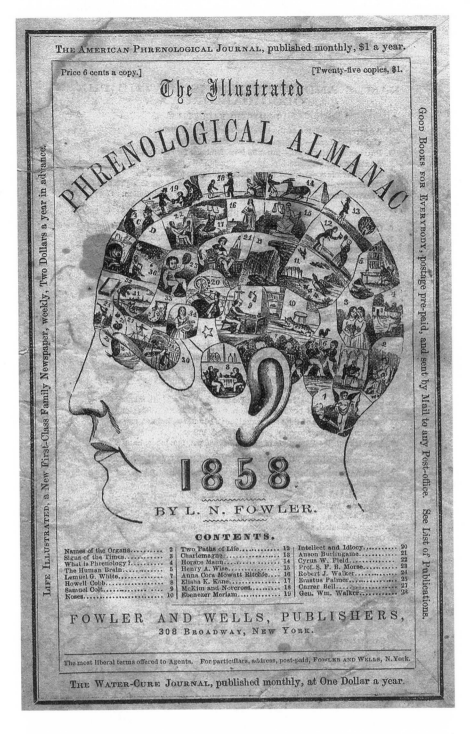

many period descriptions of Neanderthal man have a phrenological flavor. According to phrenological belief, a high forehead was indicative of advanced intellect and genteel behavior. The low profile and heavy brow ridges of the Neanderthals, on the other hand, pegged them as classic examples of violent brutes of low intelligence. The Neanderthals were seen as just one step along the way of human development.

Modern-day paleoanthropologist Ian Tattersall of the American Museum of Natural History argues that anthropologists of this era were preoccupied with the progressive single-species idea. They tended to view the story of human evolution as a simplistic linear progression from ape to angel. This helps explain why William King's argument that the Neanderthal was a separate species was at first ignored. Unlike paleontologists, who look at the wide diversity of all life and attempt to discover insights about groups across species boundaries, nineteenth-century anthropologists were looking at humans alone, with themselves at the top of the evolutionary line. Most naturalists could not conceive of it being any other way. They saw the story of man as a string from the past to the present that only need be untangled to show the "truth." Since study of ancient humans began before Darwin's ideas were published, Tattersall says, there was no satisfactory evolutionary mechanism to bring the wider picture into focus. This mind-set was about to change.

*La Chapelle-aux-Saints*

Now that naturalists knew what to look for it was not long before more Neanderthal material was unearthed. In a rapid sequence of events, discoveries were made across Europe: in Dinant, Belgium, in 1866; Spy, Belgium, in 1886; Krapina, Croatia, in 1899; and Ehringsdorf, Germany, in 1908. Neanderthals have since been found in Spain, Israel, Russian Georgia, and Iraq, showing that they were not strictly European. That so much Neanderthal material was found after 1856 makes one wonder how much material was found before then but was discarded or ignored because there was nothing to compare it to. How many skulls and jaws were found and thrown away or, like at Gibraltar, put in the dusty back room of a museum or monastery to be forgotten? It would be an interesting project to check the surviving saints' relics in European churches to see if any are Neanderthals.

In 1908 a trio of French priests found an almost complete Neanderthal skeleton lying among woolly rhino, bison, and reindeer fossils in a cave in the Corrèze area of France known as La Chapelle-aux-Saints (the church of the saints). Accomplished archaeologists who were searching for human remains, the priests speculated that the skeleton seemed intentionally buried. They showed it to another priest, Henri Breuil (1877–1961), who was becoming one of France's leading paleoanthropologists. The priests were interested in the problem of reconciling faith with scientific evidence of human prehistory. They were part of the "modernist" movement within the church. The Catholic modernists allowed for a universe that ran its own course, with God stepping in from time to time to make course corrections. Many of these priest anthropologists studied together at the seminary of Saint Sulpice, a stronghold of modernist thinking.

The cave floor at La Chapelle-aux-Saints was covered with a jumble of fossil mammal bones and Mousterian artifacts. Under this covering was the skeleton. Breuil suggested the skeleton be shown to another authority. Instead of winding up at Mortillet's more liberal École d'Anthropologie, it was shown to Marcellin Boule (1861–1942) of the Musée National d'Histoire Naturelle in Paris. Boule studied in Toulouse under archaeologist Emile Cartailhac (as did Breuil) and then paleontology under the crypto-evolutionist Albert Gaudry. As a staff member at the museum, Gaudry had to conceal his belief in transmutation to retain his job. The status quo there was still the Cuvierian denial of evolution. In the 1880s Boule began examining rock shelter sites in France where human fossils and artifacts had been discovered. He quickly rose in the ranks of French science, becoming a full professor in 1902. Boule, though politically conservative, brought the Musée National to a position more conducive to evolutionary thought.

Boule did a careful and painstaking examination of the La Chapelle-aux-Saints skeleton. This work, as did Huxley's before him, set a new standard for paleoanthropology. Boule joined the school of thought that argued for the Neanderthals being a separate species from modern humans. He could not bring himself to accept them as his ancestors. Like everyone else's, Boule's attention was riveted by the skull. Boule would later write of the skull that "we are impressed by its bestial appearance, or rather by the general effect of its simian characters" (1923, 194). In his reconstruction he curved the spine from La Chapelle-aux-Saints like an ape, not a human. He rebuilt the Neanderthal to look like a stooped-over old man, arguing that the spinal column did not have the proper curvature for a true upright stance. For Boule the Neanderthals were little better than gorillas. He said they rested on the outside edges of their feet, with their knees perpetually bent and an ample primatelike space between the first and second toes. In this reconstruction they would have tottered about fiendishly. "The crouching position," Boule said, "habitual to fossil man and savage [modern] peoples, is . . . an ancestral survival" (225). He claimed the Neanderthal must represent some early stage in locomotor development and that the skull was just too different in its proportions and anatomy and too close chronologically to be considered a direct human ancestor. The Neanderthals represented a branching off that led to a dead-end, not to modern humans.

Boule held the standard racist views of his day. He argued that compared to modern "lower races," Neanderthal man was very human, but compared to "higher," that is, white, races, he was inferior. The fact that the La Chapelle-aux-Saints skeleton seemed to have been buried was overlooked by Boule. A burial suggests compassion, a consideration of an afterlife, and other humanlike social behavior. This certainly did not fit with Boule's brutish thug image. He was intent on pushing the Neanderthals as far away from humans as possible.

The shape of the interior of the braincase suggested to Boule that the Neanderthals had an inferior intellectual capability. The bowed legs and powerful limbs, which were apparently characteristic of the group, led Boule to develop the overall, but erroneous, view of the Neanderthals many still have today. He said that the skeleton had many apelike features that suggested a stooped-over walking stance, the brain of an imbecile unable to communicate by anything other than grunts, and a robust figure that made it strong and violent. It is from Boule that we get the classic image of the caveman.

The year after the La Chapelle-aux-Saints skeleton was discovered, an almost complete Neanderthal skeleton was found in a cave in the Dordogne region of France known as Le Moustier (the Dordogne was quickly gaining a reputation as a center of early human activity). The skeleton was of a fifteen-year-old boy who may have been deliberately buried and who dated back about 100,000 years. Along with the skeleton were stone tools and other Neanderthal cultural objects in the layers above the skeleton. It is from this site that the term *Mousterian* is applied to Neanderthal tools (as opposed to the earlier Acheulian phase identified by Jacques Boucher de Crèvecoeur de Perthes). These types of instruments are known as flake tools. In the flaking technique a specially prepared stone is chipped to a certain shape in order to produce specific-size flakes that are then carefully worked to a razor-sharp edge. In the case of the Mousterian boy it is not clear if the tools were produced at the time the body was interred. As the fossil was not excavated with the proper scientific care, much important information about the site was lost.

The man who discovered Le Moustier, and did such a shoddy job uncovering it, was the controversial Swiss amateur archaeologist Otto Hauser (1874–1932). He had excavated several sites in Switzerland in the 1890s, but because of his haphazard methods he was scorned by established archaeologists. Determined to proceed, Hauser bought up tracts of land in the Dordogne and kept digging. In 1908 he found the Le Moustier teenager but kept quiet about it. Instead of hacking out the skeleton in his usual manner, Hauser invited leading archaeologists of Europe to view it in situ. The French establishment, Boule included, wanted nothing to do with someone they considered a bumbling charlatan, and besides, it was preoccupied with La Chapelle-aux-Saints. Only a handful of Germans arrived to watch Hauser remove the exquisitely preserved skeleton from its grave. Still smarting from the French rebuff, Hauser, who was deeply in debt, sold the skeleton to the Germans. After this contentious sale (human fossil material and artifacts are normally kept in the country they are found in), Hauser left archaeology for good, only later writing a few books. In his twilight years he and his wife would solemnly visit the Berlin Ethnological Museum to pay their respects to the Le Moustier boy, like parents visiting the grave of a child. Unfortunately, during World War II, Allied bombs found the museum, and much of the collection was incinerated.

Trying not to look too upset for missing out on Le Moustier, Boule kept to his grand plan. He was empire building and was determined to use the La Chapelle-aux-Saints skeleton to accomplish this end. His branching-tree approach to human lineage contradicted Mortillet's straight-line scenario. By using this approach Boule could snub Mortillet and the École d'Anthropologie as well as proponents of Neanderthals all at the same time. He was attempting to place himself and the Musée National at the forefront of French anthropology, and he succeeded. Prince Albert I of Monaco had been following the work on the La Chapelle-aux-Saints skeleton closely. He was so interested in human prehistory that he personally took part in several digs. Impressed by Boule's work, the prince offered to build him an entire academy dedicated to the study of human evolution. Boule accepted and in 1910 established the Institut de Paléontologie Humaine. He immediately brought in his friend Henri Breuil and another like-minded anthropologist, Hugo Obermaier. A contributing factor in the longevity of Boule's model for the Neanderthal was that he was so successful in taking control of the French paleoanthropological establishment that made the rules, set the standards, and brooked no opposition.

Henri Breuil spent most of his career studying the cultural artifacts that were associated with ancient humans. Following Mortillet's death in 1898, Breuil put together a much more complex theory of descent more in line with Boule's. Breuil's idea was bolstered by discoveries made years before. In 1868 six skeletons were discovered by railway workers in a cave near Les Eyzies, France, called Cro-Magnon (again in the Dordogne region). The skeletons were old, but at the same time they were modern looking. They did not have the heavy brow ridges or robust limbs of the Neanderthals. The Cro-Magnons (pronounced kro-man-yons), who date to about 50,000 years ago, were ancient but anatomically modern people. They seemed to be the next logical step in human evolution: they fitted perfectly the simple linear progression, their culture and artifacts were more sophisticated, they painted pictures on cave walls, and they created three-dimensional artwork and sculpture.

In 1901 more Cro-Magnon skeletons were found at Grimaldi, Italy. These skeletons seemed to be at least as old as the Neanderthals. The bodies were intentionally buried and ritually painted. If these Cro-Magnons were as old as Neanderthals, it put a crimp in the linear-progression pattern: How could the Neanderthals have become the Cro-Magnons if the Cro-Magnons already existed? Boule said this irregularity supported the branching-tree theory. Breuil applied the same idea, arguing that the same progressive development held for culture as for anatomy. The Aurignacian culture of the later Cro-Magnons was not a further advance on the Mousterian, he said, but something that had come into the area from outside and was therefore unrelated. It was more catastrophic, like the Cuvier model. Thus, Breuil, Boule, and Boule's student Henri Vallois promoted the "pre-sapiens" concept. Presapiens were creatures older than the Neanderthals but were unconnected to them. The presapiens were thought to be the direct ancestors of modern humans, who were little different from them yet traced their lineage back millions of years. Boule had worked for years on nonhuman paleontology and saw that descent was not a simple straight line but a complex pattern of relationships. It seemed only reasonable to apply this approach to humans. The pre-sapiens theory pushed the modern human line much further into the past. There was just not enough time for the Neanderthals to lose their apelike qualities and become modern. Therefore, they could not be our direct ancestors but instead were a branching dead-end.

Politics was as integral a part of the search for the history of humans as fossils and artifacts, and not just in France. In England Sir

Arthur Keith (1866–1955) had taken over for George Busk at the Royal College of Surgeons in 1908. Born in Aberdeenshire, England, Keith studied medicine and zoology. He went to Thailand in the early 1890s to work as a doctor at a mining company and became fascinated by primate anatomy. He did studies on the relationship of humans and apes before starting work at the London Hospital Medical School in 1895. At the Royal College of Surgeons he influenced many students with his views on human evolution. His approach to natural history, the acquisition of fossils, and his relationship to scientists of other countries suggest that he saw it all as a competitive game. He gave the French and Germans their due for the discoveries and theories—and prodded the Americans for not having any—but hinted that the British were the real leaders in the competition for fossil collections and bragging rights to the cradle of man. He used Boule's and Breuil's work to support his position. He too was empire building and wanted to show fossil finds from Britain as preeminent discoveries that would make British paleoanthropology, and him, the world leader. Until 1911 Keith accepted the Mortillet straight-line theory of human descent. In 1912, after reading Boule's work on the Neanderthals, he went with the branching-tree approach, pushed the Neanderthals aside, and accepted the presapiens theory. Keith had formed in his mind's eye a picture of how a human ancestor should look and searched for it.

Many Europeans liked the idea of being able to claim the oldest human fossils or cultures. Citizens and scientists alike in France, Germany, Belgium, and Britain often considered themselves superior to the others. These political and cultural rivalries spilled into the study of human antiquity. In the case of the Moulin Quinon jaw (an early find made by Boucher and thought to be genuine, but actually the misidentification of a modern bone), the French thought the skull real, whereas the British did not. Later, when Piltdown man was revealed, the opposite happened: the British hailed the skull, whereas the French had their chance to scoff. There were several instances during this period where a little more scoffing would have helped.

In 1888 along the banks of the Thames River near Kent, chalk workers uncovered a broken but fairly complete skull. (During this period more human fossils were found by construction workers than scientists.) The skull was brought to the attention of amateur fossil hunter Robert Elliot of Scotland, who had previously asked the men to keep an eye out for such things. The skull was quickly dug out under the protests of another amateur fossil hunter, the local schoolmaster, Matthew Keys. The late nineteenth century was a transitional period for paleoanthropology as it moved from haphazard collecting by amateurs to careful excavation by professionals. Keys wanted to photograph the skull in the ground as a way of properly recording the find. That it was not fed suspicions that Galley Hill man, as it came to be known, might not be what it was thought to be.

The modernity of a skull found in apparently ancient strata suggested to Keith that the presapiens theory was valid and that the Neanderthals could not be our ancestors. Keith accepted Galley Hill as genuine, but others (Boule included) did not. Just why Keith advocated this is unclear in light of the dubious nature of the find. Galley Hill man was not as ancient as Keith hoped. It was found to be a Bronze Age intrusion dug down into the strata of an earlier age, making the newer skeleton appear to be from the earlier time. This problem is why archaeologists and paleoanthropologists have to be extremely careful when they excavate a site and why they go through great pains to document every step of the process so that the material recovered can be dated accurately. Not doing this is why so many people were upset with Otto Hauser. This misinterpretation is what Matthew Keys hoped to avoid by photographing the fossil. A fossil is virtually worthless unless it is known exactly where it came from, what level of strata, and so forth. Like Boule, Keith was searching for a skeleton of his own, preferably a British one. What Keith wanted was a missing link.

The concept of the "missing link" has been a powerful one in Western biological science. If living things evolved from one form to another, the thinking went, then there must be an intermediate stage that was a combination of the old and new types. These intermediate forms should put an end to any haggling over whether evolution actually worked. Detractors said that proevolution forces could quiet them by showing just one genuine example. Evolution supporters were always looking for one to quash the antievolutionists. Several examples, like the part-bird, part-dinosaur archaeopteryx, had been discovered, but a human missing link was a much tougher proposition. Anthropologists like Arthur Keith argued that a form of human ancestor must have existed that had both apelike and humanlike characters. It was argued that since evolution worked slowly, a big-brained primate, or a small-brained one who could walk upright, must have existed. There were also arguments about which came first. Did our ancestors walk upright first? Did they acquire big brains first? Did they evolve modern grasping hands first? Did they come down from the trees, or did they start off on the ground? A missing link might answer these questions. The image of what a human ancestor should look like was held up as a sort of wanted poster. Have you seen this ape-man? If so, report him to your local anthropologist. Do not approach him alone! The missing-link hypothesis fascinated scientists, theologians, and the public alike.

*Impostors and Poseurs*

Arthur Keith was looking for something that fitted his expectation of what a human ancestor should be. Australian anatomist Grafton Elliot Smith (1871–1937), then working in England, had his own view. As a brain specialist, Smith believed that for early ancestors to progress to modern humans, their brains had to enlarge first. Therefore, he argued that there had to be a large braincase to any fossil. As a curator at the British Museum of Natural History working primarily on fish, Arthur Smith Woodward (1864–1944) was looking for any early ancestor that would boost his career. In 1912 all three men got what they were looking for in the same package.

Piltdown man had everything an early-twentieth-century anthropologist and human evolutionist could want: it had a modern-design skull and an apelike jaw, and it was found in an ancient layer of strata. It fitted the "missing link" hypothesis perfectly. Unfortunately, it was a fake, a forgery that haunts science in general and evolution studies in particular to this day. Like the story of Jack the Ripper, the culprit remains unknown, though there are several popular suspects. At the center of the story is Charles Dawson, a lawyer by training but a naturalist by desire. Dawson, likable, middle-aged, with a big mustache and big dreams, was an amateur who wanted to enter the rarefied world of British science as a fossil man. To that end he roamed the English countryside searching for fossils and enlisting the services of workmen at quarries and construction sites. In 1908, as the legend goes, workers at a gravel quarry on the land of Barkham Manor near Piltdown, Sussex, where Dawson had a business connection to the local landowners, discovered some strange bits of fossil bone. The term *legend* is used here because the specifics of how the bones were found are in question. In any event, the bones were given to Dawson, who recognized them as pieces of a human skull. By 1911 additional fragments had been brought out of the quarry. At this point Dawson contacted an acquaintance at the British Museum of Natural History.

Arthur Smith Woodward was a trained geologist and curator of fish at the museum who had struggled to lift himself up from his working-class roots. He joined the museum as a teenager and clawed his way to the top. He was also doubtful of Arthur Keith's evolutionary theories. Where Dawson was big and blustery, Woodward took himself seriously and was reserved to the point of being dour. Woodward realized that Dawson's energy could be made to work to his advantage, so he gave the lawyer the honorary title of "collector" for the museum. Eager for the recognition, Dawson ate up the bone Woodward tossed him and in return gave Woodward all his best bones.

In May 1912 Dawson took the Piltdown material to his benefactor. After seeing the fossils Woodward had Dawson take him and a Jesuit paleontologist, Pierre Teilhard de Chardin (1881–1955), to the Piltdown site. Like Henri Breuil, Teilhard de Chardin was a French Catholic priest and scientist. He was gaining a reputation as a paleontologist of scholarly ability and by 1905 had already taught physics and chemistry as well as studied geological strata and fossils. He would go on to a long, distinguished career writing empirical books on human evolution as well as deeply mystical works on the relationship of evolution, religion, and the meaning of life. His metaphysical writings on the existence of a "noosphere," or moral superorganism, brought him occasionally into conflict with the more traditional and conservative elements of the Catholic Church. He studied with Marcellin Boule and received his doctorate in 1922.

In June 1912 the eager, jovial lawyer, the stiff scientist, and the lanky priest headed out to Barkham Manor. They found a few promising mammal fossils and a few eoliths. Further excavation was begun at once. The following November a newspaper story came out in the *Manchester Guardian* that a human ancestor, probably the oldest ever found, had been dug up in Sussex. As Johann Fuhlrott and Hermann Schaaffhausen had presented Neanderthal man to the German scientific community in 1857, Charles Dawson and Arthur Smith Woodward presented Piltdown man to a meeting of the Geological Society of London on December 18, 1912. Unlike the two Germans, the two Englishmen met a more favorable response. Although the actual fossil comprised relatively few pieces of the skull and jaw, a reconstruction was put together that filled in all the missing parts. The fully formed skull and jaw were a striking sight. The upper skull and face were human and the jaw apelike. There was some haggling over the correct size of the skull, but in general comment was positive. With his greater knowledge of primate anatomy, Arthur Keith argued that the skull should be bigger than Woodward made it but accepted Piltdown as genuine because it fitted his preconceived image of presapiens. Piltdown was not the ugly beetle-browed Neanderthal of dim wit and growling countenance but had a graceful, even beautiful face full of budding intelligence. Though they disagreed on details, the three British anthropologists agreed that Piltdown man was a human ancestor. Not everyone was so captivated.

Aleš Hrdlička (1869–1943), a curator at the Smithsonian Institution in Washington, was uncomfortable with the awkward fit of the Piltdown skull and jaw. It made no sense from an evolutionary point of view. The creature had a modern-size brain, so why did it not have a modern jaw that would allow it to talk? Primates like apes, chimps, and monkeys can make sounds, but they cannot engage in human speech. This is because of the shape of their jaws, the number of facial muscles they have, and the movement of their tongues. The mechanics of their jaws do not allow for the subtlety and nuance of movement that gives humans speech. Piltdown had a brain like a human but no ability to articulate complex language. It was like a creature that had flippers for swimming but no way to hold its breath underwater. Hrdlička said moderns appeared as a result of a slow, steady evolution from an as yet unknown preanthropoid ancestor, not a presapien. He held to a more straight-line hypothesis with the Neanderthal as an ancestor.

Several Americans were at first skeptical of Piltdown. In particular, William K. Gregory (1876–1970) and Henry Fairfield Osborn (1857–1935) of the American Museum of Natural History in New York hesitated to accept it. In 1917, however, pieces of an apparent second skull were discovered. With this new development Osborn came around to a more sympathetic view of Piltdown. Osborn was already in the presapiens camp, and though he was baffled by Piltdown, it became easier for him to accept. Even so, no one was quite sure what to do with this strange hybrid. It did not fit easily into any accepted form of lineage. A nagging, vague disquiet led many anthropologists to drop the thing from their researches. By the 1920s only a few diehards continued to refer to it. When the deception was finally exposed, scientists' views did not change much because Piltdown had already been flushed from the system of scientific thought. The Piltdown case is often held up by antiscience and antievolution forces as the perfect example of the hubris and arrogance of science and scientists. In their headlong rush to prove their theories, it is argued, scientists either fool themselves or intentionally try to fool the rest of us. Though Piltdown man was not conclusively found to be a hoax until the early 1950s, it was found out. Either way, by the 1920s Piltdown had already fallen from its place in the minds of most paleoanthropologists. If anything, the story of Piltdown man can be held up as an example of how scientific evidence, once past an initial stage of excitement, must pass rigorous scrutiny before being accepted.

Whoever the forger was, he did his work well. The pieces were broken, stained, chemically treated, and arranged to look ancient. They were fitted together with just enough material to suggest that it was genuine, but not too much to give the game away. The claim was accepted by a wide range of naturalists because it seemed to have all the elements that they thought it should have: part human, part ape, big brain, ancient strata, and worn molar teeth. If you looked hard enough you could see whatever you wanted. British scientists were particularly proud that this important creature was one of their own. They now had a specimen that ranked with those being discovered in Europe that had seemed to upstage them. Even the taciturn Boule liked it because it was the kind of evidence that would help him push the Neanderthals even further away from him.

An enormous amount of literature was produced about Piltdown man as scientists and theologians alike tried to work it into their theories before giving up. The few voices of opposition were drowned out in the din of acceptance. It was not until 1953 that modern dating techniques, using first fluorine and then nitrogen tests, showed once and for all that Piltdown was an early modern human skull with an orangutan jaw attached to it. The tests were done by British Museum scientists Kenneth Oakley, Wilfrid Le Gros Clark, and Joseph Weiner.

The questions remain, who did it? Why did they do it? What did they gain from doing it? No one knows for sure. It could have been Charles Dawson using the "discovery" as a way up the ladder of scientific success or as a way to embarrass those who had already made it there. It has been argued that Dawson did not have the skill or anatomical knowledge to produce such a convincing forgery. In recent years some have questioned whether it really is a convincing forgery. One school of thought says Dawson did have the requisite knowledge from his university training; another blames Arthur Smith Woodward. The latter's motivation to do it was advancement to the position of director of the British Museum, a post he coveted and was actively campaigning for. Woodward also had access to all the raw materials needed to make the forgery, while Dawson had access to the site. The thirty-year relationship between Dawson and Woodward makes this scenario plausible.

To complicate the story, a discovery was made public in 1996 about the contents of a storage box. Originally discovered in the attic of the British Museum in the late 1970s, the box contained skeletal materials stained in the same way as Piltdown. The box belonged to Martin Hinton, who was curator of zoology at the time of the Piltdown discovery. Hinton had been turned down in 1910 by Woodward for a research grant. The theory is that Hinton concocted the Piltdown forgery as revenge. He knew of Dawson's incompetence and Woodward's gullible pomposity and used their weaknesses to make them look ridiculous. Woodward was enamored of the idea of a British missing link, so Hinton led him down that trail. He even created a bogus "ancient cricket bat" for Piltdown man to play with (something that would have been especially enticing to an Anglocentrist). Woodward bought the idea completely and later published *The Earliest Englishman* (1948). Since the discovery of the box of fragments, many have come to believe the case is closed, with Hinton the final guilty party. In the end it could have been Hinton, Smith, Keith, or Woodward. It could even have been Teilhard de Chardin, known for his love of practical jokes. Or it could have been someone never suspected, someone who planted the bones so that Dawson would find them and get the ball rolling and who will laugh themselves silly for eternity at the great fun he had.

Not every false ancestor was a hoax like Piltdown. Many were simple misidentifications. The nineteenth and early twentieth centuries were a heady time for discovering fossil humans. A virtual parade of "men" appeared, many of peculiar countenance and dubious integrity. The British, of course, had Galley Hill man and Piltdown. The Americans had Lansing man in California, Vero man in Florida, and Trenton man in New Jersey, among others. Even in Argentina, paleontologist Florentino Ameghino discovered what he thought were early humans he called Tetraprothomo and Diprothomo. They all turned out to be misidentifications of modern skeletons.

A close second to Piltdown man's infamy was a discovery from the Badlands of Nebraska. In 1906, Richard Gilder, a Nebraska journalist and amateur fossil hunter, was searching for human artifacts near Indian burial mounds outside Omaha. He found some unusual specimens and took them to Nebraska state geologist Edwin Barbour. An article about the discoveries then appeared in the *Omaha World Herald,* a copy of which made its way to Henry Fairfield Osborn, the head of the American Museum of Natural History in New York.

Osborn was so excited by what he read that he went to Nebraska to view the material firsthand. Osborn had only recently turned his attention to the question of human evolution. He had followed the work of Marcellin Boule, Arthur Keith, and other physical anthropologists, but he had little hands-on human fossil experience himself. He was intrigued by the fact that the Nebraska find came from a locality he was already familiar with through his study of fossil horses. Osborn examined the material—a skullcap, several long bones, and other assorted pieces. Heavy brow ridges on the skullcap and a general robustness of the bones suggested their great antiquity. Osborn published an article about the find in *Century* magazine the following month. He said that anthropologists were of two minds about the appearance of humans in the Americas. They believed they had appeared either very early or very late. He placed himself in the former camp. Since he believed a land bridge connecting the Americas to Asia and Europe had allowed for the migration of animals during the Pleistocene epoch, he concluded that early hominids must have done the same.

Some heralded Nebraska man as the oldest hominid known in the Americas. Not everyone was so enthusiastic. Sent by his boss at the Smithsonian to view the bones, Aleš Hrdlička examined all the Nebraska man material with an eye toward anatomical detail but had disappointing news. "If the present knowledge concerning these specimens is impartially considered," he said, "it is apparent that the theory of a more than recent geological origin of any of them meets with serious objections" (87). The bones were the disinterred modern burial of a Native American, not a fossil.

Unexpectedly, Nebraska man reappeared in February 1922. A paleontologist and fossil hunter from Nebraska named Harold J. Cook sent Osborn an unusual tooth he had uncovered. Upon receiving it, Osborn concurred that it belonged to some kind of anthropoid. Osborn called it *Hesperopithecus* (the ape of the Western world) and told Grafton Elliot Smith that it fell between the anthropoid apes and humans. Osborn was nervous, however, that the European press was referring to *Hesperopithecus* (he never called it Nebraska man) as a human ancestor since he did not believe it was. The June 24, 1922, edition of the *Illustrated London News* ran an article on *Hesperopithecus* with an illustration showing the creature as an archaic but clearly humanlike creature. Using Grafton Elliot Smith as an authority, the *Illustrated London News* called the find "an astounding discovery of human remains." Osborn knew it would cause trouble. He wrote Smith saying he could not agree with him that the creature be called an ape-man because there was still so little evidence to confirm it. Osborn argued that *Hesperopithecus* was neither an ape ancestor nor a direct human ancestor, though more related to hominids.

While all the public pronouncements were being made, museum staff reexamined the tooth. By 1925 Osborn's assistant, William K. Gregory, was having second thoughts about *Hesperopithecus*. Osborn had sent an expedition to the original site that discovered material showing that Nebraska man was not a man, or an ape, but an extinct peccary, *Prosthennops*. Unmasked, Nebraska man had to be explained. Gregory made an official statement at a meeting of the New York Academy of Science and in an article in the December 1927 issue of the journal *Science*. The Nebraska man incident has been held up ever since by antievolution forces as an intentional hoax.

There were other candidates for inclusion in the human family tree. Some of them were humorously charming, some genuinely intriguing. In November 1869 a farmer named Newell said he dug up a large, bizarre fossil on his land outside Cardiff, New York. The story quickly spread through the media to the outside world. It was a large figure of a man almost nine feet tall who had turned to stone through some unknown but extraordinary process. People came from far and wide to gawk at the forlorn figure and speculate on what it was. In the best American tradition of entrepreneurship the landowner put up a tent and charged visitors a fee. Protestant ministers seized on the fossil as scientific support for the accuracy of Scripture. A New York geologist, James Hall, also came to look. His statements about the thing being intriguing were taken out of context by newspapers as scientific support for its genuineness. Eventually, a young Yale University paleontologist early in a long, distinguished career, Othniel Charles Marsh, inspected the anomaly and quickly saw that it was a block of gypsum carved to look like a human body. Marsh's assessment that the Cardiff Giant, as it was known, was a hoax did not deter showman P. T. Barnum, who, unable to buy the humbug outright, simply made one himself and put it on tour.

Another anomalous example of the intense curiosity over our difficult ancestors turned up in South America in the 1920s around the time people began to question Piltdown man. François de Loys was a Swiss zoologist and explorer on an expedition up the Tarra River along the border of Venezuela and Colombia. At a campsite, de Loys and his party were allegedly attacked by a pair of strange primates. The attack was so ferocious that de Loys's men fired on the creatures, killing one and driving the other off. The creature was so unusual that de Loys propped it up on a box and took a photograph of it. He then skinned it and prepared the skeleton to bring back with him. Unfortunately, the hardships of the rest of the expedition were such that all of his equipment and specimens, including the creature's remains, were lost. All that was saved was the photograph, which caused a sensation. De Loys said the creature was almost five feet tall, was tailless, and weighed more than one hundred pounds. De Loys's friend geologist George Montandon thought de Loys had found an unknown American species. Montandon was a polygenist who also subscribed to white supremacist Aryan theory (discussed in the next chapter). He seized on the photo as evidence of the separate evolutionary line for the aboriginal Americans. The British just sniffed at this Swiss monstrosity.

Arthur Keith suspected de Loys had fabricated the whole thing. He said it was nothing more than a large spider monkey with its tail cut off and that there was nothing to show that it was anywhere near the five feet tall de Loys claimed. However, in the photo, de Loys had set the dead animal on a Standard Oil Company packing crate, which was known to be a uniform size. This allowed other scientists to extrapolate the creature's height in comparison to the box. It came out to be a little less than five feet tall. With nothing to go on but the photograph, de Loys's ape never made it into the discussion of human or primate evolution. In the 1960s pioneering cryptozoologist (one who studies unknown animals) Ivan Sanderson reexamined the de Loys photo and came to the same conclusion as Keith. Although most anthropologists dismiss de Loys's ape as a misidentification or even hoax, some still think there is enough about the photo to keep their interest. Had the creature been what de Loys claimed it was, it would have been doubly intriguing, as five-foot-tall, tailless, upright anthropoids were not supposed to have ever existed in the Americas. Supporting the hoax claim, no other examples of de Loys's ape have since appeared.

One of the things incidents like the Cardiff Giant, de Loys's ape, Nebraska man, or Piltdown man tell us is that we have an uneasy attitude about our ancestors. On one hand, we are profoundly interested in what and where we came from. Yet on the other hand, we are just as profoundly disturbed by what we find when we open up our closets. This can lead to mistakes, arguments, and questioning, but questioning can lead to growth and new knowledge. Until the twentieth century, there were few rules or established techniques for the study of human ancestry. Thanks to the work of T. H. Huxley, Marcellin Boule, and others, scientific investigation became more sophisticated and discerning. With the rise in professionalism, incidents like the ones described declined drastically. Under all these false starts and misidentifications, however, one fossil cried out for recognition but found only deaf ears.

## Java Man

Starting in the early 1890s a genuinely ancient discovery began hovering about the human line, complicating the situation further still. Eugène Dubois (1858–1940) collected fossils as a child and then attended medical school in the late 1870s. His Dutch Catholic upbringing clashed with what he learned about evolution in school, but he became fascinated by the work of T. H. Huxley and the German evolutionist Ernst Haeckel and grew increasingly interested in the question of human origins. He was especially enamored of Haeckel's argument that evidence of the earliest human relations would be found somewhere in the East Indies, in Asia, and that man had a primate lineage. As the East Indies were then a colony of Holland, Dubois would have relatively easy access to the region. There are questions as to why Dubois chose to hunt fossils in Java. Though a skilled anatomist, he had no experience with fossils. His hero,

Haeckel, was himself not particularly enamored of fossils, insisting that a good naturalist could infer biological relations without them. Ironically, it was Haeckel's rival, an antievolutionist, Rudolf Virchow, who claimed that fossil apes would most likely be found in the Indies.

From his studies Dubois formulated a series of reasons for going to the Indies: the primate loss of long hair would not be a problem in the tropics; orangutans and gibbons (which Dubois believed most closely related to humans) lived there; later versions of organisms often lived in the same range as their ancestors; most human fossils were found in caves, and Java is honeycombed with caves; and finally, a fossil ape jaw had been found in the nearby Siwalik Hills of India in 1878. It was the theory of Asian human origins postulated by Ernst Haeckel that led Eugene Dubois to Java.

Haeckel was the foremost proponent of Darwinian evolution in Germany. A prolific researcher, Haeckel coined the terms *ecology* and *phylogeny* and developed the first representational tree of life to describe the relationships of all living things. He worked out a theory that said the development of an individual organism (its ontogeny) mimicked the development of the larger group it belonged to. These larger groups of organisms linked by a common ancestor Haeckel called a phylum. The evolutionary development of these larger groups he called phylogeny. Each group was connected by a common link. Therefore, there must be a link between humans and primates. After studying the manlike apes, he concluded that there was a middle step from the former to the latter with a large brain and bipedal posture. He called this hypothetical creature *Pithecanthropus alalus* (the ape that cannot talk). He also argued that the site of the earliest stage of human ancestor development must have been South Asia, in particular the lost continent of Lemuria, somewhere between Africa and Indonesia. From there the *Pithecanthropi* spread into Asia and the rest of the world.

Failing to raise the funds necessary for an expedition, Dubois took the extraordinary step of joining the Dutch East India Army. Having done so, he was posted, along with his wife and daughter, to Sumatra in 1887. He quickly worked out an agreement with his commanding officers to get extra time away to search for fossils. By 1889 he had coaxed the Dutch government into placing him on permanent leave to fossil hunt full-time. In addition to the free time, the Dutch army also gave Dubois a pair of assistants and a work gang of local convicts to dig. Although he had already covered considerable ground, by 1890 Dubois had concentrated his efforts at the Solo River near the village of Trinil. The large number of mammal fossils he and his team began excavating suggested to him that India and Java had once been connected, allowing the easy passage of animals from one region to another. Digging a large pit down many meters to hard volcanic rock that October, the team discovered a pair of important finds: a tooth and a skullcap. The finds were made under circumstances that would later haunt the entire endeavor and threaten to ruin Dubois's reputation. The problems were that Dubois was probably not present when the fossils were found, they were found some distance apart from each other, and detailed records of their discovery were not kept. Though unsure if the skull and tooth went together, Dubois at first tentatively speculated that they came from a fossil chimpanzee. Due to the onslaught of the inclement weather season, work was halted until the next year. When work resumed, a humanlike thigh bone was found in the same strata but farther upstream. Dubois began to rethink his chimpanzee theory, as the thigh seemed to have come from a true biped.

Over the next few years the dig site was radically enlarged, but little more of this material was discovered. Based on this tiny amount of material—a skullcap, two teeth, a thigh bone, and a few scattered bone splinters—Dubois came to a startling new conclusion. The creature, he speculated, must have been a bipedal chimplike creature with a humanlike skull. Originally calling it *Anthropopithecus,* Dubois settled on *Pithecanthropus erectus* (the upright ape-man). Because of the region it was found in, it was commonly referred to as Java man. In Dubois's mind, the creature was clearly an intermediate step between the primates and the hominids—a missing link.

The discovery was made public in 1895 at the Third International Congress of Zoology, in Leiden, Holland. Heading the congress was Rudolf Virchow. The assembled meeting, though impressed by the fossils and seeing their importance, could not help but question Dubois's assertions. As with the Neanderthal fossil, three schools of thought jelled around Java man: it was an ape, it was a human, or to the smallest group—Ernst Haeckel included—it was an intermediate form, as Dubois claimed. Following the congress, Dubois engaged in a frantic schedule to show the fossils around, but the reactions were the same. This response made Dubois combative and defensive. He consistently argued that Java man was a missing link and would consider no alternative.

Although few agreed with him, many paleoanthropologists wanted to see Java man. A steady stream of visitors formed at his front door and annoyed Dubois no end. He soon shut his door and refused to show the fossils to anyone. As a result, Java man and Dubois faded from the scientific consciousness like a vaguely interesting but strangely peculiar memory. Rumors began to spread about the fate of the two. Some said Dubois had destroyed the fossil, some said he had gone insane, that he had reverted to ultraorthodox Catholicism, and still others said that he had hidden the bones under the floorboards of his house like the body in Poe's "The Tell-Tale Heart."

The reasons Dubois hoarded the fossils is a little more prosaic. He needed time to complete his research so it could be published. Upon his return to Holland, Dubois was able to obtain only a lowly post at the University of Amsterdam. If he gave up the fossils to others he would have nothing of value left to his career. Others had already begun to build careers around the work they had done on Java man, and he wanted his limelight too. Because of this absence, Java man was not embraced by the paleoanthropological community and did not play much role in the human evolution controversy during this period. It was not until the 1920s, as Aleš Hrdlička coaxed his way into Dubois's confidence, that the material was made available again. When the fossil was again examined, the conclusion was the same as years before: Java man was an early human ancestor, not a missing link.

So wedded to his conclusions, Dubois dismissed later similar finds made outside Peking, China, in the 1920s and '30s. Oddly, when more *Pithecanthropus* material was unearthed along the Solo River in 1936, Dubois dismissed it too. Anthropologist Ralph Von Koenigswald found most of a young skullcap of what he called Pithecanthropus II (also known as Mojokerto child). Dubois went so far as to accuse Von Koenigswald of either faking the skull or poorly reconstructing it. What is so strange about Dubois is that where others fought to have their finds included in the human family line, he fought to keep his out. It is now known that Java man and the finds from Peking were the same and part of a group today called *Homo erectus.*

In the end Java man was brought into the human line, but Eugène Dubois was left to die a lonely, angry old man. Symbolic of this fate, in the basement of the museum of Leiden there stands an odd statue. A creature not wholly human or ape stands holding an antler in his hand, the other hand outstretched, palm up. The creature stares at the bone tool he is holding as if absorbed in thought. On the base of the statue, which is nicked and scratched and chipped with age, it reads: "Pithecanthropus erectus." Dubois made the exhibit himself using his fossils and son as a model. Only a curiosity now, it stands sadly forgotten in a corner. Staring closely at the face and the gesturing open hand, one sees a questioning, puzzled look come over it as if asking, "Who am I, what am I, where do I belong?" For a creature that never really existed, these questions have no answers.

## Conclusion

By the end of the nineteenth century there was little doubt in scientific circles that humans had evolved. That the Neanderthals and Cro-Magnons were ancient was also a closed issue. Just what relationship the Neanderthals and Cro-Magnons or Java man had to modern people was a different debate entirely. That debate was held mostly in the halls of science. The religious debate quieted briefly during the early scramble for fossils after the initial outburst of theological concern. Most Christians, indeed most cultures around the world, stuck with their spiritual and scriptural views of Creation and bothered little with the fixation on fossils and naturalistic explanations.

Regardless of what the Neanderthals may or may not have been, few liked them as direct ancestors. Only Aleš Hrdlička continued to argue for them. Like Victor Frankenstein, anthropologists could not bear to look at the hideous progeny they had unearthed. The Neanderthals were left to scratch their beetled brows and flat heads in wonderment as to where they belonged in the human family that had passed them by. That Java man seemed to have Neanderthal characteristics, only more primitive, located it as a precursor to them. *Pithecanthropus* seemed to confirm the presapiens theory and justify the banishment of the Neanderthals. That a brutish line of humanlike creatures was being established off a sidetrack gave hope that a more acceptable ancestor lay in wait to be discovered. It was this hope that contributed to the initial acceptance of Piltdown and the burst of interest in, then disappointing climax over, Nebraska man and the other almost ancestors and near men.

In 1914 World War I broke out. Human evolution seemed something of an anachronism in a world where humans were slaughtering each other by the millions. Others questioned the notion of evolution itself. Was this what we had evolved for? Was this the pinnacle? Antagonism among the British, French, and Germans over fossil interpretations was exacerbated by jingoistic politics. Scientific boundaries based on nationalistic lines grew only stronger. With apocalyptic battles raging across France, European fossil hunting ground to a halt.

When such activities began again, something new had come to the fore in the thinking on human origins. While all the talk about fossils and relationships and evolutionary mechanics was going on, a parallel, quieter but no less important question was being asked. If humans had evolved from lower forms, if there was a point when the first humans appeared, then where on earth did they appear? Where was the first human born? The answer that came to most people's minds when asked this question was the same: Asia.

*Further Reading*

There is a large body of work on the Neanderthals. Some of the better ones are Christopher Stringer and Clive Gamble, *In Search of the Neanderthals* (1993); James Shreeve, *The Neanderthal Enigma: Solving the Mystery of Modern Human Origins* (1995); Eric Trinkaus and Pat Shipman, *The Neanderthals* (1992); and Ian Tattersall, *The Last Neanderthal* (1995). Some accessible articles are Frank Spencer, "The Neanderthals and Their Evolutionary Significance" (1984), and Michael Hammond, "The Expulsion of the Neanderthals from Human Antiquity: Marcellin Boule and the Social Context of Scientific Research" (1982). For the story of Java man, see Carl Swisher, Garniss Curtis, and Roger Lewin, *Java Man* (2000), and Pat Shipman, *The Man Who Found the Missing Link* (2001). On the origins of phrenology, see John Van Wyke, "The Authority of Human Nature: The *Schädellehre* of Franz Joseph Gall" (2002).

*3*

*The Asia Hypothesis*

The question most occupying evolutionists in the late nineteenth and early twentieth centuries concerned the mechanics by which humans came into existence through the biological process of hereditary descent. Another aspect of human antiquity was the search for that place on earth where the first humans appeared. Although researchers were initially far more concerned with the former, the latter did occupy many naturalists' thinking. The Asia hypothesis of human origins was popular with a wide range of thinkers, few of whom shared ideas on human evolution (there was more consensus on the place of origin than on the method of it). Once the story of Eden had been called into question, intellectuals were free to begin looking for the secular garden. Attention began to move away from the traditional Holy Lands of the Middle East to India, then to central Asia. This shift coincided with the growing fascination with Asia, a place little known to Westerners. Besides being free of theological baggage, central Asia became a substitute for the Garden of Eden because it seemed to solve many of the problems associated with human origins without demanding too much in return in the form of verifiable facts. The Enlightenment had inspired intellectuals to leave behind biblical explanations for more naturalistic ones for the origins of man. By turning to Asia they had a region onto which they could write a history of the human race that Judeo-Christian dogma and tradition had no hold over. Asian origins became caught up in several issues: besides helping wrest intellectual control of history away from Christian theology, it became an element in the birth and spread of fascism, led to the greatest large-scale scientific expedition before the space program, and produced the most enduring lost-treasure story in the annals of human evolution studies.

## Early Theories

The modern search for the origins of humankind, as well as the Asia hypothesis itself, began in seventeenth-century Europe as a result of a desire for national identity and a growing dissatisfaction with a literal reading of the Genesis story. Ethnology was as much political as it was scientific. Intellectuals and politicians in fledgling states looked for a heroic past to build up self-esteem and patriotism. Establishing historically deep roots could bind a people together, giving them continuity with the past and a sense of connection to it. By the late 1600s some French intellectuals claimed their people to be descendants of the Trojans, even the Titans of Greek mythology. French geographers and philosophers thought that high mountains would be the ideal locality for the first humans and so suggested the Himalayas of Tibet. Voltaire thought that Adam must have taken his culture and society from India, Diderot's pioneering encyclopedia likewise argued that the oldest science came from the subcontinent, while Immanuel Kant argued for Tibet. In his part of *Histoire naturelle* (1749–1767), Count de Buffon argued that man's birthplace must have been in a temperate zone because a good climate would breed good men. Buffon theorized that the Caspian Sea region and adjacent Caucasus Mountains would be a logical place to look for evidence of their existence. In Germany Johann Friedrich Blumenbach also believed in the Asian origins of man. Indeed, central Asia became especially popular with the Germans.

Attitudes about human origins changed as the Enlightenment gave way to the era of the romantics and neoromantics. German philosophers were unhappy with what they saw as the cold, soulless views of the Enlightenment. They sought to bring spirit, emotion, and passion back into philosophy, with nature study at its core. Friedrich von Schlegel (1772–1829), in his attempt to define the origin of his people, created stories of a glorious Germanic past that he believed better suited this sensibility. This new history became widely popular among the youth of his homeland. This led him in 1819 to develop the notion of an ancient and powerful Indian-Germanic race for which he coined the term *Aryan*. The Aryans were believed to have originated in the regions north of India and to have swept down to conquer all of Eurasia. After Schlegel, others proposed central Asia as the home of the Aryans, whereas the great philosopher G. W. Hegel (1817–1830) argued that Europe had been first colonized by these people. Their admiration for Eastern culture and civilization prompted many German philosophers to look there for the source of mankind. Some Europeans had grown uncomfortable with the idea of the Semitic origins of man. Indian origins were readily accepted because they seemed to link the Germans to a "higher" culture—and a non-Jewish race.

Since there was little or no physical evidence to support any of these theories, the emerging discipline of philology—the study of the origins of language—became an important component of the search for the first humans. Typical of this approach was French author Joseph-Ernest Renan, best known for his *Life of Jesus* (1863), who speculated on human origins based on the relationships of various languages. He wanted to substitute philology and science for divine intervention and saw language as the engine of human experience rather than God. A racist anti-Semite, Renan looked for a substitute for Christianity in a mythical Aryan Asia and argued that the structure of language revealed the Aryan origins of mankind. By the middle of the nineteenth century, the assumption that Asia was the cradle of man and the belief in the existence and superiority of the Aryan race were well entrenched in European thinking.

An illustration of human diversity circa 1830s (From J. Olney's A Practical System of Modern Geography [New York: Robinson, Pratt and Company, 1836])

Another Frenchman, Arthur de Gobineau (1816–1882), in *Inequality of the Races* (1854) and *Moral and Intellectual Diversity of the Races* (1856), also codified these ideas and argued that the Aryans were the world's superior race and that they originated in central Asia. A polygenist, Gobineau articulated the idea that history was a racial struggle and that to study it was a form of biology. He feared that what he considered mongrel races were overflowing the world and threatening to swamp the racial aristocracies he believed should be running it. Needless to say, Gobineau was not a supporter of democratic ideals. His work became a major inspiration for later racial theorists.

Although the Germans considered themselves descendants of the Aryans, they also considered themselves Nordics. The living embodiment of the Nordic ideal, Ernst Haeckel (1834–1919) loved sports, nature, and the fatherland. The creator of the first genealogical tree of life, Haeckel coined the term *phylogeny* in 1862 to argue that the embryonic forms of a species showed the stages that an organism went through during evolution. Performing dissections of a wide range of organisms, he said that in the stages of development a fetus went through prior to birth, one could see a playing out of the entire evolutionary process. He said that a human embryo went through a metamorphosis from fish to amphibian to reptile before achieving its final mammalian form. This, he said, was a playing out of how all life had evolved. To describe this process he used the phrase "ontogeny recapitulates phylogeny." In other words, the short embryonic development of an individual organism (ontogeny) mimics the longer evolutionary development of an entire group (phylogeny). He also developed the idea of monism, which stressed man's mystical oneness with the universe. He saw humans as part of, not separate from, the natural world. He argued that the closer and more in tune with nature an individual was, the better he or she was since nature was the source of all knowledge and power.

Haeckel also believed that certain races—the Nordics and Aryans, naturally—were better able to experience this oneness than others. The affinity for nature Haeckel claimed for the Aryans was just one more reason he believed them superior. Haeckel was an outspoken advocate of Aryan superiority and a mystical German past and

*Ernst Heinrich Haeckel (Library of Congress)*

believed Germans' origins could be traced back to Asia. He sought to bring to public attention an awareness of biology and what he considered the dangers of racial decline because of miscegenation. At the same time his conglomeration of nature worship, mysticism, and science gave "rational" support to the notion of racial superiority and gave racial theorists an authority to fall back on and apparent intellectual absolutes to save them from changing times.

In the late nineteenth and early twentieth centuries a wave of back-to-nature movements, akin to Haeckel's monism, sprang up in Germany. An offshoot of German romanticism that first appeared in the 1870s, the Volkish movement glorified the mystical oneness of the German people, or *Volk,* and sought personal fulfillment and salvation in self-identification with the land. Volkish proponents argued for a German soul directly connected to nature in a way unlike other ethnic groups (especially Jews). The Aryans were held up as the most imaginative and creative people, and the current Germans, it was argued, were their direct descendants. The study of human origins and the search for the origins of the Aryans went a long way toward providing a unifying history for people who felt lost in the world. Germany did not become a unified nation until the 1870s, and scholars argue that this cultural fragmentation created a space into which a unifying cultural or even biological history could appear to pull the German people together.

Haeckel and others embraced the Asian origins of man partly because it seemed a way to accomplish this goal. He combined science, politics, and religion and equated the steady march toward perfection he saw in nature with man's evolution. T. H. Huxley was so concerned with Haeckel's mix of science and mysticism that he cautioned the German against going too far with his speculations. Not to be deterred, Haeckel gave free rein to his mystical, occult proclivities and conjectured that the ancestors of the Aryans had come from the lost continent of Lemuria in the Indian Ocean. (Lemuria is a mythical continent often associated with Atlantis.) In *The History of Creation* (1879), Haeckel even included a drawing of the migratory routes he thought they had followed.

Though not a priority, the location of the first humans was given cursory attention by some British naturalists. In *Vestiges of the Natural History of Creation,* Robert Chambers hypothesized Asia was the cradle of man. In 1865 T. H. Huxley weighed in on human origins with *On the Methods and Results of Ethnology.* He took a middle road, saying that humans undoubtedly began from one ancestor, but he was not completely thrilled with the idea of the Aryans, calling them a myth and poking fun at those who held the myth so dearly. Charles Lyell generally supported the central Asian origins of man but doubted that the Aryans were still around or that their descendants could really be separated from the rest of the population. If they had existed at all, he surmised, they had intermingled so much with the indigenous peoples of Eurasia that they ceased to exist as a separate group. The British did not dismiss the Aryans out of a belief that ancestor worship itself was preposterous. Many in Britain looked as fondly to their Anglo-Saxon history as the Germans looked to their Aryan background.

Asia as the birthplace of man also figured prominently in the thinking of the late-nineteenth-century occult revival because devotees of the movement saw it as the starting point for their construction of a non-Christian creation story. This flowering of interest in the mystical aspects of life was popular among artists, poets, writers, and others in the West who felt bored and abandoned by the modern world.

The occultist most interested in human origins was also one of the pivotal characters of the revival, the Russian aristocrat Madame Blavatsky. Known as HPB to her friends, Helena Petrovna Blavatsky (1831–1891) landed in New York in 1874 after a stormy youth. Immersing herself in spiritualism, mesmerism, and other occult fascinations, she formed the Theosophical Society the next year. The society drew many trendy members, including Thomas Edison for a brief dalliance, attracted to the faddish and exclusive nature of it. Though most members eventually drifted away, a core remained loyal and devoted. Hers was a philosophical system through which adepts could allegedly gain knowledge of transcendent reality through revelations and other occult techniques. The goal of this program was the acquisition of spiritual salvation and elevated consciousness. Practitioners believed they were guided by shadowy hidden masters who chose certain worthy students to whom they imparted wisdom and instruction.

Blavatsky was a prolific writer, and her most important work was *The Secret Doctrine* (1888). In it she argued that evolution worked through a series of cycles, or rounds, that were divided into seven root races. She worked out a complex and overwrought evolutionary system with the Aryans as the current superior race. She argued that the previous race of Mongolians was guilty of miscegenation and had precipitated their fall from grace by breeding monsters. These monsters were still visible as vestiges of the "lesser races" that inhabit the earth. HPB claimed that man had not descended from the apes but the other way around. Apes, she argued, appeared because of the inbreeding of the Mongolian-Atlantians, which created the missing link in central Asia. Her form of evolution was, like many evolution theories of the nineteenth century, progressive, goal oriented, nonrandom, and always leading to a higher form or level of spiritual consciousness.

By her own accounts, however, Blavatsky did not develop this system but was instructed in its mysteries by the hidden masters. The masters themselves had masters who were the priest-kings of Atlantis who lived in the hidden city of Shamballah in the Gobi desert of central Asia. Ironically, she used the work of Darwin, Huxley, Lyell, and Haeckel, arguing that the latest scientific evidence and theory supported her system. She claimed not only that monkeys had evolved from humans but also that the human form was the source of all mammalian life. Using Richard Owen's archetype concept as a model, she said that man was the basic model all other creatures found their design in. Like the romantics, Blavatsky was enamored of India but saw central Asia as the abode of the gods and the first men. She was not alone.

## Henry Fairfield Osborn

Aside from Eugène Dubois, none of the human origin theorists actually went to Asia to determine if their ideas were valid. Although Dubois was the first to search Asia for fossil humans, because he was not affiliated with any university or museum, his effort was modest. He quietly excavated in one region for several years. In the 1920s a completely different type of expedition came to Asia to search for ancient humans. Where Dubois's operation was small, sedate, and limited in scope, this new venture was big, loud, brash, expensive, and wide ranging.

The Central Asiatic Expedition steamrolled through China and Mongolia for a decade and brought the industrial, organizational, and economic resources of the United States to bear upon the problem. The expedition was sponsored by the American Museum of Natural History in New York and was the brainchild of expedition leader Roy Chapman Andrews (1884–1960). Born in Wisconsin, Andrews was so determined to work for the museum that he began his career there in 1906 as a menial laborer. He quickly worked his way up by showing a flair for exploration and specimen acquisition. By the late 1910s he had racked up many years' experience roving Asia and had become enamored of the theory of human origins put forward by his boss, Henry Fairfield Osborn. Osborn had been running the museum since 1901 (and would continue to do so until his death). He was one of the most well-known scientists in the United States and certainly one of the most controversial. He had developed a theory of human evolution that Andrews wanted to prove by mounting a major expedition. In 1921 Andrews went to "Outer Mongolia" and the vast Gobi desert to search for the origins of man.

Henry Fairfield Osborn was born in 1857 into a wealthy Yankee railroad family and called financier J. P. Morgan uncle. His privileged position allowed him to attend Princeton College, where he studied with Swiss geologist Arnold Guyot and pioneering Scottish educator James McCosh. Both showed Osborn that one could be a Christian and an evolutionist without contradiction. After graduating from Princeton, he traveled to England, where he studied with T. H. Huxley and once briefly met Charles Darwin. With his education complete, Osborn first worked at Princeton as a professor but soon was offered dual appointments at both Columbia College and the American Museum of Natural History in New York. By 1901 he was promoted to president of the museum.

There are many examples of characters in both science and religion who go to great lengths to support deeply held beliefs about various aspects of human evolution. Osborn is one of them. He had learned from his teachers the importance of basing theories on hard evidence and direct observation of nature. He studied fossils, particularly of horses and their extinct relatives, the titanotheres. These "thunder mammals" were large lumbering creatures with ornate horns and head ornaments that had inhabited the western United States. When looking at fossil horse teeth and the horns of the titanotheres, Osborn came to believe that they showed a slow, steady, progressive march of evolution, with new characteristics appearing when and where the creatures needed them to survive. The evidence also suggested to Osborn that evolution was not the random, chance affair Darwin said it was but something with purpose and divine order. He saw what were for him clear and unambiguous lines of descent from earlier simpler forms to later more complex ones, all moving in a progressive, optimistic, inspired path toward perfection. Osborn was one of many scientists of the period who accepted evolution as a fact but were uncomfortable because it did not involve an ultimate creator or purpose: they wanted teleological evolution, not scatological evolution.

The underlying framework of Osborn's theory was a belief that when a type of organism first appeared, it was generalized in structure. It was not adapted to any specific environment but was flexible and adaptable to many types of conditions. As they radiated out from their point of origin new versions appeared that were more specifically adapted to the environments they encountered. As they became more specialized they lost that original evolutionary flexibility. As time went by these groups developed what Osborn called a race

plasm. This was a base pool of hereditary characteristics that gave the group or species its particular abilities. Every species had a race plasm, though not all were of equal value or quality (this notion would become crucial when Osborn applied it to humans). For a species or group of related species to advance along the evolutionary line, Osborn argued, they had to take their inborn race plasm and strive to go further. They could advance only by overcoming environmental obstacles. The quality of the race plasm gave each group its ability to do this. The downside was that as a species struggled to overcome its environment and adapted to it, it grew less able to do so. Its growing specialization saved it in its environment but made it less able to adapt to any new environment. Osborn believed a more generalized species was superior because it could adapt, whereas specialized species were inferior because they had lost the ability to adapt. Building on what he thought he saw in the fossil record, Osborn believed that highly specialized mammals represented the outer reaches of mammal radiation around the world. The more specialized a type of mammal, the farther it was geographically from the center of original evolution. Some mammals in South America and Africa, he thought, were at the extreme edge of their adaptation. So, if one were to follow a line backward from hyperenvironmental specialization to more generalized forms, you would find the point of original mammal evolution. For Osborn that point was central Asia.

In the early twentieth century, Osborn turned his attention to human evolution. He also worked theological ideas into his thinking. He believed that just as an organism had to strive to achieve evolutionary advance, a person also had to strive beyond what birth and position gave him to achieve spiritual salvation as well. Osborn came to equate physical evolution with spiritual evolution.

Osborn was also a believer in Nordic superiority. He justified this by saying that of all the human species and races, the Nordics were the most generalized and had the strongest race plasm. Nordics could, therefore, he believed, overcome environmental obstacles more readily than any other type of human. He gathered a large collection of human fossils and casts so he could base his conclusions on direct observation of physical evidence. Because of his belief in the notion of racial superiority and purity, however, he refused to see a direct line of descent from Neanderthals and Cro-Magnons to moderns. He separated all fossil, as well as modern, humans into different lines of descent in a model called orthogenesis. He wanted to be able to say modern humans, Nordics in particular, had evolved separately from all other groups. He was also uncomfortable with primate ancestry. To avoid all these difficult ancestors, Osborn created a complex circumlocution beginning with a hypothetical creature he called Dawn Man. These Dawn Men evolved directly into modern humans. This way he could argue that all humans, whether living or extinct, appeared first in central Asia but from different base stocks, making them separate species. It was a thinly veiled polygenesis.

Osborn received a good deal of opposition for his views. Theologians and Christian Fundamentalists knocked him for being an evolutionist who undermined belief in God, and scientists said he undermined belief in evolution and relied too heavily on theology. Even his assistant at the museum, William K. Gregory, disagreed with him and engaged in a public debate on the subject in the media. Gregory argued that it was nonsense to support a theory of evolution that did not involve primates when the evidence clearly showed it did. Osborn argued back that primate ancestry was a myth. In a telling irony, Osborn, the devout Christian, opposed the Christian Fundamentalists because they attacked evolution and were antiscience.

In 1900 Roy Chapman Andrews read Osborn's paper, with the ungainly title "The Geological and Faunal Relationships of Europe and America during the Tertiary Period and the Theory of Successive Invasions of an African Fauna," and was intrigued. It was in this paper that Osborn initially laid out his version of the Asia hypothesis. Andrews wanted to do a large-scale interdisciplinary, systematic survey of the region. He put together a well-equipped expedition of specialists—geologists, paleontologists, archaeologists, and others—who would do a comprehensive study of Mongolia's flora, fauna, and geology. Although they wanted to find evidence of human origins, they also wanted to record a wide range of data about the history of the region so that the fossils could be seen in a detailed context. When Dubois worked the Solo River, he did little contextualizing so that when fossils were found, it was difficult to make them speak with the authority they could have. This lack of a wider view led many to dismiss Dubois's findings.

Andrews was determined that the Central Asiatic Expedition was not about to fall into such a trap. They arrived in China in 1921 and made their base in Beijing (known by Westerners as Peking). The Central Asiatic Expedition included, along with the American scientists, many local Mongolian and Chinese workers. They would head out into the Gobi desert during the summers and winter in the city. Intent on doing as much as possible in the time allotted, Andrews employed a small fleet of cars and trucks to cover the vast and unforgiving desert, instead of using the traditional camel caravans. They battled bad weather, armed bandits, revolutionaries, intransigent and corrupt politicians, and other difficulties for most of the decade before political breakdown and Chinese suspicion forced them out. Andrews and Osborn bankrolled this expensive undertaking with generous donations from financier J. P. Morgan and corporations like U.S. Steel. It was also heavily publicized, with newspapers around the world covering it. The expedition discovered hundreds of tons of fossils, particularly dinosaurs (including the first known dinosaur eggs). What it did not find was human fossils. For all their work, Andrews and his team never proved Osborn's theory, and it was eventually forgotten. Though Osborn's theory fell apart, hominid fossils were found in Asia, just a little bit north of where he was looking.

*Peking Man*

Not all Asia hypothesis proponents were drawn to it because of mysticism or racial theory. A major cache of human fossils was discovered thanks to local people having what they considered a practical use for fossils. Chinese tradition held as far back as the Han dynasty that "dragon bones," as fossils were known, could be ground up and used for a wide range of medicinal and culinary purposes. One of the first Westerners to begin collecting the dragon bones was the German physician and amateur natural historian K. A. Haberer in 1899. Haberer amassed a large collection, not by prospecting or digging in the usual manner but simply by going to different drugstores and apothecaries around China and buying them. Druggists bought them from farmers and peasants who dug them up at various localities. The druggists in turn sold them to customers along with instructions on how to make them into teas, poultices, and other remedies. Haberer, forced to leave the country during the Boxer Rebellion, gave his collection to a colleague, Professor Max Schlosser of Munich, who described it in *Fossil Mammals of China* (1903). Schlosser noticed that one of the pieces in the collection was a decidedly humanlike primate tooth. Because of the manner in which the tooth was collected, Schlosser had no idea exactly where it had come from, so he could only speculate. He suggested that the tooth supported the Asia hypothesis of human origins.

During the early twentieth century it was common for Europeans with scientific and technical expertise to be employed by the Chinese government, as there were few native Chinese with their particular level of sophisticated Western knowledge. One of them was a Swedish geologist, Gunnar Andersson (1874–1960). He went to China in 1914 at the outbreak of World War I to help the Chinese find iron ore deposits that could be sold to the Allies. Andersson was an amateur fossil collector, so he naturally became interested in a local site called Jigushan (Chicken Bone Hill) outside the village of Zhoukoudian, itself some forty miles outside the capital city of Peking. He went there in March 1918 and saw that the strata from which the fossils were being taken were Pliocene and Pleistocene in age.

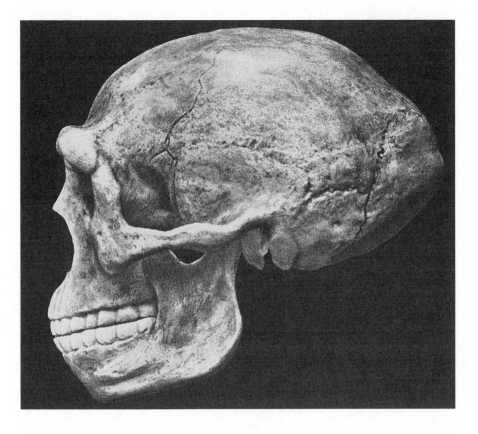

Following the war, Andersson became a senior scientist for the newly formed Chinese Geological Survey. Though it was ostensibly a Chinese operation and had a Chinese director, the survey was dominated by Swedish interests and was largely controlled out of the University of Uppsala. Carl Wiman (1867–1944), the first professor of paleontology at Uppsala, was unhappy with Andersson's collecting techniques and so sent him an assistant in the form of the young Austrian paleontologist Otto Zdansky (1894–1988).

Though Zdansky did not get along with Andersson, he quickly set to work at the dig site. In the late summer of 1921 Zdansky found a humanlike molar tooth. Because of the harder materials they are composed of, teeth are usually the parts of an organism, mammals especially, that stand the best chance of surviving as fossils. Because of their complexity, teeth can tell much about the creature they come from: whether they are carnivores or herbivores, what their general overall size is, what conditions they lived in, and other valuable clues to their existence. The tooth Zdansky found turned out to be the first piece of a creature later known as Peking man. Strangely, Zdansky did not immediately publicize this important find. It was not until the prince of Sweden, a main benefactor of the Geological Survey, paid an official state visit in 1926 that Zdansky made it public. At the official scientific meeting of the festivities, Zdansky unveiled the tooth along with a second he had since found. An American scientist, A. W. Grabau, working in Peking at the time, is said to have first used the term *Peking man*. The discovery was hailed as a major accomplishment.

Behind the unveiling of the Peking man teeth, and the wide-ranging fascination and interest they generated, was an intriguing series of events connecting Zhoukoudian and the Central Asiatic Expedition. Part of the rush by Roy Chapman Andrews to get his expedition going was that Gunnar Andersson had foolishly told him that he was planning a large expedition of his own. Andrews then quickly mobilized Henry Fairfield Osborn and the American Museum of Natural History to beat the Swedes to the punch. To justify his desire for an outside expedition, Andrews wrote an article for *Asia* magazine in which he stated that there was no institution in China with the resources to mount such an undertaking (completely ignoring the Chinese Geological Survey, which he was well aware of). Andrews's chief scientist was Walter Granger, an accomplished paleontologist, field man, and friend of Gunnar Andersson.

When the Central Asiatic Expedition rolled into China in June 1921, Andersson invited Granger to visit Zhoukoudian. Granger, Andersson, and Zdansky lost no time in getting to work at the site. They soon turned up promising fossil mammals. At this point, things get murky. As Granger was technically working for the American Museum and not the Geological Survey, he left after a few days of giving the relatively inexperienced Zdansky pointers on field technique. They may have found evidence of hominid occupation there, but they said nothing. Only Andersson hinted that Zdansky still had important work to do at the site. It was just days later that Zdansky found the tooth at what was now being called Locality I. He kept the discovery secret for some time, even from Andersson.

Granger seeing something at Zhoukoudian that piqued his interest may account for him telling both Roy Chapman Andrews and Osborn that China might prove a better place to search for the first humans. From some quick reconnaissance he did there, Granger thought the Sichuan region looked promising. Granger's hunch was right. In 1984 at a Sichuan site called Longgupo Cave, Chinese scientists discovered dental fragments suggestive that archaic *Homo erectus* had been there. The same team also discovered jaw parts of the elusive and bizarre early hominid *Gigantopithicus* (discussed later). Indeed, Granger wanted the Central Asiatic Expedition to turn its sights on China instead of Mongolia, but it was not to be. Not long after Granger left Zhoukoudian, the Chinese Geological Survey and the American Museum of Natural History worked out a "gentleman's agreement" that the Americans would stay in Mongolia and away from Zhoukoudian, even though they clearly had the better resources to work the site. The episode remains a mystery.

In the audience when Zdansky unveiled the Zhoukoudian-Peking teeth was a young Canadian anatomist, Davidson Black (1884–1934), of the nearby Peking Union Medical College. He too was interested in human origins. Born in Toronto, Black was an enthusiastic outdoorsman. Interested in nature, he received his medical degree in 1906 and then studied comparative anatomy. In 1914 he went to England as a student of anatomist Grafton Elliot Smith. This period seems to have generated in Black his interest in human origins and the Asia hypothesis (Smith was a proponent of the theory). Just as Eugène Dubois joined the Dutch army so that he could get to Sumatra, in 1919 Black took a position at the Peking Union Medical College, largely to gain access to Asia and its fossils. In 1921 he briefly joined Roy Chapman Andrews and the Central Asiatic Expedition but stayed only a short time because of his official duties at the medical school.

Chinese paleontologist Jia Lanpo (1908–2001), who was intimately involved in the Peking man story, remembers that Zdansky asked Black to write an article describing the Peking material. Originally appearing in the *Bulletin of the Geological Survey of China,* it was reprinted in the learned Western journals *Nature* and *Science*. Black based his article on photos of the fossils, along with Zdansky's written description (the actual teeth themselves had already been shipped to Sweden for safekeeping at the University of Uppsala, where they remain today). Black argued that the teeth proved the Asia hypothesis and that they were undoubtedly from the genus *Homo*. Zdansky himself was not so sure. His take on the fossils was more circumspect. He thought that a handful of teeth, as important as they were, did not constitute enough material to make such a grand statement. Zdansky's treatment of the Peking man material is a bit peculiar, almost as if he was not quite sure what to make of it. After finding the teeth he waited before showing anyone—even then having to be pushed to make them public. Once they were publicized, he wrote several technical monographs on them in 1928 and left Asia behind for a teaching post in Egypt, never being part of the study of human origins again.

The departure of Otto Zdansky from the scene ended the Swedish dominance of the Peking man story. Davidson Black then received financial backing from the Rockefeller Foundation to work the Zhoukoudian site along with the Chinese Geological Survey in 1927. To replace Zdansky, the University of Uppsala sent the paleontologist Birger Bohlin (1898–1990), who set to work at Zhoukoudian and found a tooth of his own. Black concluded that this tooth also belonged to Peking man. He was so convinced of his position that he took the critical step of giving a technical name to the fossils: *Sinanthropus pekinensis.* To name a new genus of organism, especially a supposed human ancestor, based on such a tiny amount of material was a bold move. If other evidence came along to overturn the idea, Black would have looked rash and unprofessional.

Few paleontologists initially accepted Black's assertion. Fortunately, Bohlin and the Chinese scientists working alongside him kept plugging away and turned up more material. In 1928 they found a jaw with several teeth in it. And in 1929 the prize of prizes for paleoanthropologists, a large piece of a skull including the brow ridges (known as Skull III), turned up. Black realized that this material was akin to that found by Eugène Dubois in Java years before, a point that strengthened the Asia hypothesis. (We now know that both Peking man and Java man are examples of *Homo erectus.*) Other scientists soon acknowledged Black's assertion that *Sinanthropus* was a human ancestor.

Like Gunnar Andersson before him, Davidson Black wanted to mount a major expedition to study the geology and paleontology of China. His idea was undermined when Swedish explorer Sven Hedin (1865–1952) proposed the idea to the Rockefeller Foundation first. Hedin had spent years in Asia and had other agendas: he was shipping Chinese artifacts out of the country and may have been helping the German airline Lufthansa map out a commercial route to Asia. Hedin was politically active but erratic. He was initially sympathetic to the Nazis—meeting with Hitler several times—and strongly anti-Soviet; he then became enamored of Chairman Mao after a flirtation with the Chinese Nationalists under Chiang Kai-shek.

Stymied in his attempt to mount an expedition, Black did secure funding to start a new research center, the Cenozoic Research Laboratory, attached to the Chinese Geological Survey and housed in the Anatomy Department of the Peking Union Medical College. Unlike the original Swedish operation, which sent its finds back to the University of Uppsala, the Cenozoic Research Laboratory kept all materials in China. Black also made extensive use of Chinese scientists and technicians. Tragically, however, Black would not get to see the fruits of all his work. He died of heart failure in 1934. He was replaced by the French Jesuit paleontologist Pierre Teilhard de Chardin. Two years later Teilhard de Chardin was replaced by the German American Franz Weidenreich (1872–1948).

Teilhard de Chardin went to China in 1923 after being invited by another Jesuit, Father Emile Licent, who discovered paleoliths in Gansu Province and the Ordos plateau of Mongolia. Teilhard de Chardin was sponsored by the National Museum of Paris. Together, Teilhard de Chardin and Licent explored the region, winding up back at the Great Wall in what is now the Ningxia Hui autonomous region. There they found more paleoliths similar to the Aurignacian artifacts of Europe. Continuing to work in China and a nearby section of Mongolia, the "French fathers," as the Chinese called them, found much evidence of early human habitation. They found a suspicious tooth that could have been Pleistocene that was promptly dubbed the Ordos human tooth by Davidson Black and Ordos man by the Chinese workers (more parts of "Ordos man" were unearthed in the late 1970s, verifying its existence). Teilhard de Chardin, like many involved in the search for fossil humans in Asia at this time, accompanied Roy Chapman Andrews into the Gobi desert.

To read most accounts of the discovery of Peking man, it was the result of European and American scientists doggedly working in the wastes of Asia to find what they were looking for. If Chinese scientists are mentioned, they appear almost as secondary characters moving about in the background. They did, in fact, play the major role. For example, when Birger Bohlin joined the excavation team he was the only Westerner. The chief geologist and administrator at the site was Li Jie, and the chief excavator was Liu Delin, who had been with the Central Asiatic Expedition as Walter Granger's assistant. Liu's assistant was Xie Refu. The first skullcap (Skull III) was discovered at the bottom of a cold, dark cave at Locality I by paleontologist Pei Wenzhong. The Geological Survey itself was under the direction of Weng Wenhao. Most, if not all, of the actual digging was done by Chinese workers, while Davidson Black cleaned and prepared the fossils, wrote the papers, and received the lion's share of acclaim for them. In addition, he was chief fund-raiser and cheerleader for the project to Western backers and scientists.

When Pei Wenzhong discovered the crucial first skull, he was assisted by a young paleontologist named Jia Lanpo who joined the team in 1931. Jia was in his early twenties and a graduate student at the time. He would go on to be China's most renowned paleontologist and mentor to most of the generations to follow. Jia's job was to search the site for man-made artifacts—called paleoliths—in the form of quartz points, cutters, and scrapers. The site had an abundance of these quartz chips. Jia eventually took charge of the site in 1935. By then, however, he was more or less alone. All the old hands had moved on to complete their educations or to new positions. Funding was also growing scarce because of the unstable political climate. The Zhoukoudian site did not remain open for long. In 1937 fighting between Communist and Nationalist Chinese forces and then the Japanese invasion made the location untenable. By then 14 skulls in various stages of completion, 147 teeth, 7 thigh bones, 2 upper arms, a collar bone, and parts of a wrist had been unearthed. They were dated to between 250,000 and 500,000 years old. Weidenreich had detailed drawings, photos, and plaster casts made of all the findings. In 1941, with war clouds looming, Weidenreich took the photos and casts with him to the United States.

### The Great Disappearing Act

It is easy to tell the story of the disappearance of the Peking man fossils as an adventure, mystery, and whodunit. The events naturally lend themselves to such things: a war-torn country; a collection of priceless, irreplaceable artifacts; and desperate scientists trying to hide them under dangerous conditions. Indiana Jones could only dream of such an escapade.

In 1937 Japanese troops occupied the Zhoukoudian area and took control of the dig site. They also occupied the main campus of the Peking Union as well as other sites throughout the capital. The Japanese seemed to show an interest in the fossils. The research team decided they had to do something to secure the fossils and safeguard them from the enemy. Jia Lanpo immediately began smuggling drawings out of the Peking Union building.

Meanwhile, Geological Survey director Weng Wenhao and Franz Weidenreich worked out a plan for the fossils themselves. Weidenreich rejected the idea of putting the fossils in his personal luggage to take back to the United States. He was afraid the fossils would be broken, lost, or confiscated. All involved believed that under the dire circumstances the rule about not taking artifacts and antiquities out of China could be lifted and that the United States was the best place for the relics to go. It was then suggested that the U.S. Embassy take the fossils in the diplomatic pouch that was not subject to customs inspections. Embassy staff, under Ambassador Nelson Johnson, was wary of the law about antiquities, so it turned the fossils over to the U.S. Marine Corps detachment in Peking that was about to evacuate to the Philippines. This being done, the fossils promptly vanished forever.

The loss of the Peking man fossils is one of the great mysteries of science. There is little consensus as to what happened to them. There have been books and articles written on the subject, and no two points of view are the same. There was disagreement from the start. Claire Taschdjian, a German working as Weidenreich's assistant, claims that she wrapped and boxed the fossils for transport and was thus the last person to see them. In *The Story of Peking Man* (1990), Jia Lanpo writes off Taschdjian's story as nonsense. He claims that it was a pair of Chinese laboratory technicians, Hu Chengzhi and Ji Yanqing, who did the packing. Jia states that Taschdjian's book, *Peking Man Is Missing* (1977), "is fictional and the details are therefore exaggerated" (1990, 160).

Whoever packed them, the boxes (and the number of boxes is in dispute) were sent to the marine barracks in Peking, Camp Holcomb. There they were put under the control of a marine officer who was to take them out as secret materials. This was all in the days just before the Japanese attack on Pearl Harbor and the onset of World War II proper. The United States and Japan were not yet at war, but all sensed it was just around the corner. At one point, when the marines prepared to defend their tiny garrison from the Japanese onslaught, one man used the boxed fossils as a prop for his machine gun. The marines were meant to board the SS *President Harrison* for evacuation, but the *Harrison* was run aground in a fight with a Japanese warship just after December 7, 1941. The marines themselves were eventually taken prisoner and their luggage train ransacked.

There are many theories about what happened. Did American staff at the Peking Union take them? Did the marines hide them and not tell anyone? Did Japanese officers take them secretly back to Japan? Did Japanese enlisted men, unaware of their importance, discard them as useless rocks when they looted the American baggage train? Did they fall overboard while being loaded on the *President Harrison?*

An Associated Press item in 1945 said that when the Japanese occupied the Peking Union Medical College they found only plaster casts. The *Peiping Chronicle* said in 1946 that the fossils were discovered in Japan, after the war, at Tokyo University. A series of books appeared in the 1970s that fanned the flames of conspiracy and mystery.

Harry Shapiro, a longtime curator and anthropologist at the American Museum of Natural History, released *Peking Man* (1974), which was followed by *The Search for Peking Man* (1975) by self-styled adventurer and stockbroker Christopher Janus and coauthor William Brashler.

Shapiro knew Davidson Black personally and wonders why the Japanese seemed to show such an interest in the project. He argues that "obviously, the fossils had a high priority [for the Japanese] and the looting must have been planned well in advance" (1974, 19). Shapiro recounts the great sense of loss felt by Franz Weidenreich when news of the tragedy arrived in New York. Later, the casts that Weidenreich had brought back to the American Museum were mistaken for the real thing, and rumors started that the museum had the originals. Shapiro remembers the reports being contradictory and confusing. In 1971 he came across Dr. William Foley, a heart specialist from New York City who claimed to be the marine officer in charge of evacuating the fossil-filled footlockers from Peking. Foley was to take the fossils during the fall of Peking to the Philippines, then on to the United States. When the war started he was captured. The boxes then went on an incredible, though unlikely, series of adventures and narrow escapes. No official report was ever made from this period.

Whereas Shapiro's book is sober, the Janus and Brashler volume is less so. They take the Foley material as well as many other accounts and run with them. Janus met with Shapiro and tried to involve him in some of his schemes. Although Shapiro was intrigued by some of the things he saw, he was skeptical of Janus's motivations and evidence. In a breathless account Janus interweaves his own personal search for the fossils with the historical one. He mounts expeditions, offers rewards, and meets shadowy figures atop the Empire State Building. Janus was an amateur relic hunter with his fingers in a number of pies. He also took comments Shapiro made about some of the "evidence" he was shown out of context, as endorsement of his contentions. Janus was later alleged to have defrauded funds from Peking man donations for himself.

So much excitement was generated over Peking man at this time that the popular television police drama *Hawaii Five-O* aired an episode with a story line about the footlocker turning up in Hawaii in the hands of one of the marines, now an old man, who had smuggled it out of China.

Jia Lanpo argues that all these stories and reminiscences were sheer fantasy and wishful thinking. He did, however, have his suspicions, referring to "certain Americans." The final answer, if one is ever found, will no doubt be something no one has yet thought of.

## Conclusion

Although religious dogmatism has always played a role in the study of human evolution, political dogmatism has as well. The Asia hypothesis in particular has been a magnet. Besides the Aryan-Nazi political connection to human evolution, there have been others. A fascinating example is the communist political theory that became part of the Asia hypothesis. Karl Marx and Friedrich Engels, two of the founding fathers of modern communism, embraced evolution because it seemed to fit into their belief that humans from lower social classes could pull themselves up to something better. Engels argued that humans evolved as a result of learning to work. Labor, he said, was the key factor in turning brutes into men. With the end of World War II, the old antagonisms between Nationalists and Communists in China were rekindled as the two sides fought for control of the country. By 1949 the Communist Party under Mao Tse-tung had triumphed. With the country now following a socialist political path, all members of society were expected to do the same

It was during this period that a great upheaval hit China. The Cultural Revolution lasted roughly from 1966 through Mao's death in 1976. Although it was an attempt by Mao to consolidate his power, the Cultural Revolution was a popular revolt against government and party privilege. The worst thing a person in a position of power or leadership could be accused of was being a "rightist" who used his position for personal gain and to undermine the party. In 1966 Chairman Mao unleashed hundreds of Red Guard groups upon China. Made up mostly of zealous teenagers who unwaveringly supported Mao, the Red Guards swept through society, seeking to purge it of anything not of the proper attitude. Thousands of people were imprisoned, put on show trials, or murdered in an increasing level of violence not unlike the terror that swept France following the revolution there. The mob violence reached a point of spinning out of control by 1968, and so Mao disbanded the Red Guards. For Jia Lanpo this was an anxiety-producing period. His position as a leader of the Chinese scientific establishment could have been easily used against him. He had to walk a careful line, as did thousands of scientists and intellectuals. This may account for some of his writing.

In *Early Man in China* (1980), Jia Lanpo claims that socialism "has spurred the development of this branch [paleoanthropology] of science" (1980, ii). After the Communist victory in 1949 the government contacted Jia and lavished a large budget on him to get the excavations at Zhoukoudian going again. The old institutions of scientific study were reorganized as the Chinese Academy of Science, with Jia taking charge of the Institute of Vertebrate Paleontology and Paleoanthropology in 1953.

In his books, Jia says that Chairman Mao's rule about intellectuals learning from the masses should be applied to the search for the first humans. Peasants could lead scholars to the sites where the remains are to be found. Jia congratulates the Chinese people on dropping their old religious myths and superstitions about the divine creation of humans for more prosaic and scientific ideas. He cites Engels on his suggestion, made in the late nineteenth century, that Asia was the cradle of mankind. Jia may have been an ardent Communist applying socialist theory to his work, or he may have felt obliged to pay lip service to it so that he would not feel the wrath of the party for "incorrect thought." He had watched powerlessly during the Cultural Revolution as many fine libraries were burned and destroyed in the name of socialist progress. He had kept exhaustive records of the Zhoukoudian project. In fact, it is through Jia's tireless chronicling of the events of those years that we know the details. He did not want to see his manuscripts go the way of so many other books and papers during that dangerous time. At great personal risk he ferreted away the notes and papers from the academy (in much the same way as he hid them from the Japanese) to his home for safekeeping and was just able to protect them from the ravages of the fanatical Red Guard. This fear may be what accounts for his fawning attitude toward Chairman Mao and the principles of the Cultural Revolution. In his later works like *The Story of Peking Man* (1990), published after the death of Mao and a lessening of tensions inside China as well as between China and the West, there are no such political allusions or party platitudes.

Whether religiously, racially, or politically motivated, the search for the cradle of man in Asia did produce significant finds and discoveries. Although Asia was not the home of the first humans, it certainly held important episodes in our history. Though the original cache of Peking man fossils has disappeared, many more have been found subsequently at Locality I and elsewhere. Significant in this period is that even though so many were running around China and Mongolia placing their bets that the earliest humans would be found there, very quietly in a dusty backwater in southern Africa more difficult ancestors began turning up.

*Further Reading*

For an overview of the life of Madame Blavatsky and the occult response to evolution, see Helena Petrovna Blavatsky, *The Secret Doctrine* (1893); Ellic Howe, *The Magicians of the Golden Dawn: A Documentary History of a Magical Order, 1887–1923* (1985); Peter Washington, *Madame Blavatsky's Baboon* (1995); and Malcolm Jay Kottler, "Alfred Russel Wallace, the Origin of Man, and Spiritualism" (1974). For evolution and German ideology, see Nicholas Goodrick-Clarke, *The Occult Roots of Nazism* (1992), and George Mosse, *The Crisis of German Ideology* (1964). On the life and work of Henry Fairfield Osborn, see Ronald Rainger, *An Agenda for Antiquity: Henry Fairfield Osborn and Vertebrate Paleontology at the American Museum of Natural History, 1890–1935* (1991), and Brian Regal, *Henry Fairfield Osborn: Race and the Search for the Origins of Man* (2002).

On Jia Lanpo and China, see Jia's *Cave Home of Peking Man* (1975) and *Early Man in China* (1980). For Peking man and the related scandals, see Harry Shapiro, *Peking Man* (1974) and *The Search for Peking Man* (1975).

# 4
## *Africa*

Grafton Elliot Smith was committed to the idea that brain size was inextricably linked to human development. The first step to becoming human had to be the acquisition of a large brain. Only then did any other "human" characteristics appear. Smith argued that since modern human brain size is large compared to that of the primates, human ancestors would have brain sizes somewhere in between. Any human ancestor, therefore, had to be judged as such by its brain. He also said that a model of the inside of a skull (an endocast) would give a detailed view of the brain's physical complexity and could be used to chart the level of the creature's intellectual development. Smith drilled these ideas into his students, including a promising young Australian named Raymond Dart (1893–1988). Upon graduation in 1922 Smith used his influence to have Dart appointed to the position of professor of anatomy at Witwatersrand University, in Johannesburg, South Africa. Although the position sounded impressive, Witwatersrand was an intellectual backwater founded only fifty years before. The school had little in the way of facilities (a pitiful laboratory and a few rooms for medical instruction), and Johannesburg itself was a rough frontier gold-mining town. Dart was interested in brain function and its relation to human evolution, and his new job seemed to have little in the way of resources for such studies, or so he thought. No one could have known that his appointment to the obscurity of South Africa would put him in a position to overturn almost everything that had been believed about human evolution before and to begin an entirely new chapter in the search for our ancestors.

## Taung Child

In early 1924 Dart's only female student, Josephine Salmons, brought his attention to what looked like a fossil baboon skull in the possession

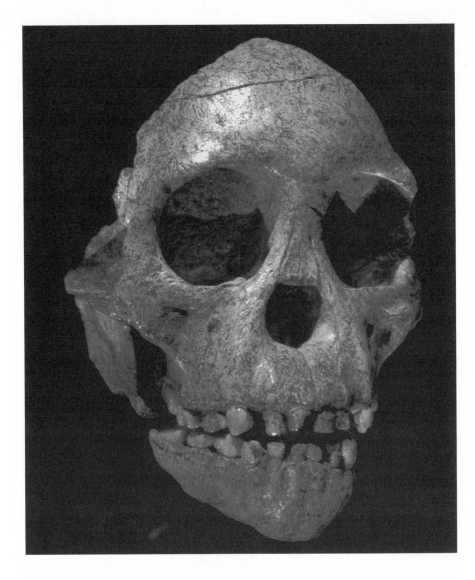

*The Taung Child. This skull showed that humans were African, not Asian, in origin. Few believed the idea at first. (Jonathan Blair / Corbis)*

of a friend. It had been found at a local lime quarry near a place called Taung. The geology professor at Witwatersrand, R. B. Young, knew the site and agreed to help Dart find more fossils. By October of that year Young had found a similar skull and sent it to Dart. In his book written with Dennis Craig, *Adventures with the Missing Link* (1959), Dart said the box arrived at his home on November 28, 1924, as he was preparing to be the best man at a friend's wedding. He became so enthralled with the skull that he almost missed the ceremony. The specimen was the fairly complete skull of a juvenile that included a magnificently preserved, and extremely rare, natural endocast. In order to establish what the creature was, Dart relied on the theories of his mentor.

One of the things Grafton Elliot Smith used to differentiate between primates and humans was the lunate sulcus, a fissure toward the back of the brain. He thought the gap between this fissure and the nearby parallel sulcus was an important marker of the advanced design of a human. These two structures are relatively close in primates and distant in humans. Due to the high quality of the Taung endocast it was clear that the separation between the sulci was more like a human than a monkey. Indeed, it was the brain cast that allowed Dart to understand Taung's importance. Dart also noted that the face did not have the heavy brow ridges or the pulled-out (prognathous) shape characteristic of primates. It had a full set of deciduous teeth with adult first molars waiting to erupt. Significantly, the skull's foramen magnum, the hole where the backbone attaches and allows the spinal cord to enter the brain, was located on the underside like a human instead of toward the back like a baboon or ape. This trait suggested that Taung child (as it was being called) stood upright as a biped. Dart was convinced that this was a human ancestor, and he began to make extravagant claims for the creature he christened *Australopithecus africanus* (the ape of southern Africa). He said it could differentiate sounds and colors and evolved the way it did by struggling against the harsh environment at the edge of Africa's Kalahari Desert. In overcoming these obstacles, he said, the little *Australopithecus* had begun the long climb to becoming human.

Dart sent a short, introductory paper to the journal *Nature*, which was published February 7, 1925. The popular press latched on to the find and trumpeted Dart's discovery as historic. Paleoanthropologists were not so receptive. *Nature* had sent copies of Dart's paper to a group of experts to assess prior to publication. Arthur Keith, Grafton Elliot Smith, and Arthur Smith Woodward (the big three of British paleoanthropology) were cautious. They saw more affinities with apes than humans. They said it was difficult to accurately make sense of Taung as it was a juvenile, and the young of a species often change their morphology as they mature. Taung's "human" traits could very well disappear after maturity. The scientific community seemed decidedly underwhelmed by what Dart had discovered. A less than complete and scrupulously detailed description of the fossil, along with extravagant claims for it, caused many to see Taung as an interesting and important ape fossil, but not a human ancestor.

Another contributing factor in Taung's less than spectacular debut was that Africa was not thought to be the cradle of man. The mid-1920s were the heady days of the Central Asiatic Expedition and the general consensus that Asia was the cradle of the human race. Stung by the criticism, Dart turned his attention to his duties at the university and returned to hominid evolution only years later, doing extensive work at a site called Makapansgat and entering the debate on how the early hominids behaved.

One obstacle to Taung being accepted as a human ancestor was its small brain. Arthur Keith, Grafton Elliot Smith, and most of the paleoanthropological community held firm in the belief that the human line began with an expansion of the brain. This assertion was supported by Keith's work on the Galley Hill and Piltdown men. Taung was bipedal—maybe—and had a small brain. Big-brain theory arose in the nineteenth century from the prevailing belief that the story of human evolution was the progressive march to perfection that would result in the acquisition of higher powers of moral reasoning. Intelligence seemed the obvious goal of evolution, and it could be acquired only by a large, complex brain appearing first. This idea fitted with the narrative quality so many looked for in human evolution. An expanded brain led to manipulative hands, which led to bipedal locomotion and eventual modernity. This sequence set up what has been called a feedback loop: large brain led to greater intelligence, which led to tool use, which led to bipedalism, which led to more brain growth, which led to greater intelligence, and so on. In other words, with a large brain appearing first, a sequence was kicked off that, once fed back into itself, created a sort of biological perpetual-motion machine. The expansion of intelligence and manual dexterity would then culminate in social and moral bearing. Keith argued that there was a "cranial Rubicon," or optimum size, the brain had to reach before the "humanization" process began. Any fossil that had a brain smaller than 750 cubic centimeters, by definition, could not be in the human line.

All was not lost for Taung, however. Robert Broom (1866–1951) had seen the Taung skull firsthand and was immediately convinced it was a human ancestor. Broom came from an impoverished Scottish background but managed to enter Glasgow University, eventually earning a medical degree. By 1897 he was in South Africa looking for fossils to aid his work on the origins of mammals, which he believed sprang from reptiles. Supporting himself as a doctor and fossil collector, he indulged his interest in human evolution. Just after Raymond Dart announced the Taung discovery, Broom visited him in Johannesburg. Legend says that when he first saw the Taung skull sitting on a table he knelt before it, claiming he was paying his respects to our ancestor. Agreeing with Dart over the role of Taung in human evolution, Broom vowed to find more material.

In 1934 Broom was offered a position as paleontologist at the Transvaal Museum at Pretoria. Two years later, at sixty-nine years of age, he went on the hunt for *Australopithecus*. He concentrated his efforts at the Sterkfontein quarry, where fossils were being sold as souvenirs to tourists. The manager there was the same man who had been in charge at the Taung quarry when the child skull was found. In August 1936 Broom acquired an adult fossil skull. Although it did contain an endocast, the face was badly crushed, which required hours of painstaking work to remove it from its surrounding rock matrix. Broom considered several names, including *Australopethicus transvaalensis* and *Plesianthropus transvaalensis* because he thought the specimen earlier chronologically than Taung. Often during this period, every time a new fossil was found it was given a separate name. Over the following two years quarrymen found more assorted pieces scattered about the region: a wrist bone, a thigh bone, sections of upper jaw with four teeth, and more facial bones.

A little boy also came to Broom's aid. Gert Terblanche had been collecting fossils in the area, and Broom went to see him. When Broom found him, the boy produced a pocketful of tooth fragments. Squatting down in amazement, Broom took out the fossil jaw and proceeded to get several broken tooth crowns in place atop broken roots still in the jaw. Gert then showed Broom the spot, called Kromdraai, where he had found the treasures. From this material Broom assembled a skull with most of the left side of the face, the palate, and most of the lower right jaw. Though similar to *Australopithecus africanus,* it was thicker and more solidly built. The Kromdraai skull seemed a different type of creature, so he eventually named it *Paranthropus robustus.*

During World War II Broom discovered several more ankle, wrist, and arm bones as he diligently continued the search. He found them near where the skull had been found, so he assumed that they came from the same individual. This situation caused a problem. Had the wrist and ankle bones been discovered separately from the skull, they would have been accepted as being from a biped. Because they were found in conjunction with the Kromdraai material, though, they were not. According to the accepted wisdom of the day, the skull found at Kromdraai could not have come from a human ancestor because of its small brain.

Throughout the war years Broom put together a meticulous description of all the fossils he had. The creature or creatures represented were genuine bipeds, he believed, who used their hands to manipulate objects, and thus were human ancestors. Finally published in 1946, Broom's description supported what Raymond Dart had initially argued. In 1947 Broom found an almost complete pelvis and vertebral column. There no longer seemed any doubt that the *Australopithecus* were bipeds and that they were human ancestors. Broom was convinced at least two types of *Australopithecus* existed: Dart's lightly built *A. africanus* and his own heartier version he now called *Australopithecus robustus*. Broom said that the new material was close to *Australopithecus* but had enough morphological difference to split it off into a new species.

In addition to Broom, influential British anthropologist Wilfrid Le Gros Clark came to accept Taung. He had been quietly researching the skull and by 1947 publicly referred to it as a hominid—something few others were willing to do. At the same time Arthur Keith, who had once ridiculed Dart and Taung, reconsidered his position and admitted he had been wrong and Dart right. William K. Gregory of the American Museum of Natural History, along with his boss, Henry Fairfield Osborn, likewise at first rejected Taung. By the late 1930s Gregory reassessed the situation and admitted as Keith had done that Dart's assertions were essentially correct. Looking at the *Australopithecus* teeth in the 1940s, Ralph Von Koenigswald (who had worked on Java man) also lined up behind Taung, though he hesitated to call it a direct ancestor because he thought the teeth too big. It was believed that organisms became larger as their genus evolved through time. The human line, however, seemed to have teeth that were getting smaller. The use of tools to work food might lead to smaller teeth, some argued. Using this logic, Von Koenigswald was able to overlook tooth size as a problem in understanding the fossils. It had taken millions of years, but Taung had finally become a human ancestor—almost.

### Louis Leakey

Taung was only the first of a long line of creatures discovered in Africa that would eventually show it was there, not Asia, that the human line first arose. The next phase of discovery was the result of the efforts of Louis Leakey (1903–1972) and his family of fossil hunters. Ironically, Leakey did not think Taung a human ancestor. Leakey was born in Kenya, the son of missionaries, and studied anthropology under Arthur Keith at Cambridge. As a child he spoke the local Kikuyu language fluently and spent hours roaming the African countryside searching for fossils and artifacts.

After his schooling, Leakey's first serious work in Africa came in 1931 related to a discovery called Oldoway man. Found in 1913 by German geologist Hans Reck, Oldoway man was thought to be ancient, judging from the fossil animals found in association with it as well as Reck's belief that the deposits where the fossils were found were 1 million years old. Reck said there were no associated artifacts with the fossils. Most archaeologists looked for flint tools, but Leakey knew from his past artifact hunting in the area that in that part of Africa tools could be found made of other materials, including obsidian and basalt lava.

Leakey scouted the Oldoway man site and found several hand axes the first day. He believed that modern humans could trace their ancestry back millions of years to creatures not far removed from them. This position was supported by finds made in 1932 of hominid fossils at Kanjera and Kanam, Kenya. Leakey had great faith in his own abilities and was sure he would find the oldest human. By the 1950s he had concentrated his efforts almost exclusively on a place called Olduvai Gorge, near the border of Tanzania and Kenya, not far from Lake Victoria, the source of the White Nile River. It was a good fossil locality because of the way large expanses of fossil-bearing strata were exposed. The gorge is part of a geologic feature known as the Great Rift Valley, itself an immense cut through the layers exposing millions of years of material and stretching halfway down the length of the African continent.

Leakey was assisted in his work by his wife, Mary, who was a distant relation of John Frere, who in the 1790s did pioneering work on Stone Age tool culture in Europe. She had an erratic and unconventional education before becoming a proficient archaeologist. She did extensive fieldwork on ancient people and preferred being outdoors rather than in a classroom. In this way she and Louis were two of a kind. She met him after being introduced by a mutual acquaintance. She started doing illustrations for his publications, became his field assistant, and in 1936 his second wife.

In 1948 a wealthy American named Charles Boise took an interest in Leakey's work and began funding the operation. This allowed the work at Olduvai to continue. The Leakeys roamed the wastes of Olduvai Gorge for years, finding many animal fossils and stone tools but no human fossils. Fortunately, the years of grueling, backbreaking work in the unforgiving African sun were about to pay off. In July 1959 Mary was scouting for fossils with the family dogs when she spotted a cranium with teeth in a layer of earth called Bed I. Simple but identifiable tools, now known as Oldowan, were scattered about. The cranium Mary found closely resembled Broom's fossils from Kromdraai, only with larger teeth. It had a small brain and a pronounced sagittal crest. Leakey named the fossils *Zinjanthropus boisei*. (Because of the large teeth, some called it Nutcracker man.)

A fair amount of *Australopithecus* fossils had been found in caves in southern Africa's Transvaal region since 1925. Some of these were like Dart's Taung Child so were added to *Australopithecus africanus,* whereas a second group, which seemed more heavily built, was named *Australopithecus robustus.* Leakey did not think either were human ancestors. As

*Zinjanthropus,* or Zinj, as it was commonly called, seemed to be associated with stone tools, Leakey believed it must be a human ancestor. He considered the heightened brainpower necessary for tool manufacture a sign of "humanness." Others, including his friend and colleague Clark Howell, thought Zinj an *Australopithecus.*

In 1960 Leakey's son Jonathan found cranial material that seemed to be neither *Autralopithecus* nor *Zinjanthropus.* Referring to this new find as pre-*Zinjanthropus,* he decided it was a genuine human ancestor that predated the other two. Leakey thought he had the whole thing worked out: the pre-Zinj creature was the toolmaker and human ancestor, whereas *Zinjanthropus* and *Australopithecus* were not. He stated that it had "become evident that the earliest known industry from Olduvai . . . already represents a stage of development in which a multiple tool-kit was in use, indicating the pre-existence of more primitive and less organized stages of tool-making" (1964, 1). In other words, Leakey thought the toolmaker–human ancestor was much older and smarter than the relatively younger *Australopithecus* and *Zinjanthropus.* To his mind, his pre-Zinj mystery creature was more ancient and had the human qualities of a large brain, bipedal locomotion, and advanced intellect.

In order to get more accurate dates for his finds, Leakey brought Jack Evernden of the University of California at Berkeley to Olduvai Gorge. Evernden had pioneered the technique of potassium-argon dating. This method tests rock containing potassium, which itself contains small amounts of potassium isotopes. Over time the potassium isotope changes, or decays, into an argon isotope. Measuring the percentages of the two isotopes gives an age to the material being tested. It is possible to determine ages over 100,000 years with this technique. Evernden, along with another dating specialist, Garniss Curtis, tested the Pleistocene Bed I and produced a date of between 1.6 and 1.9 million years. (Later, more sensitive testing equipment refined that date to between 1.78 and 1.79 million years.)

Philip Tobias had done much of the original examination of Zinj and believed it was an *Australopithecus.* His work helped sway Leakey to accept *Zinjanthropus* as an *Australopithecus,* renaming it *Australopithecus boisie.* Tobias had worked for years with Raymond Dart and had even taken over Dart's old job at Witwatersrand. He initially thought pre-Zinj was an *Australopithecus* as well. After a year or so of discussion with Louis Leakey, as well as more fossil finds of a similar nature, Tobias came around to Leakey's view that pre-Zinj was a member of the *Homo* line.

To help in the study of the accumulated pre-Zinj material, John Napier (a specialist in the anatomy of hands and feet from the Royal Free Hospital in London) joined the team. Napier's examination of the material led him to believe that the pre-Zinj had opposable thumbs and had the ability to perform what he christened a "power grip" and a "precision grip," two things needed for manipulative hands. Leakey's powerful personality may have influenced the others to see the find as more *Homo* than the fragmentary anatomy suggested. They based their assessment not on one fossil but on four different and incomplete individuals found in Bed I and Bed II and known variously by their nicknames as Cindy, George, Johnny's child, and Twiggy. This was problematic from a strictly scientific point of view: a new species is normally named for a single fossil that becomes the type specimen. The team took Raymond Dart's suggestion and named the new species *Homo habilis* (the handy man).

Tobias measured the creature's cranial capacity at 675–680 cubic centimeters, well below Arthur Keith's cranial Rubicon of 750 cubic centimeters. The idea that the creature had been a toolmaker was a factor that helped push the group to accept *Homo habilis* as a human ancestor. Leakey thought he saw the suggestion of "human" behavior in toolmaking and so included this in the assessment of the bones. To the cranial Rubicon (which was an anatomical marker of the human line that they pushed back) they added toolmaking (which was a behavioral marker). Some argued that Leakey had based too much of his assessment of *Homo habilis* on behavioral qualities not apparent in the fossils. In 1965 he said that he did not think culture or tool use should be used to determine a human ancestor. Not long after that, however, he stated that tool use had been a factor in his labeling of *Homo habilis*.

During the process of examining the *Homo habilis* fossils, John Napier showed the material to his students, including Alan Walker. His unique position to watch the process take place led Walker years later to question what had happened. As the descriptive paper on *Homo habilis* included changing the brain-size criteria to match what they had and the emphasis on behavioral elements instead of strictly anatomical ones, Walker called it "poorly conceived" and worried that all subsequent *H. habilis* finds would be measured against it (Walker and Shipman 1996, 111). Even after Tobias's lengthy monograph on the subject in 1991, Walker argued, it is still difficult to tell just what is or is not a *Homo habilis*.

The prominent scientist Wilfrid Le Gros Clark, an old Leakey friend, also had problems with the *Homo* label, saying the anatomical description of the fossils could just as easily fit an *Australopithecus*. Despite all this debate, Louis Leakey's reputation as a finder of fossils was ensured. He became world famous as the man who discovered the oldest man. He appeared on television and magazine covers and was the subject of documentary films. He had gone from being an obscure African fossil hunter to a major international celebrity. He parlayed his fame into increased funding for his projects, particularly from the National Geographic Society, and championed the cause of Africa as the cradle of the human race.

## The Hominid Gang

In the 1970s another of Louis Leakey's sons, Richard, stepped onto the stage of African human origins studies. Richard was only a teenager when he began to help his father in the field, but he did not initially take to human evolution studies. In fact, he made the conscious decision at first not to follow in his parents' steps. He later said that "I should avoid at all costs an academic life" (1983, 54). This deficiency would come back to haunt him, as some would later charge that he was simply a scientific dilettante basking in the reputation of his famous father.

As a youth Richard went out into the wilds of Africa on his own, collecting animal skeletons of which there were an abundance drying in the sun. He made a living off them by selling skeletons to universities, museums, and private collectors. Regardless of his credentials, Richard became a force in the field, especially after opening up a fossil site along the banks of Lake Turkana, Kenya, called Koobi Fora. To assist him Richard employed a group of local Kenyan fossil finders commonly known as the "Hominid Gang." Working under Leakey's supervision and team leader Kamoya Kimeu, they scoured the Lake Turkana site with tireless diligence. Few scientists could match their record of discoveries.

Richard Leakey held to the same position as his father about the relationship of the various hominids being discovered in Africa: *Australopithecus* was an offshoot and dead-end, whereas *Homo habilis* was the ancestor of *Homo sapiens*. Like his father, Richard Leakey was adept at generating publicity and funding for his projects to keep the eastern African work going. As few struggling young African countries had the money to spend on scientific research, fund-raising was, and is still, as important as digging. The National Geographic Society continued to be crucial, as did the National Science Foundation. Universities around the world gave short-term grants for individual researchers to spend time at Olduvai Gorge and Lake Turkana. As his father had done before him, Richard Leakey made the talk show circuit around the world and was featured on the cover of *Time* in 1977. In the same year he published *Origins,* a popular book on human evolution. Having good looks and an articulate way about him, the younger Leakey was sought out for his opinions on questions of the day that had little to do with human evolution. For a time he lived a jet-setting lifestyle, hobnobbing with international glitterati, a long way from the sweltering plains of Africa.

### Tough Tuff

Accurate dating is important for understanding how old fossils are as well as how they relate to one another. Richard Leakey and his team were eager to get a date for the Koobi Fora. A sample was sent to Cambridge University for testing. It was called the KBS Tuff sample, named for team geologist Kay Behrensmeyer. Tuff (pronounced tooff) was ash spewed out during volcanic eruptions to rain down and form alternating layers on the ground that in time hardened. As there had been much volcanic activity in the Koobi Fora area in the past, the region had many such layers. Dating these layers would give a good age for the fossils associated with them. The team that dated the KBS Tuff, F. J. Miller and J. A. Fitch, published their results in *Nature* in 1970. They said that "it can therefore be concluded that the best interpretation . . . of the tuff horizon in the Koobi Fora beds from east of Lake Rudolf in East Africa is that its age is very close to 2.6 m.y. (2.61± less than 0.26 m.y.)" (1970, 228). (Lake Turkana had been previously called Lake Rudolf. Following a wave of African independence movements and a desire to shed the old stigma of the colonial period, many European place-names were changed to African ones. Hence, in 1974 Rudolf became Turkana.)

In 1972 the Hominid Gang's Bernard Ngeneo turned up a skull that was labeled KNMER-1470 (Kenya National Museum, East Rudolf–1470). Richard Leakey, along with team anatomist Bernard Wood, determined that it was the oldest and largest-brained hominid ever found. They were joined in their study of 1470 by Leakey's wife, Meave, and anatomist Alan Walker. The skull was clearly a big-brained hominid of some kind, but Walker thought he saw *Australopithecus* characteristics in it. If 1470 was older than the tuff just above it, an early form of *Homo* had existed alongside *Australopithecus*. That meant *Australopithecus* could not be the ancestor to the *Homo* line.

The fact that others saw 1470 as a form of *Australopithecus* complicated the matter. When it came time for the team to publish a technical descriptive paper of 1470, the disagreement became acute. For Leakey and Wood, 1470 was a member of the *Homo* line, whereas Walker disagreed and at a strategy meeting asked to have his name removed from the publication. He did not want his name on a paper that suggested something he did not believe. As Walker had done a good bit of the work describing the fossil, when the request to remove his name was accepted, he left the meeting. Leakey and Walker disagreed strongly over what 1470 was. As early as 1973 Richard Leakey had already suggested it was probably a member of the *Homo* line, not an *Australopithecus*. In an attempt to smooth things over, Leakey agreed not to emphasize the *Homo* aspect (though the fossil had been referred to as *Homo* in some previous publications by others). Walker agreed to the compromise wording of the joint article and returned.

Dating fossils is commonly done through radiometric techniques. But fossils can be used to date other fossils. In the case of what came to be known as the KBS Tuff controversy, fossil pigs helped clear up the misunderstanding. The Omo River comes out of Ethiopia and dumps into Lake Turkana. In 1959 the young Clark Howell, inspired by Louis Leakey, planned to survey the river in order to scout the Plio-Pleistocene deposits that occurred in abundance along its shores. After some of the physical and bureaucratic hardships inherent in fossil hunting in Africa, Howell made it to the Omo and began working out the region's complex stratigraphy and fossil deposits. He believed the Omo beds were 3 million years old, as opposed to Olduvai Gorge's 2 million.

Due to other commitments Howell left after this brief journey and was unable to return to the Omo until 1967 as part of an expedition that included Richard Leakey. It was this expedition that inspired Leakey to leave the group (frustrated by the French team members' apparent treatment of him as an amateur) to go off on his own—a move that led him to the Koobi Fora site. For Howell and later paleoanthropologists, Omo turned out to be a site of major importance. The geology, though complex, comprised a "continuous record of events that is unique in the study of fossil hominid evolution" (Johanson and Edey 1981, 114). The stratigraphy and fossils of this region are in effect a giant measuring stick of time that can be read and used for comparison elsewhere. The close interspacing of the tuff layers allowed for close dating of the fossils. Extensive documentation of the fossil series found there, particularly mice, antelope, giraffes, and pigs, allowed for the dating of similar fossils found at other sites. Aiding Clark Howell was Basil Cooke, who worked out detailed histories of the various pig species that had inhabited the Omo region in the past. This record was so accurate and detailed that if a site of questionable age somewhere in Africa had fossil pigs in it, those pigs could be compared to the Omo pigs and the site dated accordingly. The Omo pigs would play an important role in working out the problem of the KBS Tuff and the age of fossil 1470.

Richard Leakey had estimated the age of 1470 to be about 2.9 million years (because it was found under and hence was older than the KBS Tuff above it dated to 2.6 million years). This made it older than the australopithecines, whose then oldest known example was 2.5 million years. So if 1470 was at least as old or older than the australopithecines, then they could not be human ancestors. A problem was that 1470 did not look old enough to some. Eventually, pigs from Koobi Fora and Olduvai Gorge were compared to the measuring stick of the Omo pigs and dated to only about 2 million years. The radiometric dating suggested 2.9 million years, whereas the pig dating suggested 2 million. The resulting tension lasted for some years until new fossils came along to help clear up the problem of *Australopithecus* as a human ancestor. If the pigs were correct, then the anomaly of *Homo* being older than *Australopithecus* would disappear. (Later radiometric dating of the KBS Tuff in the 1980s done by scientists at the University of California at Berkeley; Berne, Switzerland; and Australia confirmed the pig dating, giving dates of 1.8 million years. The discrepancies in the original dates were put down to contamination by other materials in the first samples.) What helped clear up the question to many of whether the human line found its origin in the australopithecines was the discovery of another fossil—a fossil destined to become one of the most famous since the original Neanderthal.

*Lucy*

It was Christmas Eve 1974 when it was first seen weathering out of the ground of Ethiopia. Donald Johanson and graduate student Tom Gray came across the first weather-exposed pieces of the fossil. They carefully began to excavate the site and did so for several weeks. The recovered pieces were brought back to the base camp in the evenings for examination. As the camp's tape recorder had been playing the

Beatles' song "Lucy in the Sky with Diamonds," the team began referring to the fossil as Lucy (good thing they weren't listening to "In-A-Gadda-Da-Vida"). They were working in the Hadar region of Ethiopia, north of the Turkana-Olduvai region. Though Johanson had found fossils before, this one was clearly very special. Lucy (officially, it is AL288-1) was a shortish hominid with an astonishing 40 percent of its skeleton remaining. The Ethiopian workers called it Denkenesh, or "you are so wonderful." From the shape of the pelvis, femur, tibia, and other parts, it was a three-foot-tall individual weighing about sixty pounds. The fragments of cranium suggested it had a relatively small brain. If Lucy was a human ancestor, she apparently walked upright before her brain grew large.

Donald Johanson, originally from Chicago, had come to Ethiopia in 1973 as part of the International Omo Expedition and was asked to join the Joint International Afar Research Expedition by that expedition's

*Donald Johanson, curator of physical anthropology at the Cleveland Museum of Natural History, points out some feature of "Lucy," Cleveland, Ohio, January 19, 1979. Johnson discovered Lucy, the oldest, most complete remains of a human ancestor, in the Afar region of Ethiopia, November 24, 1974. (Bettmann / Corbis)*

coleader French scientist Yves Coppens. Other team members included Maurice Taieb and Jon Kalb. Johanson quickly showed himself an able field man and theorist. After the Lucy discovery, Johanson and his coworkers spent the next several years in careful study of these and other fossils they had found and published a number of papers. Johanson's examination of the Lucy fossils and a comparison of them to fossils from other African sites led him to initially believe she might represent a new species. Working with colleague Tim White, who had previously worked with Mary Leakey, Johanson came to a different conclusion. Not only was Lucy an *Australopithecus,* but the fossils they compared it to from Olduvai and another site called Laetoli were as well. The fossils Johanson and White now thought were *Australopithecus* also happened to be fossils Mary Leakey considered *Homo.*

The conflict created by these assertions came to a head at the 1978 meeting of the Royal Swedish Academy. The academy was celebrating the two hundredth anniversary of Swedish naturalist Carolus Linnaeus. Being of Swedish ancestry, Johanson was doubly excited. He announced the new species name as *Australopithecus afarensis* (after the Afar region in which it was discovered) and suggested it was the ancestor to the human line. Johanson finished his presentation, going a bit long, and waited for a reaction. In the audience were Mary Leakey, Philip Tobias, and other major players of paleoanthropology. Afterward, several people came up to Johanson to congratulate him, but few said anything of substance. Mary Leakey, however, was angry. She claimed he had discussed material that she was going to cover in her talk later that day and that he used material that was "hers"—material that she had been working on but had not yet published. Johanson countered that although he had discussed some of her fossils in support of findings, he referred only to ones she had already published. Popular focus on this incident is usually on the assertion that Johanson had broken some kind of rule about using material not yet in the press. In reality, Johanson had observed the etiquette and had not mentioned any material that had not already been published. Mary Leakey was upset that he had mentioned her work at all but was especially taken aback that he insisted her fossils were *Australopithecus* when she said they were *Homo.* This undermined the Leakey position that *Australopithecus* was not a human ancestor and used her work to support a position she herself did not hold. In addition, Louis Leakey's old associate Philip Tobias championed *Australopithecus africanus* as the rightful ancestor to *Homo* and so was not happy with Johanson's presentation because he had essentially demoted *A.*

*africanus* in favor of *A. afarensis*. Mary Leakey distanced herself from Johanson that night after years of friendly association.

The repercussions of Johanson's presentation would last for years. When a scientist proclaims a new fossil species, they are establishing a position, staking out turf, and directly and indirectly challenging others. This is especially so for human ancestors. Each new theory has the potential to upset older ideas and established belief systems. Delicate feelings and egos can be bruised and great offense taken. Johanson eventually resigned his position in Richard Leakey's human evolution organization and started the Institute for Human Origins in 1981.

There was still more to come. In 1975 Ethiopian emperor Haile Selassie was replaced by a Marxist government. The new regime called a halt to fossil hunting while it worked out a new protocol for allowing research to take place. There were even wild accusations that U.S. and other Western scientists were operatives for the CIA, selling drugs, and stealing fossils. Richard Leakey was then a consultant to the Ethiopian government, and Johanson smelled some Leakey payback for the Swedish Academy encounter.

Johanson's colleague Tim White had worked with Mary and Richard Leakey in the 1970s and had come to feel uncomfortable with what he considered to be their attempt to force their interpretations of fossils on him. Underneath all this was the significant disagreement over the course of human evolution. Richard Leakey tended to his father's view that the *Homo* line went well into the past beyond the *Australopithecus*. For Johanson and White, the Afar material suggested that there had been one species of wide variation spread out over Ethiopia and Kenya. Lucy and her *Australopithecus afarensis* relatives were 3 to 4 million years old and part of the line leading to modern humans. This put the Leakey and Johanson camps squarely at odds.

## Footprints

Although fossils have been found there, the site known as Laetoli is best known as the place where hominid footprints were found in the mid-1970s. Mary Leakey had worked the site for some time when Andrew Hill literally stumbled across a trackway of multiple prints in 1976. More tracks were unearthed in 1978 by Paul Abell and were dated to 3.6 million years. From the arrangement of the prints as well as their shape, Mary Leakey thought they were from a creature in the

*Homo* line. An *Australopithecus,* she claimed, would not have left tracks so human in their step. Along with the footprints Mary Leakey also found fossil bones in the Laetoli area. In the early 1970s she asked Tim White to describe the material for publication (including some of the material Johanson and White later used for comparison to Lucy). She had asked him to assist her because of his advanced knowledge of anatomy and attention to detail.

White said the Laetoli hominid had teeth like *Homo habilis* as well as *Australopithecus* characters. White was then a graduate student at the University of Michigan, where he studied under a host of some of the most influential scientists of the later twentieth century, including geologist Bill Farrand, paleontologist Loring Brace, archaeologists Henry Wright and Kent Flannery, and anthropologist Milford Wolpoff. Wolpoff argued that all the different hominids that existed in Africa were variations of one species, not a collection of different ones. Originally, Donald Johanson thought that Lucy and related material represented a different species from those at Laetoli. Eventually, White prevailed upon Johanson to come around to the idea that although there were several species existing in eastern Africa, *Australopithecus afarensis* was the same as Mary Leakey's material from Laetoli, the variation in size being accounted for by temporal, geographic, individual, and sexual influences. Of the different *Australopithecus* living in Africa, it was Johanson's *A. afarensis* that, unlike *A. robustus* or *A. africanus,* led to the *Homo* line. That Johanson and White had placed *Australopithecus afarensis* as ancestral to the *Homo* accounted for much of the rift that developed between them and Mary Leakey.

Disagreement over interpretation of evidence is common in science; in fact it is expected and is generally considered healthy. Ideas over human origins are often held and promoted with a special kind of vigor. Writer Roger Lewin, who has published much on the lives and workings of the Africa human origin scientists, perceptively points out that "opinions are sometimes worn more like battle colors than scholarly points of view" (1987, 173). Whether or not their fossils are, scientists are human and can suffer all the attendant weaknesses.

*Back to Olduvai*

In the early 1980s Johanson and White's work in Ethiopia was halted temporarily while the local government hashed out research protocols. They were given an unexpected chance, however, when Tanzanian scientists and government officials asserted their right to control the Olduvai Gorge region and to decide who could work there. Prosper Ndessokia, a paleontologist for the Tanzanian Antiquities Department, and others bristled at the notion that Mary Leakey had some intrinsic right to control the fossil fields there simply because she and her husband had made so many discoveries. In 1985 the Tanzanian authorities issued permits to Johanson and White to allow them in, regardless of their relationship with the famous Leakey family. The Tanzanians had decided to develop their nation's rich paleontological sites as a national resource. They envisioned a program that included training more homegrown scientists to take charge. The resistance to Johanson and White coming in was not from local scientists but from Anglo-Americans who thought the two were perpetrating a raid upon the Leakeys' domain. By that time, though, Olduvai Gorge was considered by most to be played out, to contain no more material of importance. It was generally thought the Leakeys had found everything there was to find.

Johanson and White knew all this but could not pass up such an opportunity. Short of money, their expedition would be short as well. They were able to put together funding for four weeks in the field. On their third day, Tim White found a hominid maxilla with tooth sockets, a top end of a femur, and other tiny assorted pieces. The location was subsequently named Dik-Dik Hill (a dik-dik is a small African antelope). Labeled OH62 (Olduvai Hominid no. 62), it was the first *Homo habilis* to be found with both skull and body parts. Thought to be an adult female, it was 1.8 million years old but so broken and fragmentary that a reconstruction was out of the question. Still, it gave important information. It had apelike limb proportions. In an ape the lower arms are longer than the upper. OH62 seemed built more along these lines. Its overall height was about three feet. This showed that *Homo habilis* was more apelike in appearance than was originally thought. It also suggested that human-style proportioned limbs appeared fairly quickly afterward.

This determination brought up the question of what made a *Homo habilis*. There seemed a huge range of sizes of fossils all lumped under the *habilis* label. Johanson always thought Louis Leakey had been premature in creating *Homo habilis* and claiming it to be a human ancestor. One of Robert Broom's students, J. T. Robinson, did a study of *Australopithecus* and *Homo habilis* dentition and claimed there was less difference between their teeth than between average groups of modern humans. By the late 1980s researchers like Bernard Wood and Christopher Stringer were questioning the viability of *Homo habilis,* asking whether they were just later forms of *Australopithecus.*

## Turkana Boy

More and more, by the 1990s, Africans were part of the search for human ancestors. An increasingly multinational workforce was now scouring the countryside for fossils. Since the days of the Hominid Gang, Africans had been involved in the search, but now they were doing more than just digging. Ethiopians like paleontologist Berhane Asfaw, Tanzanian archaeologist Fidelis Masao, geologist Paul Manega, and even Japanese paleoanthropologist Gen Suwa joined Prosper Ndessokia and others in continuing to make discoveries in a place thought to have none left to make.

Richard Leakey's team was still hard at work at Lake Turkana, Kenya. In 1984 Kamoya Kimeu discovered an almost complete skeleton of a teenaged boy there. Turkana boy, as it is commonly known, was a *Homo erectus* 1.6 million years old. This *Homo erectus* youth was unusual for several reasons. First, *Homo erectus* was still seen in many people's eyes as an Asian creature. This find confirmed that there was a solid *erectus* presence in Africa as well. Also, Turkana boy was much taller than *Homo habilis.* He was as tall as a *Homo sapiens* with the long limbs associated with the modern people of eastern and southern Africa. *Homo erectus* was the first hominid to acquire the same general body proportions and height of modern people. Despite these modern characters, Turkana boy's brain was not as large as a modern person's. Once again, here was evidence that locomotion on two legs came before large brain growth. It also showed that Africa still had a lot to say about human evolution. Bernard Wood's examination of Turkana boy seemed to show that the African *Homo erectus* was distinct from the Asian version. The difference could be so great as to warrant the African variants to be reclassified as a new species, *Homo ergaster* (which will be discussed in a later chapter), in the mid-1970s.

## The Scientist as Hero

With all his important work, Donald Johanson became a scientist of world renown. Like Richard Leakey, Louis Leakey, Henry Fairfield Osborn, and even T. H. Huxley before him, Johanson became an authority in the public eye. He was courted for television interviews, documentaries, and book projects. To many people his was the last word on human evolution. It was a position Johanson did not ask for, nor was he particularly comfortable with it. He was perceptive enough to understand that his work was being received in the public as not just data relating to human evolution, but more as a new kind of creation story. Yes, he was uncovering new facts about human origins, but he was not trying to create a new mythology, only bring forth empirical evidence about the past. He was trying to uncover a new reality, not a new philosophy. Yet he fell prey on occasion. When discussing Lucy and her popularity in the public he waxed self-consciously poetic, saying, "In an elusive but powerful sense, she represents the Mother, Gaea, Isis—or whatever history has called the fertility that lingers at the beginning of our consciousness" (1996, 30).

The common human need for leadership and easy answers to tough questions pushed Leakey and Johanson to places of authority in the media. They were set up as a kind of all-knowing priesthood of human evolution. As a scientist Johanson knew he did not have, nor could he have, all the answers. He accepted that there were various possible explanations and valid theories about the meanings of fossils that might differ from his. Whereas Richard Leakey embraced his celebrity in the 1970s and '80s and used it to promote a range of agendas, Johanson tried to resist. Their careers became examples of how the finder of a fossil could become as famous as the fossil itself and forever be associated with it.

*Conclusion*

Trends that started the day Raymond Dart opened a box of rocks from Taung in 1925 continued in the finds of the 1970s and '80s. The work of Robert Broom, Louis Leakey, and Donald Johanson and their discoveries at Sterkfontein, Olduvai Gorge, Lake Turkana, and Hadar rewrote the story of human origins and evolution. As a result the Dark Continent became the Mother Continent. While not all these scientists agreed on every aspect of their work, one thing was clear: Africa was the place the human race began. The real problem now was determining how it began and what the relationship of all those hominids was to each other.

There were others issues of growing concern as well. Fossils can say a lot about our ancestors, but there are aspects of their lives that are a bit more elusive than simple morphology. While the physical origins of humans were being established, the origins of intelligence, culture, and the very idea of "humanness" were being addressed as well. These areas of inquiry can be just as controversial as the others—sometimes more so.

*Further Reading*

For the life of Raymond Dart, see Dart and Dennis Craig, *Adventures with the Missing Link* (1959). The first description of Taung is in Dart's "*Australopithecus africanus:* The Man-Ape of South Africa" (1925). For the opposing view, see Arthur Keith, Grafton Elliot Smith, and Arthur Smith Woodward, "The Fossil Ape of Taung" (1925). On Louis Leakey and Olduvai Gorge, see L. S. B. Leakey, *Adam's Ancestors* (1953) and *Olduvai Gorge, 1951–1961,* vols. 1 and 3 (1967); Philip Tobias, *Olduvai Gorge, 1951–1961,* vol. 2 (1967); and Mina White Mulvey, *Digging Up Adam: The Story of L. S. B. Leakey* (1969). For the work of Richard Leakey, see Richard Leakey and Roger Lewin, *Origins* (1977) and *Origins Reconsidered* (1992); Richard Leakey, "Skull 1470" (1973); and M. H. Day, R. E. F. Leakey, A. C. Walker, and B. A. Wood, "New Hominids from East Rudolf, Kenya" (1975). For Lucy, see Donald Johanson and Maitland Edey, *Lucy* (1981), and Donald Johanson and James Shreeve, *Lucy's Child: The Discovery of Human Ancestry* (1989). For a good general discussion of this era, see John Reader, *Missing Links* (1981); Roger Lewin, *Bones of Contention* (1987); Delta Willis, *The Hominid Gang* (1989); and Ian Tattersall, *The Fossil Trail: How We Know What We Think We Know about Human Evolution* (1995).

The study of human evolution has involved more than just fossils. While some paleoanthropologists picked, scavenged, and excavated bones, some studied the artifacts and creative works left behind by our ancestors. Others looked for the origins of behavior, intelligence, and culture. One question that had long been of interest was how our hominid ancestors became genuinely human—how did *they* become *us?* Linked to this was the problem of definition. Before the mid–nineteenth century, naturalists interested in the antiquity of man were concerned with how far back in time people went. They assumed that, regardless of how old the human race was, it had always been essentially human. With the arrival of Darwinian thinking and discoveries like the Neanderthal, this assumption began to change. Questions of how to tell the differences, if any, among modern people, the apes, and archaic people were being asked.

As the search for human origins continued, naturalists were forced to define what they were looking for. It seemed such a simple question to answer, but the more people tried to define "humanness" the more complicated it became. As late as 1981 Donald Johanson could still say that "we do not have, even today, an agreed-on definition of humankind, a clear set of specifications that will enable any anthropologist in the world to say quickly and with confidence, 'this one is a human; that one isn't'" (1981, 100). The eighteenth-century German naturalist Johann Friedrich Blumenbach began the definition process when he identified four characteristics he believed made humans unique: erect posture, flat pelvis, two hands, and closely set teeth. Later researchers added speech, intellectual capability, grasping hands, and brain size. Even with these markers the answer remained elusive. In the nineteenth century Ernst Haeckel developed the "family tree" approach to grouping living things. In the later twentieth century another way of looking at evolution came about.

## The Evolutionary Synthesis and Cladistics

Idiosyncratic theories of human evolution were rampant in the 1920s and '30s. Orthogenesis, for example, and its attendant idea of internal willpower and goal-oriented development still held thrall over many paleoanthropologists. This approach saw the organism itself consciously working to evolve. It fitted nicely with the romantic notion of human ancestors fighting against great odds to evolve into higher creatures. The growth of genetics in the early part of the twentieth century was not initially embraced by most paleoanthropologists. They were focused on fossils and thought genetics unable to show how evolution worked; geneticists thought it was fossils that were incapable of explaining evolution. What neither side realized at the time was that both held keys to explaining evolutionary mechanics.

The 1930s and '40s also saw the appearance of the evolutionary synthesis through the publication of Theodosius Dobzhansky's *Genetics and the Origin of Species* (1937), Ernst Mayr's *Systematics and the Origin of Species* (1942), and George Gaylord Simpson's *Tempo and the Mode of Evolution* (1944). This new way of thinking was partly a result of the notion of population genetics. These authors argued that evolution worked by a slow, gradual change through a process of accumulating tiny genetic variations, controlled by natural selection and the environment. This combination of Darwinian and genetic processes would alter a population of organisms in a way that would lead to speciation. Small-scale genetic changes would therefore become large-scale changes visible in the fossil record. Scientists would now think of not only how change affected individual organisms but also how it worked throughout entire populations.

Paleoanthropologists tended to think in terms of individuals (easy to understand, as human fossils are some of the hardest to find and rarely show up in large numbers). Now they could look at human evolution with a wider lens. Dobzhansky did this in 1944 when he argued that the differences between Java man and Peking man were insignificant if thought of as part of a larger population. (Today both are considered examples of *Homo erectus.*) This approach helped generate new questions concerning the nebulous boundaries between individual hominid fossils. Were the fossils being found separate species or only variations within a population? Was there a straight line from one to another, a more branching system with dead-ends, or a series of long parallel lines with many species following similar but not directly related tracks? Dobzhansky thought the hominid fossil record showed a series of local variations on one theme. Mayr argued that speciation was not a nice, clean, orderly process with one group turning into the next one en masse.

As useful as it was, the evolutionary synthesis did not seem to always fit the fossil record as well as was hoped. If the synthesis was correct in that evolution worked in slow, steady increments over vast periods of time, theoretically, you could watch the change from one species to another by following new characters as they appeared in the fossil record. Detractors pointed to "holes" in the fossil record where fossils did not appear as proof that evolution was a sham. Paleontologists argued back that holes were only caused by fossils that had not yet been discovered.

A possible answer to this conundrum was not exactly what either side anticipated. As crustaceans were more numerous and because of their circumstances more easily fossilized, their fossil record was more complete than that of most mammals. In the 1970s Niles Eldredge of the American Museum of Natural History in New York saw something fascinating in the trilobites he was studying. Trilobites existed in huge numbers and in a dizzying array of styles and are very well known from long fossil sequences. The collection Eldredge was working on covered a period of roughly 6 million years yet showed virtually no anatomical change until a point where a great deal of change occurred. He surmised that the environment the trilobites lived in had been stable for a long period but then changed suddenly. The trilobite population remained steady while the environment did, but when the environment changed the trilobites changed as well.

At about the same time Stephen Jay Gould (1941–2002) of Harvard was studying fossil snails and came to a similar conclusion as Eldredge. The two men came together and called their new idea "punctuated equilibrium." They argued that with no environmental pressure a population could remain in stasis for long periods and experience little or no evolutionary change. Once the environment changed the population had to respond to the new situation. As a result speciation would not always be a slow, steady affair ticking away like a clock, but something that came in fits and starts. This kind of sudden change could take on the illusion of a hole in the fossil record.

By 1975 Eldredge and his American Museum colleague Ian Tattersall began adapting punctuated equilibrium to hominids. Tattersall argued that hominid evolution was not just the study of individual fossils but also a study of patterns in the overall fossil record—patterns and relations that were not obvious or that could even be found. Close analysis required the scientist to be intimately familiar with the fossils so that the pattern of relationships would become apparent on an intuitive level.

Another way of hypothesizing the relations of hominids to one another had been around since 1950. German entomologist Willi Hennig developed the concept of cladistics as a way of working out evolutionary relationships and patterns. The underlying idea behind it was that all living things changed over time and that change occurred when one group split to form two new ones. In using cladistics (from the Greek word for branch) a researcher creates family trees (cladograms) by comparing characteristics that are common among groups and arranging them into logical order. There are two types of characters cladistics looks at: shared and derived. Shared, or primitive, characters are less important in a relational way because they appeared in the past and are held in common by many organisms, even ones not closely related. An example might be a five-fingered hand. The five-fingered hand is primitive for all vertebrates, but it is derived for all land vertebrates (except the very earliest ones). What are important are derived, or advanced, characters. The term *advanced* as it is used here does not imply they are "better" than primitive; it only means one appeared later than the other.

Also, characters are not inherently derived or primitive but are one or the other only within the context of comparison and the level at which one is looking at things. Derived characters are those that appeared in a group, or clade, after it split off from the common ancestor and are held in common only by those later organisms. A clade is the group that contains organisms that hold the same derived characters. As such, the more derived characters various groups hold in common, the more closely related they are. For example, if we wanted to see the relationship among forms of mechanical transport like a bicycle, automobile, airplane, and spaceship, what would the cladogram look like? The first derived character could be engines. The bicycle does not have one, so it goes off one way while the others form a new clade. Then we could introduce air travel as a new split that would send the automobile off on another path, leaving the airplane and the spaceship. Although they are all related by the shared characters, the airplane and spaceship are most closely related because they have the derived character of flight, whereas the others do not. This approach tends to do away with time relationships in favor of shared characters. By the 1980s cladistics had became a popular and widely accepted method of working out evolutionary relationships and for putting together hypothetical phylogenetic family trees.

Not everyone was completely happy, however. Mark Collard of the University of London and Bernard Wood of George Washington University argued that results of cladistic analysis could prove misleading if based on certain types of evidence. They accepted that accurate hominid relationships had to have a phylogenetic base but argued that phylogenies based upon craniodental material alone (teeth and jaw parts) would give skewed readings. Hominid fossils were commonly placed in lines of descent based solely on this kind of fossil material. Collard and Wood pointed to conflicting results from various studies that suggested there might be something wrong with the process itself. To find out what was wrong they did a series of tests on living primates. As relationships between living creatures are easier to work out, especially at the molecular level, results from them would help confirm any evidence generated from fossils. They constructed phylogenetic groups based on craniodental evidence and genetic testing. If cladistics worked the way it was thought, the two charts should show congruence: there should be overlap in the results, giving the same answer. However, they did not. Collard and Wood suggested several reasons for this, including the possibility that teeth and jaws alone are not enough to base groupings on. Their conclusion was that "cladistic analysis of higher primate craniodental morphology may yield not only 'false-positive results,' but false-positive results that pass . . . the statistical test favored by many researchers" (2000, 5005). In other words, a popular method if not applied properly could skew results and the conclusions based on them. Collard and Wood did not condemn cladistics, which they saw as a useful technique, but suggested its application to hominids be done with larger samples of data.

## Ways of Thinking

Ian Tattersall suggested that intuition based on intimate knowledge of fossils revealed information that could be analyzed. This statement brings up an intangible quality involved in the study of our ancestors. When scientists look at fossils or attempt to analyze data and come to conclusions, they do so with certain intellectual frameworks in mind. There are modes of thought and techniques of analysis that are used

both consciously and subconsciously that affect how the fossils are described and what theories are created to explain them. Fossils mean nothing without a way of interpreting them. Conceptual ideas help take the jumbled bits of rock and make a clearer picture.

Geoffrey Clark, a paleoanthropologist from Arizona State University, looked at conceptual issues related to human origins to see how these elements affected analysis. He asked why scientists had been unable to come to any overall consensus about the origins of modern humans. His answer was that because so many different disciplines were involved in human origins research—biology, paleontology, geology, genetics, and others—there were many approaches to the acquisition of knowledge involved. Each discipline looked for different things in different ways; there were no unified answers because there were no unified questions. Asking questions involves the notions of ontology (the nature of reality) and epistemology (the nature of knowledge). These areas of intellectual inquiry ask things like: Is there an objective truth that is readily apparent? How do we know what we know, and how do we determine what is or is not real? When scientists look at a fossil skull, how do they "see" it, and does that affect the way they analyze it? Do their educations, personal beliefs, or prejudices affect their analysis? And is there more to it than just measuring and weighing?

The empirical approach—direct observation and measurement—holds there is an objective reality or truth that exists and waits for the researcher to find it. Strict empiricists argue that factual data carefully collected and collated will yield incontrovertible results. The connection between data and observer (how the scientists feel about what they are doing) was not considered important. This was a standard approach to doing paleoanthropology for most of its history. Clark argues this approach had long been abandoned by most of Western science except for human evolution studies.

Along with empiricism, the idea of positivism looked for laws of behavior inherent in the fossils. Finding them was thought to allow predictions to be made about what kind of fossils might be found based on what was already known. The investigator must have no preconceived notions or inject any of him- or herself into the study; that way the individual's feelings will not taint the research. As a result, the "truth" will be attained more easily. (Historians call these ways of treating data constructionism and structuralism: simply gather the facts without preconceived notions, and they will fall together to give a clear, unambiguous truth.) Postpositivism argues there is no real objective truth to find, only endless interpretations of data. Literary scholars and historians have a similar form of thinking in postmodernism, which argues that truth does not exist and that a researcher's personal view always becomes part of their work, that the way a researcher uses language is as central to their work as measuring and weighing, and that a virtually endless number of interpretations are possible.

Clark points out that all these approaches to knowledge are only ways of organizing and hold no intrinsic truth, as they can be neither proved nor disproved, only argued over. Still, different views can bring new insights. Unfortunately, he adds, "with few notable exceptions . . . human paleontology remains mired in strict empiricism" (Clark and Willermet 1997, 65). Part of Clark's critique is that the lack of an accepted intellectual starting point for human evolution studies or a consensus on research methodology has hampered advance in the field. He says many controversies involving human origins are a result of not taking all the different intellectual issues into consideration. What is needed, he argues, is an agreed-upon focus for all the disparate fields to share.

In the 1940s Franz Weidenreich complained that preconceived notions and "axioms made sacred by tradition" had long been keeping paleoanthropologists from accepting new finds or ways of thinking about human evolution (1949, 149). The idea that researchers had allowed more into their work than just empirical data was the focus of Misia Landau's *Narratives of Human Evolution* (1991). She discovered that many of the nineteenth- and early-twentieth-century human origins researchers, like Henry Fairfield Osborn, Grafton Elliot Smith, Ernst Haeckel, and others, saw human evolution as a story of heroes battling against overwhelming odds in order to survive and become human. Their descriptions and theories were less scientific than they were literary and incorporated romantic notions of action and adventure, affecting how they saw the fossils.

Although the blatant romanticism of that time is largely gone from human origins research, personal opinions and desires are still there. Louis Leakey, for example, strongly believed the ancient lineage of the *Homo* and interpreted every fossil as supporting that belief, even when the fossil record pointed elsewhere. Scientists are human like the rest of us and are subject to the same failings. Wanting to have the oldest or biggest or most complete or smartest or best preserved can be powerful motivation to interpreting data one way or the other. Politics also played a role in fossil interpretation. British scientists, for example, accepted Piltdown man in part because they liked the idea of the earliest human being British and using it to gain political capital over their European rivals.

Human evolution research has been dominated by Western ideas from the beginning of the discipline, with European, British, and American scientific theories at the core of the field. Although Asian and African researchers were trained in the rigors of the Western tradition, they brought local sensibilities to their studies. Paleoanthropologists in Asia, particularly China and Indonesia, until recently followed the lead of the Western scientists. Despite their training, they have overlaid theory with a certain amount of traditional Asian philosophy and culture. Influenced by a strong cultural preoccupation with their own world, they tend to focus on the origin of Asians in particular as opposed to the origin of humans in general. Combining age-old Chinese interest in and reverence for ancestors and antiquities with more modern desires to shed imperialist Western influence, they examine fossil evidence as it relates to local conditions, distanced from the African experience. Asian fossils were traditionally seen as the same as archaic humans found in Africa and Europe. Western scientists saw Asia as fitting into a scenario that began in Africa; the Chinese saw Asia as the central sphere of interest. They leaned more toward the notion that hominids originated in Asia (an idea long since abandoned in the West), with *Homo erectus* being the direct ancestor to modern Chinese people. There were a number of calls for new approaches to the field in the late twentieth century.

Ian Tattersall's work led him to call into question the Mayr-Dobzhansky approach to human evolution as a straight line. He saw a much more complex branching tree with a considerable amount of diversity (multiple species) throughout hominid populations over time and argued that not enough paleoanthropologists looked at human evolution from this point of view. Humans, he said, should be looked at as creatures that came in various species often existing simultaneously like any other animal group. If scientists did so, they would be more accepting of the idea that there was great diversity among our ancestors. For example, Tattersall was not so sure that Donald Johanson and Tim White were correct to argue that the *Australopithecus* materials from Hadar and Laetoli were from the same species spread out over a wide geographic area. He argued that a closer look at the skulls and teeth in question showed something different. The *Australopithecus afarensis* material was more apelike than other hominids The canines were separated from the incisors and angled outward, more like a chimp. Tattersall believed there were several different species between Hadar and Laetoli and saw these tooth arrangements as evidence of the fact.

Tattersall believed that paleoanthropology as a discipline had started off somewhat straitjacketed in its way of acquiring knowledge. Researchers had not looked for patterns in the fossil record. The basic approach had been to link species as they appeared in time with emphasis placed on age, but age alone could become problematic for the reason that just because *A* is older than *B* does not mean *A* is the ancestor of *B*. Patterns of development and anatomical change, Ian Tattersall and Niles Eldredge argued, would result in a clearer and more accurate picture of who was ancestral to whom. They believed the patterns of human evolution supported the punctuated equilibrium concept (though they conceded that there were periods in the human fossil record where no pattern emerged). They saw the search for patterns applicable to the study of early stone tool culture as well. They shied away from the idea of linking changing tool technologies to advances in biology, as had sometimes been done. Just as the appearance of a new species did not mean existing ones vanished, the appearance of new tool technologies did not mean existing ones stopped developing. Different tool cultures could exist side by side, as could different species.

Despite their focus on pattern, Tattersall and Eldredge eschewed any notion of a grand plan or overarching theory that would explain all human evolution. In the past paleoanthropologists tended to look for big explanations for human ancestry. This was not unlike historians who sought a metahistory to explain all the human experience. Nineteenth-century historians like Leopold von Ranke (1795–1886) argued that meticulous collection and collation of facts would lead to an understanding of the past "as it really was." Paleoanthropologists seek to tell the story of the past as well. Historians, for the most part, have since departed from the metahistory approach and have dislodged themselves from the belief that they can reconstruct the past as it really was. They see history as a nonlinear interplay of different things that can have multiple, and unpredictable, interpretations. This new emphasis allows historians to broaden their view and gain a fuller and more complex and nuanced view of the past. Postmodern and deconstructionist historians argue in part that you can get "a" view of the past, not "the" view of the past.

However, to say that paleoanthropologists are all simple empiricists is overly simplistic. That human evolution is a highly complex process was discovered in part because paleoanthropologists looked for patterns in the fossils and applied creative thinking and new methods to their work. Another problem is that for most of the history of paleoanthropology there has been a relatively small amount of human fossils to study. It is difficult to see patterns in small amounts of data. During the latter part of the twentieth century the human fossil record grew considerably, allowing researchers to see a wider view of what was going on and to search for patterns. Along with the patterns, it was necessary to look at specific aspects of anatomy and behavior.

*Walking*

As complex creatures, hominids performed many behaviors. One of the more significant was the ability to walk upright on two feet. As the Lucy fossil contained a significant portion of its skeleton it became a focus of locomotor studies. Many assumed Lucy and her kind could walk upright habitually. Anatomist and locomotion specialist Owen Lovejoy of Kent State University wanted to see just how well an *Australopithecus* could walk. He saw bipedal walking as an overall survival strategy. Early hominids needed grasping hands to hunt prey (such as bugs) while in the trees and still be able to hang on. Catching with hands makes it that much more important to be able to stand and see straight. With this in mind Lovejoy reconstructed Lucy as an agile walker. He argued that early hominid walkers could already walk by the time they moved to the savannas and open plains of Africa (the traditional view was that, finding themselves on the plains, our ancestors stood upright). Free hands and bipedal walking helped the species survive because a mother could hold on to a baby and still move around in the trees. This helped ensure the baby's continued good health. Males and extended family would be able to help with child rearing, food gathering, and toolmaking, increasing social interaction and group cohesion. An awkward but useful way of locomotion in the trees became a major advantage on the plains and opened new avenues for other behaviors to develop. Anatomist Ron Clarke argued that the famous Laetoli prints (which Johanson and White believed

*Fossilized footprints from Laetoli, the earliest known hominid footprints. Do they belong to our ancestors, or are they a dead-end? (IRC)*

were made by a creature similar to Lucy) showed a separate apelike big toe, not the closely aligned toe of a human.

Another reconstruction of Lucy, made by Peter Schmid, was more apelike, with the pelvis turned out, making the rib cage more cone shaped. This allows for several possible interpretations: the stance of *Australopithecus afarensis* made it a human ancestor, or it could be seen as a characteristic of all *Australopithecus*. Just who made the Laetoli prints, and what those prints say about the printmakers, continues to be argued. Ron Clarke and Philip Tobias looked at pieces of an *Australopithecus* foot found in the 1990s and thought it was more chimplike. Found at Robert Broom's old stomping grounds of Sterkfontein, South Africa, the bones seemed to suggest that the big toe could move away from the rest of the toes, like an ape. A test of live chimps walking on sand left prints similar to those at Laetoli.

Researcher William Leonard argued that walking and eating were closely linked. Along with colleague Marcia Robertson, he studied hominid eating habits and their relationship to locomotion. They posited that bipedalism was adopted partly because it used less energy than quadrupedal locomotion. Studying living animals, including primates, they argued that a walking human uses energy at a very efficient rate in relation to weight and style of motion. Modern apes, as well as our earliest relatives, lived their lives in the trees of dense forests where movement was relatively slow and distances were short. When they ventured out on the open plains greater distances had to be negotiated. If our ancestors already had a two-legged walking ability in the trees, scampering down to the plains would have been easier, but it would have required more energy to sustain.

Walking on two legs and growing larger brains would have needed a higher intake of energy from new food sources. Leonard and Robertson calculated that *Australopithecus* needed roughly 11 percent of its total energy production to satisfy its brain at rest. *Homo erectus* used 17 percent for its brain at rest, whereas modern people use 25 percent. Leonard and Robertson suggest that brain expansion would not have occurred until the hominids had a diet rich in the required nutrients and calories. Walking on the open plains would have pushed them to eat a new diet, which in turn would have benefited both walking and brain growth. They would have likely turned to an omnivorous diet that, along with the fruits and vegetables, would have included meat. As a result of the change of diet, the mechanics of their chewing would have been affected as well. The *Australopithecus* had a pronounced sagittal crest for the attachment of large jaw muscles and thickly enameled teeth to deal with tough plant food. With the appearance of the *Homo* line, the crest had been reduced and the teeth became smaller, as did the face. Diet was one more contributing factor in the development of modern humans.

Richard Wrangham of Harvard University adds that cooking may also have appeared as part of this dietary trend. Once fire was relatively under hominid control, they would have recognized that cooking brings out not just flavor, but more nutrients (starches, for example, give off more calories when cooked than raw). Although the idea is intriguing, Leonard is skeptical of this position, pointing out that Wrangham's study assumed that *Homo erectus* had fire roughly 1.5 million years ago. This is based on evidence from sites at Koobi Fora and Chesowanja, Africa. Whether this evidence proves *Homo erectus* had fire is a matter of contention. The earliest accepted date for hominid fire use goes back only 200,000 years.

Even though the fossil evidence showed there were several types of *Australopithecus*, not all of those hominids led to the human line. There were also differences among the various *Australopithecus*. Ian Tattersall saw so much difference in some of them that he suggested there may have been more genera than *Homo* and *Australopithecus*, a claim he acknowledged was controversial. He went back to the notion that if we were talking about horses or fish, no one would have a problem with wide diversity, but because it is our ancestors we are talking about, it is controversial. In the end what the vagaries of morphology may mean is that if scientists were searching for a definition of what is human, they could have to look somewhere else.

## Cognition and Language

In the 1960s and '70s Raymond Dart argued that the *Australopithecus* were wild weapon-wielding killers fighting their way to humanness. Although that idea has been largely discounted today, Dart's killer-ape theory seemed to work well with the "man the hunter" image that had become popular. Robert Ardrey popularized the killer-ape idea in a series of nontechnical books, including *African Genesis* (1961). He argued that as we are animals, we must be as violent and aggressive as they are. Richard Leakey saw the killer-ape idea as a "dangerous fiction" and considered violence a very recent addition to human behavior, brought on by the shift from a hunter-gatherer lifestyle to sedentary farming. He saw violence as a cultural choice, not a biological imperative. To Leakey the adoption by the *Homo* of meat eating and plant gathering led to higher social organization that turned to farming around 10,000 years ago. Some members of the *Homo* survived because they began to behave like modern humans, whereas other hominids did not. These traits seem to have begun to manifest when our ancestors still had relatively small brains. Some paleoanthropologists began to think that brain size alone was not necessarily an indicator of ancestry, but intelligence was, and that brain size did not necessarily correlate with intelligence. A small-brained but smart creature might be more plausible as an ancestor than a big-brained one who was not so clever. Instead of focusing on the correlation between brain size and intelligence, emphasis was shifting to behavior and intelligence. With the growing interest in behavior, researchers began looking not just at the physical aspect of the brain, but also at its function: they turned to studying the mind.

For many, the definitive separation between modern people, our ancestors, and all other living things is our brains and how they work. It was commonly believed in the late nineteenth century that growing intelligence and a state of consciousness were the inevitable goals of evolution and that their manifestation was in man. Many human origin theorists of the day, unable to accept natural selection completely, leaned toward the idea that evolution was a kind of unfolding of God's divine plan.

One nineteenth-century evolutionist particularly interested in human intelligence was George John Romanes (1848–1894), who worked with Darwin. He argued that intelligence was not unique to humans. This argument was in opposition to men like St. George Jackson Mivart, the liberal Catholic anatomist, and Alfred Russel Wallace, the man who came up with natural selection separate from Darwin and believed that intelligence and higher mental function could not have been the products of natural selection but must be the results of divine intervention. Romanes said that language was not unique to man because other organisms communicated with each other in a form of language. He suggested that humans had reached their modern appearance of stance and body proportion before acquiring speech. Therefore, social interaction brought on speech.

Although few accepted the mute-human theory (*Homo alalus*), most believed that social interaction did play an important part in speech and language development. Friedrich Engels, one of the intellectual fathers of modern communism, in 1876 argued it was not God but work that made our ancestors human. He saw labor as the driving force in human evolution. Engels's theory was most likely an attempt to elevate the power of working-class laborers over middle-class bourgeois intellectuals rather than an attempt to explain evolution.

That the brain and mind are different is known as the computational theory of the mind. The two things our brains do are information processing and computation, both of which involve patterns of data and how things relate to each other logically. The physical substance is the brain, the mass of gray tissue, neural nets, and wiring inside the skull. The separate workings of the brain, the information processing and computation part, are the mind. Information processing and computation exist independently of what medium is used to transmit them. An idea or thought exists on its own regardless of how it is communicated.

Developed in part by scientists Alan Turig, Marvin Minsky, and others in the late twentieth century, the computational theory opened new avenues of research. It suggested that belief, desire, and other aspects of the mind were made up of symbols coded into the brain that are triggered by stimuli. It was the pattern of thought, not just bits of data, that created the mind. This book you are reading, for example, is a collection of letters and numbers strung together in the English language and written in the Latin alphabet. Without arrangement the letters are meaningless. It is the arrangement, the pattern of those letters and numbers, that gives it meaning. The brain makes a relationship between all the disparate parts, and the reader understands what ideas are being put across. That is how the brain works. The process is called cognition, and the study of it is known as cognitive science.

At the cutting edge of cognitive science and the study of language was Steven Pinker of the Massachusetts Institute of Technology (MIT), whose work also fell into the realm of evolutionary psychology (pioneered by anthropologist John Tooby and psychologist Leda Cosmides). This field joined concepts of cognition, information processing and computation, evolutionary synthesis, and natural selection. The combination of these strands of thought helped to make sense of why we have minds and how minds were even possible in the first place. Pinker argued that not only is the physicality of the brain a result of evolutionary adaptation but the elusive mind is as well. As such the mind should be studied from an evolutionary position. He was originally turned on to evolutionary psychology when Leda Cosmides applied for a job with his department at MIT. Her work spurred him to ask how humans acquired language as individuals and how they acquired it as a species.

Language skills were hardwired into the human brain from birth as evolved characteristics and aspects of human nature were "fixed." This is something of a controversial position. Since the Enlightenment, philosophers have argued over whether the human brain had certain innate abilities of intelligence and social understanding. The Englishman John Locke (1632–1704) and others posited that we were not born with any kind of character or intellectual ability, and there were no innate moral principles. Our minds were "blank slates" upon which the normal progression of life would write the character and beliefs of the individual. The blank-slate idea, also known as the tabula rasa, posits that our minds were huge expanses of nothingness at birth and that all our ability to talk, act, think, and behave as social creatures was a result of the environment in which we were raised and how we were treated and taught as children. Locke argued his idea from a political standpoint, using it to defend the notion that all people were created equal, free, and capable of reason. He opposed the divine right of kings to rule and rejected the supreme governmental authority concept espoused by Thomas Hobbes (1588–1679) and his followers.

Hobbes called for an all-powerful state—the Leviathan—to rule and keep order. In opposition to the blank-slate argument, some said that at least part of our intellect and other aspects of our behavioral selves were preprinted in our minds at birth and guided us along life's path. A person could not rise above what he started with; any intellectual ability or social status was fixed. Ever since, racists and sexists of all stripes have argued that women, and certain ethnic groups, could not hold this or that position or job or receive equal, just, and social treatment based on the "limited" aspect of their inborn traits (see the chapter on alternative theories for more on this concept). After World War II and the horrors of the Holocaust, sociologists and anthropologists backed away from the idea that people were born one way or another. They feared any acceptance of this notion of fixed inborn traits would leave the door open to intolerance and bigotry. With this in mind, some have looked warily on Pinker's assertions.

Pinker argued that language ability was a product of Darwinian evolutionary processes and as such was one part of an overall survival strategy employed by the early hominids. For him, language was in this respect no different from upright walking, stereo vision, or opposable thumbs. Parts of speech like phrase construction, syntax, sound structure, and a limitless lexicon were evolutionary products like the larynx or nasal passages. They evolved as adaptations to the environment and as a survival tactic. The physical manifestation of these abilities was the neural wiring and structure of the brain. The complex nature of speech and language became an automatic function of the brain, like breathing or blood flow; it did not need to be taught—it just worked. He saw it as an instinct, a "biological adaptation to communicate information" (2000, 5).

It was a very complex instinct, however. Humans do not speak as robots or make rote responses to outward stimuli (like sneezing when dust goes up your nose); they speak as creative thinkers using language in original ways. Because humans create language spontaneously, our brains cannot simply click out stock answers; they must be flexible enough to deal with an endless set of choices. It was speech and the higher intellectual functions that resulted from it that gave our ancestors the needed edge other hominids did not have. They were able to create images with words that suggested ideas and mental constructions well beyond the simple sounds made. That was a major advantage in the game of survival.

Language is more than just stringing sounds together; it is the response the words cause. For example, if someone asks, "How do we solve this problem?" your brain does several things. Besides understanding the question, you begin to think of possible answers, approaches, and outcomes. You then articulate the thought through the organ of speech. Speech and language are the outward manifestation of the inward organ of thought and the logical mind. For Pinker, this ability was an evolutionary adaptation like any other useful organ or appendage, not an example of some spiritual or metaphysical power, nor was it a social or cultural construction.

Pinker's work was often seen in opposition to that of the twentieth-century pioneer in the study of language, Noam Chomsky, who went against the idea that a person's character was created by his surroundings and rejected the Darwinian model of natural selection for language. He argued that syntax (the structure of language) was unique to humans and was controlled by a "universal grammar," a fundamental speech pattern and set of rules out of which all modern languages grew. He saw the fundamental structure of language as innate, not evolutionary. Pinker agreed with the former but not the latter. Humans, Chomsky argued, put language together themselves.

In addition to speaking, humans sing as well. Mario Vaneechoutte and John Skoyles saw this ability as crucial to language development. They argued that singing played the crucial role in bringing speech and language about. For them language resulted as the end product of increased cognitive ability that allowed certain hominids to be able to create song for communication. This made them "musical primates." As natural selection worked, greater vocal control entered the hominid toolbox. With these things in place, improved singing became a springboard to speech and then language. The idea that song predated speech originated in the seventeenth century, when it was proposed by the French philosopher Jean-Jacques Rousseau. In *The Descent of Man*, Darwin also postulated that an early singing ability may have led to language. The notion eventually lost favor until it was resurrected in the late twentieth century.

Speech results from a complex interplay of brain function, breath control, expansion of the diaphragm and rib cage, and vocal cord action. It is this control ability that gave the hominids song ability. It helped peer groups bond and attract mates as well as warn of danger. As something that aided in survival, natural selection would have helped push singing to greater levels of sophistication. Vaneechoutte and Skoyles see "song" as the controlled modulation of sound to create specific tones used to call to other members of the group in rudimentary communication. As song appeared first, speech and language (symbolic sounds strung together according to rules of grammar and syntax) came along later as cultural phenomena and as such were recent acquisitions of about 100,000 years ago (Pinker argues more like 2 million). Instead of Pinker's speech genes, Vaneechoutte and Skoyles look to memes (the conscious imitations of behavior) and a mental music-acquiring device. Although they agree with Pinker on the central role of natural selection in creating language, they differ by arguing that song was the crucial intermediate step without which speech would have been unlikely. They cite the failure to find a speech gene as support for their position and reject Chomsky's universal grammar. The literature on the origins of language and its connection to the brain is quite extensive, and the debate is as lively as the one over human evolution.

## The Mind's Big Bang

Years of studying stone tools had shown researchers that human mental and technological capabilities advanced slowly throughout time. Unlike today when technology changes almost on a daily basis, the change from one level of tool technology to another occurred over hundreds of thousands and even millions of years. The painful slowness of the process sped up around 50,000 years ago when the human intellect suddenly expanded radically during the Upper Paleolithic age. The reason for this explosion of human intellect and symbolic thinking has intrigued many researchers. It was such a major jump in intellectual capability that it was labeled the Mind's Big Bang (the name pays homage to the cosmic big bang astronomers believe began the universe).

The oldest tools made by hominids are from the East African Oldowan culture and date back 2.5 million years. The oldest evidence of a direct connection between tools and hominid fossils is from Hadar at 2.3 million years. The first stone tools were likely just rocks picked up and awkwardly used to break open bones for the marrow or to crack nuts. When rocks with naturally sharp edges were employed, a number of cutting purposes were discovered. Tools could be made of more than just stone. Paleoanthropologists tend to focus on things made of stone because they survive the great intervals between being made and then found again. Any tools made of wood or other perishables from early in hominid history are likely long gone or may be unrecognizable as such. There are examples of bone and wooden artifacts from the period of archaic modern people, but nothing from before then.

Tool use may have come about as another strategy to survive by improving the diet. Tools allowed the early hominids to get more of the kind of food they needed for sustained bipedalism and larger brains. Lucy and her relatives (a million years older than the oldest known stone tools), despite having superficially chimplike hands, did have opposable thumbs. As Bernard Wood points out, there is no reason to think they could not have made tools. On the other hand, Tim White argues that there is no evidence to suggest they did. By the Upper Paleolithic period, toolmaking suddenly became a highly sophisticated undertaking.

That the cognitive jump occurred is not in question, but why it did is. In *The Prehistory of the Mind* (1996), Steven Mithen suggests that in the early stages of archaic modern human development, brains acquired three different kinds of thinking ability: social intelligence, toolmaking, and a desire to organize and classify the world around them. These abilities formed separately in what Mithen calls "mental modules." They allowed the archaics to perform functions and behaviors other hominids could not. The problem was that these advanced ways of thinking were not wired together. Mithen argues that around 50,000 years ago, some small genetic change occurred in brain wiring that allowed these separate spheres of thinking to work as an integrated unit. It was this new wiring that caused the big bang.

William Calvin, in his book of the same year, *The Cerebral Code,* agrees with Mithen to a point. He believes the cognition surge did occur in some early hominids because of a genetic rewiring but is not convinced of the mental-module idea. He sees archaic humans developing an ability to deal with what he refers to as the "novelty" of the lives they lived. The often unexpected and sudden nature of these creatures' lives forced them to learn to deal quickly with different situations. This led to greater speaking and thinking ability. This in turn allowed for the cognitive jump when the requisite wiring appeared. The archaic humans' new thinking powers would have appeared without any outward anatomical change.

As a result of the brain expansion, culture would have also taken a great leap forward. Despite the advances in tool- and artmaking during the big bang, there seems to be no correlated anatomical change in the archaic *Homo sapiens.* The Cro-Magnons, who were anatomically identical to modern people, appeared around 150,000 years ago, yet the brain expansion occurred much later. This situation has given support to the notion that cultural, intellectual, and anatomical changes were not necessarily linked. Cognitive growth was unlikely to have occurred across the entire human population. As a result, there was an overall population of humans coexisting with varying degrees of intellectual capability. Though all the same species anatomically, they would have become fundamentally different due to differing brainpower.

## The Artistic Turn

The most spectacular evidence of our ancestors' cognitive jump is the cave paintings, bone engravings, and sculptures that have been found around the world. Although cave art has been found in many places, the first and most elaborate examples were found in the Dordogne region of France beginning in the mid–nineteenth century. The Dordogne has so many Neolithic sites it became a tourist area sprinkled with gift shops, museums, and scientific dig sites. The region has high cliff faces and narrow protected valleys and is crisscrossed with a series of rivers that over the years created caves and grottos that were very attractive to the early *Homo sapiens.* The most common subject of the early artists was the local animal life. These pictures were made with such attention to detail that they were originally dated by comparing the pictures of elephants, antelope, and horses to fossils of these creatures.

*The cave at Lascaux, France. These are some of the earliest known examples of human artistry. (Corel Corporation)*

The first studies of the caves in this region were done in the 1860s by Édouard Lartet (1801–1871) and his British ethnologist colleague Henry Christy (1810–1865) who made careful examinations of the caves of the Vézère River valley. The caves were often discovered accidentally by curious local children who happened upon them. The cave at Lascaux, for example, was discovered in 1940 when a dog wandered into it, followed by its owner and his friends. The paintings in particular drew attention for their accuracy, delicate workmanship, and vivid colors (still bright after thousands of years). Some assumed originally that the dynamic renderings of horses and other animals were simply artistic expressions celebrating the life the artists saw around them.

A pioneer in the study of the caves and cave art was the French priest and archaeologist Henri Breuil. He was one of the first people to study Lascaux after its discovery. His work was criticized for its tendency to the romantic rather than the scientific. His descriptions of the caves and the art contained in them conjured up images of religious and magical ritual, with people fighting a great struggle for survival under harsh conditions and against monstrous beasts. He argued that the pictures of animals had magical properties that prepared the hunter for the hunt. One picture in particular seemed to suggest magical properties. The Sorcerer, as it is called, depicts a half-man, half-antelope figure that stares at the viewer with hypnotic eyes.

Breuil's way of looking at the cave art led to some unusual interpretations that had political as well as scientific impact. When he looked at some of the art in caves in Africa he thought they were evidence of contact by classical-age Mediterranean peoples like the Minoans or Phoenicians. One example that especially stirred his imagination was known as the White Lady of Brandberg. The drawing, which depicts a figure in white pants, possible body paint, and carrying a bow and arrow, was discovered in 1917 by cartographer Reinhardt Maack as he was putting together a map of Brandberg Mountain in Namibia. Breuil saw a copy of the drawing in 1929 and was enthralled by it. Following World War II he tried to get permission to go see the Lady in person by contacting the South African prime minister, General J. C. Smutts. It was not until 1947 that the French priest was able to see the actual cave and drawing. Upon viewing the original he was even more convinced that the site, like others in Africa, was evidence of a presence of classical Greek explorers, not local Africans. It was a common misconception (fueled by racial animosity) that Africans were incapable of producing such works. Because Breuil was an accepted authority in cave art studies, his assessment was embraced by the government of South Africa, which was anxious for any evidence to bolster its contention that black Africans were degenerate intellectually and incapable of ruling themselves and thus needed to be controlled by the white minority. Modern research into the White Lady has shown it to be a male figure, and the white painted legs are a common artistic motif found in cave works throughout Africa. Had Breuil been familiar with a wider range of African cave art he would have seen the picture as part of a long prehistoric tradition, not evidence of Caucasian invaders.

In the 1960s Johannes Maringer reassessed the paintings of the Dordogne region and rethought Breuil's romanticizing. He argued that as the pictures were painted on surfaces so inaccessible that to see them required special effort in climbing and crawling through tight spaces, there must have been some more profound reason for creating them than just drawing nice pictures to look at. (Murals in some caves are in places as much as a mile from the cave opening.) Such effort to view the pictures must have resulted in a transcendent experience for the observer. Maringer was interested in the origins of religion and saw the cave pictures and figurines as the earliest examples of a great mother cult. He thought he saw parallels in the work of Neolithic tribes from Siberia and posited that they must have migrated west to Europe and eventually east into the Americas. The female sculptures found in some of the caves represented evidence that the earliest religions were maternal, not paternal. Although Maringer saw religion as the reason for the pictures, Richard Leakey has said that "why they [ice age humans] made the difficult and dangerous journey into the cave . . . will always remain a mystery" (1982, 62).

In the late 1980s and early 1990s Jean Clottes of the French Ministry of Culture and David Lewis-Williams developed another intellectual model to study the art. They looked partly to magic but more toward the religious or shamanistic mode to explain how the art was employed by those who made it. Shamanism was an ancient belief system—still practiced in parts of Asia and among Native Americans—that attempted to link the visible world with that of the spirit world. A shaman was a kind of priest–wizard–medicine man who facilitated the connection between the living with the spirits of animals, the environment, and passed ancestors. Through this technique supplicants sought help, advice, cures, and protection from the spirits. Clottes and Lewis-Williams saw the pictures as devices used by the religious workers to aid in contact with other realms for practical purposes.

Not all Neolithic cave art comes in the form of beautiful renderings of animals; some is quite simple and primitive. How these simple marks and scratchings relate to the more complex paintings is unclear. It is also unclear just how visual representation began for humans. How and why did humans begin to make symbolic marks on surfaces? In the 1980s it was argued that the simpler abstract markings and geometric forms found in some cave sites were the result of wiring in the brain that somehow caused humans to instinctively make marks and designs.

Along with this neural hypothesis was the idea that the marks also represented early people's attempts to reproduce phosphenes, the lines and dots that appear to you when you close your eyes, sit in the dark for long periods, or suffer from a severe headache. The idea was that seeing these phosphenes, early people assigned mystical relevance to them and attempted to reproduce them. Support for the neural hypothesis was that different groups of people unconnected to one another made the same kind of marks in different cave and rock outcrop sites.

In 2000 researcher Derek Hodgson argued that the shamanistic aspects of the neurophysiological hypothesis did not have enough supporting evidence. He pointed to geometric art examples made with no discernible religious connection. He saw the art impulse as much more biologically driven. It is generally accepted that it is the nervous system and more likely the visual cortex of the brain that are responsible for generating phosphenes. As the early art-making humans were anatomically and neurologically indistinct from modern people, it is assumed they reacted as we do. Hodgson argued that the attempts to reproduce the geometric images produced in the individual by the brain were the first natural step to making more representational art forms. In this way, religious and shamanistic considerations were unnecessary to the original production of symbolic art (though he does accept that mystical elements were present in some geometric marking). This ability was an evolutionary strategy to help in communicating ideas to other members of the group. In the end Hodgson decided that artmaking behavior grew from evolutionary strategies made possible by internal wiring in the visual cortex.

Like stone tool design, art ability was thought to have progressed from simple to complex over time as early humans learned to control visual, cognitive, and manual dexterity. The more complex paintings like those of Lascaux and other places in the Dordogne region were thought to date to around 17,000 to 20,000 years ago. In the 1990s accelerator-mass-spectrometry dating techniques were applied to the cave art and gave some interesting results. Using samples of the pigments as well as the charcoal used to draw the outlines of the pictures, this technique produced ages ranging from 22,000 to 30,000 years ago. This may suggest that the more complex art appeared fairly quickly after the initial simple geometric forms. The new dating also suggested that the several artistic traditions, or styles, that are evident in the caves persisted in some cases for thousands of years with little or no change. Archaeologist Jean Clottes argued that this persistence may point to a well-established teaching system with masters instructing novices in specific techniques. The new dates along with new discoveries at caves like Cosquer, Cussac, and the impressive Grotte Chauvet (discovered in 1994) support the idea that the sophisticated styles appeared early.

In modern times the caves again became popular as tourist sites. In the late nineteenth century only hardy travelers and anthropologists ventured into the darkness. After World War II and the discovery of the spectacular Lascaux Cave, the French government developed the site for greater ease of viewing. It put in electric lights, doors, and a ticket booth and urged people to visit. As a result tens of thousands began tramping through. It was then that scientists realized something was happening to the paintings. After thousands of years of vibrancy, the colors began to fade from the growth of mold and algae. Some thought it was a rising moisture level that did it, and some argued the moisture was from the leagues of visitors breathing in the unventilated caves and forming clouds of carbon monoxide. The situation deteriorated so badly that in 1963 the cave was closed to all but scientists. Some years later, a duplicate cave nearby was opened to tourists. Although meticulously re-created, the cave at Lascaux that the public is allowed into is a copy, not the original.

When we look at "cave art" we view it through what is called a "search image." This is the preconceived notion of what we think the thing we are looking at should look like. Sometimes search images are conscious constructions, sometimes unconscious. We often precondition ourselves as to what something should look like before we actually see it. We create, for example, the image of the perfect mate in our minds and then search for that specific person. Search images help us find things; they can also blind us to other possible views. If we focus on the search image, anything that does not fit that image can be overlooked. Recognizable cave art, though primitive, is still representational; it is meant to depict actual things like antelope, bears, and other people.

What if the cave people made nonrepresentational art beyond the geometric shapes? Was there ancient modern art? Modern art is an attempt to depict things beyond the representational. Things are reduced to abstract ideas and forms in order to achieve a different level of "seeing." It is such that those not used to seeing it can mistake it for something else. If they are told "that is art," they can then begin to appreciate it. The casual viewer might see only a pile of metal bits or a canvas with a few splashes of paint on it. Some modern artists cannot explain why they create their art; they only know they need to. It is a powerful creative impulse in humans. Could the cave people have been capable of this as well?

## Conclusion

Even though it may seem instinctual, there really is no currently accepted definition of what makes a human or, more important, how and when the *Homo* line appeared and how it is distinguished from similar hominids. It is an underlying problem that continues to trouble paleoanthropology. Beyond the metaphysical implications, not having a strict definition makes it difficult to place one fossil or another in the human group or to keep it out. As we have seen, there are several ways a human can be defined and several points at which humans can be said to have "appeared." When it is agreed upon, it seems likely that the way to tell a human from a nonhuman fossil will be through a complex interplay of many characteristics, not just one thing.

## Further Reading

For cognition and language, see Steven Pinker, *How the Mind Works* (1997) and *The Language Instinct: How the Mind Creates Language* (2000). For discussion of ways of analysis, see G. A. Clark and C. M. Willermet, eds., *Conceptual Issues in Modern Human Origins Research* (1997); Mario Vaneechoutte and John Skoyles, "The Memetic Origin of Language: Modern Humans as Musical Primates" (1998); and Alan Walker and Pat Shipman, *Wisdom of the Bones* (1991). For cave art, see Henri Breuil, *Four Hundred Centuries of Cave Art;* Jean Clottes, *The Shamans of Prehistory: Trance and Magic in the Painted Caves,* translated by coauthor J. David Lewis-Williams (1998); Lewis-Williams, *The Mind in the Cave: Consciousness and the Origins of Art* (2002); Lewis-Williams and T. A. Dowson, *Contested Images: Diversity in Southern African Art Research* (1994); and Shirley-Ann Pager, *A Visit to the White Lady of Brandberg* (199?).

# 6

## *The Peopling of the Americas*

I t was the last great migration of humans into an area previously de-
void of their presence. It is unclear what made them do it. There
was no fanfare when they did. They may not even have realized they
were doing it. It is not known whether it was a man, woman, or child
that did it, but at some point the first human entered the Americas.
That it happened is not in question; when and where it happened is.
As with human evolution studies in general, unraveling how humans
arrived in the Americas has been as much politically motivated as scientifically based. Traditionally, the peopling of the Americas has not
been linked to human antiquity, as it occurred long after modern humans appeared. However, if some of the arguments for when and how
humans first appeared in the New World prove correct, they could
shed new light on human evolution itself.

Like the study of human antiquity in Europe, human prehistory
in the Americas was pursued initially by amateurs who had no clear
goals, techniques, intellectual methodology, or direction. Consequently, there was a good deal of wild speculation and haphazard digging, both of which had serious repercussions for later years. Nonsci-
entific elements such as nationalism, personal avarice, and cultural
pride and anger fueled the debate. With modern archaeological techniques, a mountain of empirical data has been generated that has ac-
celerated the discussion. In the late twentieth and early twenty-first
centuries this debate became contentious to the point that some say it
is less a debate than a shouting match.

Once the province of Euro-American scientists, the peopling of
the Americas became an area of concern for the people those scientists once studied and who had little input in the discussion: the Native Americans. It is an example of the struggle between scientific
thought and traditional belief. Scientists hold that their methods of

intellectual inquiry are the key to understanding, whereas native peoples argue their oral traditions and folk beliefs are more "true" than any science could ever be. The rejection of evolution and science by some Native Americans represents a resistance to what they see as one more attempt by Euro-Americans to impose ideas and social structures upon their existence. They have certain beliefs about how they came to be and resent anyone telling them differently. This element has turned the debate from a simple scientific one about who the first Americans were, or how best to study them, to a fight for national identity and cultural pride, with Native Americans asking themselves not only "Who are we?" but also "Why are you in the nonnative world trying to steal our past?" In many ways this is a fight to see who controls knowledge and which approach is the more reliable authority.

## Armchair Speculations

Christopher Columbus was looking for India when he came upon the islands of the Caribbean in 1492. He thus incorrectly called the people he found there Indians, and the name stuck. When Europeans realized the New World was not Asia but a continent unknown to them, they tried to work out some explanation for its inhabitants. Some of the first to consider the origins of the Indians were Jesuit missionaries who accompanied the Spanish conquistadores into Mexico, Peru, and other regions in the 1500s. One, José de Acosta, wondered if the Indians had migrated to the New World from somewhere else, possibly Asia. Most of the Spanish explorers and exploiters of the New World saw the native people as barbarians and degenerates fit only for conversion to Christianity, slavery, and servitude, if not extermination.

Some saw past the superficial differences. Bartolomé de Las Casas wrote in the 1550s that he found the native people not barbarous at all, nor did he view them as intellectual simpletons. He saw them as creative, intelligent, and even civilized. He pointed to their cities, law, commerce, and other social behavior as proof. His more liberal attitude was not a widely held position. The Spanish and Portuguese conquests of the New World were for the most part confined to Central and South America. There they encountered the Maya, Aztec, and other civilizations with their grand cities, pyramids, temples, and monumental architecture. Later, up in British North America, the situation was different. The native peoples north of Mexico had cultures, ethnicity, social structure, and architecture unlike those to the south and were commonly seen as inferior.

Regardless of their perceived level of sophistication, the native people had to have come from somewhere. The problem for some intellectuals was that the Indians upset the Christian worldview: How did they get there except by a special creation not mentioned in the Bible? Well into the nineteenth century theological answers remained primary. Just as with early-man theories elsewhere, answers to questions about the origins of the Indians were expected to have scriptural reference.

By the mid–seventeenth century the common answer to where the Indians came from was Asia. This is interesting, as the Bering Strait had not yet been discovered by Europeans. Like José de Costa before him, author Thomas Gage speculated in 1648 that—aside from special creation—the only place the Native Americans could have come from was Asia. He pointed out the remarkably similar physical traits between Asiatics and the Indians. It was this apparent racial relationship that led Europeans to look to Asia as a source. Matthew Hale, in his *Primitive Origination of Mankind* (1677), assumed that Asia was the point of origin for the native people. Influential anthropologist Samuel Stanhope Smith argued in the early nineteenth century that the first humans had appeared in central Asia in a state of civilization where they were aided and instructed by God. By the time they had migrated to America they had thrown off the veneer of civilization and degenerated to a state of barbarism. Anthropological dilettantes like Thomas Jefferson also thought the Indians had come originally from Asia.

The idea that the Indians all came from Asia was originally known as the single-origin theory. It was not long before it was also thought that the Indians or their ancestors may have come from different places at different times: this was known as the multiple-origin theory. Governor of New York De Witt Clinton thought some of the Indians were originally Vikings. In the 1790s, naturalist Benjamin Barton argued that some of the earliest arrivals were Danes who eventually traveled south to become the Toltecs. What is interesting about Barton is that, during a period of reliance upon biblical literalness, he thought the Indians entered the Americas prior to 4004 B.C.

Searching for anything that seemed possible (or at least plausible) as an explanation, some late-eighteenth- and early-nineteenth-century theorists suggested the Indians' antecedents came from Korea, whereas other theories involved the Chinese, Carthaginians,

Romans, and Canaanites. American naturalist Samuel Mitchell argued that the Plains Indians were probably descended from Tartars from Asia, the Indians of the Northeast from Laplanders and Scandinavians, and the people of South America from Malaysians. Mitchell told the story of a great war that had broken out among these various peoples, with the barbarous Tartar Indians victorious.

There were numerous curiosities held up as proof of classical civilization involvement in the peopling of the Americas. As an example of a Phoenician connection, some pointed to the curious object known as Deighton Rock on the east coast of Massachusetts. It was covered with various markings thought to be an ancient alphabet. William Bollaert of the American Ethnological Society as well as James Hunt's Anthropological Society of London discounted this theory in 1863. Bollaert's reading of the evidence was that the markings were the result of the native people, not marauding Mediterraneans. He dismissed most examples of "Hebrew" writing as hoaxes. The question of the origin of the Indians was addressed for the most part by armchair theorizers of varying levels of ability. Some of these amateurs took their work seriously, even obsessively, but little of what would be called professional science was applied to the problem.

## The Mound Builders

One of the great mysteries of North America was the man-made mounds scattered across the landscape from New York to Ohio and Nebraska to Florida. The mounds, also known as tumuli, seemed strange and mysterious as they squatted in their silent, foreboding bulk. They seemed full of magical properties, mysterious suggestions, and unresolved vistas. The mounds became something of a mania for naturalists. Jefferson so admired the mound architecture that he built his house at Poplar Forest using mound symmetry as a guide. He excavated a mound on his property in Virginia. Jefferson worked in an unusually systematic fashion and concluded that the mounds were ritual burial sites. That they were graveyards did not protect them from being rummaged. They were commonly broken open and looted of their contents and the bodies in them desecrated. Unfortunately, the long history of looting Indian archaeological sites, by treasure hunters and scientists alike, continued.

Made of earth, not stone like the pyramids of Central and South America, the mounds of North America ran the gamut from simple cone-shaped structures to elaborate forms in the shape of animals, some a half mile long. When Europeans arrived in New England the native people did not seem associated with the mounds. When asked about them, some of the Indians said the mounds had been built by people they had little or no recollection of. This led naturalists to speculate that an earlier "lost civilization" had existed in the Americas, a civilization physically and culturally unrelated to the "heathen" Indians.

In his book on the tumuli, *An Inquiry into the Origins of the Antiquities of America* (1839), John Delafield Jr. argued that the mounds of North America were relatively simple because the people who built them enjoyed a lush climate and an abundant food supply. Once these people began to migrate south to Mexico and Peru, where

THE MOUNDS.

FIG. 69.   *Temple Mound.*
Intimately connected with the interesting works already described are the mounds; of these, however, little has hitherto been known. The popular opinion, based, in a great degree, upon the well-ascertained purposes of the barrows and tumuli occurring in certain parts of Europe and Asia, is, that they are simple monuments, marking the last resting-place of some great chief or distinguished individual among the tribes of the builders

*One of the ancient mounds of North America (from Ephraim George Squier's Antiquities of the State of New York [Buffalo, NY: G. H. Derby and Co., 1851])*

conditions were harsher, they built larger, more permanent stone monuments. As to the relationship between the mound builders and the modern Indians, Delafield thought they were different people. The mound builders were seen as the more advanced, whereas the Indians were inferior savages incapable of higher social and intellectual function. He also thought the Indians originated in northern Asia and the mound builders in southern Asia and Egypt.

John D. Baldwin in *Ancient America* (1872) argued that the mound builders entered North America from Mexico and found their way up the Mississippi Valley. He believed the mound builders and Indians were two different groups with separate ethnic origins. The evidence, he said, was the high level of sophistication exhibited by the mound builders versus what he considered the barbarism of the historic Indians. He stated flatly that "no savage tribe found here by Europeans could have undertaken such constructions as those of the mound builders" (34). In a telling twist of logic, many theorizers said the degenerate Indians were capable of overthrowing the mighty lost race, ousting and outwitting them, yet the production of cone-shaped dirt piles was beyond their ability.

A wide range of lawyers, ministers, explorers, and naturalists investigated the mounds. The French American explorer Constantine Rafinesque (1783–1840) wrote in 1824 that the Americas were originally populated by descendants of Noah who came from North Africa and the West Indies. Josiah Priest, in his *American Antiquities* (1837), agreed, saying the first Americans were descendants of Noah's son Shem. Priest too was convinced there had been a great civilization in the Americas prior to the arrival of the Indians. Caleb Atwater (1778–1867), a prominent American ethnologist, thought the Indians were Tartars from Asia who had migrated first and the mound builders descendants of the lost tribes of Israel. Originally from Massachusetts, Atwater was a lawyer, Presbyterian minister, and politician who became fascinated by the mounds. According to the Bible ten tribes of the original nations of the Hebrews were "lost" following an invasion. They apparently disappeared from history without a trace, and many have since tried to figure out what happened to them. A popular theory concerning the origins of the Indians was that they were descendants of these lost tribes of Israel who had somehow made it to the New World. Atwater was neither the first nor the only person to think so. It was so widely held an idea that the Puritan heretic Roger Williams as well as early American intellectuals Cotton Mather and Jonathan Edwards believed it as well. The earliest book to promote the lost Hebrew tribe theory is probably Johannes Fredericus Luminius's *De Extremo dei Judicio et Indorium* (1567), published in Antwerp. Gregorio Garcia argued in 1729 that the Indians were cowardly Jews fit only for menial labor. John Baldwin called the lost Hebrew tribe theory an idea put forward by the Catholic Church in order to fool Protestants.

Lost tribes and civilizations also figured prominently in the thinking of American prophet Joseph Smith (1805–1844). The founder of the Mormon Church, Smith grew up in New York among the mounds and was fascinated by them as a source of hidden treasure and occult power. Smith later claimed that an angel had appeared to him and, among other things, imparted to him the "true" history of the Americas. At the heart of the *Book of Mormon* (1830) is the story of a conflict between the Nephites and Lamanites. These two groups came to the Americas from the Middle East. The dark-skinned Lamanites were the ancestors of the Indians. Their skin was the result of a curse by God because of the wrongs perpetrated by their evil progenitors, Laman and Lemuel. As a result, the Indians were backward and warlike. The light-skinned and beautiful Nephites were industrious, intelligent (they were the mound builders), and superior to their swarthy cousins. In the war between them, the malignant Lamanites killed off or drove off the Nephites, who fled south, leaving the Lamanites in control. In her controversial biography of Smith, *No*

*Man Knows My History* (1945), Fawn Brodie argues that Smith took the prevailing ideas about the origins of the Indians and created a new story. More specifically, she cites Ethan Smith's (no relation) *View of the Hebrews; or, The Ten Lost Tribes of Israel in America* (1823) as Joseph Smith's direct source material.

Not everyone accepted the growing popularity of the idea that the Indians and the mound builders were different people. Samuel George Morton in *Crania Americana* (1839) argued that the mound builders and the Indians were the same people. Using skulls from his collection, which included several mound skulls as well as Indian skulls, Morton could find no anatomical differences. He did say, however, that though the Indians were all of the same origin, they were of a different origin from the rest of humanity.

Except for a few dissenting voices, by the 1850s and '60s it was accepted by most American ethnologists that the Indians and the mound builders had different ethnic origins and were thus not the same people. Regardless of their ideas, none of these researchers saw the age of the Indians as great. Historian William Stanton argued that the early-nineteenth-century American anthropologists were chronologically conservative. They did believe people in America to be ancient, but not too ancient. They were attempting to operate within a more or less biblical time frame so as not to upset Christian tradition. Stanton also argued that the reliance upon separate creations by American archaeologists was a result of the distrust of what they considered the thinly supported pre-Darwinian evolutionary systems of Lamarck and Chambers.

It can also be argued that the preoccupation with the mounds and lost civilizations by early ethnographers was an attempt to construct a glorious past for America to match the glorious future many envisioned for the country. Being a displaced people, some Euro-American intellectuals were enthralled by the idea of a great lost race having once inhabited the land. They believed God had ordained a special place in the world for America. As a matter of pride they were anxious to be able to associate themselves with a special past. The genuine early Americans, the Indians, were just not good enough in their eyes as grand forebears. It was a sad sort of history envy that juxtaposed the primitiveness of the Indians against the "obvious" higher culture that built the mounds. The Indians *had* to be uncouth barbarians. This way an excuse could be used to justify the barbarous treatment heaped upon them. The Euro-Americans contrived a long list of excuses and justifications for their rampage across the continent, from Aristotle's idea that certain people were born to be ruled, to Augustine's concept of a just religious war, to Manifest Destiny, the frontier thesis, and national security. All were little more than intellectual salve to prop up egos and soothe the underlining ache of genocide.

The early naturalists employed techniques and scientific methodology that were relatively primitive. They compiled no databases, only speculated on who may have built the mounds or where the Indians came from. Caleb Atwater (1778–1867), for example, did careful documentary work during this period but then speculated that the mound builders came from "Hindostan." In the mid– to late nineteenth century, the amateur nature of American archaeology changed. The growth of several large museums like the Smithsonian Institution in Washington, D.C., and the American Museum of Natural History in New York, as well as anthropology programs at Harvard, Yale, and other universities, helped shape a new professionalism. The U.S. government also became an active researcher into Indian origins with the creation of the Bureau of American Ethnology (BAE) in 1879. During this time the old speculations gave way to a period of systematic description and classification. As archaeology and anthropology became genuine sciences with professional practitioners, more emphasis was placed on carefully documenting the material being discovered.

A good case in point is Ephraim George Squier (1821–1888). In his work Squier paid particular attention to the mounds of New York and Mississippi and included meticulously prepared drawings and descriptions of them. A lawyer and journalist, Squier was also a diplomat who, when posted to Latin America, busied himself studying the antiquities there as well. Squier believed the various Indian groups to be of similar origin to each other but unrelated to other ethnic groups around the world. He is thought to have been the first to use organized techniques of description and preservation in his work on the mounds. He worked hard to gather reliable facts and avoid speculation. Along with his partner, physician Edwin H. Davis, Squier asked questions about the mounds based on examinations and measurements of artifacts and sites. In this way he even began to change his own mind about the origins of the Indians. Originally thinking the mound builders and Indians distinct groups, he began to wonder if at least some of the mounds were made by the modern native people or their ancestors. The Smithsonian Institution published Squier's work in large, impressive tomes beginning in 1848.

Several decades later the meticulous work of Cyrus Thomas (1825–1910), of the BAE, helped end the lost-race theory. His conclusive fieldwork and direct scientific observations brought him to the belief that the mound builders and Indians were one and the same. His work was published in the bureau's *12th Annual Report* in 1894. Appointed curator at Harvard's Peabody Museum in 1875, Frederick Ward Putnam too accepted the single-group idea and spread the belief to his students as he helped found and organize several museums and university departments of anthropology. With the likes of Putnam and Thomas championing it, the single-group idea came to dominate thinking, whereas lost races vanished from all but the most romantic minds.

## Glacial Man

Not all the theories about the first Americans died so easily. Frederic Ward Putnam (1839–1915) also had an interest in showing that people in the Americas were very ancient. He thought the first Americans must have arrived well before the close of the Pleistocene age. To this end, in the 1870s, he supported the excavations being conducted by Charles Conrad Abbott (1843–?) at Trenton, New Jersey. Abbott thought the site dated to the glacial period and believed his "Paleolithic man" unrelated to the Indians. He found what he thought were man-made stone tools like those found in Europe.

William Henry Holmes of the BAE found stone tools at Piney Branch Creek near Washington, D.C., in 1890. Unlike Abbott, he thought them "rude" stones that only looked like those from Europe or at best had been made by the historic Indians. He thought the same about the Trenton material. Holmes (1846–1943) was an artist whose work came to the attention of government scientists who hired him in 1871. After taking part in several government expeditions out West for the U.S. Geological Survey, he was promoted to geologist. He became interested in physical anthropology and worked his way up the ladder to a position of power at the BAE.

Unlike Putnam, who believed people in America ancient, BAE archaeologists routinely argued away rude tools by saying they were modern pieces. Most at the bureau were uninterested in the multiple group–entrance idea. They believed there had been a single entry of one group through Asia only a few thousand years before. Many of the government men were inspired by the work of anthropologist Lewis Henry Morgan (1818–1881), who argued that humans passed through stages of cultural development from savagery to barbarism to civilization. In the 1860s he became the first Euro-American to examine the kinship systems that linked various Indian tribes; he was instrumental, along with Edward Tylor, in establishing the study of cultural evolution. For Morgan the sign of civilization was writing, and since the Indians had no writing they were uncivilized. This view proved significant, as the power of the BAE was growing. As a government agency the BAE could count on funds to keep going as well as sources to publish findings. Non-government-affiliated researchers began to cry foul as they perceived an attempt by various government agencies to take control of the archaeological American past. Their fears were not unfounded. As head of anthropology at the U.S. National Museum, Holmes had originally hired Aleš Hrdlička. They were becoming the arbiters of human prehistory in the United States and used their positions to counter any who thought differently.

Work at the Abbott site continued until 1910 under another naturalist interested in the Trenton gravels, George Frederick Wright. Wright was a deeply religious Christian and an evolutionist who had no problem reconciling Genesis with science. In 1880 Wright, a disciple of botanist Asa Gray, went to New Jersey to study the gravels. He determined that humans had lived in the area 8,000 to 10,000 years before. He wrote a pair of books, *The Ice Age in North America* (1889) and *Man and the Glacial Period* (1892), discussing his findings and supporting Abbott's conclusion about a Pleistocene presence. By the late 1890s, however, Wright's Christian liberalism began to turn more conservative. Later, Frederick Ward Putnam hired a digger to work the Trenton site who in 1899 found a human femur. Putnam sent the femur, already being referred to as Trenton man, to Hrdlička for inspection, hoping it was proof of an ancient arrival. Hrdlička promptly dismissed it as a recent burial, and interest in the Trenton site declined.

Despite the overturning of the Trenton man theory, dreams of finding ancient humans in the Americas would not go away. One of the most notable dreamers was Henry Fairfield Osborn. His enthusiasm, as discussed in chapter 2, led to the Nebraska man incident. The problem was that none of the various "men" put forward held up to Aleš Hrdlička's scrutiny, and as curator of physical anthropology at the Smithsonian's U.S. National Museum, his opinion held great weight. In his defense, Hrdlička believed that ancient bones should have certain anatomical traits not found in recent ones. Thus, if the bones did not look ancient, then they were not, even if the stratigraphic evidence said they were. As the bane of "early man in the Americas" theories, Hrdlička staunchly held that humans had entered the continent very late, no more than a few thousand years before at best. Hrdlička (pronounced Hurd-lishka) was born in what is today the Czech Republic and came to New York City as a teenager. He took a position at a hospital, where he was found by Putnam, who gave him an entrée into the world of government anthropology. He eviscerated, with great glee, any and all theories he deemed groundless. His meticulous attention to detail and thorough knowledge of human anatomy could quickly pick out the intellectual holes in arguments and spot inconsistencies and shaky evidence. In *Early Man in South America* (1912) and *Recent Discoveries Attributed to Early Man in America* (1918), published under government auspices, he lined up all the "early man in America" theories then known and systematically destroyed them. Even Osborn, intimidated by no man, was forced to back off the idea. The evidence of ancient people in America was there; it just had to be found.

*The Folsom Blues*

In August 1908 George McJunkin, foreman of the Crowfoot Ranch and amateur fossil collector, was inspecting his land on horseback after a devastating flood. Located outside the New Mexico town of Folsom, the ranch covered a wild and beautiful region. In a newly washed-out ravine he spotted some bones that he recognized as being from a bison, but an unusual one. McJunkin took the bones home and displayed them in his living room. A friend tried to interest local paleontologists in the bones, but none paid attention. It was years before some of McJunkin's fossil-collecting friends went back to the site and found more large bison bones.

In 1925 the bones came into the sympathetic hands of Denver Museum of Natural History president Jesse Figgins and paleontologist Harold Cook (who had worked with Osborn on the Nebraska man case). Cook immediately saw that the bones were of an extinct bison. Adding to the excitement, stone tools were found with the bones. Cook and Figgins estimated, based on this evidence, that humans must have entered the Americas an astounding 55,000 years before. Unfortunately, the artifacts and bones from the site, known as Wolf Creek, had not been professionally excavated. This called into question whether they were contemporaneous. Artifacts and bones had to be carefully documented in the ground in order to be taken seriously.

*Clovis arrowheads. These artifacts were once thought to be evidence of the earliest human habitation in the Americas, but recent discoveries have thrown the Clovis Hypothesis into some doubt. (Warren Morgan / Corbis)*

In March of the next year Figgins and Cook, along with the two amateur fossil hunters who had found the site from McJunkin's description, Carl Schwacheim and Fred Howarth, returned to the scene of the crime and discovered bones and archaic spear points in the same layer of matrix. Hrdlička showed the pieces to William Henry Holmes. Planning to play a trick on the country rube Figgins, he asked Holmes to comment on the material without telling him where it came from. The trick blew up in Hrdlička's face when Holmes promptly and confidently said they must have come from Pleistocene deposits in Europe. Figgins was elated, Holmes was embarrassed, and Hrdlička quietly fumed. Backpedaling, Holmes said he would never verify such a thing until he saw them in situ and embedded in a bone. He had a distaste for amateurs like Figgins who he believed were diluting science. This is interesting, as Holmes was himself not a trained scientist but an artist.

That August more spear points were found embedded in bone, just as Holmes had demanded. This time Figgins and company called people to the site to see the finds prior to excavation. Barnum Brown (1873–1963), a well-respected paleontologist from the American Museum of Natural History (the discoverer of the Tyrannosaurus), came and was convinced. He said the evidence showed man in the

Americas to be contemporaneous with the extinct bison. A. V. Kidder of the Carnegie Institute in Washington and Frank Roberts of the BAE also came, looked, and were convinced. The site clearly showed that early humans had butchered as many as thirty bison on the spot at least 10,000 years before. The distinctive spear points with their precision fluting (serrated edge), from the spot originally found by the cowboy George McJunkin, are now known as Folsom points.

In the face of such evidence Hrdlička was still reluctant to give in. He was convinced that humans were recent arrivals. Unfortunately, more Folsom-style sites were being found. The most important of these sites was 150 miles away, at Clovis, New Mexico. By 1933 scientists from the Academy of Natural Science in Philadelphia and the University of Pennsylvania began excavating there. The teams found points that were related to yet different from the Folsom points. These Clovis points were older and heavier than the Folsom versions and represented, at 10,900 to 11,500 years old, the earliest example of human habitation found in the Americas. The Clovis-Folsom culture is thought to have lasted about 600 years and stretched from New Mexico well into the southeastern United States. Aleš Hrdlička and the late-arrival theory had met their match.

The Clovis people have been commonly characterized as hardy, tough explorers and courageous hunters who braved incredibly harsh conditions to tame a continent with their advanced technology and determination. It was believed they first entered North America about 12,500 years ago as the Ice Age eased. Lower water levels created a land bridge between Siberia and Alaska, while an ice-free corridor appeared to create an avenue straight into what are now Washington, Oregon, and the Dakotas. The "story" of humans in the Americas is, in its narrative form, not unlike that of early human evolution theories. Humans were said to have appeared as primitive primates fighting against a series of harsh environments, who, through their struggle to overcome obstacles, eventually evolved into modern humans. It is a heroic, inspiring story of beating great odds to achieve success. The conventional story of the peopling of the Americas is similar. Here we have the tiny band of intrepid explorers coming out of Asia and crossing into the Americas under adversity and hardship. They stalked monstrous beasts, such as the bison, mammoth, and other megafauna, with their deadly, efficient spears. They were so good at hunting that they ran several types of animals to extinction along the way. Dynamic and aggressive, they followed a manifest destiny to become the masters of this strange, alien land from Alaska to Tierra del

Fuego. This scenario became the paradigm, or underlying assumption, for the peopling of the Americas.

As is common in science, and in all intellectual endeavors, a single idea came to dominate explanations for phenomena. Whereas initially the Hrdlička-Holmes late entry for humans held sway, the Clovis hypothesis now became the norm. Once at the forefront, Clovis would become as unassailable as Hrdlička and Holmes. By the middle of the twentieth century, anyone promoting the idea that humans came into the Americas before 12,500 years ago was ignored or dismissed. In the later part of the century the "Clovis hypothesis," as just described, came under increasing pressure by those who believed it had taken on a life of its own.

*Trouble in Paradigms*

In his landmark work, *The Structure of Scientific Revolutions* (1970), Thomas Kuhn expounded on paradigms and paradigm shifts. A paradigm is an underlying belief, or set of related beliefs, that is widely accepted as the answer to a central question and around which all study in a field is based. Kuhn argued that once established it was difficult to overthrow a paradigm (pronounced para-dime) because it had become part of accepted scientific thinking, it had evidence to support it, and careers were built around it. New ideas are forced to go up against an entrenched worldview. Accordingly, they must have great weight and a preponderance of evidence and must be ready to be shot down in their long uphill climb to acceptance. But, Kuhn argued, if the new idea has what it takes, eventually it will be proven and accepted, and it will become the new paradigm. Classic examples of paradigm shifts—the shift from an old to a new paradigm—are the Copernican view of a sun-centered solar system and Darwinian evolution. They fought against great odds to overthrow old ways of thinking. This was the situation facing anyone arguing that humans entered the Americas before 12,500 years ago.

A common notion is that what initially kept Clovis from acceptance was the power of the late-arrival idea as a "paradigm bias." When Clovis finally replaced late arrival, it then became the established paradigm. Anthropologist David Meltzer, of Southern Methodist University, argues that there was no such paradigm bias against the original Clovis hypothesis. He says it was more a clash between men of the naturalist tradition and those of the modern scientific tradition—in essence, a conflict between amateurs and professionals. In Hrdlička's defense, though he staunchly defended his idea, the early Clovis and especially Folsom material was at first scientifically untrustworthy, being badly collected and poorly documented. Scientists must work with carefully measured and testable evidence. If they do not, it is not science. Once acceptable Folsom evidence came to the attention of scientists, they saw its merits and with further professional work accepted it. Meltzer argues that historical perceptions of bias against Clovis grow from oversimplifications of the facts in the case and a stereotyping of Aleš Hrdlička's role in it. In addition, there were expectations and preconceived notions about what should or should not be found. Unfortunately, expectations are not proofs. Genuine paradigms have evidence to support them; neither the recent nor the early-man theories in America had much. In this way it can be argued there was no paradigm bias because there was no paradigm.

By midcentury a series of new theories and discoveries had gone up against the Clovis barrier. In 1942 a site was unearthed at Calico Hills, California, outside Barstow. Originally worked by archaeologist Ruth Simpson of the San Bernardino County Museum, Calico was a trove of stone tools. Simpson contacted Louis Leakey to come and look at the site. Leaky was interested in the peopling of the Americas and had been offered a temporary teaching position at the University of California at Riverside. In 1963 he visited the site and was impressed. Further excavation brought out artifacts Leakey argued were 50,000 years old. Later uranium-thorium-dating tests confirmed they were as much as 200,000 years old. Many scoffed at Leakey's pronouncements and dismissed Calico as a fantasy. Calico Hills is still being excavated and is still controversial.

At another California site, carbon-14 and amino-acid racemization tests gave dates of 28,000 to 48,000 years for a skull called Del Mar man. Originally discovered in 1929 near San Diego, the skull drew new attention with its apparently ancient provenance. Anthropologist Spencer Rogers argued that "the skull gives evidence of a population not strongly Mongoloid in character which occupied the Southern Pacific coast perhaps shortly after the first migrations Eastward from Asia into the lands of the Western hemisphere" (1974, 6). Alan Bryan, of the University of Alberta, claimed humans entered the New World 40,000 years ago and that they may even have been a late form of *Homo erectus*. He based this assertion on the allegation that he had photographed a *Homo erectus* skull in Brazil in 1970, which later disappeared without a trace.

A far more serious contender for pre-Clovis stardom was Meadowcroft Rockshelter. The life work of anthropologist James Adovasio of the University of Pittsburgh, Meadowcroft Rockshelter is located in the wilds of western Pennsylvania near the Ohio River and the border of West Virginia. The rock shelter—a glorified cave—was a natural living space 700 feet above sea level, with good ventilation and a magnificent view of the surrounding valley. Adovasio first began excavating there as a practice exercise for his students in 1973. They dug down several layers of cave floor that indicated several periods of human habitation. Starting with the layer of beer and soda cans and other modern detritus, they traveled back through artifacts to colonial times. Amazingly, the layers continued down past the point of initial European contact and kept going. The cave quickly showed itself to have been attractive to humans for thousands of years.

As they went deeper they found older yet still recognizable artifacts. Reaching a level they dated to 10,000 years ago, they began to encounter artifacts of unknown styles. At the 12,000-year level they found a type of point known as a lanceolate. Christened a "Miller point," after the name of the man who owned the land, it was a major discovery. The flint used to make many of the tools came from quarries in the nearby Ohio countryside. Meadowcroft was turning into something very special indeed, a pre-Clovis site in Pennsylvania. And it just kept going. At what they calculated to be the 15,000-year layer they found a fire pit, animal bones, shells, and the remains of basketry, along with knives, choppers, and other tools.

In order to avoid any discrepancy, a whole battery of radiometric dates were taken and meticulous care exercised in the excavation and documentation. Adovasio did not want to be accused of slipshod work. He and his team studied not only the contents of the cave but also the geology of the outside surrounding area in addition to the paleontology of ancient animal and plant life that also lived in the region. Meadowcroft Rockshelter was becoming the most carefully excavated archaeological site in North America. It was a multidisciplinary project that brought in different specialists to amass a mountain of data that would support the claim of ancient provenance. The various carbon samples taken from the cave, including those from what was clearly a fire pit that had been used for generations, dated back 19,000 years. Adovasio knew he was going to not just break the Clovis barrier but smash it to pieces. He wanted his data to be beyond question.

Despite his careful attention to detail, doubts arose. C. Vance Haynes and others questioned the dates, saying they must have been contaminated from carbon seeping into the cave through the water system. Water percolating through the hillside, they said, would have dumped carbon all over the site, thus throwing off the readings. Any dates from the site were therefore not to be taken at face value. When the Clovis-first forces sniffed at Adovasio's dates he countered by arguing that they did not understand the geologic data. The region, he said, superficially looked as if it had been glacial and inhospitable to animals or people. In reality, the glacial maximum (the farthest extent of land that a glacier covers) was well north of the rock shelter. Far from being inhospitable, the area would have been quite inviting to both animals and people. That there were not more stone tools at the site is also explainable. Adovasio argued that the first Americans would have entered the continent with perishable or soft technology, things that would not last once discarded. He claimed there is a "preservation bias" on the part of anthropologists who feel only stone technology is worth anything (Adovasio and Page 2002, 71). The soft-technology model, he said, opens up dates for the first entry of humans into the Americas to go into the tens of thousands of years. To many, Meadowcroft Rockshelter was more than proof enough that people were in North America far earlier than what Clovis suggested.

At the forefront of pre-Clovis sites in South America is Monte Verde, Chile. First excavated by Tom Dillehay of the University of Kentucky in the 1970s, the site is a village containing bone and stone artifacts. Stores of seeds, fruits, and shellfish as well as fowl and extinct camels and mastodons have been discovered, along with a child's footprint left over in mud. Dillehay dates the site to 12,500 years ago. Located on a hill overlooking what was a lagoon or pond, Monte Verde is actually several sites on top of one another. The second level could be as old as 30,000 years. However, Dillehay is properly reluctant to make such a claim seriously without more work.

Dillehay first began working Monte Verde in 1976 while he held a position at Southern University of Chile. Lumbermen uncovered the site while clearing an area along Chinchiuapi Creek. The stone tools found there were not impressive, but Dillehay saw that the site held some promise and began excavating. The site was well preserved because in the years prior to discovery the area had been covered with a thick layer of moist peat. This effectively sealed the site off from the harmful effects of the atmosphere. After scraping off the peat layer Dillehay and his team found arrowheads, animal tissue, and pieces of huts and other dwellings. As the apparent age of the site upset the Clovis barrier, careful attention to detail had to be paid to the excavation to keep objections to a minimum. The National Geographic Society, which was supplying financial support to the dig, sent an auditor to determine if the site merited further funding.

In 1979 Junius Bird, a Paleo-Indian specialist, arrived to check out Monte Verde. Unfortunately, Bird questioned the antiquity of the site, and National Geographic cut its funding. Upset, Dillehay argued that pro-Clovis thinking was prejudiced against anything that rocked the status quo. As a result, few scientists came to look at the site for years after that, even ones from Chile. It was not until 1997 that a reevaluation of Monte Verde was undertaken by the Dallas Museum of Natural History and the National Geographic Society. They looked at the data again and decided Monte Verde was 12,500 years old. It was a vindication of all the years of hard work and the neglect heaped upon Dillehay, though later C. Vance Haynes of the University of Arizona claimed he felt pressured into agreeing with the majority of the panel when he disagreed about the site's age. Although he thought it was an interesting and valuable one, Haynes did not think it pre-Clovis.

C. Vance Haynes is considered a central figure in the Clovis-first school. A geologist who studied archaeology, he looked at the strata of sites to determine their age. He joined the Clovis-first school after working a site in Nevada called Tule Springs. It was originally discovered in the 1930s, and the Nevada State Museum did excavations there in the 1960s that went over the site in great detail, including what were thought to be the remains of a campfire that dated back 23,800 years. Campfires are prized at dig sites because the carbon can be used to get accurate dates. Haynes at first supported the dates but was embarrassed to find that the campfire was in reality a deposit of naturally occurring carbon. He thus turned away from ancient Americans, arguing that all such dates must be incorrect. He argued that one group of people had entered the Americas across the Bering land bridge, bringing Clovis technology with them. Using their "Clovis tool kit" of spear points, scrapers, drills, and other sophisticated accoutrements, they were able to radiate across the landscape, very quickly taking control of the continent.

But why are there no indisputable artifacts that date prior to 12,500 years ago? There are several possible reasons. The simple explanation is that there are none to be found. Clovis may be the oldest evidence because it is the oldest evidence. The conspiratorial view is that the "Clovis police" have quashed every piece of evidence that goes against their shaky control of the situation. Some believe that the

Clovis-first forces know they are wrong but will not admit that someone else might be right or allow anything that might dislodge them from their vaunted positions.

Another reason could be that there are no artifacts to find, but not because there are none. Anthropologist John Alsoszatai-Petheo argued that if early people came in pre-Clovis times with a "simple material culture of stone and perishable bone artifacts, cultural change would not be archaeologically visible until significant climatic change occurred at the end of the Pleistocene" (Dillehay and Meltzer 1991, 15). In other words, if early people entered the Americas with culture of a type that was relatively simple and artifacts made of materials that did not last, or were unrecognizable as such, traces of them would be particularly difficult to find, suggesting to archaeologists that they never existed. He said that if the classic "man the hunter" story was replaced with something else, the evidence would make greater sense. His idea of a more "steady state" lifestyle for the early Americans would have them living off the easily accessible bounty of the land. This would result in a slow rate of technological change, a rate that would leave little of the kind of evidence archaeologists normally look for. It would not be until the late Pleistocene age that climatic change would force people to acquire hardier and more substantial technology to survive. Impelled to create greater technology, they would have begun to leave behind permanent evidence of their existence.

The Euro-American tradition looks for signs of progress. Archaeologists have traditionally looked for evidence of a simple to complex rate of development to chart human history. Older civilizations and cultures had to look old, whereas newer ones were expected to look more sophisticated. Any artifacts or ways of thinking that did not fit the pattern, Alsoszatai-Petheo argued, were overlooked or ignored. As was charged with Folsom, pre-Clovis sites are often looked down upon because of preconceived notions of shoddy excavation and documentation. Although Alsoszatai-Petheo admitted that some sites have been badly excavated, most have been worked by competent professionals whose data must be confronted. There is so much evidence for pre-Clovis entry, he argued, that all of it cannot be tainted, fabricated, or the result of poor recovery work. He claimed that there is a distinct bias against pre-Clovis material by post-Clovis supporters. Dillehay agreed with Alsoszatai-Petheo that people arriving very early to the Americas would have brought perishable material culture with them. Harvard anthropologist Carole Mandryk also called for an abandonment of the Clovis mighty-hunter scenario, arguing that the hunter–meat-eater theory was the result of modern male scientist wishful thinking and action adventure–story preoccupation. She saw the perishable-artifact gentle-entry scenario as much more likely.

## The Dating Game

An important part of modern archaeology and paleoanthropology is accurate dating. A common chemical dating technique is known as carbon 14. Discovered during research into the atom bomb, this technique measures the level of carbon 14, a radioactive variant of the carbon present in all organic material that is absorbed through respiration and the consumption of food. Once the organism dies, it ceases to take in carbon 14, and the carbon 14 already present begins to break down. Since the rate of decay is relatively constant, measuring the amount of carbon 14 shows approximately how long the organism has been dead. The time it takes for a radioactive material to lose half its strength is called a half-life. The half-life of carbon 14 is 5,730 years. Every 5,730 years after a thing dies, it loses half of its store of carbon 14. (Potassium 40's half-life, for example, is 1.35 million years.) The carbon 14 content of cut wood, charcoal, bones and tissue, and the remains of other organic material at a site gives a date for when the site was active. Dates have been contested because carbon 14 tests (as well as other similar radiometric techniques) can be contaminated by outside materials, giving false readings, as was the accusation in Louis Leakey's Tule Springs case as well as the KBS Tuff controversy. If clean samples are taken, the dates are reliable.

Ancient people left behind more than just tools, artifacts, and bones. Within those bones may be the key to finding out when they came and where from. DNA analysis has suggested some interesting things about the origins of the first Americans. DNA (deoxyribonucleic acid) is the series of long strands in the shape of a double helix in each cell of every living thing that carries the genetic blueprint for that organism. Along with nuclear DNA there is also mitochondrial DNA (mtDNA), which is a smaller structure that produces energy for the cell. MtDNA is preferred by geneticists for study because it exists in larger quantities and thus is easier to extract for dating purposes. It also mutates in such a way that one can make a rough estimate of how long one group has been separated from its nearest biological relative. MtDNA can be used to tell how closely one population of humans is related to another. Different ethnic groups share similar lineages of mitochondrial cell structure. Modern Native Americans share genetic lineages with northern Asian people but are at the same time distinct from most other populations. It is thought that lineages differentiate from each other at a rate of about 2 to 3 percent per million years. In the mid-1990s Emory University anthropologist Theodore Schurr used these calculations to determine how long it had been since Old World and New World populations parted ways. If his calculations are correct, the split occurred between 20,000 and 40,000 years ago.

A range of genetic data has been used to argue that only one group came to the Americas and produced the modern Native Americans, whereas others argue that the same data show several groups must have come along. There could have been one group that had a wide genetic diversity, or several groups could have arrived at roughly the same time, mixing with each other to form a homogeneous population. There could have been simultaneous populations in competition, with only one surviving. The mixed-population theory seems logical, as an unusual mtDNA lineage, known as *X,* appears in both living and ancient American remains. Who the original source for this *X* is remains unclear. It is also found in Middle Eastern populations, the Iberian Peninsula, and regions around the Caucasus Mountains. Any idea that Caucasians may have been early arrivals to the Americas has been greeted with screams of racism and Eurocentrism. The difficult nature of such ideas became all too apparent in 1996.


## Kennewick Man

Anomalous sites that seemed to break the Clovis barrier are not the only issues confronting ancient American studies. Since the lost-race idea was discredited in the 1890s, anthropologists thought they were sure of at least one thing: regardless of when they did it, the first people came into the Americas from Asia and were therefore all ethnically related. It seemed obvious from simply looking at Native Americans that they shared affinities with the people of northeastern Asia.

By the 1990s what consensus there was began to break down. A series of problematic skulls and skeletons came to light that undermined the single-migration theory and ignited a firestorm of debate that has complicated the situation in ways never thought of before. These remains date back to 11,500 years ago and suggest to some that the modern Native Americans may not have been here first, or at the very least that they were not alone. One of these problematic individuals was

Spirit Cave man (actually a mummified individual with hair and skin). Spirit Cave man was first discovered in 1940 in a rock shelter in Nevada that was thought to be a burial of only 1,000 years. In 1994 radiocarbon dating pushed that date back to 9,400 years. He was wearing a sophisticated capelike blanket made of rabbit skin, his stomach revealed he had eaten fish (which suggests he was a fisherman instead of a meat-eating bison hunter of the Clovis model), and he wore moccasins. Most peculiar was that he had a skull that did not conform to the typical Asiatic type one would expect of a Native American. Instead of the usual roundish head, he had a longer, narrower head with flat cheekbones and a pointy chin.

Spirit Cave man and other anomalous skeletons came to light as a result of an attempt by the U.S. government to give back what it had taken so long ago. It was common practice for anthropologists to dig up skeletal remains in the United States for shipment to museums and universities for study. In response to Native American demands that the material be returned, Congress passed the 1990 Native American Graves Protection and Repatriation Act (NAGPRA). The act said that any Native American remains collected from federal lands must be returned to the affiliated tribe from which the material came. Records made at the time of collection made repatriation a straightforward matter for most skeletons. When that information was no longer available or was unclear, specialists would be brought in to make an examination and disposition as to where the remains should be sent.

Anthropologists Doug Owsley of the National Museum of Natural History in Washington, D.C., and Richard Jantz of the University of Tennessee were often the ones called to make the determinations (Owsley has worked many high-profile cases, including helping to identify the remains of Branch Davidian leader David Koresh). They had spent twenty years compiling measurements and other morphological information on skull shapes of modern native peoples. This base of craniometrical data was used to create an average profile for various Indian groups against which a skull's measurements would be compared to the chart in order to assign it to a native ethnic group.

Spirit Cave man and several other skulls were not even close to any of the standard profiles. Some variation was expected, but these skulls went off the scale. Owsley and Jantz were not the first to see this deviation. Anthropologists at Texas A&M University, the University of New Mexico, and the University of São Paolo made similar findings on skeletons that dated from the same period. Walter Neves of São Paolo suggested that one of the skeletons he worked on (dated to 11,500 years old) resembled people from southern Asia or even Australia. Complicating the matter, not only do these problematic skeletons not resemble modern Native Americans but they do not even resemble each other. They seem to be from many different places.

The one skeleton that became the lightning rod for ancient American disputes was Kennewick Man. Discovered by hiking college students in late July 1996 along a branch of the Columbia River near the town of Kennewick, Washington, the skull was at first thought to be the remains of a murder victim. The police were called, and the coroner took possession of the skull and other parts found in the mud. The coroner sensed something was amiss and called local forensic anthropologist James Chatters to come and give an opinion. Chatters taught at the University of Washington and served as a part-time coroner and forensic anthropologist for Benton County.

After a cursory exam, Chatters thought the skull might belong to an early European settler. What moved him in this direction was the shape of the skull and the fact that the hip had the point of a spear lodged in it. This suggested that the man had fallen victim to an encounter between himself and Native Americans (if correct, it is the earliest known example of such an encounter in the Pacific Northwest). A second opinion also said that the remains were those of a European. Chatters thought the spear point could have been an example of a "cascade point" dating back 5,000 to 9,000 years. He now found himself in a tricky situation. If the skeleton was an early settler, it would be held up as some kind of heroic pioneer who died at the hands of Indians. If it was a Paleo-Indian, as Chatters was beginning to suspect (it was unlikely that a 9,000-year-old spear point would be lodged in the hip of a nineteenth-century European settler), local Native American groups would claim the skeleton as their ancestor under NAGPRA and take it away for burial before it could be studied. If he did a radiocarbon-dating test on it to prove its great antiquity and it turned out to be modern, he would be accused of desecration. Taking the chance, Chatters ran a quick carbon 14 test that determined the skeleton was 9,500 years old.

Word spread that Chatters was claiming the skeleton to be an ancient European who had come to the Americas long before the Indians. This upset him, as he had claimed no such thing. He said that the skeleton had certain morphological affinities shared with Europeans but was clearly from the Americas, not a recent immigrant. Anthropologist

C. Loring Brace examined photographs of the remains and said they had characteristics of the aboriginal Ainu people of Japan.

Chatters's worst fears quickly began to materialize. He had worked with local tribes previously on anthropological issues; he thought he had a good working relationship with them and wanted to keep it that way. Unfortunately, the situation was rapidly deteriorating, as a group of scientists as well as local tribal groups began to fight over ownership of the remains. The Army Corps of Engineers then said that since the skeleton had been found on federal land, it belonged to them, and they would decide who would take possession of it. The government then sent agents to Chatters's lab and confiscated the bones. A group of scientists brought a suit in court, saying the government was applying NAGPRA too broadly. They claimed that since the skeleton was 9,500 years old, it could not possibly be affiliated with any modern tribe. The media played up the science-versus-tradition angle and continued to refer to the remains as those of an ancient white European. This problem was not helped when a reconstruction of Kennewick man appeared that seemed Caucasian (some wags chortled that it bore a striking resemblance to actor Patrick Stewart, Captain Picard of *Star Trek: The Next Generation*). The Umatilla Tribe claimed ownership and ethnic affiliation and wanted no tests done, as they would be considered sacrilegious. They claimed that their tribe had occupied southern Washington literally since the beginning of time; thus, any skeleton found there was automatically theirs. They were so adamant about it that Chatters claims they engaged in a smear campaign to ruin his reputation and his business.

This type of animosity was unusual prior to this event. There have been many examples of Indians and scientists working together closely and amicably on the repatriation of remains, even incidents where local tribal councils were uninterested in remains that were not directly and historically affiliated with them. Some native groups, the Senecas of Pennsylvania, for example, see the use of scientific investigation of remains as useful to both themselves and science. The problem seems to have started when James Chatters innocently used the C word: *Caucasian*. James Adovasio has commented that in the Kennewick man case, things were said by both sides that aroused the ire of the other, as passions spiraled out of control. Extravagant claims were thrown around, few having any evidentiary support. The government then stepped in to do what governments do best: it mucked it up and tried to sweep it all out of sight, literally. The Army Corps of Engineers inexplicably, and some say criminally, bulldozed the Kennewick man site, destroying its archaeological value. The entire mess was exacerbated by people being unable to remain calm in the face of an emotional situation.

The battle went on like this for years. Not only did Kennewick man experience the indignity of being shot with a spear and dying along a riverbank, but he was now also being used in a political and cultural tug-of-war. Chatters and others argued that only folklore connected Kennewick man to the modern Native Americans of the Washington area. Ironically, in September 2000 a government publication, *Human Culture in the Southwestern Columbia Plateau, 9,500–900 BP,* said the same thing. That month the government awarded custody of Kennewick man to a collection of Nez Perce, Umatilla, Wanapum, Yakima, and Colville tribes. A suit was immediately filed to hold up repatriation. At the time of this writing, Kennewick man rests quietly in a storage facility, awaiting the final disposition of his remains.

## Native Ideas

One aspect of the Western scientific anthropological approach to the study of the peopling of the Americas is that few scientists ever bothered to ask the Indians themselves what they believed about their origins. Although a general prejudice against the Indians certainly contributed to this, another obstacle was a clash between two fundamentally different approaches to the acquisition and retention of knowledge. The Western tradition relies on the written record for history, whereas the Indians rely on the spoken word, particularly in North America. The Native Americans developed an oral tradition for holding on to information. It was easier that way, as they did not have books or papers to cart around with them as they moved about the landscape. Instead of writing, they developed a complex mythology and oral tradition. As a comparison, the classical Greek stories of *The Iliad* and *The Odyssey* started as elaborate oral traditions, possibly hundreds of years before they were transcribed. When the Indians of Central and South America settled down into urban lifestyles they quickly adopted writing techniques and began producing books and other visual symbolism. When Europeans first came to the New World they brought a written tradition with them. As a result they looked down on the native oral tradition and saw it at best as charming and quaint and at worst as faulty, unreliable, and just plain backward. With a few notable exceptions, most Euro-American scholars thought they had nothing to learn about Indian origins from oral histories. Many anthropologists, archaeologists, and historians believed myth and legend could be intriguing and could say a good deal about the cultures that produced them, but ultimately they were useless because they could rarely be proved or disproved.

But to believe the Native Americans do not contribute to scientific knowledge is erroneous. There have been Indian anthropologists and archaeologists since the nineteenth century. For example, Arthur Parker of New York, first state archaeologist and a Native American, was mentored by Frederick Ward Putnam and briefly by Aleš Hrdlička. He was active in American archaeology and Indian political affairs. Along with another important early Native American archaeologist, Francis La Fleshe, he established the Society of American Indians in 1911. There have been, and still are, many anthropologists and archaeologists who are Native Americans and who have contributed greatly to recording Indian history and languages and bringing the Native American point of view to science.

Some Native Americans, however, have taken a more critical view of Western science. Long forced to accept scientists seeing them as things to be studied, by the 1970s native people were becoming more outspoken about their past and how it was viewed. Partly an outgrowth of 1960s radicalism, the American Indian Movement (AIM) was formed. Originally intended to keep an eye on police treatment of Indians in Minnesota, AIM soon turned its attention to anthropologists, archaeologists, and other non-Indians who were looking into Indian history and origins. It stressed a return to traditional Indian values and culture and espoused "red power." It viewed scientists not as investigators or chroniclers of the past but as evil interlopers bent on destroying Indian culture. AIM deeply resented archaeological digs as desecration of sacred lands.

One of the more vocal and controversial voices in the pro–Native American, antiarchaeology movement was Vine Deloria Jr., a Standing Rock Sioux law student turned activist. Deloria's 1969 *Custer Died for Your Sins: An Indian Manifesto* was a discussion of the sad state of Indians in their own country and how they were treated by the larger Euro-American culture. *Red Earth, White Lies: Native Americans and the Myth of Scientific Fact* (1995) is a blistering attack on Western science and archaeology. Anthropologists in particular, whom he derisively called "anthros," were called into account. He made powerful cases against them, asking why, if they were so interested in the welfare of Indian culture and history, they had turned a blind eye to years of neglect, oppression, and the systematic destruction of the subjects they studied.

A central aspect of his work is a critique of the fundamental methodology, what he called the hypocrisy, of Western science as it sets itself up as the authority of "truth." Deloria said scientists were priests of a dogmatic religion who brooked no outside or alternative view. The higher the academic degree one possessed, he argued, the more likely a person was to lie, cheat, and mislead. His own career, in addition to his work as an activist lawyer for Indian causes (he defended Russell Means over the infamous Wounded Knee incident), has been a series of teaching posts at UCLA, the University of Arizona, and the University of Colorado. He pointed to examples of scientific fudging of evidence, intellectual intransigence, incompetence, and other flaws that all too human scientists are sometimes guilty of. Balanced against this, Deloria based his knowledge on Indian tradition and oral history, which he cited as more reliable.

Like many antiscience advocates, however, he engaged in some of the same flawed practices he accused his enemies of. For example, he held Indian tradition as sacred and truthful, allowing for little in the way of metaphorical interpretation and arguing a thinly veiled infallibility. He claimed that whereas science is untrustworthy (a cabal of scientists controls the field and forces other scientists to toe the party line), Indian tradition is not. If you asked an Indian elder about the past, Deloria claimed, he would give "as closely as possible a literal description of the event" (1995, 252).

His view of tradition over empirical evidence can be as dogmatic and myopic as the anthros, simply from a favored viewpoint. He called science a collection of beliefs (though he admitted it is sometimes backed up with solid evidence) and said that if the Bering land bridge and migration route actually did happen, then we should be able to point at the actual footprints—a sort of fossil roadway—of the people who made the crossing. Others could counter that if the story—popular with many Native American histories—of the Indians emerging in America by exiting the earth from the spiritual underground is true, then where is the hole they emerged from? Deloria argued that a shared memory of continental drift and catastrophic geological change accounts for these stories, and therefore oral tradition is supported by geologic evidence. His reliance on oral tradition is much like Fundamentalist Christian reliance on biblical inerrancy. Deloria, in fact, held many beliefs dear to the hearts of Fundamentalists: dinosaurs were contemporaneous with early humans, mammoths and other presumably extinct megafauna of North America lived well into the colonial period, radiocarbon dating is undependable due to contamination, and Darwinian evolution is an ill-conceived and unwarranted theory. His work, not surprisingly, has been championed by native supporters and has been called "largely ill-informed" by anthros (Adovasio, 2002, 124).

Deloria's style of mixing oral tradition and geology was part of Jeffrey Goodman's *American Genesis* (1981). An anthro with a background in geology and archaeology who worked with Louis Leakey at Calico Hills, Goodman argued a reversal of the traditional "into the Americas" scenario with an ingenious and quirky "out of the Americas" scenario. Appearing first in California, the early Indians spread out of the Americas to populate the world. Claiming that fossils in North America are "twice as old as the oldest fully modern skull from Europe," Goodman said that humans must have originated in the Americas (19). He attempted to show that the Indians were not only the first Americans but also the first humans. Although he allowed that hominids did appear in Africa, modern *Homo sapiens* are Indian in origin. He cited Leakey's work at Calico Hills as well as Del Mar man. He was a little vague as to the evolutionary relationship between the Indian humans and the non-American humans originating in Africa. To Goodman, the Indians did everything first: domestication of plants and animals, toolmaking, pottery making, even the creation of calendars and the use of electromagnetism. In 1983, Goodman tackled human evolution in general. Discounting natural selection, he offered several possible substitutes, including God and spirits.

It has been argued that the Kennewick man controversy stems from Native American fears that if they were not the first Americans, then they will lose their special place in history and become just another immigrant group. Even worse, they could lose what protection from the government they have as indigenous peoples. They would also lose their place as sovereign nations within the United States. In his excellent study of the first-Americans question, *Skull Wars* (2000), David Hurst Thomas, a curator at the American Museum of Natural History, pointed out that loss of sovereignty was not an issue directly affected by Kennewick man's origins. Indian law and U.S. government law are written in such a way as to preclude tribal affiliation from threatening sovereignty. There were some in government, however, who were attempting to use Kennewick man as a catalyst to put forward legislation to curb tribal sovereignty, so these claims were not without merit.

There is another reason that can be considered to help explain Native American reactions over the peopling of the Americas. Indian reactions to archaeology are not unlike the reactions of Europeans when the question of human evolution was first raised in the nineteenth century. Darwin, Huxley, Neanderthal man, the Cro-Magnons, and others were originally rejected, and in many ways are still rejected, because they threatened people's view of the universe and their connection to the spirit world. If humans appeared through the forces of natural selection and random chance, then what role does God play? Scriptural and traditional beliefs were called into question and people's identities threatened. Those who held to Judeo-Christian tradition reacted violently to these new ideas and worldviews. Imagine how you would react if someone told you everything you ever believed about who you were and where you came from was wrong. The Euro-American archaeological view of the peopling of the Americas can be seen as undercutting the "Indianness" of the Indians. It would seriously question their personal beliefs and religious as well as cultural history. The basis of the Indian religious nexus is that God created them *in* the Americas. Undermining a people's connection to time and space has considerable intellectual consequences. That some Indians and Christian Fundamentalists (a group that does not actually have the greatest track record with Indian culture) espouse similar antievolution and antiscience feeling should not be seen as unusual. They both oppose anything that threatens their deeply held theological paradigms.

## Clovis and Beyond

In response to charges that all archaeologists and anthropologists do is disturb and loot Indian burial sites, some anthros pointed out that during various intertribal conflicts throughout history the Indians themselves have been guilty of raiding Indian dead. They also claimed that archaeologists have done a great deal to protect Indian graves from looters by putting the material behind the safety of museum walls. Indian activists countered by saying if it matters by whom or for what reason graves are disturbed, they are still disturbed and the damage done. Anthros claimed not all Indian people agreed to their origins. For example, Amy Dansie, in her review of James Chatters's book, said that while she was at the Nevada State Museum during the Kennewick man controversy, some Paiute Indians told her that their history says they are originally from Australia, and they resented other

Paiutes claiming Kennewick man as one of their own. Both sides have argued they are doing what they think is right and best to promote and save Indian culture.

Independent of the Kennewick man fiasco, research and theories continue to be produced and attitudes changed. In 1999 a scholarly conference was held in Santa Fe, New Mexico, to discuss the state of archaeology in the United States. Most of the major names were in attendance, and it was clear that dates as much as 30,000 years or older were being considered for the initial human entry to the continent and that people had sailed as well as walked in. While the pre-Clovis forces seemed in the ascendancy, ancient American proponents still spoke of having their books, articles, and funding applications rejected by the Clovis-first forces. Alan Bryan of the University of Alberta, who has said people go back in the Americas at least 40,000 years, complained that when a pre-Clovis site is discovered, it is immediately labeled "controversial." This, he said, undermines the site's credibility and unfairly prejudices it in people's minds.

One of the more radical and startling proposals of recent years is the suggestion that genetic and artifact evidence shows connections to Europe. Dennis Stanford of the Smithsonian's National Museum of Natural History has been looking for the Clovis trail into North America. If the Clovis people brought their tools with them, as some argue, then there should be traces of them in Asia. After years of searching, Stanford could find no trace of Clovis culture there. Clovis points are found mostly in the American Southwest. Clovislike artifacts found in Virginia resemble those of Solutrean Spain from 24,000 to 16,000 years ago. (The Solutrean connection has been hinted at for years.) Stanford argues that this evidence—not yet conclusive—suggests part of the pre-Clovis culture of eastern North America came from the Iberian Peninsula. He has been quick to add that this does not mean that people from that region traveled to the Americas, only that the technology somehow made it there.

There is the problem of how people of Europe might have ventured to the Americas. They would have to have come by water. To make such a trip would require a substantial maritime culture. In the 1970s the idea of people sailing from the West began to appear. If North America was cut off from Asia by ice up until 12,500 years ago or so, how could people have arrived before then? If they had learned to build small boats, they would have paddled their way along the coast. That would account for the oldest sites being in the South.

Although originally dismissed, the maritime hypothesis started gaining more acceptance. There is abundant food along the shoreline in the form of fish, shellfish, and marine mammals, making a coastal cruise viable. Water is also a faster mode of transport and would allow people to cover a vast area quickly without rapidly changing technology. Circumstantial support for this comes from evidence that people made it to Australia 40,000 years ago by crossing water, that there was island-hopping going on around Japan about the same time, and that humans were on islands in the Mediterranean by 14,000 years ago. Ancient people around the world had learned to deal with large bodies of water. Thor Heyerdahl's controversial *Kon-Tiki* voyage of the late 1940s, and others through the 1970s, showed that at the very least a sea voyage across the Pacific in primitive balsa wood or reed boats was possible. Heyerdahl argued that Polynesia had been populated by people sailing from the Americas, not Asia.

The mysterious *X* genetic marker found in some early Americans is also found in small portions of some European populations. Doug Owsley pointed out that ancient Americans do not resemble any modern people, not even modern Indians. In 2001 C. Loring Brace of the University of Michigan reproposed some ideas that had already been floating around. He argued that multiple waves of people had come from Asia and that the earliest were genetically related to the Ainu aboriginal people of Japan and Polynesia, who themselves can be traced back to Pleistocene western Asia. He suggested that the Ainu of Japan as well as modern Europeans could be the result of the Neanderthal line breaking up into these groups. This Eurasian-post-Neanderthal connection would account for the European characteristics some saw in Kennewick man and other problematic remains. Brace based these assertions on extensive craniometrical study of skulls from around the world as well as genetic findings. This interpretation is controversial, as many but not all paleoanthropologists believe the Neanderthals were an evolutionary dead-end that did not lead to modern humans.

By the end of the twentieth century controversies over the peopling of the Americas were about more than just the ages of bones and artifacts. There are still legal battles being fought over ownership and affiliation. The U.S. government had essentially reached the point of saying any human remains that date from before 1492 are by definition ancient Americans and therefore should be repatriated to Indian hands. Most archaeologists agree now that many different types of people were coming to the Americas at different times throughout history, just as they still do today.

## Further Reading

For early theories on the peopling of the Americas, see Raymond W. Murray, *Man's Unknown Ancestors* (1943); William Stanton, *The Leopard's Spots: Scientific Attitudes towards Race in America, 1815–1859* (1960); Robert Wauchope, *Lost Tribes and Sunken Cities* (1963); L. E. Huddelston, *The Origins of the American Indians: European Concepts, 1492–1729* (1967); and Gordon R. Willey and Jeremy A. Sabloff, *A History of American Archaeology* (1975). For some original sources, see Samuel Stanhope Smith, *An Essay on the Causes of the Variety of Complexion and Figure in the Human Species* (1810); and Richard Harlan, *Medical and Physical Researches* (1835). For the modern debate on the origins of the Native Americans, see David Hurst Thomas, *Skull Wars* (2000), and James Chatters, *Ancient Encounters: Kennewick Man and the First Americans* (2001). The best popular description of Meadowcroft Rockshelter and its attendant debates is James M. Adovasio, *The First Americans: In Pursuit of Archaeology's Greatest Mystery* (2002). C. Vance Haynes's objections are in "More on Meadowcroft Rockshelter Radiocarbon Chronology" (1992). For the paradigm argument, see David Meltzer, "On Paradigms and Paradigm Bias in Controversies over Human Antiquity" (1991), and John Alsoszatai-Petheo, "An Alternative Paradigm for the Study of Early Man in the New World" (1986). An excellent source for the most up-to-date discussion of the controversies of the peopling of the Americas is the *Mammoth Trumpet,* the house organ of the Center for the Study of the First Americans, based at Texas A&M University, which is available on-line. For alternative Native American views, see Vine Deloria Jr., *Red Earth, White Lies* (1995), and Jeffrey Goodman, *American Genesis* (1981).

# 7

## *Picturing the Caveman*

The crowds shuffling through the Hall of the Age of Man at the American Museum of Natural History in 1925 found the skulls, fossils, and stone tools in the display cases interesting. What really captured their imaginations, however, was a triptych of murals depicting the lives of Neanderthals and Cro-Magnons. The large, impressive pictures—commissioned by museum president Henry Fairfield Osborn and executed by artist Charles R. Knight—told the story of ancient man with an immediacy and power that cold fossils and rocks could not. Knight's pictures were reproduced innumerable times for postcards, popular articles, and textbooks so that they became the image of prehistoric people for generations. Many visitors had come to view this exhibit because of the controversy then roiling over it in the New York press. Protestant clergy claimed that Osborn and his museum were corrupting the souls of American youth with their unholy depictions of the barbaric human past and the suggestion that humans had evolved from lower animals without the help of God. The controversy only boosted the attendance of people wanting to see what all the fuss was about.

Knight's pictures were part of a long tradition of picturing ancient humans. From the moment the remains of ancient humans were discovered, speculation as to their appearance and lifestyles began. Visions of our ancestors have been based on our perceptions of what they should look like as much as the actual fossils. Whereas fossils remain, perceptions change with each generation. Renderings of ancient humans often say more about the people who produced them than the people they depict. Earlier ideas and representations of wild men, barbarians, and primitive races helped prepare the way. Preexisting images and stereotypes of ragged hair, rude tools and weapons, fur clothing, and bestial behavior were simply laid down over the fossils. When visitors to the American Museum saw the visual representations of cavemen, they recognized the already established stereotypes of what a caveman should look like. The image of the caveman was so familiar that it had become an icon: a picture that needs no words to understand and that represents an entire range of ideas. That icon was partly the result of empirical examination of fossils and partly a search for the intangible meaning of those fossils. Although many volumes have been written on human evolution, it is the pictures that make up most people's knowledge base, not the text (remember Huxley's skeleton lineup). So understanding visual presentations is just as vital as understanding the science behind them.

## The Bible

Images of cavemen (and in this discussion *caveman* refers to any fossil hominid) have varied greatly since Hermann Schaaffhausen first described the Neanderthal remains. The tradition of depicting the past did not start there but traces its lineage back much further. In the Christian tradition the past meant the biblical past. No other past existed outside of what was described in Scripture. Church decorations and illuminated manuscripts brought with them a whole list of pictorial conventions and visual cues for interpreting the past. A visual cue is any element or symbol in a picture that conveys an idea that the audience is familiar with and that has special meaning. For example, in medieval Christian paintings a saint was recognizable because of a ring of light, or halo, that hovered over his head. Viewers knew what the halo meant; no explanation was necessary. With the introduction of printed books in the 1500s conventions like these were brought to an increasingly large audience who learned how to "see" the past through them.

Creating images of the past posed certain problems for artists. They were being asked to render events that no living person had ever seen. For biblical scenes artists had only words as a guide. Details such as clothing, faces, and environment had to be put together from their own imaginations. There was little knowledge of how people of the past had dressed. Renaissance artists solved this problem by abandoning any pretense of historical accuracy and placing Bible stories in a contemporary context with clothes and other details taken from the artists' time and culture. Following the discovery of the ruins of classical Greece and Rome, attitudes began to change.

*Figurier's idealized image of Anglo-Saxon cave people (from Louis Figurier's* Primitive Man *[London: Chapman and Hall, 1870])*

Artists now tried to be more visually accurate. As historical artifacts became more accessible, a mania for historical pictures arose among Western artists. *Visual accuracy* became the operative words for depicting the past. By the eighteenth century biblical imagery was sporting fossil animals and plants as relics of the antediluvian world. Techniques like oil painting, perspective drawing, and other rendering methods made Western art more visually representational, if not always philosophically so.

By the beginning of the nineteenth century, artwork that could be called "scientific illustration" was being produced. Art was becoming essential to the communication of scientific and technical ideas. Scientific art eschewed many of the standard conventions of traditional art. For example, where a nontechnical artist might paint flowers in a vase or with some pleasing background, the scientific illustrator rendered the botanical specimen with the highest level of detail achievable without any background to distract from the communication of scientific information. The advantage of scientific illustration was that art could express quickly and succinctly what it might take pages of text to accomplish. An image could be less ambiguous than words, more direct, and in some ways more important than the text. It is here that art crossed over from simply conveying information or scientific ideas to helping build them. Art was now a full partner in constructing ideas. An illustration, however, could also be misleading: it could put across not just empirical evidence but also ideological agendas and political viewpoints. It could also make it appear that more information was available than really was. Artists were no longer depicting existing facts about the past but were adding their imaginations and conjectures about what the past looked like. When artists began to stray from solid evidence—the shape and size of a skull, for example—to conjecture of what that meant for the creature's behavior (its habits and intelligence), more subtle concerns came into play. Religious belief, social standing, and preconceptions both benign and malignant created a vision that more accurately reflected the feelings of the creator of the image than the fossils it was based on.

Depicting the past was neither the province nor the creation of the Western world. All cultures through time have created scenes of their past. They too taught moral lessons or were used to honor the dead and the Almighty and to hold on to cultural norms and accepted paradigms for future generations. Even fossil reconstructions were nothing new. Cultures throughout human history have made pictorial representations of their ancestors. The oldest known modern forms of this are rock paintings done by aboriginal people from Australia to Africa and the Americas. Though unsophisticated to the modern eye, these works meant as much and said as much to those people as Charles R. Knight's complex, detail-oriented works did to his audience.

The Greeks made attempts to understand the human past and even its development. They saw their ancient ancestors as superior to themselves. The gods and heroes of the past were larger-than-life entities who lived in a golden age of existence. By the time humanity reached the contemporary age it had fallen into relative degeneracy. Greek mythology is a long parade of wild men in fur and swinging clubs; giants and Titans; the Cyclopes; half-man, half-horse creatures; and winged babies. The Greeks looked back on these creatures with awe and respect as their predecessors. Their world was populated with mythological creatures and, as we now know, full of fossils. The region around the Mediterranean was home to a wide range of creatures like mammoths, mastodons, camels, horses, and others from the Miocene, Pliocene, and Pleistocene eras that left fossil remains.

It was once thought that fossils were not recognized as such until the seventeenth century. But recent scholarship has discovered that the Greeks collected, studied, and even exhibited fossils. Folklorist

Adrienne Mayor argues that the Greeks were "the first fossil hunters," as described in her book of that title (2000). Her study of Greek texts and mythology shows that when the Greeks discovered fossils after floods or earthquakes, they equated them with the remains of the Titans, not extinct animals. Their descriptions of fossils, the earliest we know of, were as sacred remains of deities in the same way that medieval Christians venerated as relics the bones of saints. The question is why the Greeks would see these bones as ancestor, not animal. Mayor argues that when the Greeks were looking at fossils they did it with a certain "search image" in mind. The Greeks had no real conception of extinction as we understand it today. For them, what lived in the past were Titans, giants, and monsters. When they deliberately looked for fossils, they were searching for the remains of the gods. They assumed their ancestors would have huge bones, and that is what they found. Added to this, many of the fossil bones were discovered in places where Homeric legend said they should be. Mayor adds that some Greek legends may have been based on the discovery of Titanic fossil bones. The Greeks were putting together the story of their past; they wanted to know where they came from, and these bones helped them make sense of it.

As early as the eighth century B.C. there was already a market for these relics for personal and public devotion. Shrines throughout the Greek world contained such relics as Pelop's Shoulder, the Giant Hero of Messenia, and other mythological characters. The ancient Greek approach to the giants and manlike beasts that populated their mythology was not unlike how Christians in Europe explained fossils as biblical giants killed off in the Deluge. Johann Scheuchzer, of *Homo diluvinii* fame, believed fossils were relics of Noah's Flood. In 1709 he published *Herbarium of the Deluge,* which contained depictions of fossil plants and animals. His later *Sacred Physics* (1731–1733) was a massive multivolume tome with hundreds of illustrations of natural objects and animals.

Another problem in the construction of visual representations of the past was that fossils are rarely found completely intact. They are usually broken beyond recognition. Like the hapless egg man of the children's story, all the king's horses and all the king's men could not always put these shattered remains back together again. A method was needed. The technique of fossil reconstruction attempted first to reconstitute the actual skeletal parts of a creature and then visualize what it looked like in life. This approach was pioneered by Georges Cuvier as an outgrowth of his development of comparative anatomy.

He saw that by comparing organisms you could gain insight into how biological structures functioned. Along the way Cuvier realized that one part of an organism gave clues to other parts and to overall lifestyle. Certain body proportions could suggest a fast runner or a swimmer, whereas big molar teeth suggested an herbivore. Cuvier applied this logic to reconstructing fossil animals when only a portion of the overall creature was known. The progression went like this: parts of a skeleton could suggest the rest of the skeleton, which in turn could be used to show muscle structure and even skin. From there the creature's lifestyle could be roughly deduced. From the geologic area the fossil was discovered in, an environmental setting could be put together. In this way a relatively small amount of fossil material could give a picture of what the creature had looked like. Although this technique did not always work perfectly, it was a beginning. With this reconstruction technique, books began to appear in the nineteenth century that contained what historian Martin Rudwick calls "scenes from deep time" in his book by that name (1992).

With more material to work with, a number of artists turned their talents to the creation of such scenes. In the 1830s Frenchman Johann-Baptiste Pfitzer produced a series of engravings of the marine plesiosaurs and flying pterodactyls. One of the most well-known paleontological artists of the period was Benjamin Waterhouse Hawkins. His renderings of dinosaurs, like Gideon Mantell's iguanodon and megalosaur, have an almost giddy quality. These denizens of the past lumber and bellow and slouch through primeval landscapes. He created his captivating scenes based on scant fossil material. As a result his reconstructions were woefully inaccurate but popular. What was needed next was a way to depict ancient people as well as ancient animals.

*The Monstrous Races*

All cultures around the world develop ways of seeing other people. They represent them in pictures, words, and oral traditions. Often strangers are viewed as just that: strange, not of us, the "other" to be feared and marveled at. Europeans were no different in this respect. By the Middle Ages Christians in Europe were comparing themselves to other groups around the world in order to differentiate themselves from what they called the monstrous races. These were people known or understood only from legend, classical mythology, travelers' tales, and half-remembered stories. In the eleventh century a picture book called the *Marvels of the East* was produced as a catalog of weird and wild people from India, Ethiopia, and other exotic locales. It contained representations of giants, long-haired fish-eating people, dog-headed men, the *Homodubi* (half man, half donkey), and other fantastic creatures. Certain visual cues and motifs were employed to show the primitiveness of monstrous people: they carried clubs as a symbol of their nontechnological state, were hairy and unkempt, and almost exclusively were naked. All these were signs of their cultural, intellectual, and spiritual backwardness and inferiority. When Hermann Schaaffhausen attempted to describe the Neanderthal man it was to the tradition of monstrous races that he turned.

Images of the monstrous races merged with European legends of barbarians and wild men. Starting in the 400s the "civilized" societies of the old Roman Empire were ravaged and toppled by successive waves of barbarians from the East and Central Asia. The Huns, the Goths, the Vandals, and other groups that moved into Western Europe were terrible not only in behavior but in appearance as well. They wore fur skins, were uncouth and uncivilized, were not Christian, and engaged in behavior that was, well, barbaric. Just as Europe began to recover from this onslaught, the Vikings of the North swept down in the 900s to scourge it again. As a result European mythology is full of crazed, rampaging, fur-covered nightmares.

The idea of the barbarian and the creatures of the *Marvels of the East* and similar books can themselves trace their lineage back to the classical world and before. One of the two main characters of the Babylonian *Epic of Gilgamesh* is Enkidu the wildman. Like his medieval relatives, he is hairy, carries a club, and represents all that is barbaric, uncivilized, and outside society. By the thirteenth and fourteenth centuries the wild man had become a common motif in European, particularly German, tradition. A stained-glass window produced in Germany in the late 1400s, in the collection of the Cloisters Museum in New York, contains a classic wild man. Ceremonial drinking vessels of the same collection from the Germanic Lowlands of the 1500s have wild-man figures worked into them, complete with long hair and knobby clubs. Barbarous races like the Celts, Picts, and ancient Britons and Germans seemed everywhere. In the Americas, the native people had Sasquatch; Tibet had the Yeti; and China had a host of wild men as well.

The wild man was as close as scholars could get to understanding man's primitive early state. A series of illustrations that depict early people discovering fire and building the first structures appeared in Vitruvius's *De architectura* (1511) and look uncannily like twentieth-century depictions of the same scenes except that the characters are anatomically modern. What must be remembered is that although legends and depictions of barbarians and wild people were attempts by scholars to account for and make sense of man's early development, they were not evolutionary in intent. As wild as wild men might be, they were still anatomically no different from modern people. Their primitiveness and ancient status were cultural and societal, not biological. These images were popular, and the motifs of barbarians and wild men were copied over and over for an entire range of books and pamphlets.

By the 1700s scholars were becoming more reliant on careful technical descriptions of the natural world. That did not put a crimp in the fascination with weird and wild people. Victorians could not seem to get enough human oddities. Fat boys and girls, dwarfs and giants, legless and armless people, and others were shown in circuses, museums, and other public attractions. They were feted as celebrities by royalty and commoners alike. The connection between these natural oddities and human evolution was discussed and wondered at. They were usually not seen as "wild," being more likely to be dressed in contemporary clothing than furs. But old ways die hard. When the first Neanderthals were discovered, the wild man reappeared, flashing his toothy grin.

Initially running parallel to the image of the caveman, but then melding with it, was the image of the ape that was becoming more and more caught up in the discussion of human evolution. If European intellectuals were disturbed by how closely people of color stood next to them on the ladder of life, they were more so about the primates. This seemed the most disturbing relationship of all. Though ape and evolution cartoons and references in literature had been appearing in England since the 1840s, with the appearance of *The Origin of Species* the ape, and the image of the brute, became a popular device to insult individuals and entire groups. The fascination with brutes, both real and imagined, grew steadily. Popular culture began to sag under the growing weight of the monkey imagery of novels, newspaper articles, learned books, and cartoons that alternately ridiculed, satirized, supported, and condemned evolution. Authors as diverse as H. Rider Haggard, Joseph Conrad, and Edgar Allen Poe all explored the interaction and relationship of men, monkeys, human society, and politics. They questioned the fine line between the civil and the savage. Robert Louis Stevenson's story of *Dr. Jekyll and Mr. Hyde* (1866) literally turned a man into a monkey. The ape as an icon was used to disparage ethnic groups from Africans to the Irish, to poke fun at inept politicians and brutal military leaders, and to sell products. Evolution dredged up man's relationship to God, race, class, the spread of empire, and gender issues. The ape and the caveman became the metaphor of everything dark and troubling in Western minds, not only about evolution but about themselves as well.

## The Neanderthals Appear

Along with the ape, the other perfect target for satire and racial commentary was the Neanderthal. Archaeologist Stephanie Moser argues in *Ancestral Images* (1998) that once human fossils were unearthed, a new problem arose. There was already the tradition of showing wild people in primitive settings. What would the difference be between these scenes and ones with Neanderthals? Louis Figurier's 1867 revised edition of *Earth before the Deluge* gave one answer. He included more "ancient" backgrounds—fossil plants and animals—as well as a yawning chasm to physically separate the people of the modern world from the beasts of the ancient world. The renderings were done by Edouard Riou (1833–1900), a Parisian landscape artist who also did illustrations for the works of Jules Verne. Adam and Eve were rendered as wild people with the conventions of clubs and fur. In his later *Primitive Man* (1870) Figurier (1819–1894) continued using modern people in "ancient scenes." This approach, however, was growing increasingly unsatisfying.

Though originally described in 1856, the first life reconstruction of the Neanderthal was not produced until 1861 when Pierre Boitard included a full-length portrait in his *Études antédiluviennes Paris avant les hommes*. The creature swings his ax menacingly at an unseen foe as he guards the entrance to his cave home, where his mate and child cower. The layout of this scene is identical to a rendering of a wild man from a French book of 1500. The creature is very apelike in its facial features and feet. Several years went by before another illustration appeared. In July 1873 the American publication *Harper's Weekly* ran an illustration labeled *The Neanderthal Man*. He has all the stereotypes: fur, club, cave home, trusty canine companions.

With the age of Darwin and Huxley, depictions of ancient people began to change. They started to look more like monkeys and apes. Where "ancient" people were characterized as modern Caucasians, fossil men now took on a darker complexion both physically and philo-

*Figurier's Adam and Eve as stone age people (from Louis Figurier's* Primitive Man *[London: Chapman and Hall, 1870])*

sophically. Figurier's characters were benign travelers; now cavemen became terrible monkeys chewing up the countryside. Primate physiology was worked into depictions of cavemen, Africans, and other people of color as a way to accentuate primitive bestiality. In 1894 artist Gabriel Von Max created a painting called *Family of Ape People* as a present for Ernst Haeckel. A bizarre rendering, the creatures have dwarflike proportions and are covered with blond hair (possibly as an homage to Haeckel's Aryan beliefs). While the mother has a somewhat sympathetic look, the father has an imbecilic expression. Haeckel was so taken with the painting that he used it to illustrate his *Natürliche Schöpfungsgeschichte* of 1898. It was not until February of 1909 that the first really influential Neanderthal picture appeared in the popular *Illustrated London News.* Based on Marcellin Boule's descriptions, this image seared the Neanderthal into the public eye. He stands before his cave, club in hand, hairy, muscular, powerful, with a fearsome expression. He is a nightmare come to life, a smiling Paleolithic serial killer.

The next time he appeared, again in the *Illustrated London News,* a transformation had come over the Neanderthal. Artist Amadée Forestier presented the Neanderthal in May 1911 in a far more sympathetic light. Gone is the wild man of ancient myth, replaced by a thoughtful toolmaker and housekeeper. Forestier did a series of illustrations on ancient human themes for the *Illustrated London News* in the early twentieth century. The editors of the paper had an interest in archaeology and human evolution and routinely ran articles on the latest discoveries. Forestier did many reconstructions of ancient humans during this period, including Arthur Keith's Galley Hill man in 1911, which the paper labeled *The Briton of 170,000 Years Ago,* as well as the infamous Nebraska man picture. The iconography of ancestral humans was now firmly established: cave homes, rude clothing, tools and weapons, fire building, ritual eating, and eventually primitive art creation. They battled the elements and fierce beasts. The cave bear, woolly rhinoceros, mammoth, and of course the incorrectly named saber-toothed tiger became the arch-nemeses of the cavemen.

In the 1880s an interesting variation on the caveman theme appeared. Some depictions of the lives of cave people took the standard conventions of brutishness to another level. French academic artists like Leon-Maxime Faivre and Paul Jamin began to use the caveman motif to address other subjects. Fernand Cormon did saloon paintings of cavemen and murals for the Paris Museum of Natural History. They addressed such ideas as bravery, honor, family, race, and gender relationships. Faivre's *Deux meres* (1888) is typical of this genre. The very white, presumably Cro-Magnon, woman with one provocatively bare breast shields her children from an approaching menace, her stone club at the ready. It is a touching display of raw courage and motherhood in the face of danger.

These artists and others were preoccupied with realism in faithfully reproducing the visual look of the real world. The core of this attitude was careful attention to detail in rendering objects and people and other minutiae of existence. When Cormon and his contemporaries turned to the ancient past as subject matter, they brought the sensibilities of realism with them. The idea of using the historical past as a metaphor for the present was popular among academic painters of the late nineteenth century. The Briton Lawrence Alma-Tadema (1836–1912) painted scenes of the classical world that were carefully researched. He made painstaking studies of Greek and Roman artifacts and architecture so he could add lush detail to his paintings. All the togas, polished marble floors, and period musical instruments were exotica to ornament comments on contemporary Victorian culture and society. The pictures were less about second-century Rome than late-nineteenth-century London. A similar mind-set worked its way into a good deal of caveman depictions as they became morality plays dressed up in bearskins.

## Charles R. Knight and Anatomical Accuracy

More than Marcellin Boule's written descriptions of cavemen, the work that most fixed the idea of what ancestral humans looked like was that of New York artist Charles R. Knight (1874–1953). Most caveman renderings were the results of collaborations between artists and anthropologists. Knight's scientific partner was the president of the American Museum, Henry Fairfield Osborn. Knight had done work for *Century* magazine and others on nature topics and was ready for more. He originally became known around the American Museum because of his extensive use of the museum's exhibits and holdings as subjects for drawings and paintings during the 1890s. After making the acquaintance of museum paleontologist Jacob Wortman, Knight was introduced to Osborn. They shared views on art, politics, and the state of U.S. society and so quickly became friends. Osborn liked Knight personally and admired his work to a considerable degree. Theirs was a relationship that would mold and dominate the public's perception of what dinosaurs and cavemen looked like, one that lasted throughout most of the twentieth century.

Osborn's early work on human evolution culminated in *Men of the Old Stone Age* (1915), which Knight illustrated. The book was meant to be the foundation of his human evolution theory, yet it contained little of his own original work. It was primarily a survey of the latest paleoanthropology done by Marcellin Boule and Henri Breuil. Breuil worked with Osborn regularly and gave Knight pointers on the illustrations for the French edition. The book proved a popular success and went through several reprints and reissues. People brought it with them when they toured the museum, author Edith Wharton carried it with her as a guide when she toured the Cro-Magnon sites of France, and H. G. Wells used it as a source work for his widely read *Outline of History*. Although his depictions were not as animalistic as Boule's picture, Knight kept to the general idea of Neanderthals as brutish inferiors.

In 1924, in order to bring his human evolution theories even more before the public, Osborn opened the Hall of the Age of Man at the museum. He had always seen the museum as an integral tool for teaching science and culture to the masses through a combination of ideas and images. The hall included several large impressive murals by Knight. Osborn wanted the ancient humans to be seen as pristine wildlife that lived naturally and in harmony with its surroundings according to the rules of nature.

Knight threw himself into the project, doing a series of preliminary drawings from live models at the Art Students League in New York. He created figures far more dynamic than what he did for Osborn's book. Knight based his work on a thorough fine arts training, good knowledge of human anatomy, and the actual fossil material to produce accurate renderings. He emphasized sticking closely to the biological reality of how they looked. This approach set new standards. Although Knight was anatomically accurate, his depictions of how the cavemen behaved were open to more subtle qualities.

Though they were ostensibly ancient people, Osborn wanted the pictures to be analogous to modern racial distinctions. The Neanderthals were depicted as robust and tough, their skins dark, their stances brutish, their attitudes lacking advanced thinking or creativity. Their society had cohesion but was not as efficiently organized as it could be. By contrast, the Cro-Magnons were shown in their two murals as far better organized. They were thoughtful, intelligent, and creative as a group. They hunted not on a whim but with careful planning and foresight. They created art. Their weapons were more advanced, their clothing better made. They had tamed wild animals as allies and of course were much lighter skinned. They are the picture of Anglo-Saxon, Nordic superiority.

Though Osborn claimed the hall was to present empirical evidence of mankind's evolutionary progress "and not to confuse the visitor with theories and speculations," it was arranged to support his human evolution theory (1925, 2). The exhibit was organized with a clear message that all the races were separate species. Nordic whites occupied the pinnacle of a line of evolution that began from an early protohuman, nonape ancestor. In this world everyone knew their place and was happy there. The order of human evolution was slow, steady, and predictable. Man went from base origins to the height of human evolution as modern Caucasians.

There were those inside and outside the museum who were uneasy with the politics involved. Anthropologist Margaret Mead and even Osborn's assistant, William K. Gregory, squirmed a bit. There were claims that Knight had made up all the details, a notion that made him bristle. He said he had consulted experts and even actual Neanderthal and Cro-Magnon material in preparing his drawings. Not one to pull racial punches, Knight shot back at a visitor who said he had made the Neanderthals unrealistically brutish by saying that there were plenty of people roaming the streets of Manhattan more brutish and degenerate than the ones he depicted.

Following Knight, the next artist to specialize in renderings of humanity's past was the Czech Zdeník Burian (1905–1981). Working in a style and philosophy similar to Knight, Burian created a series of paintings, the best known of which make up *Prehistoric Man* (1960). Though a century had gone by since the first discovery of fossil humans, Burian still used the narrative approach that had become the standard tradition. The mammoth hunting was still there, with bearskins and communal life emphasized. Clubs were still carried. Although Burian did try to be as archaeologically correct as possible, he was unable to shake the visual baggage of earlier traditions completely. He also helped contribute to another popular staple of Neanderthal life: cannibalism.

In 1899 Croatian anthropologist Dragutin Gorjanoviæ-Kramberger discovered a Neanderthal site at Krapina that seemed to expose the truly dark side of human ancestry. The Krapina cave was the largest collection of Neanderthals found in one spot. Almost eighty individuals in their late teens and early twenties (dating to about 130,000 years ago) were there. In his examination of the remains Gorjanoviæ-Kramberger saw that most were broken as if eaten, but he could find no evidence of predators. If a big cat or bear had eaten the bodies, it would have left obvious signs of biting and chewing. Finding none, he determined that this was evidence that the Neanderthals had been cannibalized.

Years before, French anthropologist Edouard Dupont had denied that the Neanderthals were cannibals, without anyone having claimed they were. This suggests that although Gorjanoviæ-Kramberger was the first to publicly accuse the Neanderthals of that most revolting of human behavior, the idea must have been circulating unofficially since the 1860s. Being eaters of human flesh seemed perfectly appropriate for the grunting, homicidal Neanderthal image. Few opposed the idea at first. One of Burian's most well-known paintings is of a Neanderthal clan that is in the middle of enjoying a cannibalistic feast. He based the painting on the Krapina finds. Later researchers have called Gorjanoviæ-Kramberger's analysis into question. They argue that there are plenty of predator marks on the Krapina fossils that more than put the myth of cannibalism to rest. The picture, however, remains.

In the late 1970s and early 1980s a reassessment of the historical and archaeological record suggested that the evidence for cannibalism among Paleolithic and modern people was poorly documented or simply wrong. Critics of the cannibalism scenario called for a more rigorous examination of the data. They said many cultures treat their dead in ways that, to outsiders, could look like cannibalism when it was not. More recent examinations of the data, however, showed that Gorjanoviæ-Kramberger was right after all. At Krapina at least, the Neanderthals did engage in this activity.

In 2000 evidence was published suggesting that the Anasazi of the American Southwest had done the same. This claim generated much resentment from Anasazi descendants uncomfortable with the idea that their forebears did such things. Work begun in the 1960s showed that many Anasazi sites contained bone fragments with signs of cannibalism, including evidence of having been cooked in pots. The bones had been processed in the same manner as they processed their animal kills. Another study of Anasazi sites from Colorado dating to A.D. 1150 included similar evidence as well as human feces. Biochemical analysis of this material showed it contained human myoglobin, which is present in heart and muscle tissue (myoglobin was also present in the remains of cooking pots). This showed that the individual who produced the fecal matter had consumed human tissue. Why people like the Neanderthals or Anasazi engaged in cannibalism is unknown. It could have been ritual or survival. There is no convincing evidence either way.

A more favorable claim was that the Neanderthals had elaborate religious cults that included the worship of cave bears. Between 1917 and 1921 Swiss amateur Emil Bächler came across a Neanderthal site in the Swiss Churfirsten Mountains at a cave known as Drachenloch. He found Mousterian tools and artifacts. Although he found no human bones, he did find a large cache of cave-bear bones, many piled in neat order in little depressions dug in the cave floor and behind stone walls. Most striking of all, he found a pile of cave-bear bones with a skull mounted on top with a leg bone carefully positioned through the cheek. The entire arrangement made the cave a kind of Neanderthal church. Bächler saw it as clear evidence of religion. If the Neanderthals had a cult of the cave bear, it suggested they had some appreciation of metaphysical ideas or at least a spiritual consciousness. Unfortunately, Bächler's work was, as it was for many amateurs, sloppy. Most of the excavation was done by unskilled laborers. Bächler based many of his assertions on the descriptions of the work foreman instead of his own observations. Today, most paleoanthropologists dismiss Bächler's analysis as misinterpretations of naturally occurring conditions: the rock wall was a natural cave-in, the burial pits were those dug by live cave bears as they prepared for hibernation, and the skull and leg bone were just a coincidence of scavengers throwing them around. As there are no other examples of Neanderthal ritual activities, aside from the intentional burials, the vision of the cave-bear cult has largely vanished from anthropological thinking.

*Popular Culture*

In the early twentieth century the new medium of film became a prime arena in which the cavemen could romp. Several films like *The*

*Lost World* (1925) and *One Million B.C.* (1940) included caveman themes. Although there have been many subsequent films throughout the twentieth century, the golden age of caveman movies was the 1950s through the 1970s. Exploitation films like *Teenage Cave Man* (1958), *Eegah!* (1962), and *Trog* (1970) filled theaters on Saturday mornings and often generated more unintentional humor than horror. Some films used the motif as an excuse for cheesecake and scantily dressed women with plot lines only vaguely involving genuine cave people. The 1967 remake of *One Million B.C.* put Raquel Welch in a tight-fitting fur bikini in which she could flee from various marauding people and creatures. *Iceman* (1984) took a more serious tone. In the film a caveman (presumably a Cro-Magnon) is discovered frozen in ice and thawed out in modern times. The scientists are then faced with an ethical dilemma. What do you do with a 40,000-year-old man? In one poignant scene the hapless iceman breaks down as he attempts to make sense of the strange surroundings and new environment. *Clan of the Cave Bear* (1986), based upon the novel of the same name, explored the interaction of a beautiful Cro-Magnon girl, played by actress Darryl Hannah, as she tries to fit in with her adoptive Neanderthal family. "Serious" films like *Clan of the Cave Bear* and *Quest for Fire* (1981) were attempts at making the lives of ancient people come to life and seem "real" in the same way Charles R. Knight or Zdenìk Burian tried to do in their paintings.

Pop culture was full of caveman imagery. The year 1949 saw the introduction of Alley Oop and his friends in comic strips and comic books. Arthur Conan Doyle had Sherlock Holmes crack the case of *The Creeping Man* (1927), in which a scientist uses monkey-gland serum to give himself renewed virility in order to marry a young beauty. *King Kong* (1933), though not a caveman movie, did use deep-time scenes of dinosaurs, and the ape himself had much anthropological and racial baggage attached to him. Edgar Rice Burroughs created not only Tarzan but also a host of novels like *The Moon Maid* (1923) and *The Moon Men* (1925), in which apelike humanoids battle degenerate races, Anglo-Saxon heroes, and beauteous Nordic princesses. Second only to Tarzan as Burroughs's best-known character, John Carter, the fighting man of Mars, found adventure, struggle, and interplanetary sex in a series of novels and magazine articles throughout the 1920s by battling alien protohumans.

An attempt to portray cavemen in a realistic fashion was Stanley Waterloo's *Story of Ab* (1923), which took a sympathetic and somewhat melodramatic view of our ancestors making the final step to truly modern people. In the 1960s and '70s television produced the most famous caveman since the original Neanderthal: Fred Flintstone. The animated show he starred in was hugely popular—a cave version of the live-action *Honeymooners*—and included a host of wild caveman devices, from cars and trucks to airplanes and refrigerators. The problem was that, whether teenage exploitation film, comedy, or drama, popular culture recycled the same old stereotypes. Although more sophisticated filmmakers tried to create faithful reconstructions of the past—employing experts to guide the visual look—there was not much difference between *One Million B.C.* and *Clan of the Cave Bear*.

## Three-Dimensional Presentations

Museum displays are another area that has contributed to our view of the lives of cavemen. Like films and illustrations, three-dimensional presentations (dioramas) have often hindered as much as helped our understanding of human evolution. Taking their lead from the illustrators, museum designers kept the same visual canon, or fixed set of images, as they did. Museum display designers simply took the stereotypes established by the two-dimensional artists and made them life-size.

The other extreme is that in the rush to design new and up-to-date high-tech exhibits, an "edutainment" mentality took hold. Displays were often put together with more emphasis on entertaining the audience than transmitting accurate information. In an attempt to compete with theme parks, museums began to adopt methods from theme parks. Even when museums resisted doing this there were certain inherent problems that any museum has. The way the display is set up determines how information is presented and understood by the viewer. Museum curators create an interpretive framework that directs knowledge in a certain way. For many visitors, the display became the theory. Finally, because of the lag time between scientific discovery and when museum displays are built or updated, viewers often see displays they assume to be technically accurate but may be well out-of-date.

The first caveman dioramas were put up at the Field Museum of Natural History in Chicago in 1933. Like its counterpart in New York, the Hall of the Stone Age of the Old World was as hugely popular as it was clumsily titled. Through a combination of lifelike mannequins, meticulously re-created artifacts and scenes, painted backgrounds, and cinematic lighting, the story of human evolution was presented in dramatic style. Innovative in its day, the Chicago exhibit was copied around the world, creating a widespread uniformity. Later designers, either unable to create imaginative scenes of their own or simply trying to duplicate Chicago's success, copied what came before them. It is not unlike what happens in films when an imaginative or compelling scene is done for one movie and is then copied so many times in later movies that it is noticed only when it is not used (think of the shot of the hero walking toward the camera as a great explosion goes off behind him).

Archaeologist Stephanie Moser has studied this problem and argues that to break the cycle of mediocrity and poor information transmission a few changes should be made. She claims in part that the old display canon of visual standards has to be abandoned, that too much reliance has been placed on the narrative approach, and that the past and present must be linked. She also contends that the underlying racial and gender issues involved should be brought into the open. Adding to this, human evolution displays in the West have a Euro-American flavor that is often very different from how non-Western cultures see the subject. The old notion of Africans and other people of color being a somehow more primitive form of human development still echoes in some displays.

Although public displays continue to recycle old ideas, changing scientific views have been addressed at some larger institutions. In the early 1990s the American Museum of Natural History, for example, conducted a major overhaul of its fossil and evolution halls. Old displays, which showed evolution as a straight line from simple to complex, have been replaced by ones that show the great complexity of evolutionary change. In order to help museum visitors understand, the new display on horse evolution was partnered with the old simplistic view for comparison. It was explained how the old idea had been discarded in favor of the more accurate presentation and why.

Human evolution displays can be problematic for other reasons. They are often arranged in a way that suggests straight-line progression and simple development from earlier, simpler, unsophisticated forms to modern humans in an "*A* leads to *B* leads to *C*" configuration. Human evolution is presented as a "story" of people fighting their way from crudeness to modernity, a sort of rags-to-riches story of hard work leading inevitably to success. The American Museum of Natural History's human evolution exhibit tries to break up the misleading chronological connections.

Misia Landau, in her *Narratives of Human Evolution* (1991), showed that the idea of storytelling played a central role in nineteenth- and twentieth-century human evolution theories. The main character of the story was early man battling the elements and overcoming obstacles to achieve the rewards of bipedalism, a large brain and increased intelligence, and life on the ground instead of in the trees. They were presented like Greek hero stories where battles are fought, tests given, goals obtained, and ethics and morals enforced. The early-twentieth-century renderings of humans in a prehistoric world, particularly the Cro-Magnons, suggested an optimistic, progressive approach. These humans might have been culturally or spiritually primitive, but they were only at the beginning of the great adventure to modernity. They looked to the rising sun and knew what their destiny was. Whatever *they* were in the past, *we* were the culmination of that effort. Whatever obstacles, adventures, or hardships they had to encounter, they would ultimately triumph, as we would. The Neanderthals were never in such a position. The separate-species idea locked them out. Over and over the visual cues were different for them. The Neanderthals struggled against great odds for every inch. Their lives were not joyous celebrations of unlimited possibilities but mind-numbing workaday experiences that rarely raised a smile or happy moment. Their world was brutal, an ultimately wasted effort that went nowhere. Although it is ultimately pessimistic for them, it is optimistic for us. As we were not their descendants we were not tainted by their failure.

Landau saw that to make sense of facts and theories, some scientists organized their information like a literary work, describing the life of a fictional character. The preoccupation with narrative could often obscure scientific accuracy. As I mentioned in the introduction, even now as I the author of this book have used the narrative structure, it is playing a part in how you the reader make sense of this topic. The use of the narrative can give the impression that there is only one story, only one "truth." In reality, there is no metahistory, or single grand story. Human evolution in its cultural aspect is just as complicated as it is in its biological aspect. It is so complicated that it is doubtful any one picture or museum display could do it justice. It might only muddy the waters to the point where some argue whether human ancestors should be depicted at all.

Other approaches were taken, however. The *Missing Links Alive* exhibit that toured the world at the end of the twentieth century used the innovative tactic of placing a model of a Neanderthal in modern clothes standing innocuously outside the diorama looking in where museum visitors were likely to end up standing next to it, thinking it a live person. The idea was to show that despite the stereotype, Neanderthals did not look that much different from us. This harkens back to the 1930s when anthropologist Carleton Coon created an illustration of a Neanderthal in a business suit. He claimed that if dressed in modern clothes, a Neanderthal would blend right in. With the *Missing Links Alive* figure it is interesting that it is dressed in jeans and a casual jacket, not a suit. These clothes suggest a certain class and economic situation. The old stereotypes still exist: a Neanderthal might blend in with us, but as a "working stiff," not a corporate CEO.

Also in the latter part of the twentieth century a new group of artists, led by Jay Matternes, began producing caveman reconstructions to an even higher degree of scientific accuracy than previously. They stressed technical accuracy, as Knight and Burian did, but made a conscious effort to abandon the old caveman conventions in favor of a more sophisticated knowledge of hominid behavior. Gone were the knobby clubs and battles against beasts. New evidence suggested a much more complex and less violent lifestyle. In addition, in the 1960s and '70s attitudes about gender roles in the United States worked their way into reconstructions of the past. In several of Matternes's illustrations females take the lead in performing what are usually thought of as male activities. Children also began to appear, not just helpless infants. Increasingly, Neanderthals were seen as people living in harmony with the landscape as modern aboriginal people do. This is a fascinating twist. As was shown earlier, anthropologists in the nineteenth century saw cavemen as simply old aborigines. The new view of Neanderthals as 1960s-style "flower children" living like the Native American Indians simply changed the idea to a more sympathetic angle. Influenced by the counterculture that many paleoanthropologists of that generation came out of, the Neanderthals were changed from drooling killers into wise people with a connection to and harmony with nature that put "modern" people and society to shame. The men were more understanding, and the women got out of the kitchen into the workplace and leadership roles. His drawings of Lucy did as much to publicize the creature as did Donald Johanson's scientific research. Matternes was more successful than his predecessors at showing something of the complex and multidimensional lives of the cavemen.

Picturing the caveman being what it is, there is still room for a little drama. In the American Museum of Natural History's diorama of the famous Laetoli footprints, a simple but momentous gesture takes place, one so simple and unassuming that it is often missed at first glance. The exhibit designers depicted the scene as two adults, with the male's arm tenderly and protectively around his partner's shoulder as they walk. This simple gesture suggests a huge array of social interaction and emotional development that is not known from any fossil evidence. It is a "human" act that can never be ascertained from fossils alone, yet it is a touching and powerful sight. Although possibly suggestive, the trackway gave no indication of any behavior other than bipedal walking. Many such intangible qualities are often depicted in fossil reconstructions, some more subtly than others.

## The Problem of Hair

The touchy-feely *Australopithecus* couple from the American Museum's Laetoli exhibit highlights an important point. What evidence do we have for any behavior depicted in any caveman illustration or diorama? We know a good deal about the later Cro-Magnons and their culture, as they created art in the form of cave paintings, jewelry, and even three-dimensional sculptures. Often the later Cro-Magnon culture is confabulated with that of the Neanderthals, suggesting they too had these tools and accoutrements. There are other reasons that depicting the lives of cavemen is problematic still today. For example, what color hair did they have? What color skin did they have? Did they wear clothes? We know they had scrapers and cutting tools for processing leather, so they probably did make things to protect themselves from the elements.

When Charles R. Knight was working on his Neanderthal murals, French anthropologist Henri Breuil suggested to him that he paint them naked to be more in line with what was known about them. Henry Fairfield Osborn insisted they be clothed. He did not want to upset the social sensibilities of museum visitors. This is a problem with most of the stereotypes of cavemen. What we think we know about them from artwork and tradition is commonly not known from reality. Maybe more than any other accoutrement, the knobby club is most associated with Neanderthal males. Like an American Express card, they never seemed to go anywhere without one. Yet there is no evidence that Neanderthals or Cro-Magnons ever actually carried clubs. This is the power of imagery to alter what is "real" and "true" about the past. Unfortunately, except for a few tantalizing bits, the cavemen did not leave us any pictures of what they looked like.

Anthropologist Judith Berman has focused on hair in her examination of how cavemen are pictured. Of the three great stereotypes of caveman life—fur clothing, clubs, and wild hair—it is the hair that is most telling. She asks why cavemen are always shown with long, shaggy hair. Like the wild men, barbarians, and monstrous races, a caveman's shaggy hair locates him as an outsider, not of us, uncivilized. Depicting cave people with hair of no style suggests that they were incapable of or uninterested in combing their own hair. If there is one thing we as humans worry about it is our appearance. Hair is a visual signifier of our place in society. The way we keep it says much about who we are. Why would the cavemen not have cared about their appearance as well? Giving them specific hairstyles would make them look modern. That could throw off the delicate balance between us and them.

Facial expressions are another human trait that poses problems for cavemen. They had the same ability to make faces as modern humans do, yet when they are pictured it is either with a grimace or a blank expression. They might have been great practical jokers. Sitting around a campfire all night with nothing else to do may have produced caveman stand-up comics who helped the clan laugh the night away. Although it may make us feel better to portray cave people as wise and ecologically correct, living utopian existences that neither exploited nor destroyed the land, we have relatively little to base much of this on one way or the other.

Artist John Gurche, like Jay Matternes, stressed great reliance on scientific accuracy and the employment of the latest theories and ideas of scientists in his meticulously crafted illustrations. His illustration for Roger Lewin's *In the Age of Mankind* (1988) shows a mother-and-child group with the father and a second child in the background. She looks confidently at the viewer, a hint of a smile on her lips. It is a far cry from Gabriel Von Max's 1894 rendering of the imbecilic Neanderthals. Mauricio Anton's cover illustration of *Homo erectus* for the August 2002 issue of *National Geographic* shows the creature sporting an almost impish grin.

## Conclusion

Like their scientific colleagues, historians attempt to reconstruct the past in order to learn from it. Some argue that, try as we might, we can never get all the facts. Even when we collect mountains of data about the past, any image or conclusion we draw is part artificial construction. We cannot help but bring our personal views, prejudices (both good and bad), and preconceptions to how we describe what went before us. Therefore, no definitive picture of the past can ever be attained, only a series of views of what might have been. Postmodernist scholars argue meaning is not derived from facts as much as the language (or imagery) we use to describe those facts. We can never know if it bears any resemblance to what actually happened. All we can hope for is some kind of workable approximation. Influential paleoanthropologist David Pilbeam agreed in 1978 when he said that much of the image of human evolution has been influenced by modern social attitudes as much as by fossils.

The image of the caveman has evolved over the years as much as the cavemen themselves. In the early twenty-first century they are enjoying a vogue of good press and a positive image. This change is similar to the changing attitudes about Native American and other aboriginal peoples. Where once the Indians were savage red men, now they are the noble caretakers of the Americas and are seen as fundamentally wiser than the European invaders who displaced them. That makes sense. No one wants ancestors who are stumbling, muttering fools. The ancient Greeks saw their ancestors as mighty heroes and larger-than-life characters. It made them feel better about themselves. We do the same thing today. It is not unusual for someone to want their grandfather to have been a powerful king, not a court jester. When cavemen were stupid brutes no one wanted them. Now that we view our difficult ancestors in a better light, we accept them more easily. We feel a certain pride in saying we have tough Neanderthal blood in us. In this way the image of the caveman can be used to sort our feelings about ourselves. As Judith Berman pointed out, "the cave man can be both debased and noble, expressing nostalgia for our noble animal nature, as well as the negation of civilized society" (1999, 290).

Cavemen can also help us get in touch with our primitive selves. In the nineteenth century, Europeans, like the artist Paul Gauguin, traveled to the island of Tahiti to live with the "natives." Living among "primitives" was a way of escaping the modern world. A growing number of people today have embraced the "modern primitive" movement. They use tattoos, body piercings, and other methods to separate themselves from the affluent Western tradition they are products of in order to restore a sense of humanity they feel they have lost. By attaching oneself to an ancient culture the chic of the primitive is sought. Others search for their roots of ethnic and family background. Picturing the caveman is part of the search for ourselves as much as hunting fossils is.

*Further Reading*

For excellent histories of ancient life and caveman imagery, see Martin Rudwick, *Scenes from Deep Time* (1992); Stephanie Moser, *Ancestral Images: The Iconography of Human Origins* (1998); Judith Berman, "Bad Hair Days in the Paleolithic: Modern (Re)Construction of the Cave Man" (1999); and Annemarie De Waal Malefijt, *Images of Man: A History of Anthropological Thought* (1974). For the role of art in science, see B. Baigrie, *Picturing Knowledge: Historical and Philosophical Problems Concerning the Use of Art in Science* (1996), and D. S. Berkowitz, *In Remembrance of Creation: Evolution and Art and Scholarship in the Medieval and Renaissance Bible* (1968). For monsters, see John Block Friedman, *The Monstrous Races in Medieval Art and Thought* (1981); Michael Mitchell, *Monsters of the Gilded Age: The Photographs of Charles Eisenmann* (1979); and Rosamond Purcell, *Special Cases: Natural Anomalies and Historical Monsters* (1997). For the life of Charles R. Knight, see Sylvia Massey and Donald Glut, *Dinosaurs, Mammoths, and Cavemen* (1982). On museums, see Stephen Asma, *Stuffed Animals and Pickled Heads: The Culture and Evolution of Natural History Museums* (2001), and Douglas J. Preston, *Dinosaurs in the Attic* (1986). On realism in art, see Linda Nochlin, *Realism* (1971). For David Pilbeam's comments on representations of cavemen, see *Discovery Magazine* (1978). On cannibalism, see Tim White, *Prehistoric Cannibalism at Mancos 5Mtum4-2346* (1992).

# 8

# *Alternative Theories*

It was a rainy night in August 1979 as Jack Cuozzo steered the rental car crazily through the streets of Paris. He was being pursued by at least one carload of shadowy intelligence agents intent on stopping him. His wife was in the passenger seat; the children were in the back. He ducked and weaved through traffic, desperately trying to shake the pursuing desperadoes who would do unspeakable things to them if caught. The agents were after the secret Cuozzo carried. He had been gathering evidence in museums around Europe that would rock the belief in human evolution to its very core. The pursuing agents, who Cuozzo (a dentist from New Jersey) speculated were a CIA type of group who carried out the orders of the "evolution establishment," would do anything to keep that secret from being made public. What the dark forces of human evolution did not count on was Cuozzo's dogged determination to get the word out. He had discovered the key to the "truth" about human evolution. He was going to put that key in the lock of righteousness, give it a turn, and kick the door wide open.

Most of the theories of human evolution discussed so far in this book are considered "mainstream": they fall within the parameters of science. Generally speaking, science is the pursuit of abstract knowledge of the universe based upon physical evidence gathered according to rigorous rules and methods. The thinkers and ideas in this chapter, however, tend to fall outside those parameters and into the twilight world of pseudoscience. These definitions create a dilemma: although some of the people in this chapter clearly do not follow scientific norms, others think they do. They believe they base their findings on physical evidence and follow rules of scientific inquiry. These thinkers are dismissed by the mainstream as unworthy of serious consideration because their findings and claims are too sensationalistic and speculative.

Mainstream scientists tend to dismiss fringe thinkers—or "outsider thinkers," as they will be referred to here—because, among other things, they often do not have higher degrees, are not affiliated with a recognized academic institution, base their findings on faith as much as empirical evidence, disregard accepted modes of scientific thought, are too narrowly focused, and are too wedded to their convictions to allow for other views. Fringe thinkers often dismiss mainstream scientists for the same reasons: they accuse the mainstream of being too educated, of being too worried about pleasing their masters at the colleges and universities they work for, and for being too narrowly focused and too wedded to their theories to be able to think outside the norm. The last accusation is particularly intriguing, as the fringe thinkers claim it is they, not scientists, who are looking at the "real" evidence and accuse scientists of holding their positions on faith and belief in a scientific dogma that is indistinguishable from any other religion.

The difference between science and pseudoscience is not always as clear as we would hope. The extreme ends of the spectrum are clear enough, but toward the middle things become less so. Not all mainstream scientists dismiss fringe ideas completely. Any scientist would love to meet a space alien or travel through time. In addition, not all fringe thinkers are lonely eccentrics working in their basements; some have degrees and try to work within the confines of scientific protocols.

This chapter will examine some of the more unusual and quirky theories of human evolution that came about in the twentieth century. Some are religious, some secular; they range from the occult to the empirical. Some are comical, whereas others are homicidal. Some are from self-taught geniuses; one or two make mainstream scientists take notice. And some are just plain crazy. They are all fascinating in what they say about human behavior, if not human evolution.


*Eugenics*

The dark underbelly of human evolution theory was eugenics. First introduced in the nineteenth century by Charles Darwin's cousin Francis Galton (1822–1911), eugenics was the concept of controlled human breeding and the attempt to clean up society by promoting the procreation of certain groups over others. Galton referred to his work as "racial improvement." He devised a series of statistical studies on how to measure the hereditary makeup of a population and how hereditary traits are transmitted from one generation to another. Indeed, Galton was a pioneer in the development of statistics as a working methodology for studying various problems. He believed that members of a society who carried positive hereditary traits—courage, honor, wealth, intelligence, and such—should be supported and encouraged to breed. Those members who had less than admirable qualities—poverty, alcoholism, illiteracy, or criminality—should be discouraged from breeding. The idea of marrying "the right sort" has a long history that transgresses national boundaries and ethnicity. Royal houses and just plain folks alike from one corner of the globe to another have carefully chosen who could and could not marry in their respective worlds. Eugenics was simply the modern attempt to organize and give official sanction to age-old beliefs and practices.

The idea of racial inequality goes back as far as human civilization itself but was codified into its modern form in the work of the Frenchman Joseph-Arthur de Gobineau, who argued in the 1860s in books like *The Inequality of the Races* that human society was a struggle between superior and inferior races: he was antidemocratic as well as anti-Semitic. Gobineau and other like-minded individuals saw racial inequality as a staple of the human experience. To them Caucasians were biologically, intellectually, and culturally superior to other ethnic groups. Within the wide range of what were believed to be Caucasian types—Nordics, Mediterraneans, and Alpines—the greatest were the Nordics, who could trace their lineage back to the mythical Aryans (Galton spoke in terms of Anglo-Saxons, the British variation of Nordic). They were the best form of human evolution, the cream of the evolutionary crop. Non-Caucasians were considered of different and hopelessly degenerate origins.

Eugenics took its first practical form in the United States in the late nineteenth and early twentieth centuries. There were many factors that led to this. In addition to the large numbers of southern blacks and poor whites who moved north following the Civil War, successive waves of Irish Catholics, Russian Jews, Poles, Italians, and others came to the United States. Urban populations exploded between 1860 and 1910, causing already established groups to feel threatened by the newcomers. An example of this trend is New York City, where many members of "old" society saw tradition and authority breaking down. The new groups were said to undermine wages, take scarce jobs, and compete for the bare necessities of survival, all of which created tension.

Opened in 1892, Ellis Island was by 1900 the key entry point for new arrivals. Between 1880 and 1919, 17 million immigrants came through New York alone. Most of these newcomers crowded into the city, unable to go farther, doubling its population. By 1907, for example, almost 300,000 Eastern European Jews were living in the city, which led to an increase in anti-Semitism. Whereas Catholics had been the bogeymen of nineteenth-century American politics, now the Jews took center stage in eugenic nightmares.

By 1905, 70 percent of New York's public school children were immigrants; by 1910, 40 percent of the city's entire population had been born outside the country. One way to assimilate these people into mainstream society was to "Americanize" them. They were inspired to adopt American dress and ways of behavior. This initiative came from both inside and outside the immigrant communities. Immigrant aid societies were often arms of various religious organizations. Churches and synagogues routinely paid for paupers and the working poor to come to the United States. Although these organizations could sometimes transplant Old World religious strife, they also helped the newcomers make the process of Americanization easier. Americanization came to mean, as it did for such old-line patriotic groups as the Daughters of the American Revolution, not just learning English and U.S. government and culture, but also giving up connections to old lives. Though it appeared as a liberal response to the growing immigrant population, it soon became a conservative attempt at forced conformity. For some, these measures were not enough.

The nativists—those of Nordic Anglo-Saxon ancestry born in the United States—were deathly afraid of the large number of new immigrants. The eugenicists felt the same way but brought to the discussion what they saw as a practical remedy. Beginning in the 1890s the nativists and eugenicists claimed they would apply "scientific" techniques of cleansing sterilization. The eugenicists added to the basic nativist fear of foreign culture a fear of foreign biology in the form of what they called "feeblemindedness." Feeblemindedness was a catchall expression meant to describe mental disabilities. Its meaning was soon made so elastic that it could be used to cover almost any social ill the eugenicists wanted it to, from severe mental impairment to simple illiteracy or poverty. In addition, miscegenation, or race mixing, was raised to the level of biological warfare. As eugenicists believed blacks to be of a different and inferior evolutionary origin, they wanted the races kept apart. Any such mixing, they argued, would throw off the delicate balance of human evolution.

Impetus was given the eugenics movement by the rediscovery in 1900 of mid-nineteenth-century Hungarian monk Gregor Mendel's (1822–1884) laws of heredity. He had done extensive work on botanical heredity and learned how to manipulate the color of pea plants. This suggested that physical traits were the result of "unit characters"—single hereditary units that were responsible for single characteristics like color and height. His work was published in an obscure local journal and did not become known to the wider scientific community until the end of the century. Many researchers interested in heredity took Mendel's law to mean that if a particular trait was unwanted, it could be eliminated from the population. Confusing social with biological traits became a cornerstone of eugenic thought: to clean up a population biologically, they argued, identify unwanted traits and then eliminate those individuals who carried them or keep them from procreating or mixing their blood with those who did not have the traits.

Along with Mendel's work, the germ-plasm theory of German cytologist (one who studies cells) August Weismann (1834–1914) was also adopted by eugenicists. In the 1880s Weismann discovered that the human body contained two types of cells: somatic and reproductive. He showed that only hereditary material contained in reproductive cells was used to create the next generation. Eugenicists fixed on this as proof that it was blood that carried superior and inferior traits, making the mixing of bloodlines harmful. They saw it as evidence that biology alone (nature), not environment and upbringing (nurture), was responsible for transmitting traits through the bloodstream.

Possibly the most notorious purveyor of eugenics in the United States was Madison Grant (1865–1937). A wealthy New York lawyer, Grant argued in *The Passing of the Great Race* (1916) and *The Conquest of a Continent* (1933) that the country was being swallowed up by hordes of degenerates whose inferior origins were destroying the fabric of society. Grant used as an underlying framework the central-Asia hypothesis of human origins put forth by his friend Henry Fairfield Osborn. He said Aryans evolved in central Asia under separate and different origins than the other races. They then swept across Europe, becoming Nordics and Anglo-Saxons to create a great civilization that found its highest expression in North America.

*Madison Grant, ca. 1918. Grant believed that non—Nordic Americans should be closely restricted and even eliminated so that they would not contaminate his own precious bloodstream. (Courtesy of the Save the Redwoods League)*

Grant and other prominent American eugenicists lobbied the U.S. government to enact stricter immigration reforms to stem the tide of unwanted masses they feared were entering the country, polluting Anglo-Saxon blood and ruining Anglo-Saxon society. The result was the Johnson/Reed Act of 1924 that restricted the numbers of Asians, Irish, Slavs, southern Italians, and other groups Grant and his cronies both in and out of the government deemed undesirable. This was the first permanent immigration law in the U.S. and lasted until 1952.

In his books, Grant put forward a three-tiered plan for dealing with this evolutionary threat. The first was to restrict new immigrants from coming into the country. Second, any undesirables in the country should be segregated into special areas so that they could not mix with the Anglo-Saxon population. Finally, all undesirables should be sterilized, by force if necessary, to ensure they would die off without issue. Sterilization was a favored remedy of eugenicists for fixing all the country's ills. They thought they could sterilize the country to cleanliness. Local miscegenation laws, mostly in the South, were already widespread. The first state sterilization law came from Indiana in 1907.

The pivotal moment in the sterilization issue in the United States was the *Buck v. Bell* case. Seventeen-year-old Carrie Buck was an institutionalized woman from Virginia. Deemed "feebleminded" because she and her mother, Emma, became pregnant out of wedlock, Carrie was placed in the Virginia Colony for Epileptics and the Feebleminded in 1927. The State of Virginia decided to sterilize her and her child, Vivian, so they would not reproduce again. A legal action ensued that went to the Supreme Court. The state argued that it had the right to sterilize any citizen posing a threat to the state economy through reproduction.

The Eugenics Record Office (ERO), a biological laboratory on Long Island, New York, came to the state's defense. The ERO was started by biologist Charles Davenport (1866–1944), with money from the influential Harriman family, as a center of eugenic research into how to control and modify the American breeding public (Davenport was a friend and ally of Madison Grant). They collected data on thousands of Americans in an attempt to chart the country's hereditary disposition. These data would then be used to construct a plan to carefully control breeding. This meant finding ways to keep "degenerates" from procreating and to promulgate the births of the "right sorts."

To aid the State of Virginia, Davenport sent Dr. Arthur Eastabrook to testify. After a brief exam of Carrie's daughter, Vivian, he declared her "backward" (she was, in fact, a straight-A student). The head of the colony, Dr. Albert Priddy, testified the entire Buck family was a tangled bush of degenerates badly in need of some pruning. The defense argued that the state had no right to sterilize anyone against their will. In the end the Supreme Court sided with Virginia, allowing the procedure to take place. In his majority statement, Chief Justice Oliver Wendell Holmes Jr. said the state did have the right to perform such operations to protect itself. He argued that if too many mentally handicapped or degenerate people were allowed to breed, they would adversely impact the entire nation.

The *Buck v. Bell* case was a watershed for sterilization in the United States. Almost immediately, states across the Union began passing sterilization laws that resulted in the forced sterilization of tens of thousands of Americans. (In the year 2000, the State of Virginia publicly apologized for its role in the eugenics movement and erected a remembrance of the Buck family in Lynchburg.)

## Romantic Genocide

Eliminating whole groups of people because of their ethnic origins resulted in genocide in Turkey during World War I and in Bosnia and Africa in the 1990s, to name just a few examples. The fight over ethnically superior and inferior evolutionary origins and eugenic concepts had its most notorious moment in Germany. By the latter part of the nineteenth century, the romanticism of philosophers like G. W. Hegel was revived into the new romanticism that was eccentrically mystical. At the same time Ernst Haeckel's conglomeration of nature worship, the occult, and science gave "rational" support to the notion of the "re-creation" of the German Man into a new being in tune with nature. Under Haeckel, the Monist League sought to bring an awareness of the importance of biology and the dangers of racial decline brought on by miscegenation.

As a result, science and the occult began to merge into a hybrid. Germany's political upheavals and economic crises had intellectuals searching for a unifying principle they believed German people lacked. The study of human evolution contributed to that unifying history. Many German intellectuals became obsessed with their supposed Aryan origins. This philosophical trend was partly a result of the German middle class's fear of slipping into the obscurity of lower-class status brought on by economic hardships. Aryan mysticism, the occult, and ideas about man's central-Asian origins all seemed to prop up their social status. They saw themselves as surrounded by degenerates who were trying to destroy them and their culture. The people at the focal point of this worry were the Jews. Scapegoats are necessary for nations in crisis, and the Jews of Europe made the easiest target. Their supposedly inferior evolutionary origins and biology became the hook on which many hung their fears and hatreds.

In this climate pro-German social philosophies flourished. An offshoot of German romanticism that first appeared in the 1870s, the Volkish movement glorified the mystical oneness of the German people, or *Volk*, and sought personal fulfillment through exposure to nature. Volkish proponents rejected Christianity as not addressing the specific concerns of Germans and argued for a cultural soul directly connected to nature in a way unlike other races (especially the Jews). Volkish theory emphasized a natural spirituality that thrived on race-based imagination and creativity and a superior biological origin. The Aryans were believed to have been a race of supermen who evolved in central Asia and then spread out to conquer the world, and the modern Germans were their direct descendants. After Madame Blavatsky's *Secret Doctrine* was translated into German in 1901, it quickly became a blueprint for budding German mystics. Occult evolution is about advancing not only physically but spiritually as well. Progressive levels are attained that lift the initiate above the pale of everyday existence and allow the lower orders to reach a superior position in the cosmos. Spiritual evolutionary struggle was thought to make a better spirit in the same way it was thought that physical evolutionary struggle makes a better organism.

The preoccupation with mysticism in Germany was epitomized in the life of Guido Von List (1848–1919). A third-rate would-be aristocrat, Von List created a mythical history for himself as well as for the German nation in a series of novels. The occult world he created was inspired by German mythology, the music of Richard Wagner, Madame Blavatsky's evolution theory, and occultism, and it was full of mist-shrouded castles, dark foreboding forests, magical powers, and racially superior Aryan *übermenschen.*

In addition to individuals like Von List, groups such as the Germanen Orden and the Thule Society, all of whom ascribed to the Aryan myth and the Asia hypothesis, flourished. This hodgepodge of occult spectacle was adopted by many of the key members of the early Nazi Party as the basis for their new religion. Under Hitler, Nazi ideology embraced a form of Aryan biology. Hitler's close ally Heinrich Himmler constructed the SS, Hitler's personal bodyguard, around the pseudohistory of Aryan evolution as mapped out in the works of Von List and others. Himmler also created a special archaeological unit, the Ahnenerbe (Ancestral Heritage Society), expressly to search for "scientific" proof of his beliefs. He sent expeditions to Tibet, Venezuela, and the Antarctic to search for Atlantis and holy relics to aid the Nazi war machine.

Human evolution and the North Pole had a history the Nazis tapped into. Jean-Sylvain Bailly (1736–1793) argued that the learning of classical Egypt and India were all that was left of an earlier and more advanced civilization that had its origins at the North Pole. In 1779 he linked the North Pole, central Asia, and the Bible by claiming that following Noah's Flood, an advanced civilization moved out of the temperate paradise of the Arctic to the plains of central Asia and then spread out around the world.

Himmler was intrigued by the idea and worked it into his philosophy. The headquarters for this fringe thinking was the imposing Wewelsburg Castle. He took it over and turned it into a Nazi monastery. Within its massive, dank walls, Himmler and Hitler created a fantasy world and dreamed their noxious dreams of Aryan evolution, Holy Grail legends, and world conquest. Although eugenics was popular in the United States, Britain, Sweden, Argentina, and other places around the world in the 1920s and 1930s, it reached its insane extreme under the Nazis. Taking their lead from American eugenicists, the Nazis added the final step—the Final Solution—to the process of how to deal with "undesirables" by putting the Holocaust into operation. Adding industrial, assembly-line thinking to the idea—Henry Ford was one of Hitler's heroes—the Nazis created factories of death in which millions were murdered because of a perceived flaw in their evolution.

*The Aquatic Ape*

A less foreboding alternative human evolution theory, and one of the more successful outsider concepts in the field, was the aquatic-ape theory (AAT) of Elaine Morgan. She argued that following their descent from the trees, human ancestors in Africa went not into a savanna living phase, but into a semiaquatic phase in lakes and rivers. The evidence for this lost moment in our history is in certain aspects of human morphology: bipedalism, hairlessness, fat layers in our skin, and other characteristics. Morgan pointed out that marine mammals, like dolphins, whales, and the walrus, have many of these same characteristics. She also claimed that no other mode of life could possibly account for these things.

Elaine Morgan came of age in the world of 1960s radicalism, where war and violence were being repudiated in favor of a new approach to the world's problems. Women everywhere were stepping out of traditional roles to seek careers, make their voices heard, and take their rightful place within the decision-making apparatus of modern society. It was a liberating time for millions of women, and it left its mark on Morgan. Not a scientist, she became enthralled with a controversial theory put forward by British marine biologist Alistair Hardy (1896–1985), a professor of oceanography at Oxford.

Hardy did extensive studies of plankton and developed techniques for studying and collecting microscopic marine life. In 1960 he presented an academic paper to the British Sub-Aqua Club and later wrote a series of articles for *New Scientist* in which he put forward the idea that some human traits were the result of an aquatic way of life. The idea was not new; in 1942 German scientist Max Westenhöfer proposed essentially the same idea in *The Unique Road to Man.* As Nazi Germany had become a pariah, his ideas generated little interest. Hardy did not advance his work with much energy, as it was so controversial he feared it might have adverse effects on his career.

Morgan came upon the idea through Desmond Morris's popular book, *The Naked Ape* (1967), in which he mentions and then dismisses the idea. Morgan, who had no academic career to protect (she was a television documentary writer in her seventies), was intrigued, adopted Hardy's basic thesis, gave it a feminist spin, and christened it aquatic-ape theory. Her first book, *The Descent of Woman* (1972), played off Darwin's 1873 *The Descent of Man,* which stressed the importance of sexual selection in human evolution. The idea of peaceful females having vital if not leading roles in human development was greatly satisfying to Morgan and her supporters. In her text, Morgan is palpably angry and sarcastic at what she perceives as the trivialization of the role of the female in human evolution. She points out that for more than a century the story of human evolution had been thought of in terms of "he" and "his," not "she" and "hers" or even "theirs." She sniffs that the male-centered view of evolution "not only causes [the scientist] to overlook valuable clues to our ancestry, but sometimes leads him into making statements that are arrogant and demonstrably nonsense" (1972, 3). She shows the classic outsider contempt for academics, saying that "the trouble with specialists is that they tend to think in grooves" (4)—which is, of course, what the specialists said about fringe thinkers.

In 1982 Morgan refined her thesis in *The Aquatic Ape*. She argues that a lack of thick body hair, bipedalism, and other characteristics were the result of an intermediate aquatic stage between the trees and the open plains. The only primates, she says, that exhibit secondary bipedalism are proboscis monkeys, who live in swamps. The other aquatic mammals—dolphins, whales, and walruses—are essentially naked like humans. Her scenario asserts that the arboreal environment suddenly changed about 5 million years ago and pushed populations of primates in the Great Rift Valley into the local waterways for survival. A part of this population somehow survived by adapting to a semiaquatic lifestyle. Having learned to frolic in their African water world, these swimming hominids were then dislocated again when the water dried up about a million years later. This pushed them out onto land to resume their terrestrial evolution. (One critique of AAT is that this is a lot of activity for a fairly short period of time.) The changeover to an aquatic lifestyle was, of course, led by females. Presumably, though Morgan is a little vague on this point, the ex-aquatic now landlubberly apes evolved into *Homo habilis* or *Homo erectus*. Although the aquatic ape theory has some intriguing aspects to it, much of it seems built on the same types of inferences and speculations Morgan and her supporters disparage mainstream paleoanthropology for using.

Morgan set her position in opposition to what was then the popular hunter-killer view of human development. This was done less as an alternative than as an elixir to it. Increasingly, however, mainstream anthropology has questioned the nature of the killer-ape theory in favor of a more subtle and nuanced view of early hominid development. The main sticking point for nonbelievers in AAT is the lack of any concrete evidence in the form of fossils. Morgan counters this by saying that the morphological changes would have occurred in the soft parts of the aquatic hominids: parts like skin and fat that would not fossilize. The theory has been rather briskly debated, and a conference on it was held in 1987 in the Netherlands by the Dutch

Association of Physical Anthropology. The conference resulted in a scholarly anthology of the papers presented there, *The Aquatic Ape: Fact or Fiction?* (1991).

The theory is not completely discounted by members of the mainstream. Some, like respected scientists Glyn Isaac and Philip Tobias, have given grudging respect to some aspects of the argument that seem more difficult to reason away. Saying a theory has intriguing aspects is far from acceptance, however. That mainstream scientists do not accept her work Morgan puts down to male scientist ego and refers to them as Tarzanists. Mary Leakey did not particularly care for the aquatic-ape scenario, and not a few of Morgan's detractors have been female. She says they are sexist in their support for the hunter-killer theory of human development. Men see themselves, she contends, as primordial characters living vicariously through the lives of the ancient humans as heroes providing food and protection for the family while females are relegated to the status of docile sex objects. As an adjunct to the aquatic-ape theory Morgan argues that it was females performing the necessary tasks of child rearing and food preparation who really gave humanity its edge in the evolutionary struggle and that only a woman could understand the importance of child rearing. Although Morgan claims, as many outsider anthropologists do, that her ideas are based on facts, they emphasize the intangible qualities of male ego and motherly instinct. She runs up the standard outsider flag that scientists will not support her because they have careers to protect, and that they know she is right but refuse to admit it. The more the "establishment" scoffed at her idea, the more convinced she was of its validity. Morgan gained a further level of respectability in 1995 when paleontologist and Olduvai Gorge alum Philip Tobias invited her to speak at a conference on human evolution at the University of London (she first encountered the academic community when she gave a presentation at a conference in 1968).

In recent years AAT supporters have developed a new variation on the theme, called aquatic hybrid ape hypothesis (AHAH). This was an attempt to address the criticisms of AAT and turn it into a more scientifically acceptable theory. Melding AAT and the out-of-Africa theory, AHAH argues that although an aquatic phase did take place, it was not a fully aquatic one. The watery hominids lived in lakeshore environments, venturing into the waves less than was originally thought. The theory also claims that *Homo sapiens* are a hybrid of two aquatic-ape variations: one freshwater and one marine. AHAH proponents say this system helps explain certain human characteristics, particularly bipedalism. One point of contention among scientists, for example, is explaining the posture of Lucy and her relatives. Some think she walked essentially like modern people do, whereas another camp thinks she would have moved more like an ape. AHAH says that her odd-seeming stance makes perfect sense if she was spending time in the water. Aquatic-ape theory in its different guises, however, is still being worked out and has yet to reach a form that genuinely challenges orthodoxy.

### Bigfoot and the Anomalous Primates

Elaine Morgan and other AAT supporters were not alone in looking at current conditions to learn about humanity's past. The idea of being able to find a still living human ancestor has given rise to some of the more dramatic aspects of outsider evolution studies. The search for these creatures falls under the category of cryptozoology. This is the study of animals thought to be extinct but that are still alive, as well as mythical creatures that may have actually existed. The classic example of this phenomenon is the coelacanth. Paleontologists thought the coelacanth—a large bony fish up to three feet long—had gone extinct at the same time as the dinosaurs. In the 1930s it was discovered that fishermen on the east coast of Africa had been catching live coelacanths for years. Since then a number of the creatures have been brought up.

The term *cryptozoology* was coined by the French-born Belgian scientist Bernard Heuvelmans (1916–2001). Becoming interested in strange and unusual animals after reading Jules Verne and Arthur Conan Doyle as a youth, Heuvelmans earned a doctorate in zoology and began a writing career. By the late 1940s he was collecting printed references to unusual fossils and unusual animals. He was convinced there were many animals, once thought extinct, still alive around the world. His research led to the publication *Sur la piste des betes ignorees* (1955), better known by its English translation version, *On the Track of Unknown Animals* (1958), in which he laid out the tenets of cryptozoology and his extensive evidence. The book was hugely influential and has been in publication ever since. Heuvelmans then began an extensive correspondence with like-minded scientists and amateurs around the world who were inspired to delve into the subject.

Heuvelmans became involved with the search for the Asian Yeti in the early 1960s. The Yeti is a supposedly anomalous primate that roams the snowy wastes of Tibet. Mountaineer Sir Edmund Hillary had discovered on one of his trips to Mount Everest a "Yeti skull-cap." Yeti hunter Tom Slick put together a team of scientists and naturalists to quietly study the fur hat with an eye toward determining if it was what it was purported to be. Heuvelmans's meticulous examination showed it to be made of the hair of a goat indigenous to the Himalayas.

Heuvelmans's other anomalous primate encounter was with the Minnesota Iceman in 1968, along with friend and fellow crytozoologist Ivan Sanderson (1911–1973). An Edinburgh-born naturalist who, like Heuvelmans, became intrigued by unusual animals at an early age, Sanderson was by the 1950s a well-known author and television personality. His book *Abominable Snowmen: Legend Come to Life* (1961) became a standard text on the subject. His work led him to believe that many "ape man" or "wild man" legends—particularly the Wodewoses of western Europe—had a basis in ancient hominid survivals to the modern era.

The Minnesota Iceman's mysterious and strange story began when a carnival exhibitor named Frank Hansen claimed that he had been approached by the agent of a millionaire who had purchased a frozen hominid in Hong Kong. The creature was sealed in a block of ice and was reputedly discovered floating in the Sea of Japan. The millionaire wanted to exhibit the thing but not have his name associated with it. Hansen agreed and began shuttling the Iceman around county fairs and circuses throughout the American Midwest in 1967. The next year, at the Chicago International Livestock Exposition, a local herpetologist, Terry Cullen, viewed the creature and became obsessed with it. He wanted someone else from the scientific community to look at it and determine what it was (Hansen had billed it as an Ice Age throwback). Cullen contacted Sanderson, who by coincidence had Bernard Heuvelmans visiting him. They were given a private viewing by Hansen at his farm in Minnesota and were astonished by what they saw. The creature appeared to be a hairy, bipedal hominid slightly smaller than a human. It was naked and had its arm pathetically draped over its head as if to ward off an attack. Indeed, it seemed to have some type of head wound. Sanderson and Heuvelmans tried to make as careful an examination as they could but were hampered by the fact that the creature was under several inches of foggy ice. Despite the cramped and awkward conditions, both men were convinced the Iceman was a genuine Neanderthal survival. When they made their findings public, a brief storm of interest swirled around the hapless frozen hominid.

*What former rodeo rider Roger Patterson claimed to be the American version of the Abominable Snowman, October 1967. He said pictures of the creature, estimated at seven and a half feet tall, were taken northeast of Eureka, California. (Bettmann/Corbis)*

Thinking the creature's wound a gunshot through the eye, Heuvelmans speculated that the creature had been killed in the war in Vietnam and clandestinely shipped to the United States, possibly masquerading as a dead GI. Sanderson was able to persuade Smithsonian Institution scientist John Napier to conduct an examination. Upon hearing the gunshot rumor, the Smithsonian contacted the FBI. The bureau's interest did not last long, as it decided that if it was not a true human then no crime had been committed. Hansen then disappeared with the creature before further inquires could be made, turning up later carrying what he claimed was a rubber copy of the Iceman. He eventually said there had never been a "real" Iceman, only a dummy. After that and several other outrageous claims about the creature were made, Napier and then Heuvelmans and Sanderson backed away from the creature, and it slipped into the obscurity of anomalous legend.

The most popular candidate for a living human relative is the Sasquatch of North America, or Bigfoot, as it is commonly known. More than any other anomalous primate, the evidence for Bigfoot is considered convincing by some (though the idea of an eight-foot-tall hairy bipedal hominid roaming the Pacific Northwest without being seen or leaving few signs precludes its existence for many others). Tracks are the most abundant Sasquatch evidence. Numerous oversize tracks (hence the name) have been found, the first discovered in the 1950s by lumbermen. They are found singly and in groups. They are normally twice the size of a human print, in the fourteen-by-six-inch range. A few have shown intriguing morphology. For example, one set had a pair of bumps just behind the big toe. These were interpreted as evidence the creature had broken its foot. A set found in 1982 had detailed skin structures called dermal ridges (a sort of toe fingerprint). These details are used to argue for authenticity, as no hoaxer, it is presumed, could fake or even think to fake such things. There have also been claims of found hair, an audiotape of a Bigfoot howling, and numerous photos.

The most well-known evidence of Bigfoot's existence is the Patterson-Gimlin film. Roger Patterson and Robert Gimlin were Bigfoot enthusiasts on an expedition to search for tracks in northern California in the Six Rivers National Forrest. On October 20, 1967, at Bluff Creek, traveling at a leisurely pace on horseback, the two men came around a corner to an open area surrounding the creek. Patterson's horse reared, throwing him. He quickly recovered, grabbed his camera, and began filming what had so startled his mount. The all too brief and jumpy sixteen-millimeter footage shows a large primate more than seven feet tall and 700 pounds walking erect and dashing off into the woods upon its detection. Supporters hold up the Patterson-Gimlin film as the best possible proof of the creature's existence. For example, some see the creature as a female because of what they perceive to be breasts. Also, the way it walked is said to be "right" for such a creature. If it were simply a man in a rubber suit, supporters argue, it would have looked that way. It is said to be so anatomically correct that a mere hoaxer could not have put it together in such a convincing fashion (the same things were said about Piltdown man). This film forces the issue: either it is a hoax or the real thing; there is no chance of a misidentification.

There is other circumstantial evidence to support the idea that a large unknown primate may lurk and skulk and peep about the trackless expanse of North America. *Gigantopithecus blacki* was a large Pleistocene primate that inhabited parts of Asia. Unlike most fossils that are discovered in the ground, this creature was found in a jar in a Hong Kong drugstore in 1935 by Ralph Von Koenigswald. He knew of the use by Chinese herbalists of "dragon bones" and was always on the lookout for them. What he found was a large primate molar, much larger than any he had ever seen. By comparing the teeth with known fossils mixed in with them, he estimated the creature to have existed roughly 125,000 to 700,000 years ago. He named it for friend and colleague Davidson Black. Analysis of *Gigantopithecus* fossils—which came to include many teeth and four jaws—suggests it ranged from China through Vietnam to India.

Franz Weidenreich thought *Gigantopithecus* showed "characteristic human features" and that although this position was controversial, it would eventually be accepted. He prophesied that *Gigantopithecus* would be admitted by paleoanthropologists to the human line by the year 2000 (1949, 149). It also shared its range with *Homo erectus* and probably lived off the same diet of bamboo. Bigfoot supporters suggest that late populations of *Gigantopithecus* could have migrated from Asia to the Americas across the Bering land bridge, following the routes of other animals and humans to become the Sasquatch of Native American folklore. Unfortunately for this theory, no *Gigantopithecus* fossils have been found in the Americas as of yet.

The problem of Bigfoot is that, like so many fringe ideas, there is little evidence for it that is accepted by the mainstream. One of the few mainstream scientists to disagree with that assertion was anthropologist Grover Krantz (1931–2002) of Washington State University. Krantz was an outspoken supporter of the existence of Bigfoot. He outraged many by publicly stating that the best thing to happen would be for someone to shoot a Bigfoot and bring the carcass in for study. Krantz was a traditionally trained academic holding a post at a prestigious university who wrote a series of books and papers on Bigfoot as well as other aspects of human evolution and did careful studies of numerous Bigfoot tracks. He did not shy away from the spotlight; indeed, he was a common sight on television programs on the subject. He was annoyed that so many of his colleagues dismissed Bigfoot. He remarked that when he would hand one of them a Sasquatch track cast to examine, they would hand it back quickly as if trying to avoid catching some malady by simply touching it. His analysis of the Patterson-Gimlin film led him to argue that the gait the creature exhibits could not be performed by anything other than a seven-foot-tall, 700-pound creature. He often demonstrated that a human could not approximate the bent-kneed walk the creature uses in the film. Also, he pointed out that in the film the creature turns to look at the camera. When humans look behind themselves they tend to turn their heads only. This is possible because a human's chin is above the level of the shoulder. When a gorilla wants to look behind itself, it must turn its entire upper body. This is because the gorilla's chin is below its shoulder. When the creature in the Patterson film turns, it does so with its entire upper body in a way a gorilla would.

Krantz's last project was examining, along with several other naturalists, an artifact known as the Skookum Cast. This object was the product of an expedition mounted by the Bigfoot Field Research Organization (a group of enthusiastic amateurs). In September 2000 the group spent several days in Gifford Pinchot National Forest in Washington placing pheromone-soaked lures in the woods in the hopes of attracting a Bigfoot. Pheromones are agents given off by animals when they are trying to attract a mate. At some point during the second night, they claim, a Bigfoot was drawn to one of the lures and sat down in the mud to investigate it. This left a large imprint in the mud that the searchers quickly made a cast of. Krantz saw prints of a forearm, hip, thigh, and heel. He was joined in his examination by Jeff Meldrum, an anthropologist from Idaho State University; Canadian biologist John Bindernagel; and others. In addition to the impression, hair was found that defied identification with known animals. Jane Goodall, the legendary primatologist who spent years in Africa living with a group of apes in order to study them, though not totally convinced, thinks enough evidence exists to warrant a study by mainstream science to determine whether Bigfoot really exists. University of Iowa paleoanthropologist Russell Ciochon, who did pioneering work on *Gigantopithecus,* finds it all difficult to believe, however. In the end, Grover Krantz may have been right in saying the only way to clear up the mystery of Bigfoot would be to catch or kill one—something Sasquatch researchers hope will not happen. Until then, Bigfoot will remain hidden.

## Hidden History

Much outsider thinking on human evolution contains an element of what can be called hidden history theory. This is the idea that there is a vast unknown storehouse of knowledge that has been forgotten or suppressed. This takes the conversation on human evolution even further into folklore, mythology, and the ever continuing epistemological battle over how knowledge is gathered, held, and transmitted. Hidden history is allied with romantic notions of the past as a fantasy more attractive than the reality of the present: the concept of the golden age. Golden age theories almost always include not only a physical decline but also a loss of precious knowledge that only the purity of a return to past conditions would allow. Talk of lost knowledge and hidden histories is juxtaposed against contempt for the modern industrial world with its loss of spirituality and prevalence of corrupt Western decadence. Hidden knowledge remains hidden, not only because of its great age but also because of modern forces that work to actively keep it hidden. These nefarious forces want to keep this information out of the hands of those who would bring it to the masses or use it for their own purposes. It is also hidden because its acknowledgment would undermine accepted modes of thought.

Part of the hidden knowledge concept is the collecting of empirical evidence that supports the "lost" wisdom and contradicts mainstream thinking. It is commonly held that the mainstream is aware of the existence of contradictory data but ignores them or keeps them suppressed. Possibly the greatest collector of such data was Charles Hoy Fort (1874–1932). A sort of thinking man's Robert Ripley, Fort spent most of his life gathering and pondering what he called "damned" knowledge. He looked for evidence of experiences that did not fit contemporary scientific and intellectual paradigms and as such had been discarded, or damned, by science. He ransacked the world's newspapers at the New York Public Library and the British Museum for accounts of strange phenomena, artifact discoveries, and other anomalous flotsam and jetsam of the human experience. He collected accounts of frogs and fish falling from the sky, strange lights seen at night, ghostly encounters, unaccountable fossils, odd coincidences, strange disappearances, and mysterious visions. Taken in the aggregate, Fort believed such reports constituted an alternative body of data not easily waved off by mainstream thinking. He believed that if enough evidence existed for a thing to be, regardless of how strange it sounded, then it must at least be considered possible. He dismissed explanations based on faith alone, even from scientists. Fort argued that much of what was called science was a constructed way of looking at the cosmos that often bore little relationship to facts. For him, modes of analysis and theoretical frameworks came and went, but facts always remained to challenge explanation. In *The Book of the Damned* (1919), *New Lands* (1923), *Lo!* (1931), and *Wild Talents* (1932), he marshaled textural evidence that things were happening in the world that science had no explanation for. Fort's work gained a cult following in the latter part of the twentieth century as a new generation in both the fringe and mainstream reexamined his philosophy of the importance of strange phenomena in understanding the universe.

Like Fort, William Corliss collected newspaper and journal accounts of anomalous artifacts and other paradigm-bending information that contradicted accepted scientific wisdom. Although his interests were wide ranging, he published a series of books on material related to human evolution. In *Ancient Man: A Handbook of Puzzling Artifacts* (1978), he reproduced a brace of articles about human footprints found where they had no right to be. There are examples of footprints and even shoe prints in limestone, sandstone, and rock older than humans are thought to have existed. Although he accepts that this evidence is rarely found, "down the years, though, a few apparently human traces have been discovered deeper, in rocks millions of years old—far older than current anthropological theory allows" (636).

One interesting entry came from the *American Journal of Science* in 1822. Henry R. Schoolcraft, a well-known anthropologist of the day, discussed a pair of human footprints found in a limestone deposit in St. Louis. He reported clear heel and toe prints in the solid rock. Similar reports are found in *Scientific American* (1882), *American Antiquity* (1957), and *Archaeology* (1973). Another intriguing report came from Edward Drinker Cope (1840–1897) in *American Naturalist* (1883). Cope was one of the more important and respected paleontologists of nineteenth-century America. He personally discovered an entire array of dinosaurs and did pioneering work in American prehistory from his base in Philadelphia. Cope referred to an artifact discovered during excavations for the Nevada State Prison. A sandstone trackway of footprints was found containing various mammals from the Pliocene era (5–1.8 million years ago). Along with the horse tracks were ones that, Cope believed, were "clearly those of a biped" (Corliss 1978, 645). Though he would not say it was a set of modern human prints, he thought it was from some kind of human ancestor. Standard wisdom says our earliest ancestors appeared during this period in Africa, but this is millions of years before modern humans entered the Americas. As such these prints were out of time and place. Corliss balances Cope's remarks with a set from an anonymous correspondent in *Nature* of the same year. This reviewer analyzed the same material and said they were not human prints at all but misidentified mammal prints. There are numerous reports like Cope's of human presence in odd places and times. The nineteenth-century versions tend toward the vague. Those from the 1960s and 1970s come mostly from Christian creationist sources and rarely have photographic evidence to support them.

Another collection of anomalous material put forward as proof that paleoanthropology has it all wrong comes from the unlikely source of the Hare Krishna religious sect. Michael Cremo and Richard Thompson are a pair of Hindu creationists based in San Diego. Their controversial nonape ancestry theory argues that modern humans are as much as 55 million years old. According to their theory, humans appeared well before the advent of the other primates. As followers of Krishna Consciousness, Cremo and Thompson claimed that the hidden history of human evolution was written in Indian Vedic literature and mythology. They rolled out many classic "proofs" like footprints in limestone, modern hammers and tools embedded in rock, and other nineteenth-century accounts of odd discoveries, accounts that are unreliable because of the primitive way they were made and documented.

Cremo and Thompson's book, *The Hidden History of the Human Race* (1994), has been criticized for a common anomalist pitfall: they tend to give the same level of scientific trustworthiness to mid-nineteenth-century reports from newspapers as to those done in late-twentieth-century refereed technical journals. They also tend to focus on specific finds without seeing them in wider context. One of the reasons it takes so long to earn a doctorate in science or history is because the student must learn a wide range of information so that individual facts can be seen as part of a larger picture. This larger picture gives a better analysis of a theory, phenomenon, or historical event.

Cremo and Thompson also do not seem to understand the fluid and changing nature of science. Just because a prominent scientist said something twenty years ago does not mean that assertion is accepted today. They filled their work with quotes from famous paleoanthropologists of the past who said things that were accepted at the time but are not now. Their knowledge of the political motivations of historical scientific personages is weak. For example, they quote Henry Fairfield Osborn on stone tools and modern humans appearing very early in geologic history. They accept his words at face value as if he said them in some sort of state of grace in which obfuscation, overeagerness, or lack of knowledge was nonexistent. Historians today know that he had a bundle of political agendas when it came to human origins data. Osborn often skewed his work to support his idea of humans being very ancient. Modern scientists, however, are portrayed as inherently evil liars, cheats, and destroyers of knowledge. In the introduction Cremo and Thompson boldly assert that "once a discovery is made, key elements of the evidence are destroyed, and knowledge of these elements depends solely on the testimony of the discoverers" (1994, 8). At this rate neither side may be able to accept the work of the other. Some have held all this anomalous evidence up as a sign that existence itself is in danger of disintegrating forever and that humans are on the fast track to nowhere.

## Devolution

The universe is falling apart. We humans are turning atrophied and degenerate and stupid and are on the verge of total breakdown. That is the basic tenet of devolution: things are not spiraling upward to glory but downward to an abyss. What young person has not heard an older person speak of "the good old days"? The longing for the perceived greatness of the past over the degeneracy and breakdown of the present is a story as old as humans themselves. The Greeks looked to their ancestors for historical greatness. They saw the past as a golden age of heroes, gods, and Titans. Thinking in terms of a fall from grace, Christians too saw the past as a golden age with modern man racing headlong to decline. The Garden of Eden story is an archetype of devolution: because of various transgressions (worst of all the search for knowledge), Adam and Eve are banished from the garden to grow old and infirm and finally to die. For Christians the past was light and beauty, whereas the present is dark, dreary, and fit only to end in an apocalyptic cataclysm that will cleanse the world and restore our sublime existence. As folklorist Donna Kossy points out in her work on what she calls "kook" literature, the line of thinking devolution comes from is that of a spiritual discontent or emptiness. It stems from a desire to shed the cold, dark, uncertain present for the warm glow of a romantic past or the hope of a brighter future once the period of degeneration is over and rebirth occurs.

Devolution is usually brought on by some type of adherent behavior, as in Oscar Kiss Maerth's *The Beginning Was the End* (1970). Originally published in German, this work drew little attention until it was translated into English. Maerth argued that although humans did evolve, at some point early hominids took up eating the brains of their primate cousins. This increased the intelligence of the protohumans and pushed them faster along the line of evolutionary development. Traits such as hairlessness, bipedalism, and a big brain came about because of this peculiar eating habit. Whereas Elaine Morgan said these traits were the result of an aquatic lifestyle, Maerth claimed they came from cannibalism. Although humans may have gained certain advantages from brain eating, they lost the lofty position of moral and physical superiority they had prior to cannibalism. Their higher intelligence was offset by the loss of the extrasensory perception, better known as ESP, they had as protohumans (in much the same way Adam and Eve lost the ability to talk to animals after being expelled from the garden). The technological world made possible by their greater intelligence and increased humanity doomed them to lose their humanity.

Maerth's ideas never caught on, but he did inspire a group of American art students to express their views on the human condition. Shortly after *The Beginning Was the End* was released it was discovered by some college friends from Kent State University. They had been discussing where art could go in the future and were questioning how Western society might be mismanaging the world. They had experienced the Kent State massacre of students who were protesting the Vietnam War on campus by Ohio National Guardsmen. They found Oscar Kiss Maerth's ideas fantastic but intriguing. They happily used the devolution concept to satirize musical, artistic, and cultural conventions. With their tongues planted firmly in their cheeks, they founded a musical group that took the name Devo and went on to create some of the most innovative pop music and videos of the 1980s.

Devolution is an underlying element of much religious funda-mentalism. It has a central but unarticulated role in the work of bibli-cal creationist and New Jersey dentist Jack Cuozzo. His 1998 *Buried Alive* tells of his research into Neanderthal dentition and the startling discovery that the Neanderthals are really the long-lived but recent denizens of the Old Testament. Humans, according to Cuozzo, are getting weaker, are living shorter lives, and are less able to survive their environment. Adhering to many of the unwritten protocols of hidden history, he claims the scientific "establishment" is trying to keep this information secret. Subtitled with great pathos *Hidden, Suf-focating from the Pain of a Story Left Untold . . . ,* the book is part science text, part adventure novel, part religious sermon (though it never ex-plains just who is buried alive or why the Neanderthals would suffer from the pain of a supposedly untold story).

Cuozzo based his thesis upon a survey of Neanderthal teeth in various museum collections. Though he claims that the forces of evo-lution were determined to stop him from studying the material, in the introduction he thanks many scientists and museum people for graciously granting him access to their prized specimens. (Appar-ently, the left hand of the conspiracy did not know what the right hand was doing.) He believes a dental expert could see things in the fossil teeth others had missed. He argues that "no person with a cre-ationist world view . . . has ever penetrated behind the evolutionist's lines to study their fossils with X-Ray equipment" (1999, 79).

Cuozzo is convinced that the Neanderthals were not ancient hu-mans but recent people from the historic past. They were unique in that they had physiques and longevity far in excess of what humans have today. They were impervious to many of the medical ills that plague modern humans, including radiation poisoning. He found that Neanderthal teeth were exactly like those of modern humans. This shows that modern people are not evolutionary advances over earlier Neanderthal physiology but the results of devolution and degenera-tion from the ancient ideal. The Bible speaks of people who matured slowly and lived for hundreds of years. Cuozzo believes the Nean-derthals are these people. In essence, Cuozzo argues that Neanderthal anatomy proves the Bible correct. Having appeared just after Noah's Flood, the Neanderthals lived their long lives, in some cases as long as 400 years, but eventually began to degenerate as the Bible says they did. Modern people, on the other hand, had lost all those advantages the Neanderthals had acquired from God and were continuing to run down by the process of devolution.

In addition to the dental evidence showing the modernity of the Neanderthals, Cuozzo points to other anomalous evidence. He takes the skull of a Neanderthal commonly called Rhodesia man as a case in point. Found in the early part of the century in Zambia, Rhodesia man—also known as the Broken Hill Skull—contains a hole that anthropologists have puzzled over. Most think it the scar of an abscess or lesion the individual suffered from in life. Others have asked whether it was the result of trepanning, which was a practice known to have been performed by early historic people. Trepanning involved cutting holes, using stone tools, into the skulls of patients suffering from various brain disorders. There are many examples of these successful early brain operations. Cuozzo waves off all these explanations, claiming that the skull of this supposed ancient human ancestor was pierced by something else entirely. To Cuozzo the wound looks "as if it had been made by a high velocity projectile, a bullet" (70). Thus, this individual lived hundreds of years only to be ignominiously dispatched by a shot through the head just like the Minnesota Iceman.

Cuozzo believes God himself was guiding him on his mission and was, through his diligent efforts, thwarting the work of the scientific establishment. His proof is that he was being chased by evolution's dark agents. At one point during their Parisian adventure he and his family stopped in at a pizza parlor to catch their breaths. Looking around, Cuozzo was horrified to see a man who had been following them munching a few tables away. He scooped up his family and raced wildly back to their apartment through the rainy Parisian night and barricaded the door. Somehow they managed to make it safely back to the United States with themselves and their evidence intact.

Cuozzo's efforts had the desired effect, for he had forced a bleat from the behemoth of evolution science. He claims that the well-known evolutionist Christopher Stringer was intrigued and worried by his work. Cuozzo had contacted Stringer with the results of his work in 1986 and jolted him out of his arrogant complacency. According to Cuozzo, Stringer was so taken by his data that he "rushed into publication by the threat of my results" (75). According to Cuozzo, Stringer and his coauthors argued that tooth-eruption rates for Neanderthals were the same as for modern humans. Cuozzo argues that slower than modern tooth-eruption rates were an indication that Neanderthals matured slowly and lived longer than modern people. He is convinced that Stringer was covering himself, and evolution science, by preempting Cuozzo's work. The dentist feels the entire weight of the evolution conspiracy being laid upon him. Like a true missionary, Cuozzo will not be deterred from his sacred task, despite the efforts of the establishment to keep him from publishing his book reinforcing a belief in a supernatural God. According to some, there are otherworldly agents involved in evolution but not always God.

## Space Brothers

The alien intervention theory may be the logical extreme of the difficult ancestry concept. The search for ancestors among the stars has something for everyone: it fits well into the devolution idea, the golden age, and hidden history. It argues that we humans were given great gifts as the children of the stars but as usual squandered them all and must now wait like Wally and the Beaver for our cosmic parents to come home and set us straight. Snarling apelike ancestors grubbing in the mud are replaced by "intellects vast and cool" from a far star.

Some researchers see alien visitations throughout history. They cite legends of gods, beings of light and similar occurrences in mythology, and Holy Scripture from cultures worldwide to show this has been happening for some time and is not some recent delusion. Everything from Ezekiel's wheel of the Bible to the Bimana of Vedic scripture has been held up as evidence of early visitations. Believers also point to pictorial representations of alien beings from cave art to the medieval period.

Regardless of whether those are actual historical moments, the modern unidentified flying object (UFO) era began June 24, 1947, when American businessman Kenneth Arnold saw a crescent-shaped craft near Mount Rainier, Washington. Flying a small private plane, he watched in amazement as a formation of silvery objects flew by at great speed in a way he said resembled a saucer skipping across water. Hearing Arnold's description, a local newspaper man coined the term *flying saucer*. Suddenly people around the world were seeing all sorts of strange things in the sky and speculating as to what they were. Although early reports concerned objects alone, discussions of who might be inside those objects began in earnest when Polish immigrant George Adamski (1891–1965) claimed he had been taken aboard such a craft.

Adamski was an eccentric amateur philosopher who studied Eastern mysticism and the occult and alternately referred to himself as *professor* and *doctor*. In 1952 he went into the Mojave Desert of California with some friends to look for UFOs. They were greatly rewarded when a disk appeared and Adamski was invited aboard. Inside he met the ship's captain, Orthon, who said he was from Venus. The aliens were unusually attractive humanoids who apparently bestowed certain favors upon the bewildered but grateful earthling. In *Flying Saucers Have Landed* (1953) and *Inside the Flying Saucers* (1955), Adamski told of his wondrous adventures with the aliens. It was an optimistic tale full of galactic bonhomie and wise beings ready to help humans take the next step in their evolution. His books were a mix of fanciful make-believe, light philosophy, and giddy delusion that, as a package, were rather endearing in their naïveté. He gathered a large following of those eager to become "contactees" as he had been and became something of a guru. Adamski has been alternately praised as a man who changed the world for the better by his contacts with aliens and denounced as a misguided charlatan who made belief in UFOs ridiculous, scaring off the scientific community, which could have solved the mystery.

The contactee movement, with its air of hopeful possibility, soon took on a darker aspect. By the 1960s, particularly after the Betty and Barney Hill case, contactees became abductees. Gone were the days of benevolent humanoids in silvery jumpsuits giving lucky humans joyrides in their saucers. Now truly "alien" creatures were snatching up helpless humans in order to perform unspeakable cruelties upon them.

Within the UFO community there was always talk that the aliens were somehow related to us. The space brother concept argues that in the distant past, beings from another world came to Earth and began the human race. This was done in one of several ways: the space beings landed here and liked it so much they stayed; they came here as "astral beings"—creatures with only spiritual form; or they arrived and somehow mated with early hominids to produce *Homo sapiens*. The result of any of these scenarios is that we are the progeny of the stars.

A number of groups appeared in the 1950s that capitalized on this idea. The Unarians began in California when an alien entity called Uriel came to San Diego in the guise of the grandmotherly medium Ruth Norman. Through Norman, Uriel claimed to be a representative of a galactic federation of planets that would approach Earth officially in 2001. Uriel claimed that he and his colleagues originally came to Earth in humanity's early days and instructed the cavemen in how to behave and took them in their ships.

Dana Redfield, in *The ET-Human Link: We Are the Message* (2001), written with Jenny Randles, claimed to be an abductee whose personal experience at the hands of aliens gave her a special insight into our alien origins. Along with our physical selves, Redfield saw the origins of our consciousness among the stars. She mixed in all the paranormal favorites of hidden history: Atlantis, flying saucers, government involvement, and even the American Indians. A lapsed Mormon with a series of broken relationships behind her, she wanted everyone to know that we are all human-alien hybrids and that humans as a species are about to go through a major period of change because of this connection. "Golden children" will appear and show us how to get back to proper thinking about the need to love one another and look after all the creatures of Earth. It is an upbeat mix of Judeo-Christian ethics and nature worship common in these types of works.

Amorah Quan Yin also believed she was an alien. She considered herself a "Pliadian" Emissary of Light who entered her existence through "the birthing canal of earth" (Yin 1996, 3). She and her fellows are on a mission to show the rest of us we are astral beings. At the heart of her teachings is the notion that humans are the result of an evolutionary process begun on Venus and Maldek (the supposed planet that exploded to become the asteroid belt between Mars and Jupiter). "Astral" beings from these planets traveled to Earth to join with the already present early human population. These new beings (she is never clear whether these are *Homo sapiens* or some other hominid form) were primitive in their behavior but soon evolved higher function. Not all was paradise, however, as infighting, eugenic struggles, and racial prejudice were soon rampant. These problems were eventually worked out, and bliss reigned. Over the years the new humans forgot their antecedents and slipped out of their perfect forms to be the version of humans around today. The Emissaries of Light are ones who remember and who work to get the rest of us do likewise.

Another example of an alien entity taking over a human and channeling good news about human evolution from beyond was Rael. The Raelian movement began in December 1973 when a French auto-racing journalist, Claude Vorilhon, was contacted by aliens who told him he was to be the "embassy" between them and Earth. He changed his name to Rael and started preaching. His following has become a rather large, sophisticated UFO cult with pretensions to philosophy and claims to have 50,000 members. Rael claims the aliens told him that humans were not the result of typical biological evolution, or divine intervention, but DNA experimentation on the part of aliens. The aliens were known as Elohim (the Elohim of the Bible, Vorilhon claims, are the result of half-remembered knowledge of the aliens, not Old Testament characters). After the human-alien clones began to grow and prosper, the Elohim departed, allowing their experiment to flourish on its own. They are now preparing to return for a family reunion and make us all feel very special.

The desire to rejoin our alien parents led to the mass suicide of the Heaven's Gate group in 2000. Lost souls searching for answers to the mysteries of life, Heaven's Gate members took on celibacy and other ritual behavior in order to prepare themselves to meet the space brothers they believed were in a ship trailing the Hale-Bopp comet then approaching Jupiter. The group's members happily launched themselves up to the mother ship by committing suicide.

In an effort to help along our genetically altered evolution and union with aliens, Rael and his followers formed CLONAID in 1997. This organization would develop the necessary technical know-how to clone humans as an ill-defined way to get closer to our cosmic parents. The scientist in charge of CLONAID is French biologist Brigitte Boissilier (also a "bishop" in the Raelian church). They planned to offer cloning services to couples so that, according to their Web site literature, "cloning will enable mankind to reach eternal life." Setting up their laboratory facilities in a secret location, the Raelian "scientists" began their work and in 2002 announced with great fanfare the first cloned human. The scientific world met these pronouncements with a fair amount of skepticism and asked for proof of such a feat, one that mainstream geneticists say is still many years off. The Raelians countered that in the interest of the baby and its family's privacy, no such detailed information would be forthcoming. With that, the mainstream dismissed the Raelian news as publicity-seeking nonsense. As of this writing the Raelians have provided no proof that they have cloned anything, let alone a human. Evidence of the existence of the space brothers remains just as elusive.

*Conclusion*

What do these fringe theories tell us about human evolution? They may not say anything tangible about our origins, but they illuminate a deep need to explain what those origins are. This entire book is one long discussion, not so much about evolution itself but about how humans react to it. When Louis Leakey or Donald Johanson looked for evidence of human evolution, they unconsciously did so for some of the same reasons Elaine Morgan, Oscar Kiss Maerth, and Jack Cuozzo did. They followed, or were drawn to, the most basic human desire to know from whence we came. Although the fringe thinkers cannot be ranked with Leakey or Johanson on the same level of scientific acumen, intellectual respectability, theoretical plausibility, or even simple logic, they were looking for the answers to our origins. Fringe thinkers never had more than limited success in promulgating their ideas—some were never accepted by anyone other than those who thought them up. They represent the extreme lengths the human mind can go to in order to explain our difficult ancestry and how questions of who we are and where we come from cross all human boundaries.

## Further Reading

A good introduction to fringe thought on human evolution is Donna Kossy's *Strange Creations: Aberrant Ideas of Human Origins from Ancient Astronauts to Aquatic Apes* (2001). For eugenics, see Daniel J. Kevles, *In the Name of Eugenics* (1985), and Diane B. Paul, *Controlling Human Heredity: 1865 to the Present* (1995). For evolution and German ideology, see Nicholas Goodrick-Clarke, *The Occult Roots of Nazism* (1992), and George Mosse, *The Crisis of German Ideology* (1964). For the complex and little-discussed history of the North Pole and its role in human origin theories, see Jocelyn Godwin, *Arktos: The Polar Myth in Science, Symbolism, and Nazi Survival* (1996). For the aquatic-ape theory, see Elaine Morgan, *The Descent of Woman* (1972) and *The Scars of Evolution* (1990). On Bigfoot, see Grover Krantz, *Bigfoot Sasquatch Evidence* (1999). For *Gigantopithecus,* see Russell Ciochon, Dolores Piperno, and Robert Thompson, "*Gigantopithecus blacki:* Implications for Paleodietary Studies" (1990); and Ciochon, John Olsen, and Jamie James, *Other Origins: The Search for the Giant Ape in Human Prehistory* (1990). For the Space Brothers, see Donna Kossy's *Kooks* (1994).

# 9

# *A Question of Relations*

long with where fossils were found, what species they were, and how old they were, one of the issues that paleoanthropologists had to address in understanding human evolution was how the various fossils related to one another: Who descended from whom, who was a dead-end, and who was or was not a human ancestor? Actually finding hominid fossils—something akin to finding a needle in a haystack—was only the first step. Once the fossil was found, it would be carefully cleaned and repaired if possible and then carefully examined. From the early days of paleoanthropology it was widely believed that the sequence of human development ran in a linear fashion from oldest to youngest and simplest to most complex. As researchers came to grips with the apparent diversity of the hominid fossil record, they began to realize that human evolution was far more complex than originally thought. As a result, more complex theories began to appear to explain it.

Within the overall study of human evolution in the latter part of the twentieth century, increasing interest was being focused on the moment when archaic humans became modern. Early ideas about the appearance of modern people had the Neanderthals as central players with two strains of thought as to what to do with them. One side argued the Neanderthals were a closely related but essentially different group that formed as an offshoot to the main human line that eventually died off, leaving no modern relatives. In this view they were not in the direct line of our evolution but a curious lost set of cousins. The other side argued that the Neanderthals played a direct role in our own evolution and contributed much to what makes us what we are today.

Early supporters of the Neanderthal phase of human evolution, particularly Aleš Hrdlička and Franz Weidenreich, based their position on European Neanderthal and Asian *Homo erectus* fossils. In 1943

Weidenreich, who was involved with Peking man and had done extensive research into the hominids of Asia, formulated an idea that the modern races were a result of several different hominid groups in divergent parts of the world transforming into modern humans separately. His study of Asian fossils led him to believe that there was no one place humans had appeared. Instead, "there must have been several centers more or less independent of each other" (1949, 152). He believed Neanderthals in Europe evolved into Caucasians, *Homo erectus* in Asia into Asians and Australians, and hominids in Africa into Africans. In other words, all modern human races were local variations but were still all the same species. If scientists accepted that different types of modern people evolved in different places at different rates at different times, he said, all the problems of understanding human evolution would disappear.

Weidenreich's idea proved intriguing to American Carleton Coon (1904–1981). A Harvard-trained anthropologist, Coon specialized in the study of human racial differentiation. He believed race was biologically based and expounded on this position in *Origin of the Races* (1962). He began this project as an attempt to rewrite William Zebina Ripley's *Races of Europe* (1899). It was Ripley who helped introduce the concept of multiple versions of Caucasians—Nordic, Alpine, and Mediterranean—into racial anthropology and so influenced eugenicists like Madison Grant.

In the early stages of the project Coon decided to write an entirely new book that would explain the concept of regional continuity, an idea that supported Ripley's categorization of the races as inherently different. He agreed with Weidenreich that some modern people appeared before the first *Homo sapiens*. Coon felt such a debt to him that he dedicated the book to Weidenreich. In the introduction he stated that "each major race had followed a pathway of its own through the labyrinth of time. Each had been molded in a different fashion to meet the needs of different environments and each had reached its own level on the evolutionary scale"(1962, vii). Using language and lifestyle as markers, Coon reasoned cultural achievement was linked to evolutionary advance, noting that Australian Aborigines still lived lifestyles Europeans had given up a hundred thousand years before. It was this sort of evidence that Coon said proved the two groups diverged in the Pleistocene age. In Coon's mind these differences were accounted for by the fact that not all the races evolved at the same rate. African and Aboriginal populations evolved much later than Caucasians; hence their relatively primitive culture. The Africans had yet to catch up to Europeans on a cultural level because they started down the evolutionary path later. To some this sounded as if it were an attempt to formulate a scientific justification for calling non-whites inferior.

## The Multiregional Hypothesis and Eve

The changeover to modern *Homo sapiens* indistinguishable from people today has been called the "quiet revolution" by British paleoanthropologist Christopher Stringer of the Natural History Museum of London. As he saw it, part of the debate over human evolution was whether it was the result of a single local population or of several lineages combining their characteristics to produce modern people in several locations. In other words, do humans have one point of origin or many? He believed there was only one point of origin for all modern people. To this end Stringer created the out-of-Africa hypothesis that argued that a population of humans first appeared in Africa and radiated out around the world in a single wave, replacing any hominids that had preceded them (William Howells of Harvard originally called this the "Noah's Ark" hypothesis, though he did not mean for the connection to the biblical character to be taken seriously). In the 1980s two strains of thought came to dominate the discussion.

Population replacement, as Stringer's out-of-Africa scenario was also known, had the support of an allied theory known as the Eve hypothesis. Traditionally, human evolution theories were based on fossils. The late Allan Wilson (1934–1991), his then student Rebecca Cann, and Mark Stoneking turned to genetic evidence taken from living populations to work out human ancestry. Their groundbreaking work first appeared as a 1987 *Nature* article titled "Mitochondrial DNA and Human Evolution." Their argument was that modern people could be traced back to a relatively small group of females in Africa about 200,000 years ago. Moderns evolved from this group, then left Africa to populate the world. They claimed fossils alone were inadequate for determining species relationships and that it was genetics that would give the most information on the course of human evolution. Genetic data, they claimed, were "a set of characteristics that is complete and objective" (68). Wilson was a pioneer in the genetic research into human evolution. Born in New Zealand and educated at the University of California at Berkeley, Wilson introduced the idea of the molecular clock and extended genetic research into the realm of fossil species.

The turn toward genetics to solve questions of human evolution was in itself a revolution. A key case used to support the efficacy of the genetic approach was that of *Ramapithecus*. Paleontologists claimed this primate fossil, originally discovered in India in the 1930s, was crucial because it appeared just after the archaic primate line split to go on to be the modern primates on one hand and hominids on the other. Paleontologists dated *Ramapithecus*, known from only a few jaw and tooth fragments, to about 25 million years ago, making it important for understanding the earliest moments of human evolution.

In 1967 Wilson and student Vincent Sarich began comparing human and chimpanzee blood proteins. They understood that the number of genetic mutations in two related groups gave an idea of how long it had been since the two lines diverged. Both groups would have many mutations in common but also a number of mutations that had appeared in each respective group after they separated. The greater the number of different mutations in the two groups, the longer they have been separated. These genetic differences gave paleontologists a kind of "molecular clock" with which to date fossils. Wilson and Sarich's work showed the primate-human split had occurred only 5 million years ago—far too recently for *Ramapithecus* to have been a human ancestor and subsequently making it less important than was thought. Later fossil discoveries in the 1970s confirmed the genetic findings that *Ramapithecus* was not a human ancestor but was in fact a member of *Sivipithecus,* a species related to the orangutans and only 12 million years old or so.

Geneticists argued that molecular evolution was the result of mutations that accrued in a genus (a collection of related species) at a steady rate. It was mitochondrial DNA that gave the best results, they said, as it came from the maternal line only, it was easier to read because it was not in the form of a double helix, and the mutations formed faster. Cann and others said that all human mtDNA came from a tiny population of females. They were quick to point out that even though many refer to this idea as the "Eve" hypothesis, there was no one individual responsible for all later humans. Genetic research supports the idea that all modern people sprang from the same original population. Every time Cann and her colleagues attempted to construct a human family tree based on their data, it always led back to Africa. They used different populations of modern people from Papua New Guineans to Asians to African Americans as subjects. Always the trail stopped in Africa. Because of this they felt confident that Africa was the point of origin for human mitochondrial DNA.

After Gregor Mendel's initially unacknowledged work on pea plants, modern genetics took off in late-nineteenth-century Germany aided by advances in microscope design and the chemistry of textile dyes. Better microscopes allowed scientists to see deep inside cells. Unfortunately, there did not seem much to look at. Cells appeared to be empty. This made no sense, as researchers knew by inference that a great deal had to be going on inside a cell. By staining the interior of a cell with chemical dye it was seen that cells were indeed full of structures and activity. Cells were packed with long strands of material that were dubbed chromosomes (colored bodies) that reproduced themselves to make new cells. The work of German cytologist August Weismann and others in the 1880s helped establish the link between chromosomes and heredity and that there were two kinds of cells in the human body—somatic (body) cells and reproductive cells—and that it was the reproductive cells only that accounted for the passing on of hereditary material.

By the early part of the twentieth century some of the mechanics of heredity had been worked out, but it was not until decades later that the structure of chromosomes was discovered. In 1953 a pair of British scientists, James Watson and Francis Crick, made the breakthrough. Using the technique developed by their associate Rosiland Franklin (1920–1958) of bombarding strands of genetic material called DNA with X rays, Watson and Crick were able to build a model of the pattern they found. Most people thought DNA too simple a structure to be responsible for heredity; they pointed to the more complex protein structure of a cell as the likely candidate. Watson and Crick eventually worked out the structure of DNA as the famous double helix and discovered that it was the source of human genetic makeup. DNA carried all the information necessary to make up an individual organism and multiplied by stripping itself in half, creating two identical pairs. From here on genetics would play an increasing role in the study of human evolution.

The main opposition to Eve and population replacement was Alan Thorne and Milford Wolpoff, who developed the multiregional hypothesis. Wolpoff, of the University of Michigan, based his work on an exhaustive firsthand study of most of the human fossil material then known. He and Thorne, along with their Chinese colleague Wu Xin Zhi, argued that modern humans with their ethnic differences were the result of local evolution and interbreeding between different groups of hominids. Around 1.5 to 1.8 million years ago various modern and near modern hominids left Africa and fanned out over the planet. These groups—versions of the Neanderthals and *Homo erectus*—then evolved into modern *Homo sapiens* as a result of local climatic conditions as well as interbreeding. This would have mixed genetic material (a process known as gene flow) from diverse groups to form a final version. Modern Caucasians, Africans, Asians, and others evolved in the places they are traditionally linked to in modern times, with all of them one large species made up of many closely related subgroups. There was no replacement of one group by another, only a continuous series of linked evolutions and subtle transformations. So while the basic early hominid stocks formed in Africa, it was not until after they spread across Africa, Asia, and Europe that they came back together to form modern humans. They contended that archaic African populations did not have the same facial features as modern Africans. The ancient Africans had a mix of features that was both archaic and modern. In other words, not even modern African people looked like early humans. What accounts for today's African facial features are the same sort of processes that formed modern Europeans and Asians: evolutionary adaptations that occurred in their respective regions much later.

Although Wolpoff admired the work of the geneticists and accepted that it formed important new insights on human evolution, he rejected the idea that it gave conclusive evidence supporting population replacement theory. He claimed fossils and human artifacts gave the best evidence for the correct circumstances of human evolution. Multiregionalists like Wolpoff opposed replacement theory in part because they found it hard to believe one population could have completely replaced another without some interbreeding or that it happened in the relatively short period of 150,000 to 200,000 years ago. They found no archaeological or fossil record of such an event occurring and claimed that "only fossils provide the basis for refuting one idea or the other" (Wolpoff and Caspari 1997, 65).

Geneticists argued that fossils were prone to theoretical conclusions and interpretation, whereas fossilists argued that genetics was dependent upon theoretical assumptions. Wolpoff said that accepting the Eve idea was to accept the assumptions that modern African humans completely replaced all other existing hominids, that early humans must all have had African features, and that no interbreeding went on.

The continuity people could not accept these assumptions without fossil evidence. In fact, they said the archaeological evidence supported the opposite. They pointed to artifacts and fossils found at sites in Israel known as Skhul, Tabun, and Qafzeh. These sites, first discovered in the 1930s, were considered the oldest human evidence outside Africa. The fossils and artifacts there suggested the Tabun cave had been the home of Neanderthals, whereas Skhul and Qafzeh had housed archaic moderns. This arrangement seemed to prove that the archaic moderns had appeared after the Neanderthals, making them descendants of the heavy-browed ones. The modern human artifacts, the multiregionalists argued, were identical to nearby Neanderthal sites. If the population replacement theory was correct, there should be more advanced technologies that would be indicative of an outside invasion by more advanced people. Wolpoff argued there were none.

Multiregionalists were aware that some opponents leveled charges of racism against them. Opponents argued that multiregionalism was just a new version of polygenesis: the nineteenth-century belief that all the races were actually different species with different origins. The polygenists argued that as different species, some races were superior to others. Wolpoff argued that what looked like separate branches of a tree were actually closely connected vines and interconnecting limbs.

Wolpoff and Thorne came up with the notion of "center and edge" to further explain their theory. The core of any population had little gene flow with neighbor populations. The outer edges of that population, however, had increased gene flow because they were in closer proximity to the edge of the neighbor. In this way populations mixed their hereditary material. Both groups, and any other nearby populations, thus remained the same species but with enough difference to create races.

Wolpoff bristled at the notion that he was following in the racist shoes of Carleton Coon, arguing that he was not a polygenist. He was particularly annoyed by the critique of his work by the late influential biologist and writer Stephen Jay Gould, who often referred to multiregionalism as a thinly veiled polygenesis in the Coon mold. Wolpoff thought Gould was misinterpreting his work and did not understand it. He thought Gould opposed him because multiregional continuity flew in the face of Gould's theory of punctuated equilibrium—the idea that most species remain static for long periods of time and then suddenly make short bursts of evolutionary change before returning to a kind of evolutionary dormancy. Gould gained a worldwide reputation based on this theory, after which he spent the rest of his career as a kind of self-appointed historian of evolution and popularizer of science for the masses, publishing a bewildering array of books.

Replacement proponents continued to say genetic evidence ruled out the widespread interbreeding needed for continuity. It may have been disease that kept interbreeding from happening, or the advanced language skills of the invaders may have effectively kept the groups apart. In 2000 scientists from the University of Uppsala, in Sweden, and the Max Planck Institute of Evolutionary Anthropology at Leipzig, Germany, did further mtDNA testing using fifty-eight subjects and a computer modeling program to look at the gene sequences of current African and non-African populations. The computer created family trees based on the genetic material. The data showed that both Africans and non-Africans could be traced to a common ancestor. This work also pushed the African breakout date forward from 200,000 to 50,000 years ago. Eve proponents said this confirmed their view. Rick Potts, director of the Human Origins program at the Smithsonian Institution, added that genetics alone could not answer everything, though the fossils and artifacts, in this case, supported the geneticists' study. He cautioned that modern human genetic material did not just appear overnight 60,000 years ago but was likely a gradual process. He also allowed for a certain amount of gene flow. Further muddying the genetic waters, a 1991 test of Neanderthal mtDNA at first seemed to confirm that modern Europeans shared no Neanderthal traits. A rival analysis of the same data, however, argued that the difference between Neanderthal and modern European mtDNA was not as pronounced as was thought.

In Christopher Stringer's estimation the earliest human relatives to leave Africa—*Homo erectus* and possibly the elusive *Homo ergaster*—did so around 2 million years ago. These populations reached Russia and Southeast Asia about 1.8 million years ago. The 1.5 million years saw increasing diversity among these groups (though just how this diversification occurred is part of the replacement versus continuity debate). He developed the replacement model with its waves of creatures issuing forth all having originated in Africa in order to explain the evidence. The most important of these waves occurred about 100,000 years ago. He argued that roughly 35,000 years ago late Neanderthals and Cro-Magnons were contemporaneous in Europe. What level of interaction there was, if any, is hard to say. A child burial found at Lagar Velho, Portugal—dated to 25,000 years ago—had attendant pendants and red ochre paint. Paleoanthropologist Erik Trinkaus argues that this little skeleton, along with some other European material, showed a mixed ancestry of Neanderthal and Cro-Magnon. This kind of mixing, or "hybridization," of morphological characters, as he called it, was the result of the two groups inter-breeding. Hybridization theory and "assimilationist" theory are two ideas that fall between strict replacement and continuity. Stringer was dubious of these middle ways as well as pure multiregionalism in that while he was willing to accept that some mixing went on between ar-chaic people and moderns, it was not enough to leave any real traces, or at least not enough to create a hybrid subspecies. For Stringer and others an appearance of mosaic characters like the Lagar Velho fossils was less an indication of hybridization or assimilation between groups than an indicator that human lineages formed slowly. Wolpoff saw in the Lagar Velho remains evidence supporting the idea of interbreed-ing populations.

In an attempt to work out which model was the most likely ex-planation of human diversity, Marta Lahr examined both the replace-ment and multiregional theories. She argued that in order to under-stand modern human diversity it was important to include human origins in the debate. Whatever mode of origins was accepted would naturally dictate what the source of the diversity was. She pointed out that the single-origin model had the most significant evidence to sup-port diversity. She cited, among other things, the genetic evidence that pointed to an African origin and the apparent fact that some pop-ulations that were thought to be ancestors and descendants lived at the same time. She also determined that there was no convincing evi-dence that modern Chinese or Australian Aboriginal people showed the genetic markers expected if they were the direct descendants of Asian *Homo erectus*. In the end, though she believed the single-origin theory, Lahr concluded that "discovering the specific history of each modern population, including all whose existence we can only infer from the fossil record, remains the greatest challenge" (1996, 340).

## The Bottleneck

One of the things that puzzled geneticists about modern humans is that although they exhibit superficial variation, they show little genetic variation. Some saw this as evidence that the human population grew and expanded at some point in the past from a geographically isolated population. One mechanism employed to resolve the question was the concept of the genetic bottleneck. Initially put forward in the 1970s to explain species expansion, the bottleneck concept argued that at some point, as recently as 50,000 years ago, some geologic, climatic, or biological event occurred that profoundly impacted the hominid populations of the world. As a result, many perished, leaving only tiny populations that somehow survived. Once the difficult period passed, a compact population of modern humans radiated out to take their place as the surviving hominids. Many think this happened in the late Pleistocene age. This, proponents argue, accounts for the small range of genetic variation found in modern humans regardless of ethnic background.

The number of genetic mutations in DNA increases as time goes by. If a population goes on its way unhindered, it should show a wide genetic variation. If the population is hit with a bottleneck, it would leave the survivors with a similar genetic makeup. In 1998 geneticists David Reich and David Goldstein argued there was something wrong not with the idea of the bottleneck but with the methods used to explain it. They argued that the normal procedure of looking at what are known as genetic "loci" (specific spots on a strand of DNA) was limiting. They said taking a broader genomewide view gave a more accurate reading. (A genome is the total genetic structure of an organism.) This approach would overcome the inherent difficulties of the loci-focused approach because evidence for population expansion would stand out from the evidence for natural selection that is also present. They devised a series of tests involving complex mathematical formulae. Using modern populations as subjects, Reich and Goldstein tested to find the amount of expansion evidence left over from the past. As they suspected, African populations showed a considerable amount of expansion, whereas non-Africans showed almost none. This "signal" of expansion seemed to indicate a period during the Paleolithic during which this event occurred, leaving only a small group (maybe as few as 7,000 individuals) to account for the entire modern human population.

In the 1990s, however, doubts began to grow over this explanation. As genetic testing techniques became more sophisticated and easier and less expensive to perform, a flood of data was accumulated on human genetic history. The data seemed to show conflicting views. Some samples displayed all the earmarks of population expansion, whereas some did the opposite. MtDNA shows evidence of two things: the effects of natural selection upon its evolution and how genetically linked populations grow. The problem is that expansion evidence and selection evidence are hard to tell apart. This is the problem that Reich and Goldstein were trying to overcome with their phylogenetic approach. The conflicting condition suggested that natural selection played a major role in the evolution of mtDNA and genetic variation and that genetics might not be able to say much about population growth. In the late 1990s further genetic research indicated that something did happen to affect human genetic variation, pointing once again to a bottleneck event and its aftermath in the late Pleistocene age. If the genetic evidence for the bottleneck is correct, the modern human population is much more closely related than previously thought.

## Getting out of Africa

Just as it did for people entering the Americas so many years later, the moment came when the first human ancestors, whether in one wave or several, left Africa. They likely walked into the Sinai Peninsula. It was a momentous occasion, and the accepted wisdom is that the first humanlike creatures to leave Africa were *Homo erectus* or some closely related group.

In 2001 a skeleton was found that could alter this view. The Dmanisi skeleton, dated to 1.75 million years ago, was strange because it had a relatively small brain, a large set of canine teeth, and an apelike face. It was more primitive than scientists thought the earliest hominids leaving Africa should be, looking more like a *Homo habilis* than *Homo erectus*. The Dmanisi site is located in a small village in Russian Georgia along what would have been one of the routes for hominids leaving Africa and heading into Asia and Europe. Discovered in the late 1980s by scientists from the local Georgian State Museum at Tbilisi, the site has produced several fossil individuals dating back between 1.6 and 1.8 million years, but oddly all their faces were missing (something not unusual for fossil hominids). Researchers working the site believed they had found *Homo erectus* fossils. The 2001 find changed that. This skull had the face almost completely intact. What it looked like stunned those who found it because it looked much more like *Homo habilis*. The more apelike *Homo habilis* characteristics were matched by more primitive tool technology: simple choppers and scrapers, not the more sophisticated hand axes normally associated with *Homo erectus*.

Once again the question of brain size and intelligence was raised. If small-brained *Homo habilis* were the first to leave Africa, then they accomplished a great deal. The question is still open as a full or at least nearly complete skeleton of the creature has not been found

David Lordkipanidze of the Georgian Academy of Sciences shows, July 8, 2002, the 1.75-million-year-old skull and jawbone excavated near the town of Dmanisi, some 85 kilometers southwest of Tbilisi, August 2001. Bones of a slightly built early human with a small head suggest that the large brains that characterize modern humans did not necessarily evolve before our ancestors began migrating all over the world. Lordkipanidze's team believes it is an example of Homo erectus, thought to have been the first hominid species to leave Africa. (David Mdzinarishvili/ Reuters/Corbis)

to date. Milford Wolpoff saw the Dmanisi material as support for regional continuity. He thought paleoanthropologists should have eliminated *Homo erectus* from the rolls and called all post–*Homo habilis* hominids *Homo sapiens*.

In addition to the fossil- and genetic-based claims for human antiquity, there are also the archaeological. In fact, of all the evidence for the course of human evolution, the largest part is made up of artifacts, not fossils or genetic material. In the 1980s archaeologists Robert Foley and Marta Lahr argued for an artifact-based analysis of human evolution. Traditional reading of the archaeological record said that hominid biology and technology advanced roughly parallel. As a result, advances in technology were used to chart advances in biology and to compare the relative status of hominid groups: simple tools with simple hominids and complex tools with complex hominids. Replacement proponents used archaeology to show distinctions between Neanderthal and modern behavior, arguing that modern human behavior is, well, modern, something only recently developed. Multiregionalists used an apparent similarity in the technology of these groups as proof they were closely related.

Foley and Lahr suggested that this simple linear reading had been giving faulty conclusions for both the replacement and the multiregional schools and suggested that a phylogenetic approach to reading tool development would yield better results. A phylum is a group of related genera and their associated species. The phylogenetic approach, instead of looking at stone tool development for a particular site or even a particular species, focuses on how technology developed broadly over all hominid groups. This would produce evidence of behavior as well as simple mechanics. Artifacts would be used to chart the behavior and history of entire populations, not of individuals. Foley and Lahr used as the central mechanism of their theory the "mode" system of archaeologist J. D. Clark. Developed in the late 1960s, Clark's system assigned ascending values to increasing levels of Stone Age technological sophistication. Mode 1 was the pebble tool system of the East African Oldowan culture. Mode 2 included Acheulian hand axes (flakes and core stones with sharp edges on two sides, known as bifaces). Mode 3, of the middle Paleolithic age, was exemplified by carefully prepared cores that were used to fashion sophisticated axes and knives. Mode 4 of the Upper Paleolithic consisted of long, sharp blades of great finish made into a wide range of cutting implements. Finally, Mode 5 included small blades of great delicacy and finish that were used to make composite tools.

Foley and Lahr were more interested in the Mode 3 and 4 technologies. It is during this period that the human mind "big bang" is thought to have occurred, with the growth of language and symbolic thought. During this period there is evidence at the Skhul and Qafzeh sites that Neanderthals and archaic moderns shared similar technologies and even instances where the Neanderthals may have had a slight lead. It is this situation that is seen by multiregional supporters as proof of their idea. It has also been argued that the less sophisticated Neanderthals learned how to make superior tools by observing their modern neighbors and mimicking them (employing cognitive memes).

From this apparent jumble of biology and behavior, Foley and Lahr pointed out that "the fact that two distinct groups of hominids with apparently different ancestry share the same broad technological system remains a major problem for modern human origins" (1997, 10). Their analysis suggested that early hominids developed both Mode 1 and then Mode 2 technologies in Africa, and some carried that technology off the continent. Then Mode 3 industries appeared back in Africa as well as in Europe as an indication of a shared intellectual capability between 300,000 and 250,000 years ago. Mode 4 technologies seem to have appeared in Africa and spread to the Middle East around 50,000 years ago and by 30,000 years, after which only Mode 4 artifacts are found there.

It is the dispersal of tools during this latter period that the archaeologists saw as crucial. They argued that Mode 2 tools were made in Africa by early *Homo erectus* who carried them to the outside world, after which a new species, *Homo heidelbergensis,* appeared in Africa, also using Mode 2 tools. The Israeli fossils suggest that later hominids, notably the Neanderthals, reached that area 100,000 years ago with Mode 3 technology. Later, back in Africa, other archaic modern Mode 3–possessing populations, close cousins to the Neanderthals, acquired increased brainpower. Improved cognitive ability allowed them to use the same tools in new and different ways than the Neanderthals.

Foley and Lahr put all this together and developed the "Mode 3 hypothesis," arguing that early moderns and the Neanderthals shared a common ancestry in Africa. As a result of this shared ancestry they shared intellectual capabilities, at least early on. This accounted for the Israeli sites with the same tool assemblages but different groups. The moderns, who left Africa in a later wave, or "dispersal event," as it is sometimes called, had a slightly more elevated cognitive ability and were able to use their Mode 3 technologies more efficiently and then advance to Modes 4 and 5. So although they were separate groups that did not interbreed, the Neanderthals and moderns lived side by side and for a time shared technologies. According to the Mode 3 hypothesis, the Israeli sites only looked on the surface to be a case of gene flow and interbreeding but were a snapshot of a brief moment when different people used the same tools.

## *Who was* Homo ergaster?

As rare and hard to find as they are, not every hominid fossil turns the world upside down. Most quietly support one theory or another or add to our knowledge about an already known species. Caught somewhere between *Homo habilis* and *Homo erectus, Homo ergaster* (the working man) appeared in the scientific literature in the mid-1970s out of the confusion between Asian *Homo erectus* and the more recently discovered African and European versions. Those who accepted *Homo ergaster* as a valid species believed it appeared in Africa around 2 million years ago and was the close African and European relative to *Homo erectus.* It was *Homo erectus,* they said, that went extinct, whereas the African and European *Homo ergaster* led to modern humans.

Also thought by some to be the African *Homo erectus,* fossils of *Homo ergaster* have recently been found in Asia. If they are from *Homo ergaster,* it means they moved out of Africa soon after coming into being and quickly hustled into Asia, where they may have evolved into *Homo erectus* proper like Java man and Peking man. These recent Asian finds were made in the late 1980s at a Chinese site called Longgupo Cave (Dragon Bone Cave) by a team from the Institute of Vertebrate Paleontology and Paleoanthropology at Beijing. The cave is not far from the mammoth Three Gorges Dam project on the Yangtze River in Sichuan Province (the site also yielded a *Gigantopithecus* tooth). The fossils, three teeth and a bit of jaw, were found along with a pair of artifacts. Joined by a group of Western scientists in 1990, the team found mastodon, horse, and panda fossils that dated the site to 1.5 to 2 million years old. Electron-spin resonance testing—which counts electrons in the tooth enamel of an animal—confirmed these dates. This material seems to show a pathway out of Africa into Asia, lending credence to multiple waves of migrants.

But multiregionalists have also used the *ergaster-erectus* debate. In 2000 a team of Australian and Chinese scientists dated Nanjing man to 580,000 to 620,000 years ago. They believed this supported the multiregional view that Asians evolved out of *Homo erectus* in Asia, not Africa. The dates were the result of thermal ionization mass spectrometry that measures uranium decay. Nanjing man—actually a pair of male and female skulls—is a *Homo erectus* found outside Shanghai in 1993 at a site called Tangshan Cave. If correctly dated, these specimens would show *Homo erectus* to have been in China much sooner than originally thought. The team envisions small groups of *erectus* scattered across Asia, evolving according to local conditions, mixing their DNA, and eventually becoming ethnic Asians.

Several questions arose in relation to *Homo ergaster*. Was it the Euro-African variant of *Homo erectus?* Was it ancestral to *Homo erectus;* or did it ever really exist at all? This last question implies that there was a wide variation of *Homo erectus* across Africa, Europe, and Asia but that they were all the same species. In 2002 Tim White of the University of California at Berkeley and his team announced a collection of fossils they thought cleared up the nettlesome question of what *Homo ergaster* was. Originally found in 1997, cranial and postcranial material dating to 1 million years ago from the Dakanihylo Member section of the Bouri formation of the Middle Awash, Ethiopia, raised expectations. "The new 'Daka' hominid fossils afford unique insights into unresolved spatial and temporal relationships of *H. erectus*" (Asfaw et al. 2002, 317). Acheulian tool technology and a wide array of other fossil life forms found with the hominid bones indicate the region during this period was a savanna. Large mammals, particularly bovids (ancestral cows), found with the hominid remains also indicated a grassland environment. Many of the bovid fossils showed evidence of butchery at the hands of the hominids. Ironically, some of the hominid bones showed gnawing marks by feline predators, indicating that some of the animals in the area were living off the *Homo erectus*. When they compared the Dakanihylo material to other African, Asian, and European *Homo erectus*, White's team concluded there was little difference. There was not enough separating the fossils to warrant them being labeled anything other than *Homo erectus*.

The "Daka" material, as White and his team called it, seemed to show that there was no real difference among Asian, African, and European *Homo erectus* populations. What looked like different species, they argued, was only the natural variation that would be expected of any species ranging across a great geographical area. They took the twenty-two most common characteristics used to distinguish *Homo erectus* and its close relatives from other hominids and compared them. A series of computer modeling programs was used to create lineages and family relationships to see how they separated as distinct groups. The results were that they did not but remained together. Thus, separating *Homo erectus* populations into different species, they say, would be misleading, and creating or using a new name—that is, *Homo ergaster*—to differentiate between early and late *Homo erectus* wrong. This would effectively eliminate *Homo ergaster* as a species. These findings did not go unchallenged. Bernard Wood of George Washington University cautioned that this fossil may simply be a genuine *Homo ergaster*. Christopher Stringer was impressed by the Daka finds but also cautioned that real comparisons cannot be made until the creature's teeth are found.

Ian Tattersall, for one, thought it was *Homo ergaster* who led the exodus from Africa. Tattersall saw the diversity of the fossil record, *Homo erectus* included, as an indication of many different species living side by side. Several types of *Australopithecus* and *Homo habilis* are known. Some are robust, some gracile. Some *Homo habilis* show facial features reminiscent of early *Homo erectus*. Not all Neanderthals were the same; some had the classic "caveman" face but others less so. *Homo heidelbergensis* was older than the Neanderthals and had morphological characteristics that caused some to think it was the immediate predecessor to them. Tattersall saw most paleoanthropologists taking what he called a "minimalist" approach to species classification, arguing that there were as many as twenty or more hominid species, many living at the same time. Tattersall pointed to the many different types of *Australopithecus* then known: *A. anamensis, A. africanus, A. afarensis, A. boisie, A. robustus, A. bahrelghazali,* and *A. garhi.* This type of diversity should not be thought of as limited to just this genus but must have been the case for all the various hominid groups. He placed emphasis on looking at human ancestors as no different from any other animal group where there was great diversity that often grinds down to a few or just one species.

One of the central questions for Tattersall was how did all those species come down to just one? How do we find the "roots of our solitude," as he put it? Eschewing simple replacement theory, Tattersall argued that it was more a becoming than a replacing; in other words, there was no outside invasion, only already existing populations becoming more human than their neighbors and slowly taking over. For all the Neanderthals' supposed modernity, Tattersall contended that there is little or no evidence they engaged in ritual or culture. Although they did bury their dead in some cases, there is really nothing to suggest they were doing anything more than burying out of sanitary considerations rather than metaphysical ones. The contemporaneous *Homo sapiens* had a greater capacity for intellect but initially were on a par with the Neanderthals. At some point language, culture, and the cognitive expansion of the big bang commingled to give some *Homo sapiens* a considerable edge. What brought about that sudden growth we may never know, Tattersall suggested, but it happened nonetheless. In this way, no evidence of an invasion and wholesale replacement would ever be found because no invasion occurred.

Lending credence to the wide-diversity hypothesis, in the same issue of *Nature* in which the Dmanisi skull was described, *Sahelanthropus tchadensis* was announced. Dated to 7 million years old, this creature existed close to the time when hominid and primate groups were forming out of a common ancestor. It is at least 1 million years older than the oldest previously known hominid and has been hailed as an important find. The fossil consists of a good part of the cranium, lower jaw, and a clutch of teeth. Discovered in the north-central African country of Chad by a French-led team from the University of Poitiers under Michel Brunet, it sports both primate and hominid characters, unlike *Australopithecus* (local Chadian technicians began referring to it as Toumai, or "Hope of Life"). The brain is chimp size at 350 to 380 cubic centimeters, but the face is far more humanlike in its vertical flatness. Some saw it as being more "human" than Lucy (who appeared much later). Noted anthropologist Bernard Wood concurred that by all that is known of human evolution Toumai should not have looked like it did for the time in which it existed. Reasons for this apparent oddity are that it could have been the common ancestor to chimps and hominids, it could be the ancestor to either the chimps or the hominids, or, as Wood suggested, it could have been the ancestor to yet another evolutionary dead-end related to neither group. Its missing pieces, once found, could show it to be another species.

Toumai being discovered in Chad, a long way from the legendary haunts of Olduvai Gorge, Laetoli, and the Middle Awash, suggested an entire chapter of human evolutionary history may be waiting to be found. As most hominid finds are traditionally made in the Great Rift Valley along the eastern to southern axis of Africa, most research has focused there. The Chad finds may be an indicator that our earliest relatives and their contemporaries ranged far and wide across the immense African continent. Milford Wolpoff as well as Martin Pickford and Brigette Senut agreed that Toumai was an ape, not a human ancestor. The Toumai discovery was just one of a group of finds that have fueled controversy at the beginning of the twenty-first century.

## A Barrelful of Hominids

Up through the middle of the twentieth century students of human antiquity assumed the earth was occupied by one hominid species at a time. One arose, lived, and went extinct, leading to the next rung on the ladder. That view began to change in the 1960s with the discoveries made at Olduvai Gorge and others. In the 1990s and early 2000s a series of impressive and important finds came in quick succession that suggested that at different times the world reverberated with the sounds of many different hominid types.

In July 2001 it was announced that a new fossil had been discovered by an Ethiopian doctoral student from the University of California at Berkeley at the Middle Awash River valley. It was symbolic that this Ethiopian fossil should be found by a young Ethiopian scientist, Yohannes Haile-Selassie. The site was one well known to paleoanthropologists and only fifty miles from Hadar and the place where Lucy was found. Haile-Selassie and his coauthor, Ethiopian geologist Giday WoldeGabriel, described the creature by its jawbone with teeth, several hand and foot bones, a section of arm, a collar bone, and a toe and dated it to an astounding 5.5 million years ago. The toe received a great deal of attention, as it suggested that even our earliest ancestors moved in some kind of upright posture. The toe's positioning shows an angled back edge that is characteristic of modern human bipedal toes. This angled aspect allowed modern humans to push off with their feet for a more powerful and controlled step. David Begun, a primate specialist from the University of Toronto, thought the toe too long and slim to be from a biped.

Haile-Selassie and WoldeGabriel named the creature *Ardipithecus ramidus kadabba*. They took this name as they thought their find a subspecies of their mentor Tim White's 1992 discovery *Ardipithecus ramidus,* which dated to 4.4 million years old and which White believed to be the oldest human ancestor. White originally assigned the fossil, found at Aramis in the Middle Awash of Ethiopia, to the genus *Australopithecus.* The next year, however, he and his colleagues reassigned it to the new genus *Ardipithecus* because further study led them to believe there were too many differences between this find and the accepted *Australopithecus.* The foramen magnum was more forward, like that of a hominid. The arms seemed rather powerful and had details that suggested they were used for steadying and holding the body up rather than walking. This also suggested that even as a tree dweller, *Ardipithecus* was a biped. Ian Tattersall was not so sure about the niche *Ardipithecus* filled. He thought most of the teeth "unhominid."

In 2001, at the same time as Haile-Salasie's find, a French team led by Brigitte Senut and Martin Pickford of the College de France announced its find from Kenya. At 5.8 million years old, it had the potential to topple current views. Discovered in the Tugen hills by Kiptalam Cheboi of the Community Museums of Kenya (CMK), it was christened *Orrorin tugenensis* (the original man from Tugen). Senut and Pickford argued that it, and not *Ardipithecus,* was the oldest ancestor. This creature was significant because of its dentition. Its front teeth were apelike, whereas its back teeth were more human in design. The arm sections found were more apelike in their proportions, whereas the legs seemed more modern (the femur showed a bone density consistent with a more humanlike walker). With these characteristics Senut and Pickford used *Orrorin* to push the primate-hominid divergence back to 7 or 8 million years ago instead of the commonly thought 5 or 6 million of the geneticists. They also argued that the attendant fossil and geological evidence found with *Orrorin* told a great deal about what the circumstances of this period of human evolution were like. They said that hominid evolution must be seen not as an isolated event but as integrated into the wider overall picture of the changing conditions of Africa and the world itself.

This idea is gaining acceptance among many paleoanthropologists. The old savanna scenario is being undermined by increasing evidence to the contrary. Where once it was generally assumed that our earliest ancestors developed their more human characteristics as a response to life on the open plains, it is increasingly thought that our earliest human attributes began to appear in the arboreal or forest phase.

Senut and Pickford argued that the evidence they uncovered with *Orrorin* shows that around 7 to 8 million years ago there was a major climatic and faunal change. Increasing ice coverage in the Arctic changed weather patterns worldwide and pushed cooler northern climes south. As a result, deserts began to spread, particularly in Africa, where a decrease in forested belts was followed by the appearance of grasslands. All this changed the types of food available. Some mammals like the elephants and rhinos reacted by developing large enameled teeth to deal with the tougher food sources. The early hominids in this environment were able to hold on to their traditional diet of fruits, allowing them a respite in the dwindling forests. Instead of making wholesale dietary changes like the horses, the hominids developed a new locomotor skill: bipedalism. Still in the trees, they learned to walk upright by walking from one branch to another, balancing on two feet. This then allowed them to travel from one food center to another, and by the time the savannas had taken over, the hominids could successfully negotiate the large open spaces with a trait acquired in the branches. In other words, they had assumed a more or less human posture before entering the savanna phase, giving them a greater chance at overall survival.

Despite Senut and Pickford's excitement over their find, *Orrorin* was a bit of a tough sell. Some questioned whether it really was a hominid. It might simply have been a primate that achieved bipedal locomotion in parallel with other hominids but was unable to capitalize on it. Another event throwing doubt on the acceptance of *Orrorin* as our earliest ancestor was the discovery of more *Ardipithecus* fossils that seemed to pull focus back to them and away from *Orrorin*.

In addition to the morphological questions some have over *Orrorin,* there may be other intrigues involved. The Leakey family, who wielded something of the power of a dynasty in the world of African paleoanthropology, had been involved in a number of the greatest discoveries in the search for humanity's origins. They were also involved in some of the more intense animosities of that world. We have already discussed the falling out between Donald Johanson and Mary Leakey as well as the resentment shown Richard Leakey over his perceived lack of credentials. Human fossils are rarer than diamonds, harder to find, and more valuable. When they are found they create excitement and interest. As a result, the places they are found are jealously guarded by the scientists who work them and, increasingly in the latter part of the twentieth century, by the local governments whose national borders they fall within. A scientist cannot just go to Africa and start poking around: permits are required; rules must be followed.

*Richard Leakey (Liz Gilbert / Corbis Sygma)*

In 1999 Meave Leakey, head of the department of paleontology at the National Museums of Kenya (NMK) (and Richard's wife) continued the family's tradition by leading a team that unearthed *Kenyanthropus platyops* (the flat-faced man from Kenya) not far from where *Orrorin* was found. Discovered by African team member Justus Erus, *Kenyanthropus* dated to 3.5 to 3.2 million years ago and was officially announced in 2001. Some saw in its flat hominid-style face a precursor to *Homo habilis*. Erus made his find on the western side of Lake Turkana at a site along the Lomekwi River.

With many of the finds so far back down the ancestral line, *Kenyanthropus* exhibited that tendency to combine both primate and hominid features, particularly in the skull. Its flat face was backed by small hominid teeth and a small primate-size brain. Some *Australopithecus* had more prognathous, or pulled-out, faces to accommodate bigger teeth. Big faces are associated with the big teeth needed to crack nuts and crush tough vegetation. A flat face with smaller teeth could be evidence of a relatively softer diet. The difference in teeth and diets suggested that while *Kenyanthropus platyops* and *Australopithecus afarensis* (Lucy and her kin) occupied the same range, they did not compete for the same food sources. They may have occupied different environments that were geographically close, or they might have occupied the same area but exploited different niches within it. This, Leakey pointed out, is just what other mammal groups did: they co-existed fairly easily.

Most paleontologists have believed that the characteristic flat face of humans did not begin developing until around 2 million years ago. *Kenyanthropus platyops* undermined this notion. In addition, Leakey and her team thought that their find was very similar to *Homo rudolfensis,* of which the most well-known example is Skull 1470, first discovered by Bernard Ngeneo in 1972 as part of a team led by Richard Leakey. By 1986 Russian paleontologist Valerii Alexeev tried to rename 1470 *Pithecanthropus rudolfensis.* There were others, in particular Richard Leakey, who thought 1470 a member of the *Homo* genus and so referred to it as *Homo rudolfensis,* the name that has persisted. In addition, there were those who thought they saw more *Australopithecus* characteristics than *Homo* and insisted it be included in that genus. What was needed to clear up the problem of 1470—*Homo rudolfensis* was either postcranial material being found or the appearance of another fossil that would make better sense of it.

Meave Leakey participated in the first attempt to reconstruct 1470 and some of the *Homo rudolfensis* material. She thought she had found the answer in *Kenyanthropus.* Leakey suggested that researchers accept that *Homo rudolfensis* descended from *Kenyanthropus.* From her point of view this would make quite a bit of material snap into place: *Kenyanthropus* led to *Homo rudolfensis,* which led to *Homo habilis* and then on to moderns. If it goes Meave Leakey's way, Lucy and the rest of the *Australopithecus* would be removed from the direct line of human evolution to be shunted off to a dead-end.

The discovery of *Kenyanthropus* was met with general approval, and Meave Leakey's access to the region was not an issue. Pickford and Senut's work on *Orrorin* was not greeted with quite the same enthusiasm. Alan Walker, by now a prominent human evolution researcher in his own right, dismissed the idea of *Orrorin* as a biped, saying the evidence did not support it. Controversy immediately erupted over *Orrorin,* most of which said more about human nature than the nature of humans.

In order to understand the *Orrorin* episode better, the career of Richard Leakey should be examined a bit more. By the 1980s Richard Leakey had all but left the field of paleoanthropology to become increasingly involved in Kenyan politics. He was named director of the Kenyan Wildlife Service in 1989 by the country's longtime president Daniel arap Moi and used his celebrity to publicize the plight of African elephants and to stem the tide of the ivory trade as well as clean up the service's reputation for corruption. By the mid-1990s he had become critical of Kenya's government, including his benefactor, President Moi. So concerned was he that he helped found an opposition party called Safina and openly attacked the government, accusing it of corruption and incompetence. He was alternately called a racist, an atheist, and an imperialist in return by the president. In 1993 he lost both his legs in a plane crash yet vowed to keep fighting.

A good deal of the criticism of Leakey came from the small but affluent white population in Kenya, including his own brother Philip Leakey. They were afraid racial strife might tear the country apart. Some violence did occur. Richard Leakey was assaulted by government thugs and beaten in the town of Nakuru. He was eventually elected to Parliament in 1998. The next year President Moi turned around and appointed Leakey to head the Kenyan civil service with a mandate to clean it up. He took to the new position with zeal and began rooting out government corruption. Following resistance to his reforms, he left the post in 2001, the same year Martin Pickford announced the discovery of *Orrorin.* Donald Johanson had been initially friendly with Richard Leakey, but they became estranged. Johanson put it down to a clash between two exuberant "Young Turks," each with something to prove. By 1999 he publicly hoped that reconciliation could be reached and friendship once again hold between the two.

Scientists jealously guard the places where they do their work. Paleoanthropologists are especially keen to protect the hunting grounds they find fossils in. Pickford and Senut were accused of fossil poaching by Andrew Hill, the British-born Yale University paleontologist. He said they were excavating without the proper authorization at a site he claimed he had been working, near where *Orrorin* was found. As he had been working the site for two decades, *Orrorin,* Hill claimed, fell under his control. Pickford countered that he had received a permit in 1998 directly through the office of the president, Daniel arap Moi. His sponsoring institution was the Community Museums of Kenya. The usual granting institution for work in Kenya was the National Museums of Kenya. The older National Museums were in large part a creation of the Leakey family; Meave was its chief paleontologist, whereas her husband, Richard, was its one-time director. The newer Community Museums had been begun by Martin Pickford and a group of Kenyans and foreign scientists uneasy over what they thought was control of Kenya's fossil sites by the Leakeys. The Community Museums of Kenya had the backing of Moi, who traced his personal ancestry to the Tugen hills where *Orrorin* was found. The director of the CMK was Eustace Gitonga, who had previously been head of the NMK's exhibits department and who had been let go from that job under allegations of appropriating money for himself that was earmarked for an exhibit on dinosaurs. Pickford and Gitonga accused Leakey of being the one who was out for personal wealth and glory. The CMK board of directors included Pickford, Gitonga, Senut, and Donald Johanson's old colleague Yves Coppens.

Pickford and the Leakeys had been acquainted for years. Pickford had been a high school mate of Richard's in Nairobi and considered him a friend. Pickford went to graduate school at the University of London with Andrew Hill but did not consider him a friend. In the late 1960s Pickford found some fossils kept in a museum for years that completed a skull, known as Proconsul, Mary Leakey had found back in 1947. She complimented Pickford for having a "keen eye" for having spotted the hominid fragments in a collection labeled as turtle parts (Mary Leakey 1984, 99). Pickford and Hill worked together at the NMK under Richard Leakey, who was then director.

By the 1980s Pickford and Hill had gone their separate ways, to the United States and France, respectively. According to a report in

*Science* in April 2001 Pickford and Hill had a chance encounter in Nairobi in 1985. Leakey then accused Pickford of stealing documents from the NMK. A researcher's career can be destroyed by charges of theft. Museums and libraries would thereafter be wary of allowing such a person into their collections. Leakey charged Pickford had stolen notebooks of William Bishop, a professor who had been mentor to both Pickford and Hill. Pickford said he had only taken the notebooks—which he claimed he signed out according to procedure—to make copies of them for his research. Pickford thought Hill had prompted Leakey to make the accusation out of spite, forcing him to spend the better part of the next decade trying to clear his name. Leakey banned Pickford from ever entering the NMK again.

In addition to his animosity toward his one-time friend Richard Leakey, Martin Pickford had, over the years, grown wary, even resentful, of Louis Leakey and his methods. In 1997 he published a scathing critique called *Louis S. B. Leakey: Beyond the Evidence*. The book was Pickford's version of the search for human origins in East Africa from the 1920s through the 1960s. He argued that there were two problems with the way paleoanthropology was conducted in Africa. The first was that most field teams had traditionally been led by anatomists and paleontologists without the necessary geologic knowledge to properly understand the context in which fossils were found. The other problem was the Leakey family and its attitudes. *Louis S. B. Leakey* was a laundry list of supposed Leakey family wrongdoing. According to Pickford, Louis Leakey began the dynasty by his amateurish bumbling and outright misrepresentation of fossils. In addition, Leakey was "the most aggressive of territorial scientists" in the way he controlled the fossil fields and restricted outside access, a trend some argued has continued by the family (1997, x). Pickford accused the Leakeys of being poseurs who, because of their lack of scientific training, should never have been let anywhere near fossil humans. More seriously, Pickford accused Richard and Meave Leakey of reconstructing skull 1470 so that it would look less like an *Australopithecus* and more like a member of the *Homo* and that Alan Walker accepted this faulty reconstruction because not doing so would have resulted in his being banished from the fossil sites the Leakeys "controlled."

For his part, Walker admitted he was "acutely uneasy" with the Leakeys' reconstruction. Walker and Meave Leakey made the first tentative reconstruction of 1470 in 1972. They made it have a more protruding *Australopithecus*-like face. Walker had become intimately familiar with the skull from working so closely on its recovery and preservation and believed there was only one way it could go together. Richard ordered their reconstruction reassembled to be flatter and more humanlike. He wanted to be able to put 1470 forward as the oldest member of the *Homo* line. Walker did not think it was, arguing that the deceptive *Homo* look was from deformation, not natural morphology. Anatomist Bernard Wood, who was then part of the team, agreed with Leakey. It was this conflict (discussed in chapter 4) that caused Walker to want his name removed from the official descriptive paper of 1470. He said they "were trying to squeeze the theory to fit the anatomy" (Walker and Shipman 1996, 120). Walker left the meeting where this decision was made in frustration but returned shortly after. Upon his return, amends were made and they went on. Later he was informed by Richard Leakey that had he not returned, he would have been removed from the team—which would have excluded him from the fossil sites. Walker said he saw no insidious threat, only the disagreement among colleagues about a scientific interpretation of evidence. Martin Pickford, however, saw darker implications in their behavior and felt compelled, whether legitimately or not, to sever ties with the Leakeys and accuse them of impropriety.

Following the charges of excavating without a permit, Martin Pickford was arrested in 2001 near Lake Turkana. He was sure Richard Leakey was behind the arrest. When Pickford originally received the permit to dig in 1998, officials from the NMK tried to have it rescinded. The office that gave the permit was then housed in the same building as the president. Some time later the permit office was moved to the building containing the Ministry of Education, Science, and Technology. It has a copy of a letter purporting to show that Pickford's original permit had been rescinded. Pickford claimed this letter was a fake. The Kenyan prosecutor's office dropped the charges against Pickford, and he sued the NMK and Richard Leakey. Pickford regretted having to do this but argued he had no alternative. In an odd addendum to this event, Martin Pickford's colleague Brigitte Senut did have a valid permit to dig, as did Andrew Hill. This effectively allowed two teams to work the same area, a condition many find worrisome. If two teams work the same locality there is the chance that their presence will contaminate what the other is doing, making both teams' work suspect. In the end, this incident could prompt the Kenyan government to create legislation making working the country's fossil site beneficial to all. Despite the rivalries and conspiracy theories, work continued.

In March 2002 Tim White announced more finds from the Dakani-hylo Member. Pieces of as many as seven *Homo erectus* individuals had been found and dated to 1 million years ago. He saw this as further evidence that *Homo erectus* ranged across Europe, Asia, and Africa as much as 1.8 million years ago. Since his days in the 1970s working with Donald Johanson in Ethiopia, White has continued to contribute to the field. As a leading teacher in paleoanthropology at the University of California at Berkeley, he has taught many of the up-and-coming students of human evolution, including many from Africa. His students, from Gen Suwa of Japan and Berhane Asfaw to Yohannes Haile-Salasie, have made major contributions to the human fossil record. White pointed out that one of the problems with African fossils was that despite the wealth of known material going back millions of years, there was space between the relatively recent dates of 100,000 to 300,000 years. What little comes from this period is problematic because of poor condition and unreliable dates. In 1997, not far from where *Ardipithecus ramadas kadabba* was found, something appeared to fill that gap.

White's team, which included Berhane Asfaw, now of the Rift Valley Research Service, found several individuals' worth of material. Potassium argon dating put them at 160,000 years old, making them contemporaries of the Neanderthals. The material was found 140 miles from the Ethiopian capital of Addis Ababa near the village of Herto. White and his colleagues believed the creature, which they named *Homo sapiens edaltus,* evolved in Africa independent of its European cousins and helped confirm the African origins of modern people. It seemed to form a transition from older African to newer Middle Eastern fossils. Christopher Stringer was delighted at the news, as it seemed to confirm his population replacement theory, whereas Milford Wolpoff conceded it was a human ancestor but only one of a group of simultaneous ancestors. At this writing, however, only a child's skull and a pair of adult males have been reconstructed. The fossils were badly damaged and required several years of painstaking work just to prepare them, so they were not announced publicly until 2003.

The Herto skulls show modern human characteristics of a high, rounded braincase; small brow ridges; and a flat face. Respected paleoanthropologist Clark Howell, who was involved in the initial study of the bones, argued pointedly that *Homo sapiens edaltus* showed with little doubt that there was no Neanderthal phase of modern human evolution. One of the male skulls had a series of curious grooves cut into it. The cuts did not seem consistent with cannibalism or butchery but suggested to some religious ritual and possibly ancestor worship. The skull also showed signs of natural polishing, as if it had been carried around for some time as a relic or even a trophy. If this theory is correct, it has startling ramifications for the origins of human culture. If these hominids were practicing some kind of religious rituals at the same time that the Neanderthals were not, then modern human behavior may have its roots outside the Neanderthal or even Cro-Magnon line. It is still a bit early to tell whether the cuts in this skull actually represent planned ritual behavior.

Not only was Tim White a major contributor to paleoanthropology, he was also one of its toughest critics. He argued that there were just too many named fossil hominids and that this condition was causing problems of interpretation and relational organization. He saw diversity systematics as inherently problematic in a kind of "can't see the forest for the trees" way. Focus on too many hominid groups was obscuring the larger picture. The tendency of the 1990s to accept that there was a wide diversity among hominid groups all running around in happy coexistence was misplaced because he did not see it in the fossil record. Questioning widely held beliefs is part of science and is expected, and White did just that when he pointed to specific methodological flaws and a specific fossil that he believed were major contributing factors to the problem.

Human fossils rarely pop out of the ground completely assembled. They are not like recent burials where skulls and bones can be removed from the ground intact. They are normally found in pieces. The very process of fossilization and the inexorable geologic forces at work over tens of thousands and even millions of years bend, break, and crush bones beyond recognition. Seemingly rock-hard fossils can be slowly twisted into pretzels, as if made of rubber. This is called postmortem deformation. Smaller bones and bits and pieces do not have this problem as much, but larger bones like skulls are especially susceptible. Fossils are embedded in stone—known as the matrix—that is often indistinguishable from the fossil. It takes a trained and experienced eye to be able to tell fossil from rock and talented and patient hands to remove the matrix from the fossil back in the lab. Even then the matrix sometimes cannot be removed because it is all that holds small pieces together and to do so would destroy larger pieces. The presence of the matrix keeps the bones from fitting back together properly. Not all the pieces of a skull are always found, forcing scientists to make educated guesses about how missing parts should look. With deformed pieces, missing pieces, and the matrix getting in the way, hyperaccurate measurements and reconstruction of fossil skulls become difficult. (It's not like assembling an IKEA entertainment center with just a screwdriver.) Some characteristics and measurements may be from the matrix and deformation and not from an actual part of the fossil. Exacting measurements are crucial to telling whether one fossil is the same as another. Without them, White argued, fossils are classified as separate species when they may not be. This causes an artificial level of diversity on which others build theories.

As more fossils are found, they are not always very different from one another. The increase of fossils with only subtle differences in morphology posed more questions than they answered. Just because two fossils seemed to have the same characteristics does not always mean they are the same species or even that they were related. White pointed to the example of the oreodonts. In the early twentieth century an enormous number of oreodont fossils were found in the western United States. Oreodonts were sheep-size quadruped mammals. So many species were named, often based on small differences, that it became bewildering. Eventually, paleontologists recognized that many of the characteristics and measurements they used to separate oreodont species were phantoms brought on by matrix accumulation and deformation and so cut down the number of species by combining many with dubious distinctions. Suddenly, what looked like wide oreodont diversity was not as widespread as was thought. If this could happen with the numerous oreodonts, how must it affect hominids, with their fewer numbers and more personal connection to us?

White saw it as unnecessarily confusing and misleading to name an entire hominid taxon after one incomplete fossil (something all too common). For a case in point more direct than the oreodonts, White singled out Meave Leakey's *Kenyanthropus platyops,* which had garnered considerable attention in the press as an important find. In an article and an address at the April 2003 meeting of the Paleoanthropology Society at Tempe, Arizona, he argued that Leakey and her colleagues' conclusions for *Kenyanthropus platyops* had been skewed by postmortem deformation and what he called expanding matrix distortion. He said the claims made were for a species that did not exist because the readings and measurements were off. He contended

Leakey's team had finessed the issue by calling the skull "well preserved" when in fact it was made up of several thousand tiny shards of bone fragments. The *Kenyanthropus* holotype (the example skull future *Kenyanthropus* fossils will be measured against) will now be used by other paleoanthropologists to compare new finds, which will in turn create more diversity that does not exist.

The popular press and media too used *Kenyanthropus platyops* as one more example of the diversity idea. With the spate of spectacular finds, human evolution had become a "hot" topic in the early twenty-first century. Television documentaries and popular books were everywhere. Magazines like *National Geographic* and *Scientific American* devoted cover articles and entire issues to the subject, and *Time* magazine ran a cover story on the Eve hypothesis. When the Toumai skull was announced, the staid *New York Times* and the tabloid *New York Post* ran full-page articles with pictures. Scholarly journals like *Science* and *Nature* bulged with papers on all the latest discoveries. White feared the emphasis on diversity would help enshrine a concept that in his estimation had no validity.

White saw too much of a rush to name new hominid groups and make extravagant claims for them like "oldest," "most important," and so on. Although these announcements make for publicity and media attention, they do little for the study of human origins, as these adjectives are often dropped after the initial frenzy over a discovery dies down and the media goes on to the next story. In his review of Ian Tattersall's 2002 book, *Monkey in the Mirror,* White discussed paleontology and the public and the fascination with diversity systematics. White saw Tattersall's series of popular books on human evolution as having helped "to promote the striking ease with which new and often invalid hominid genera and species are now reported in prominent journals even on the basis of single distorted specimens" (2002, 767). Diversity was made to seem like an end in itself, as some kind of organized program. As White saw no fossil evidence for widespread diversity, he and others have wondered if there were other factors involved in the pursuit of this ideal. White did not say there was no diversity of hominid populations; he questioned the kind of hyperdiversity being widely promoted, especially for the early stages of hominid evolution. He did not see the bushy thicket of most modern-day depictions of the human line but rather a solid trunk diversifying only at the upper reaches.

Beyond the physical problem of distorted fossils there may be less tangible issues at work. In a *New York Times* article in March 2001 the science writer John Noble Wilford suggested another possibility for diversity's popularity. The picture of our ancestors and their many relatives ambling through the ancient world in happy harmony with each other took hold in science and the media in the early twenty-first century. The notion that our ancestors differed ethnically and biologically yet lived side by side is a satisfying idea for Anglo-American culture. It makes people think that if they could do it, so can we. Fossils are being used, this line of thinking suggests, not to learn about our past or the course of evolution but to make modern people feel better about themselves. Whether this is the case and whether it is a conscious or subconscious occurrence is unclear.

## Conclusion

In the opening years of the twenty-first century, much had been learned about humanity's ancestors. The age of the earliest ones had been pushed back millions of years, and we learned that, at least sometimes, there were several hominid groups coexisting. And although the replacement theory was in the ascendant, there were important questions about the specifics of how it occurred: Was it a slow, incremental process, or did it occur at punctuated intervals? Just what role, and at what point, did genetic structure play? Did genetics lead behavior, or did behavior lead genetics? Were the Neanderthals only just smart enough to reach a certain level and mimic others, or did they think for themselves? Was human evolution in Africa something that happened across the continent or in just some isolated eastern pocket? Christopher Stringer, the man who helped promote the population replacement theory, pondered whether there may have been "an African version of multiregionalism, with modern morphology coalescing from various populations across the continent" (1990, 693).

In addition to the ideas noted here, a form of neo–Asia hypothesis appeared. David Begun of the University of Toronto argued that the only place fossil great apes (those represented by the large chimpanzees, orangutans, and gorillas) were found was Eurasia, not Africa. He says our most distant primate ancestors therefore must have formed in Asia. Around 9 million years ago, populations of primates existed in Asia, some of which were evolving generally in the hominid direction. Some of them, because of climatic change, entered Africa and kicked off the trend that led to primates and hominids. He pointed to the mosaic characters of *Orrorin* and Toumai as just the sort of creature that would result from such a scenario. Time will tell if Begun is correct. As normally happens in science, theories come and go, the survivors being any that are supported by a preponderance of evidence. And of course there are still the religious implications.

*Further Reading*

For replacement theory, see Christopher Stringer and Robin McKie, *African Exodus* (1996). For multiregionalism, see Milford Wolpoff and Rachel Caspari, *Race and Human Evolution* (1997). For popular works on the Eve theory, see Michael Brown, *The Search for Eve* (1990), and Bryan Sykes, *The Seven Daughters of Eve* (2001). Also see Marta Lahr, *The Evolution of Modern Human Diversity* (1996). The best place to look for the latest discussions of this material is in the recent scientific literature. *Nature* and *Science* are often the grounds upon which new ideas and discoveries are argued.

For Tim White's complaints, see "Early Hominids—Diversity or Distortion?" (2003), and John Noble Wilford, "Fossil Find: The Family of Man Grows a Little Larger," *New York Times,* March 25, 2001. An overview introduction to some of the problems with genetics and human evolution is Alan Rogers, "Order Emerging from Chaos in Human Evolutionary Genetics" (2001). For the Leakey-Pickford feud, see Martin Pickford, *Louis S. B. Leakey: Beyond the Evidence* (1997); Alan Walker and Pat Shipman, *Wisdom of the Bones* (1996); and Michael Balter, "Paleontological Rift in the Rift Valley" (2001). For a good overview of human evolution studies in the opening days of the twenty-first century, see the special edition of *Scientific American* for July 2003, which contains a series of articles by many of the people discussed in this chapter.

# 10

## *The Elusive Hand of God*

This book began with a discussion of how people in Western society, the Victorians in particular, dealt with the idea that humans are a very ancient species and the result of a process that operated over vast periods of time through a system called natural selection. One reason that cultures around the world had, and still have, trouble accepting the concept of human evolution was that they were steeped in the theological traditions of a divinely created universe into which people were placed whole and modern by God or the gods.

In the West it was mostly Protestant Christians who opposed human evolution. However, although the Catholic Church as a corporate body, through the office of the Papal Academy of Science, eventually accepted evolution as a factual but divinely powered process, there have been individual Catholics who were vocal in their opposition to evolution. William Crofut, for example, published *Creationism Is for Catholics* (1984) and *Does Chemical Evolution Explain the Origin of Life?* (1985). An earlier Catholic denunciation of evolution was A. N. Field's *Evolution Hoax Exposed* (1941), which carried what is surely one of the most vividly wonderful antievolution lines ever. Field described evolution as "a very low-grade religion, with its hymns played in jazz and syncopated cacophony, and its sanctuaries adorned with cubist art" (McIver 1992, 79). *Pathways to the Torah* (1985) was a Jewish antievolution book published by the Arachim organization for the furtherance of Jewish awareness. Although ostensibly a guide for Jewish discussion of evolution, it used mostly Christian antievolution arguments. In the last years of the twentieth century individual Muslims slowly began to take more interest in the topic. In some interpretations of the Koran, Islamic scholars argued there was room to accept that animals may have appeared through evolution and that archaic humans did as well. True humans, however, came into being only when Allah gave them souls. This allowed for the presence of fossil hominids of great age without upsetting the core of Islamic belief. As it was impossible to tell whether the australopithecines or Neanderthals had souls, the question of their place in creation was left open. Harun Yahya's *Evolution Deceit* (1999) was an argument built largely of Christian Fundamentalist points with little that was uniquely Islamic.

Despite the modern antagonism to evolution there were attempts in the past by both naturalists and theologians to put evolution and religion into a context in which they could coexist peacefully and even enhance each other's position. In the pre-Darwinian period of human antiquity research, reason and religion were allies: both worked to prove the Genesis story and to show God's presence in the natural attributes of the world.

An attempt of this type to address questions of the origin of the human race was Matthew Hale's *Primitive Origination of Man* (1677). Hale (1609–1676) was an influential British lawyer who was also interested in history and anatomy. The England of Hale's day was one of great upheaval, as struggles for control of the government swung between an ousted monarchy and a secular parliament. Hale believed that an officer of the court had to avoid taking sides in disputes in order to apply the law properly. This philosophy allowed him to prosper under both the Commonwealth of Oliver Cromwell and the restored monarchy. He rose in political ranks, eventually becoming chief justice of England. His nonpartisan attitude is clear in the *Primitive Origination of Man*. He wrote the book in parts over several years as a kind of philosophical hobby (it was published posthumously the year after his death).

At first Hale argued that the earth must have had some beginning, and so man could not be ageless. Then, using the tactics of a lawyer, he set up a premise that a reasoned argument, separate from simple religious belief, supported the Christian view of divine origin. He made reference to past authors and argued that there was more than enough evidence to support the Mosaic account from Genesis. Although he was in no way a transmutationist, Hale thought that if one were to believe in special creation, it should have a rational basis. Man's reason for being was to witness God's handiwork in nature. God had given man his intellect to praise creation; this was man's final cause. Examination of the natural world would lead to the realization that the laws that governed the operation of the universe were divine. Hale accepted that some creatures had appeared through spontaneous generation, but not man. Having accepted this premise, he argued that aside from spontaneous generation there was no other way of coming into being but divine creation; therefore man was a product of the hand of God.

Hale opposed belief in "mechanism," an idea popularized by Robert Boyle (1627–1691) and others who believed that God was the First Cause, having created the universe and all the laws by which it operated but then let it run by itself without further interference. Hale saw God's influence continuing in every aspect of life. The universe was more than just a machine and man more than just a cog in that machine. In the end Hale argued that reason and the study of nature showed man was divinely created.

Well into the nineteenth century science and religion had a fairly cordial relationship. The most popular technique for reconciling religion and human evolution continued to be variations of the idea that organic change and the appearance of humans were the results of divinely inspired laws. In other words, evolution was part of God's plan. This allowed for the two ideas to coexist without much conflict and was called theistic evolution. After the publication of the *Origin of Species* in 1859, it became increasingly difficult to hold a no-conflict point of view, though some tried. Some wanted to accept natural selection but could not bring themselves to accept that the mind and human consciousness could have evolved. Men like Alfred Russel Wallace, St. George Jackson Mivart, and others held that although the physical body of man had arrived due to biological development, it was the hand of God that had placed consciousness in the shell. Although there was resistance to Darwinian theory in England and Europe, the place the creation-evolution debate was most vigorous was the United States.

*Human Evolution in America*

Evolutionary thinking came somewhat slowly to the United States. There was little discussion of evolution (or transmutation, as it was then called) in America before 1859. After that most intellectuals and naturalists were eventually converted to a general belief in evolution, though not always to Darwin's central idea of natural selection. The dissatisfaction with natural selection caused some Americans to adopt the more comfortable explanations for organic change put forward earlier in the century by Jean-Baptiste Lamarck, who theorized that organisms changed through the accumulation of hereditary traits brought on by adaptation to environmental pressure and that changes to any aspect of the organism's structure were passed on to its offspring, creating a new species. For some, Lamarck's law of acquired characters was a simpler, more straightforward alternative to Darwin's selection and variation. They called themselves neo-Lamarckians.

Some historians have argued that lines between the neo-Lamarckians and neo-Darwinians (those who modified Darwinism by adding germ theory to it) were clearly drawn and amounted to a rivalry between opposing forces. This view may be misleading. One problem is that there was little consensus during the nineteenth century about what was meant by Darwinism (or Lamarckism, for that matter). Many naturalists and other intellectuals claimed to be Darwinists, but what they actually believed about evolution varied, not only from each other but from Darwin as well.

The line between evolution and religion was likewise not so clear. The early American geologist Edward Hitchcock (1793–1864), in his pioneering studies of the rocks and fossils of New England, was attempting to reconcile geology with Scripture. Hitchcock, a professor of geology and theology and president of Amherst College, discovered a trove of fossil footprints in Connecticut that he attributed to a race of giant antediluvian birds.

Many nineteenth-century religious movements made clear efforts to support their beliefs with science. Spiritualism and Christian Science, for example, did and saw no contradiction; in fact, they saw science and religion as compatible. Their work either incorporated current science or claimed that the scientific method of verifiable demonstration could prove the validity of their beliefs.

An attempt to bridge the gap between evolution and religion was in the work of George Frederick Wright (1838–1921). He studied at Oberlin College in Ohio for the ministry. The college's president was the legendary Charles G. Finney (1792–1875), a prime mover of the Second Great Awakening of spirituality in America. Finney stressed the idea that the Bible was the ultimate authority and that religious belief was supported by evidence from nature. Becoming a minister upon his graduation, Wright began to teach himself natural history by reading Darwin and Lyell, whose books' central themes were in direct contradiction to what he had been taught as a religion student. He also read the botanist Asa Gray and came to believe he could accept both religion and evolution. Gray had corresponded with Darwin before 1859 and was sent a preproduction copy of *The Origin of Species* for comment. For Gray, a New York Presbyterian, and a host of other Victorian naturalists, God was the first indisputable cause of evolution, with random chance left out of the equation. This theistic evolution approach gave them a way to accept evolution and Christianity together.

Gray and Wright were soon corresponding, and Gray became something of a mentor to Wright. They wanted to formulate evolution in such a way as to be able to put both Darwinians and anti-Darwinians in their place. They believed strict religionists who denounced evolution as anti-Christian were just as wrong as strict evolutionists who denied religion. Wright thought that God created the first few species and then let natural selection take over. This way biological transmutation did not violate the argument from design and vice versa. Unlike many Fundamentalists, Wright did not view Scripture as literal or infallible at first.

By the 1880s Wright began to move more to the conservative side after taking a position at his old school, Oberlin. In that more conservative environment he slowly changed from defending science from religion to defending religion from science. He grew to fear that science and evolutionary thinking in particular were seeking not just to coexist but to undermine religious faith. He lost his liberal view and adopted an increasingly literalist stance. In 1892 he wrote *Man and the Glacial Period* as an explanation for how a single ice age had inundated the earth and included some of his musings on the fossil humans and artifacts being found in Europe. However, reviews of the book were not encouraging. He was accused of badly misreading the geology and was told to keep his nose out of science and in theology where it belonged. The stinging critique of his work by some geologists pushed Wright more and more into the traditional Christian camp.

In the following years Wright engaged in a series of exercises to find scientific explanations for events like Noah's Flood and the destruction of Sodom and Gomorrah. Yet he interpreted the line about man being made from the dust of the earth as meaning that after evolving from the lower primates (who could be seen as coming from "dust"), man became man when God put the spark of spirituality in him. Like Alfred Russel Wallace and others, Wright could accept the bodily evolution of humans, but when it came to consciousness he believed the only explanation was divine intervention. The contradictory nature of Wright's thinking was symptomatic of an age where intellectuals were hard-pressed to accept two such different philosophies as Christianity and human evolution but wanted to. Wright's attempt to support religion with scientific thinking and geological and archaeological evidence was a step toward what would eventually be known as creation science.

As the twentieth century progressed, the conflict between evolution and religion began to heat up. This was partially a result of the rise of Christian Fundamentalism. Scholars have disagreed over how this intense and strict interpretation of Christian doctrine came about. Christian Fundamentalism was traditionally thought of as having emerged in the United States in the early part of the twentieth century as an anti-intellectual backlash against the rise of other approaches to Christian worship known as modernism. In the 1970s and 1980s this was shown to be an oversimplification. One school of thought argued that Fundamentalism was a development that grew out of revivalism, which itself originated in the early twentieth century, not over political or social concerns but over what was considered the growth of false Christian doctrine. Another argued that Fundamentalism could be traced back to the millennial (end of the world) movement of the early nineteenth century. Either way, Fundamentalism broke into wider public notice over its leaders' battles to stop the teaching of evolution in the public school system.

The Christian Fundamentalist movement can be generally categorized as one roughly held together by belief in the literal meaning of the Bible, opposition to evolution, and a desire to return to traditional forms of worship. Adherents considered themselves pious Christians in a world turning away from God and proper Christian belief. Modernists, on the other hand, held the Bible to be symbolic, not literal; accepted the teaching of evolution as compatible with Christianity; and followed a fluid, liberal view of Christianity that they believe had to be "modernized" by each generation in order to stay viable.

Easy generalizations about these groups were formed in part because of the grand generalizations made by both sides about the other. Anyone even loosely associated was blindly labeled a Fundamentalist or modernist, even though the two sides constituted relative minorities. As a grouping of diverse individuals and denominations—including Presbyterians, Baptists, and others—Fundamentalism was not a homogeneous block. Some were radical, while others were moderate. Many Fundamentalists insisted that they were making scholarly studies of the Bible and that their methodologies were more "scientific" than the theoretical work of scientists. The simplistic reading that all the Fundamentalists were uneducated hillbillies is inaccurate.

Their emphasis on gathering and studying facts in the traditional Baconian method led them in part to their opposition to human evolution because they thought it was theoretically and not empirically based (still an antievolutionist argument). The modernists were likewise more diverse than often assumed. The Reverend Harry Emerson Fosdick of the First Presbyterian Church of New York said that science and Darwinism were not incompatible with Christianity. He opposed the growing power of the Fundamentalists and was eventually forced out of his position in 1924 by a coalition of them. Modernist leaders were comfortable with evolution.

One thing the Fundamentalists latched on to was the teaching of evolution in schools. They thought evolution, human evolution in particular, was a false belief that undermined Christian civilization. As a result, Fundamentalist-supported bills were put before the legislatures of several states to ban the teaching of evolution throughout the 1920s. A Kentucky initiative was spearheaded by the Nebraska politician William Jennings Bryan (1860–1925) and strove to outlaw the teaching of human evolution in any school receiving public funds, including universities. Although the measure was struck down, diehard supporters kept fighting for antievolution legislation.

Beginning his career as a Nebraska congressman, William Jennings Bryan served as an officer in the Spanish-American War and ran unsuccessfully for president three times, in 1896, 1900, and 1908. The economic depression of 1893 led to the virtual destruction of the Democratic Party, allowing Bryan to rise to the upper levels of what was left of it. An important moment in his career was his speech called "Cross of Gold" given in 1896. Many had questioned why gold was used as the basis of American money instead of silver. Using silver, he argued, would allow poor farmers to pay off their crushing bank loans more easily. His stance drew support from rural farmers and objections from everywhere else. When the Democrat Woodrow Wilson was elected president, he made Bryan secretary of state.

By the 1920s, Bryan became associated with Christian Fundamentalism and stepped to the forefront of the antievolution movement. In February 1922 he ran an editorial in the *New York Times* excoriating what he saw as the teaching of the heretical belief of Darwinism. Claiming evolution to be an unproven theory, Bryan said that he opposed its teaching because he thought it a theory without merit. The *Times* then asked Henry Fairfield Osborn of the American Museum of Natural History to write a rebuttal. Osborn said that what Bryan was asking in his article was whether God used evolution as part of His divine plan. Osborn's simple answer was yes. Osborn was one of the last major evolutionists in the United States to continue to believe evolution and Christianity could coexist peacefully. Osborn tried to convince Bryan that evolution was a divinely inspired law that operated slowly and methodically and that its tenets were in no way antithetical to spiritual belief.

Bryan was not the only Fundamentalist who had it in for evolution. In New York another erstwhile antievolutionist set his sights on the activities at the American Museum. John Roach Straton (1875–1929) of the Calvary Baptist Church on West Fifty-seventh Street was also a leader in the antievolution movement. He took issue with the museum's newly installed Hall of the Age of Man, the first major display on human evolution. In addition to Charles R. Knight's murals, the museum had collected casts and actual hominid fossils from collections around the world to put on display. Straton fumed that this exhibition was ruining and warping the minds of impressionable New York schoolchildren. Straton wanted the exhibition dismantled or at least to include a reference to the biblical story of the Creation. Osborn did not want religion introduced into the exhibition because he feared that average people already did not understand the workings of evolution, and religion would only confuse the issue further. The public tended to side with the museum, which saw attendance climb as a result of the controversy.

Osborn became a major public defender of evolution during the Fundamentalist controversy. Evolutionary thinking, he said, was not modernist but had a long history of Christian acceptance; he cited Saint Augustine as a church father who would have been amenable to transmutation. Bryan referred to Osborn and others like him as "tree men" swinging by their tails and chattering like monkeys. He dismissed Osborn's argument completely and claimed Osborn thought the discovery of fossils more important than the birth of Jesus Christ, an accusation that enraged the devoutly religious Osborn.

One way the Fundamentalist position can be understood is by looking at the question of pessimism versus optimism. The Fundamentalists were eschatologists; they believed in the imminent end of the world as prophesied in the Bible. They also placed emphasis on proper doctrine and right thinking. Whereas their view of humanity's future was pessimistic, that of the evolutionists was optimistic. "Endtime" beliefs viewed humanity as being on a downward slide to an oblivion from which it could be saved only by Christ. Although there were many stripes of evolutionist in the late nineteenth and early twentieth centuries, most held that the human race was moving in a basically progressive and upwardly mobile fashion (unlike evolutionary belief today). This optimistic bent made evolution a false doctrine in the eyes of Christians. The verbal sparring between Osborn, Bryan, and Straton over evolution was only a warm-up for things to come.

## The Scopes Monkey Trial

The pivotal moment in the warfare between supporters of human evolution and those of special creation in America came with what journalist H. L. Mencken called the monkey trial. The state of Tennessee passed its antievolution law, the Butler Bill, in March 1925, and the fledgling American Civil Liberties Union (ACLU) of New York went after it. The ACLU advertised in Tennessee newspapers asking for volunteers to help fight the law through a test case. The city fathers of the small town of Dayton saw a chance for national publicity and approached the ACLU, offering Dayton as the site to hold the trial. They then enticed Dayton public school physical education and general science teacher John Scopes to volunteer as the accused.

As the primary defense counsel the ACLU called in the legendary Clarence Darrow (1857–1938). Darrow had become infamous over his 1924 defense of the child murderers Nathan Leopold

*Clarence Darrow at the Scopes evolution trial, Dayton, Tennessee, July 1925 (Library of Congress)*

and Richard Loeb. That the two spoiled rich kids from Chicago society had brutally killed little Bobby Franks was not in question. Darrow fought to keep his charges from receiving the death penalty by arguing that they had been morally corrupted by society and that as a result, though guilty, they did not deserve to die. His gambit worked, and Leopold and Loeb were spared. In 1925 Darrow took on the cause of teaching evolution. Although superficially about whether John Scopes taught evolution and broke the law, the monkey trial became an epic battle between William Jennings Bryan, who would be acting as special prosecutor, and Darrow over the freedom to teach unpopular ideas in the public school system in the United States.

Part of Darrow's strategy was to call various well-known scientists, including Henry Fairfield Osborn, to the stand to explain evolution and why teaching it was not a cause for worry to the people of Tennessee. Doing this was central to Darrow's case, but the judge denied the opportunity, saying scientific explanations were irrelevant to the case. Frustrated, Darrow took a desperate gamble and called William Jennings Bryan to the stand as an authority on the Bible. Over objections from his coprosecution, Bryan accepted Darrow's challenge and confidently took the stand. Darrow proceeded to grill Bryan on such classic atheist questions as "Where did Cain's wife come from?" and other anomalous and contradictory aspects of Scripture. He was also able to make Bryan admit that the biblical "days" of the Creation might not have been twenty-four hours but days of indeterminate length. Bryan stumbled and stammered his way through the cross-examination, raising the eyebrows of even his staunchest supporters. His simplistic view of Creation and unlettered understanding of evolutionary mechanics made him an easy target for Darrow's sharper analytic mind. When it was over, Bryan was exhausted and visibly shaken. Despite Bryan's poor performance on the stand, Scopes was convicted. The conviction was later overturned on a technicality, but the trial had a lasting effect on American religion and its relationship to the idea of human evolution and public thinking.

The popular image of the trial was based on H. L. Mencken's description of it in a series of articles for the *Baltimore Sun*.

*Darwin's work perverted in an American cartoon to promote hatred, from around the time of the Scopes trial (undated souvenir postcard, collection of the author)*

THE DARWINIAN THEORY.

Mencken was a well-known syndicated journalist and political commentator. He outraged many by arguing that religion was a curse upon society that clouded people's minds and led them to believe in and do irrational things. In "The Hills of Zion," written during the trial when he attended a local revival meeting, he saw hypocrisy everywhere and chuckled in self-satisfaction as he watched the attending gentlemen behave. "They were all hot for Genesis," he said, "but their faces were far too florid to belong to teetotalers, and when a pretty girl came tripping down the main street, which was very often, they reached for the places where their neckties should have been with all the amorous enterprise of movie actors" (1925).

Mencken saw the people of the South in general as fools and rural simpletons. He saw the trial as a battle of forward-looking intellectual sophisticates stemming the tide of advancing hordes of backward, clawing barbarians. This picture was advanced by the appearance of the play based on the trial, *Inherit the Wind* (1955). Playwrights Jerome Lawrence and Robert E. Lee constructed a tragedy of Greek proportions and in stark black and white that, though powerful, missed all the subtleties of the actual events by rolling out the stereotypes of big city versus backwoods and the enlightened versus the closed-minded. In one dramatic scene, the withering cross-examination by Henry Drummond (the Clarence Darrow character) forces Matthew Harrison Brady (the William Jennings Bryan character) to lose his composure. Increasingly unable to answer questions coherently, Brady jumps to his feet and in desperation quotes Proverbs, "He who troubleth his own house shall inherit the wind!" The play was a great success and inspired a major motion picture a few years later. However, this image is deeply misleading and inaccurate. To accept it on face value makes it impossible to understand what was, and is, going on.

### After Scopes

Following the Scopes trial, some antievolutionists stepped away from a purely scriptural point of view and began building what they thought would be a scientific refutation of human evolution. Creationism was the belief that the earth and all life on it were the result of divine intervention. There were many varieties of this line of thinking. Creation science was a Fundamentalist belief in a literal interpretation of the Genesis story of a six-day creation week occurring no more than 10,000 years ago, which could all be proven by scientific methods. Not all creationists took the "young earth" position.

Some allowed the earth may be billions of years old. This "gap theory" allowed that after the creation week, a period of indeterminate length passed before the historical period began. Strict literalists rejected this notion because it did not fit biblical accounts and contradicted God's word. Gap theory traces back at least to Scottish theologian Thomas Chalmers (1780–1847), who used it as a way of reconciling Scripture with the knowledge geologists were producing about the nature of the earth. In the nineteenth century William Buckland and Hugh Miller both adhered to the idea. Along with gap theory was "day-age" theory that argued that the days of Genesis were not twenty-four-hour days but were of indeterminate length. Again, strict creationists saw this as a cop-out to try to get around scientific evidence. Although these different lines of thought did not constitute a single block (they actually feuded with each other as much as they did with mainstream science), in this study they will be grouped together, for the sake of convenience, as creationism.

Generally, Jews, Catholics, and Muslims did not get as worked up about human evolution as Fundamentalist Christians did. Indeed, some of the most vocal proponents of human evolution have been Catholics like Teilhard de Chardin and Henri Breuil, Jews like Stephen Jay Gould, and even devout Presbyterians like Henry Fairfield Osborn. In the early part of the twentieth century few mainstream scientists of any stripe were willing to support creationism. Though he tried, William Jennings Bryan could not recruit scientists to support the prosecution at the Scopes trial. Even those few scientists who held a place for some kind of divine intervention in evolution would not support Bryan's blanket condemnation of it. The one "scientist" Bryan had been able to interest in the case was unable to attend, as he was in England at the time.

George McCready Price (1870–1963) was likely the most influential scientific creationist of the early twentieth century. He grew up a millenarian in a Seventh-Day Adventist sect in New Brunswick, Canada. The Adventists were an offshoot of the original American millennial group, the Millerites of 1840s New York. Under the leadership of William Miller, the Millerites waited for the world to end at Albany but were deeply disappointed when it did not happen. The group eventually broke up over this, and the Seventh-Day Adventists appeared out of the remnants. The leader of the Adventist church was the charismatic Ellen White (1827–1915), who claimed that God passed information to her followers through her while she was in a trance. She stressed a literal belief in Genesis without any of the nuanced interpretations, like the day-age and gap theories.

As a young man Price dreamed of being a writer, but his life did not go well. He suffered through a series of economic and professional disappointments and low-paying jobs within the Adventist church that left him intellectually as well as monetarily unfulfilled. In the 1890s he briefly attended a small New Brunswick school, taking a few classes in natural history (these were the closest he would ever get to formal training in anything approaching science). By the turn of the century he began to fixate on the geologic aspects of evolution as the key to the whole system: if the geology was right, then evolution was right; if the geology did not make sense, then evolution did not either. Price did considerable soul-searching and vowed to follow the geology wherever it led. He paid particular attention to stratigraphy and the explanation for why younger layers were occasionally found below older ones. Geologists had long argued that the strata of the earth went in a progression from youngest at the top to oldest at the bottom. The concept of uplift was used to explain why the sequence was not always so simple: geologic forces could sometimes lift older layers above younger ones, making them seem out of sequence. Price found this explanation unacceptable. As to the initial formation of the layers, Price found Charles Lyell's steady-state, uniform-action explanation also unacceptable. His Adventist upbringing led him to Georges Cuvier's catastrophism. Price modified Cuvier's many periods of catastrophic upheaval and reduced them down to just Noah's Flood. It was the Flood that accounted for the geology of the earth and the fossils were remnants of those animals that did not get in the Ark. He called this system flood geology and published his theory in 1923 in the book *The New Geology*. The book went on to become a basic "science" text in creationist circles, and Price himself became the grand old man of the movement, sought out by others for advice and approval.

Price was representative of many scientific creationists in that he disparaged science and scientists but was desperate to gain their recognition, if not their approval. He disliked scientists and their "pagan" ways, yet he wanted to be one. He mistrusted their extensive training and was self-conscious about his lack of any. As a result, he downplayed the importance of formal academic education yet at times claimed to hold a master's degree and was proud of his bachelor's degree, even though it had been awarded to him by the College of Medical Evangelists—not for actual course work completed but for his publications. He continued to publish and remained a central figure in the fray throughout his long life.

After the Scopes trial mainstream America and the media lost interest in creationism, but followers did not. In the 1930s the first in a series of societies was formed to keep the work going. Groups like the Religion and Science Association and the Deluge Geology Society came into being and, though small, were hotbeds of creationist activity and debate. Squabbling among believers grew intense, partly as a result of younger enthusiasts getting better conventional science educations. With their new knowledge and what they saw in the field they found it increasingly difficult to reconcile some of the more extreme claims of other followers. The new generations were not quite armchair theorizers like Price. Their deeper understanding of the natural world gave them a different insight. Unable to overcome the validity of biology and geology, some creationists began giving ground, accepting scientific tenets as long as they could hold on to the ultimately divine origin of humans and their souls. Some accepted an ancient earth but held for a literal creation week after that, some accepted God creating the basic groups of organisms that then evolved on their own according to a form of natural selection, and some allowed for natural selection after the period of the Garden of Eden. This reconciliatory approach did not attract mainstream scientists and enraged many true believers. By the 1950s Price and the circle of Seventh-Day Adventists who had played such a crucial role in the development of creationism descended into back-biting, internal warfare, and obstinacy. The societies they created broke down, and an already marginalized movement slipped into a period of deeper obscurity.

A late-twentieth-century successor to William McCready Price was Duane Gish. A "gracious Christian gentleman," Gish toured, lectured, and wrote extensively in the cause of creation science and helped bring it back to life. Unlike Price, he studied science formally, eventually receiving a doctorate in biochemistry from the University of California at Berkeley in 1953. He worked as a corporate chemist and researcher until 1971, when he joined Christian Heritage College, an institution founded the year before. The next year the college changed its name to the Institute for Creation Research. Gish eventually became the institute's associate director and vice president.

*Evolution: The Challenge of the Fossil Record* (1985) is representative of Gish's work and one of the most quoted of the genre. Originally published as *Evolution: The Fossils Say No!* it was an examination and undermining of the idea that fossils support the evolution model. He followed a common creationist technique of taking quotations of evolutionists out of context to show that what they said did not make sense and that they themselves did not think evolution proven. For example, when influential evolutionist George Gaylord Simpson said it was difficult to find fossils of the Precambrian era even though the sediment suggested they should be there, Gish argued that this meant the evolutionists were condemning their own idea. Difference of opinion or unanswered questions became "proof" that evolution was a false doctrine. Gish used many of the standard arguments of creation science thinking: there were no transitional forms in the fossil record; evolution was not really science but was just as faith based as any other religion; and fossils actually proved the creation, not evolution, model.

Like many creation scientists, Gish, despite his technical training, used some awkward examples. He pointed to the Tasaday people as proof that archaic humans were degenerates. The Tasaday were a group of primitive people found in the jungles of the Philippines in the 1970s that was supposedly "untouched" by civilization. They were thought by anthropologists to be a fascinating example of Stone Age people surviving into the modern era. Much was written about the Tasaday, and they and their discoverers became a sensation. It was later found out that the entire case had been an elaborately contrived hoax put together by unscrupulous individuals within the Ferdinand Marcos regime to defraud the government. Gish also argued that evolutionists believed and still taught the "molecule-to-man" theory. This approach, which argued evolution was a goal-oriented process leading to the advanced form of man, was popular in the nineteenth century but had long since been abandoned by mainstream paleoanthropology. Gish lamented that "it is incredible that the molecules-to-man evolution theory be taught as a fact to the exclusion of all other postulates" (1985, 19).

In the end Gish made no bones about what was really going on in evolutionist circles. The reason anyone, especially scientists, believed in evolution was because they were unbelievers and materialistic. Gish also had a peculiar fixation on scientists becoming famous along with their fossils. He referred to Donald Johanson as a once obscure anthropologist who "became famous overnight" because of his discovery of the Lucy skeleton. Gish seemed particularly peeved at Johanson's fame, which, he said, was manufactured by institutions of higher learning in league with the media in an attempt to produce a world of unbelievers.

## Man Tracks and Fossil Hammers

Creationists often pointed to geologic formations and conventional fossils to argue that far from supporting evolution, they actually supported the creation model. They also pointed to more dubious examples of fossils and artifacts. Like the anomalists discussed in chapter 8, creationists searched the world and written record for peculiar fossils, ones that would topple and upset accepted notions about the course of human evolution. One of the most often cited of these anomalous fossils was the "Meister Print" from Utah. This strange artifact was found in 1968 by fossil hunter William Meister. He was prospecting for trilobites in 500-million–year-old strata known as the Wheeler Formation when he cracked open a slab to find what looked like a human shoe print that had crushed a live trilobite under its heel. Creationists seized upon the print as evidence that humans had trod the earth during a time scientists said they did not exist. The creationists held the Meister Print as proof that the fossil record, the geologic time scale, and the very notion of human evolution were false. Several studies showed the print was in reality an example of a common geologic occurrence known as spalling, in which slabs of rock break away from each other in distinctive patterns. This particular case of spalling had created a simulacrum vaguely suggestive of a shoe print. After this determination of prosaic natural causes, some creationists stopped acknowledging the print in the 1980s, while others continued to do so.

Similar fossil "footprints" have turned up fairly regularly since the nineteenth century, and each time creationists got excited that this may be the one that would destroy the edifice of evolutionary thinking. There have been supposed human skulls found under lava millions of years old; in the Americas coins were found embedded in stone from ages before coins were first manufactured; and, one of the most popular creationist artifacts, a modern hammer was found locked in a mass of sedimentary rock. These were gleefully put forward with calls for scientists to explain them. When examined, they all turned out to be misidentifications of other things, hoaxes, or simply examples of people not understanding what they were looking at.

A major compendium of such anomalous fossils and other evidence of the falsity of human evolution theory was *Forbidden Archaeology* (1994) by Michael Cremo and Richard Thompson. Besides the sheer mass of material they collected, what made this book unique within the genre was that the authors were not Christian Fundamentalists but Hindu followers of Krishna Consciousness. Although they cited much the same material as the Christians and other antievolutionists, they argued the human race was not very young but immensely old—far older than even evolutionists are willing to allow. They claimed modern humans appeared through divine intervention more than 55 million years ago and that ancient Vedic scripture told the "true" story of how humans came to be. That their thesis was different from other antievolutionists did not keep them from falling into the same traps. They quoted evolutionists out of context and accepted vague century-old accounts of anomalous fossils while dismissing modern scientific ones backed up with meticulously gathered documentation. It was a common notion in anomalist circles that if science did not have all the answers to a problem, or if one scientist disagreed with another or harbored some doubts, this was de facto proof evolution was a sham.

Cremo and Thompson argued that there was a concerted effort on the part of the "evolution establishment" to suppress any evidence that contradicted mainstream thinking, especially mainstream human evolutionary thinking. They shared this notion with others. In their seminal work on anomalous artifacts and events, *Phenomena: A Book of Wonders* (1979), John Michell and Bob Rickard argued that "some of these evidences have been actually suppressed and deliberately ignored: some have quietly and mysteriously disappeared from museum stores and records" (75). Yet they gave the devil his due by saying that accepting that humans were around hundreds of millions of years ago based on such scanty evidence was "irrational." Since the 1990s Christian creationists have claimed that the Smithsonian Institution in Washington has a collection of artifacts that were obviously intelligently designed, but who the designers were and what purposes the artifacts served were unknown. The Smithsonian disavowed having any such collection.

An enduring belief within creationist circles has been that humans coexisted with the dinosaurs, and if proof could be found that they did the entire human evolution edifice would crumble. To support the contention, many creationists pointed to the so-called man tracks of Texas. They argued that what paleontologists called dinosaur tracks were in reality human footprints frozen forever in mud turned to stone. The tracks were first discovered in 1917 along the banks of the Paluxy River outside the town of Glen Rose, Texas. This region of Texas had been a floodplain 70 million years ago, as the Gulf of Mexico extended much farther inland than it does today. Many of the tracks were clearly those of dinosaurs, but a few took on odd shapes because of the distortion caused by the animals slipping and sliding in the wet mud. It was these tracks that creationists argued were human footprints. Roland T. Bird (1899–1978), the American Museum of Natural History excavator who did the first extensive work at Glen Rose in the 1930s, tried to convince people that the prints were just deformed dinosaur tracks. Creationists ignored him and happily measured, photographed, and discussed the "man tracks" regardless. Bird threw up his hands in frustration.

Although most creationist evidence, like the Paluxy tracks, was brought forward by individuals and groups with a shaky understanding of the science they were criticizing, at the end of the twentieth century traditionally trained scientists with a religious bent began taking to the creationist cause.

### Creationism Evolving

The creationist argument was not having much effect in overturning belief in human evolution. Flood geology, hammers embedded in stone, and shoe-crushed trilobites succeeded only in making mainstream scientists view them as even bigger jokes. By the late twentieth century they changed gears again and brought out an old friend. Dressed up in a modern suit, the argument from design took on a new life as "intelligent design." Assaults on evolutionary belief were becoming increasingly sophisticated.

Phillip Johnson wrote *Darwin on Trial* in 1991 and attempted, like Matthew Hale so many years before, to formulate a purely intellectual and legal argument. Johnson became a Christian late in life and attacked evolution with all the zeal of a recent convert. He came to believe that modern culture was responsible for a growing secularization of the education system that was resulting in a general breakdown in American society. At the heart of this breakdown was the teaching of evolution. He claimed his examination of evolutionary mechanics was on its own terms, not in light of any religious framework. According to the tenets of science and the words of evolutionists themselves, he said, natural selection as a scientific explanation for life on earth was unscientific. Johnson worked hard throughout his discourse at retaining a judicial objectivity and began by stating that "'evolution' contradicts 'creation' only when it is explicitly or tacitly defined as *fully naturalistic evolution* [his italics]—meaning evolution that is not directed by any purposeful intelligence" (4).

Johnson was willing, in the light of scientific evidence that was irrefutable, to accept evolution as long as it was acceptable as divine law. Conversely, he added that creation contradicted evolution only when it meant sudden creation rather than progressive development. He then ran out the tried-and-true objections: Darwinism was really a religion, the fossil record was misleading and actually supported creationism, evolution is a tautology. This last was popular among antievolutionists because it was a nondenominational argument. A tautology is a way of saying the same thing twice, to prove something is by its own being, not outside arguments. For example, a favorite point within the tautology argument was the line about survival of the fittest. Antievolutionists said that evolutionists said that the fittest organisms leave the most offspring because they are the fittest. This has been admitted by a number of evolutionists as well as the twentieth-century philosopher Karl Popper. This circular argument was used as proof that evolution was a speculative idea no more empirically based than any other religious contention. Johnson questioned the very notion of fitness (modern evolutionists tended to use the word *adapted* instead of *fittest*) and wondered how some traits could have been advantageous to organisms that had them. For this Johnson went to Darwin's own example of the peacock. In *The Descent of Man* Darwin used the example of these brightly colored birds as evidence for sexual selection. Johnson wondered why such a thing would have occurred, as the bright colors would have attracted predators as well as mates, which would have eliminated the peacock population. Johnson mused that "it seems to me that the peacock and the peahen are just the kind of creatures a whimsical Creator might favor . . . but natural selection would never permit to develop" (31).

For all his lawyerly acumen and metaphorical adroitness, Johnson ended by arguing that evolution should not be accepted because evolutionists had not worked out all the problems and did not have all the answers. And despite his pleas for objectivity, Johnson is well within the religious Fundamentalist antievolutionist camp, so much so that he became something of a spokesman for the cause.

At the close of the twentieth century the strongest concerted challenge to evolution was the idea of intelligent design. This phase of antievolution polemic came not from Bible-thumping backwoods preachers but from university-trained scientists, particularly from the fields of biochemistry, molecular biology, and mathematics. Intelligent design goes back at least to the mechanists of the 1600s like Robert Boyle and his *Origin of Forms and Qualities* (1666). He argued that the universe was a vastly complex machine with a first but not a final cause. As such the only way to account for this device was by an intelligent designer who put the whole thing together and started it working. The idea took off with William Paley's *Natural Theology* (1802).

In its current manifestation, intelligent design is a belief that combines the traditional idea that the great complexity and interconnected nature of life on earth are evidence that it was designed and adds to it the apparent hypercomplexity of life at the cellular level and that the various systems needed to sustain life could not have resulted if they appeared according to evolutionist doctrine. Just as geneticists began to argue in the early twentieth century that fossils alone could not answer how evolution really worked but genetics would, intelligent design people, though respectful of their elders like Duane Gish and his focus on fossils, saw genetics as the key to proving why evolution did not work.

A lightning rod of the intelligent design school was Michael Behe and his book *Darwin's Black Box: The Biochemical Challenge to Evolution* (1996). A professor of biochemistry at Lehigh University in Pennsylvania, Behe argued that what he called the "irreducible complexity" of a cell showed that life was designed. Irreducible complexity describes biological systems that consist of connected parts that must all be in place for the larger system to operate. The title came from Charles Darwin's reference to the cell as a black box inside of which he could not see or work out why it worked.

Building upon an old antievolutionist argument about what good was half an eye or half a heart while it waited for all the necessary parts to evolve, Behe claimed that since an eye would not work unless all the constituent parts were present, that alone would prove a designer had to have put the whole thing together at once. To explain this concept, Behe used the analogy of the mousetrap, which consists of several interlocking parts that must all be present for the device to function; take one out and it does not work. If the mousetrap (if it were a living thing) had evolved one piece at a time, what good would it have been until it could perform its function? But evolution does not work that way. If the wooden board of the mousetrap were to evolve first, it would have performed some action. As each piece was added the device would take on other functions. Once enough parts were present it would then be possible to start catching mice. As more parts were added, the trap might lose its ability to catch mice and would then perform yet some other function. What many antievolutionists often relied on was the notion that evolution was trying to do something specific, like catch mice. The trap was not meant to catch mice; it did so only when the circumstances of structure and environment made it possible. It could just as easily have performed some other function.

Though Behe's answer to explaining the hypercomplexity of life is intelligent design, he resists going that last step and saying who the designer is. Some antievolutionists who want to avoid being seen as religious Fundamentalists often invoke a sort of shoulder shrugging over this last bit, saying they do not know who the designer is, afraid to say the *G* word.

Adding to Behe's work was the philosopher-theologian-mathematician from Baylor University William Demski. He wrote extensively on complex systems and their relation to evolution and argued that microorganisms and their parts, though superficially simple, are still highly complex creatures, too complex to have been formed by chance. He employed statistics and other mathematical systems to show that the odds of life evolving were so astronomically high as to be impossible. As a result, the only alternative answer to why life was here at all was that it was designed by a higher power. Intelligent design became so popular that the International Society for Complexity, Information, and Design was formed, as its Web site says, to retain "the scientific imagination to see purpose in nature."

Numerous critical reviews of Behe's work appeared, most making the same points. Although intelligent design comes mostly out of biochemistry, not all molecular biologists are supporters of it. A critique by molecular biologist David Ussery of the Danish Technical University in Denmark is illustrative of the objections voiced over *Darwin's Black Box*. Written for *Bios* magazine in July 1998, his review noted several problems with Behe's approach and conclusions. For example, Behe argued that the scientific literature on molecular evolution was scanty. He also argued that if evolution were to be proven at the molecular level, only biochemistry would be able to do it. So far, Behe claimed, it had been unable to. Ussery countered that the scientific literature of biochemistry and molecular biology was full of papers on evolutionary explanations, that many conferences of biochemists dealt with the origins of life, and that evolution had been explained at the molecular level. He saw Behe's use of the mousetrap analogy as misleading. As these contentions made up the heart of Behe's critique, there was not much left in the book. Ussery was troubled by Behe's acceptance of the normal give-and-take of scientific inquiry as somehow evidence that scientists did not believe evolution worked. There are genuine questions being asked about the mechanics of evolution within proevolution circles and debates over the finer points. Debate and disagreement do not mean scientists secretly believe evolution invalid or that there is a conspiracy of silence.

### More Monkey Trials

The Scopes trial was not about John T. Scopes; it was not really over whether evolution was a valid scientific law of nature or even whether it was proper Christian doctrine. What the trial hinged on was who would be the purveyor of knowledge in American schools: science or religion. After World War II the question came back, and so did the courtroom appearances of monkeys and their uncles.

In order to teach evolution, textbooks were needed. The first book in the United States to deal with evolution was Asa Gray's *First Lessons in Botany,* originally published in 1857 and reissued after 1859. Gray, despite his relationship with Darwin, did not embrace Darwinism completely. His thinking remained theistic, and his textbook reflected it. He argued that God had created a number of species that then went on to become others. Initially, Gray did not accept common descent, but by the 1880s he had done so. The other leading naturalist in the United States turning out textbooks was Louis Agassiz. His high school text on zoology did not take the evolutionary stance. He was an ardent opponent of transmutation and based his books on the concept of special creation. Edward Hitchcock also took the creationist line, arguing that the fossil record contained no transitional forms. Throughout the 1860s and 1870s old-school science textbooks either adopted a theistic approach to evolution or avoided it altogether.

The first high school textbooks to accept evolution as the operating principle of biology began to appear in the 1880s written by the generation of naturalists raised on it. Charles Bessey's *Botany for High Schools and Colleges* (1880) and Joseph LeConte's *Compend of Geology* (1884) both aggressively taught evolution, stressing the importance of the scientific method. Around the turn of the century more proevolution texts appeared that also emphasized the part evolution played in human history. Authors like David Starr Jordan, Vernon Kellog, and Charles Davenport all made a point of connecting biology, heredity, and racial hierarchies in the development of the human race. They were also eugenicists. The most popular high school biology book of the first part of the twentieth century was George Hunter's *Civic Biology,* first published in 1914 and going through numerous editions. Besides having evolution as the driving force in the progression and appearance of life on earth, Hunter, like the other eugenicists, saw Nordic humans as the end product of evolution. This was the book that was the standard-issue biology text in the Dayton, Tennessee, school system.

Since the 1950s there had been a virtually nonstop war in the United States waged by Christian Fundamentalists and their allies to eliminate the teaching of evolution in the public school system. Textbook publishers also became the targets for the wrath of the Fundamentalists. Texas and California are the country's largest consumers of school textbooks. As such, publishers allowed themselves to be influenced by these states and rearranged their books to suit the sensibilities of creationists in those states who exerted pressure on the publishers to remove "objectionable" materials before they would buy them. As many other states followed Texas's and California's lead, considerable sums were involved. Fearful of losing lucrative multimillion-dollar contracts, publishers eagerly excised discussion of evolution in order to curry favor.

The courts also became the stage for antievolutionist activity. In states from Michigan to Georgia, Kansas to California, and places in between, local governments were bombarded with antievolution proposals and bills. In Tennessee in 1973 the state's General Assembly voted unanimously to prohibit the use of textbooks that supported evolution and attempted to make the Bible a biology reference book. The defeat of all these bills forced Fundamentalists to rethink their approach.

In the early 1980s constitutional lawyer, Christian Fundamentalist, and director of the Institute for Creation Research Wendell Bird, along with colleague Paul Ellwanger, a "repertory therapist" and president of a group calling itself Citizens for Fairness in Education, pioneered a new tactic. The main problem of creationist legislation from a purely legal point of view was that, as religiously based proposals, it violated the First Amendment of the U.S. Constitution. This amendment contains the famous "separation of church and state" rule, one of the nation's most cherished concepts. Bird and Ellwanger put together a version of creationism they believed was not religious in nature. Bird called it the "theory of abrupt appearances" and argued that organisms had appeared suddenly without the need for a common ancestor and with no mention of a deity. It was not that much different from intelligent design, but what was innovative and more important was that when presenting it, the authors would stress the idea of in-

tellectual "fairness." If evolution were to be taught, then it would be fair to give creationism equal treatment in the classroom, allowing the students to decide which to believe.

The first test of this new approach came in Arkansas in 1981. ACT590 was the legislative designation for Bird's idea. It proposed a "balanced treatment of creation science and evolution" be adopted by the state (Nelkin 2000, 137). The proposal was brought to a sympathetic "born-again" senator, James Holsted. Impressed by what he read, Holsted bypassed the state Department of Education and the attorney general and put it forward as a bill. Governor Frank White, also "born again," signed it into law without reading it or initiating any debate. The ACLU immediately launched a suit to repeal it.

Although theoretically viable, this approach of removing God from a religious precept had its downside. In order to rework their beliefs into a more constitutionally palatable form, the antievolutionists had to systematically water down, at least publicly, their beliefs. Ironically, they argued that in their version of creation, God was not God. They tried to explain that just because they used the word *creator* it did not necessarily imply a deity. The gambit failed, and the law was defeated. In a final irony, the attorney general's office that had been given the unenviable task of defending an unconstitutional law was accused of wrongdoing, not by the secular press but by the creationists. In addition, televangelist Pat Robertson and Moral Majority Leader Jerry Falwell accused the attorney general's office of siding with the ACLU and the forces of darkness. Even though the Arkansas case fell apart for the creationists, they did not give up.

In 1999 the Kansas Board of Education decided to delete mention of evolution from the state's science curriculum and standardized tests. On August 11 of that year the board voted 6 to 4 to remove most references to evolution from the state's educational standards. Although it was not an outright ban, it eliminated the need to teach the subject by removing any evolution questions from the school system's standardized tests. Grade school and high school teachers regularly concentrated on subjects that were tested on all-important state exams. With evolution not on the tests, teachers would be less likely to spend time on it. Although creationists across the state vowed they would ensure that the ruling was obeyed, many districts continued to teach evolution regardless. Their feeling was that in an attempt to give their students the best education they could, evolution would be taught.

As an example of the strange bedfellows the religion-evolution debate sometimes created, Republican governor Bill Graves, though not having any direct power over the board, urged it to repeal the ban. He feared some board members were using their position to promote personal agendas. Not wanting to antagonize voters for his upcoming presidential bid, Vice President Al Gore, who had been very vocal about the importance of science education in the past, refused to condemn the ban. In Texas, another presidential candidate wanting to curry favor with the religious right, Governor George W. Bush, said he thought creationism should be taught in public schools.

The Kansas situation came about partly as a result of a set of standards for teaching science put out by the prestigious National Academy of Science (NAS) in 1995. In a move to bring the state up to those standards, as many states did, increased emphasis was placed on the teaching of evolution in the Kansas curriculum. The Kansas Board of Education implemented most of the requirements, but some members balked at how the curriculum explained large-scale biological change and speciation. They considered it too speculative and allowed local boards to deal with the question. That is where the trouble started. The board was called backward and anti-intellectual by pundits and science advocates all the way to London. Some suggested not accepting Kansas high school science credits when students applied to college. The NAS along with the American Association for the Advancement of Science disallowed the state to use their copyrighted materials. Debates raged in the media and in both the science and creation camps as to what should be done and how this would affect the future. By 2001 several of the more conservative board members were voted off, largely as a result of the publicity generated by the evolution ban. The new board reversed the ruling and brought evolution education in Kansas back from extinction.

### Keeping a Scorecard

With all the various protagonists, keeping track of the evolution versus creation debate in the United States could get confusing. One important question at the end of the twentieth century was just who was mad at whom? Physicist Mano Singham attempted to work out the larger camps in 2000. He saw it coming down to a complex relationship among four basic groups: elite science, popular science, elite religion, and popular religion. This intellectual class system, as Singham saw it, operated in such a way that different classes might have had their differences but aligned themselves over the evolution issue. Elite science is the mainstream: it accepts evolution as a proven fact, follows established modes of inquiry, and separates itself from popular science and its more lax attitude toward rigorous examination. Elite science refers to popular science as pseudoscience because of its embrace of such topics as UFOs, Bigfoot, ghosts, and spontaneous human combustion, topics that elite science sees as spurious and without empirical support. Elite religion is mainstream religion with its established churches, positions of power, and cultural influence. Popular religion is that of the masses who believe in ghosts, a personal God, miracles, the "unseen" world, and other related ideas. Elite science and religion rarely fight, Singham argued, because as the holders of power they are in no hurry to threaten their positions. Their respective positions could accommodate each other if they had to with little fundamental change, theistic evolution being a prime example of a middle ground between evolution and religion. Singham, though, saw sinister implications in this accommodation. He asked if the middle ground was just a way for the elites to retain their power. Or as he put it, "does this middle ground survive by not posing awkward questions" to each other (2000, 430)? Popular science and religion likewise share much common ground in their acceptance of anomalous occurrences and the "unexplained." Elite religion and popular religion also find common ground. Aside from such things as weeping statues or appearances of the Virgin Mary in office building windows and packages of sticky buns, they too rest fairly easily together.

It is accepted wisdom that during the Renaissance, "science" began to dethrone religion as the seat of intellectual authority in the West. This process continued until Darwin completed it. However, that science ever really dethroned religion outside elite circles is in question. Polls regularly show that more people in the industrial world believe in some sort of general creation (as opposed to the more specific creationism and creation science discussed here) than they do in evolution. So, in the end, the fight comes down to elite science versus popular religion and to some extant popular science. The populists discount the work of the elites and try to keep them from "taking over." Elite science is generally worried about the level of pseudoscience accepted by people. Whether or not such an agreement exists or entire intellectual blocs can be made to think as one bloc is difficult to accept. This doubt aside, Singham illuminated the important question of defining who is who and what they believe and oppose—the same kind of problems that came up during the original Christian Fundamentalist movement and the Scopes trial.

## Conclusion

Underneath all the "science" of creation science, and creationism in general, is a core problem. In many ways the antievolution movement is about geology, genetics, and fossils less than it is a way of protecting a dearly held paradigm. The underlying fear of antievolutionists is that accepting evolution means there was no divine creation and hence no creator and therefore no fall from grace, no breath of divine life, no chance for salvation, no heaven and no hell, no reason to believe or go on. The preoccupation with proving Genesis is that if the introduction of the Bible is undermined, so is the conclusion. One thing evolutionists fear is that teaching creation alongside evolution will only undermine what they see as an already crumbling level of scientific and technical literacy in the United States. They see this as an important issue because as a person's knowledge of science, technology, and critical thinking deteriorates, belief in pseudoscience and the supernatural increases. Unquestioning belief in spirits, UFOs, and the like make people easy prey to be used and taken advantage of. Although scientists do not see themselves as having all the answers, they believe the scientific worldview teaches one to think critically and skeptically and to base understanding and conclusions on fact, not blind belief. Scientists are afraid that most people's knowledge of science and technology comes from the popular media like the *X-Files* or *The Matrix* instead of solid educations in thinking and reasoning.

In the late twentieth and early twenty-first centuries scientists were, for the most part, uninterested in making science more religious, yet creationists were interested in making religion more scientific. They may not have admitted it openly, but they intrinsically knew that science was the best way to explain how the universe operated. Complicating this stance, some scientists insisted that there was no conflict between religion and evolution. For all their ravings, the extreme creationists are correct in that they understand there is no way both sides can coexist. If one believes God created the universe and all the living things in it, then how could organisms have evolved on their own? If one believes that life is the result of naturalistic forces working through the vagaries of the environment and genetic mutation, then there is no need for a creator.

Although some creationists brought this point up, some scientists did as well. Where Steven Jay Gould could ridicule Phillip Johnson and still claim there was no real conflict between the two sides, British zoologist Richard Dawkins leaped upon the creationists "red in tooth and claw" and savaged them with a gleeful smile and a twinkle in his eye. In *The Blind Watchmaker* (1986), *Climbing Mount Improbable* (1996), and a series of reviews of Behe and Johnson as well as various public statements, Dawkins gave no ground and took no prisoners, stating that evolution was the only answer and anyone who believed otherwise was a fool. He argued that there was no room for design in nature and thus no room for a designer. Intelligent design was a flawed idea because it was the result of people believing there was no way to explain complex biological design by natural means. In a radio interview in 1996 Dawkins singled out Behe's example of the flagellum, a hairlike appendage on a microscopic animal that when whipped around at high speed acts as a wheel that propels the creature through the water. Behe argued that there was no other way to explain this structure other than through intelligent design. Dawkins countered that Behe's use of the flagellum was a "cowardly, lazy copping out by simply saying oh, I can't think of how it came about, therefore it must have been designed." He completely discounted any supernatural elements and was proud of it. As a result of his candid position, creationists stood agape, their fears of an evolutionary conspiracy to undermine God confirmed, and pointed feverishly at him, shouting, "Atheist, atheist!" That only made Dawkins's grin widen and grow toothier.

But Dawkins did not stop there; he went after his ally Stephen Jay Gould. Although admiring Gould's work, Dawkins was troubled by what he thought was a tendency to oversimplify and make grand statements over commonly accepted ideas. In his *Sunday Telegraph* review of Gould's book *Wonderful Life* (1989), Dawkins called it a "beautifully written and deeply muddled book." Gould argued that the strange fossil creatures discovered in 1909 in a Canadian formation known as the Burgess Shale were more diverse than any in modern times and that this condition overturned previously held assumptions about evolution. Dawkins argued the previously held notion Gould referred to was the idea that evolution was a progressive march from simple to complex forms reaching a pinnacle with man, an idea Dawkins pointed out was no longer accepted by evolutionists. Gould had done the same thing as Duane Gish and other creationists had been doing: they made arguments against ideas that were fifty years out-of-date. For Dawkins, scientists' poor transmission of their knowledge was just as big a part of the problem as the creationists' faulty understanding of it. It is unlikely that the conflict between religion and evolution will ever end.

## Further Reading

On Christian Fundamentalism, see Ernest Sandeen, *The Roots of Fundamentalism: British and American Millenarianism, 1800–1930* (1970), and George Marsden, *Fundamentalism and American Culture: The Shaping of the Twentieth-Century Evangelicalism, 1870–1925* (1980). For the Scopes trial, see Edward Larson, *Summer for the Gods* (1997), and Paul Conkin, *When All the Gods Trembled* (1998). For creationism history, see Ronald Numbers, *The Creationists* (1992); for its philosophical aspects, see Langdon Gilkey, *Blue Twilight: Nature, Creationism, and American Religion* (2001). For evolution in the United States, see Peter J. Bowler, *Evolution: The History of an Idea* (1983), and Ronald Numbers, *Darwinism Comes to America* (1998). For a compendium of antievolutionist literature, see Tom McIver, *Anti-Evolution: A Reader's Guide to Writings before and after Darwin* (1992). For the trials and other judicial aspects, see Dorothy Nelkin, *The Creation Controversy: Science or Scripture in the Schools* (2000), and Edward Larson, *Trial and Error: The American Controversy over Creation and Evolution* (2003).

# *Conclusion*

People around the world and throughout time have wondered where they came from. For most of human history that wondering led to the construction of various supernatural explanations couched in terms of parables and lesson stories meant to teach proper behavior and respect. Angry gods, happy gods, and indifferent gods appeared to look after us and keep us on the straight and narrow and to offer some kind of reward once the grueling slog through life was over. In the seventeenth and eighteenth centuries, those explanations had grown unsatisfying to some, and a new search for our origins began. The growth of the scientific method and its reliance on the collection of facts instead of simple belief or tradition became the best alternative to understanding the universe. Some looked at the geology of the earth and the strange and wonderful creatures found in it and dared think new thoughts. Human fossils suggested what had been unthinkable before. Maybe we were floating through space on our own, without being watched over. Maybe it was up to us to look out for ourselves.

Why study our own past? We do it in order to find out about ourselves. We seek in our fossil ancestors answers to questions. Can fossils really give us what we want, or can that be given us only by ourselves? We want our ancestry, or at least our study of it, to bring us to some profound conclusion. We search for meaning in ourselves because we have noplace else to look except in the mirror. But what if there is no profound statement? What if there is no big secret or deep wisdom? Darwinian evolution argues that there is no end point, no goal to be reached, just constant changing. That's not much, but there you are. It is enough just to know, which is, after all, the definition of science: the search for the abstract nature of the universe.

Despite the squabbles and disagreements over the details of how human evolution progressed, or what the relationship among different fossils is, paleoanthropologists do not question that evolution works or that humans descended from a long line of succession going back millions of years; the evidence of that basic point is unambiguous. There is no Darwinian "theory" anymore, only the fact that evolution occurs. There will always be those who strive for more than storybook explanations, who will continue to study the bones and genes of the human animal in order to figure out how it started. The greatest ability we humans have is the ability to acquire knowledge, and the thing we will want to know the most about is ourselves.

By the late twentieth century more sophisticated techniques of radiometric dating, MRI scanning, and genetic testing were being employed in the search for human ancestors. Along with all these new ways of generating evidence and working out theories to explain it, differences of opinion, debate, and controversy ensued. However, this is how knowledge is generated. Constant questioning and resistance to just taking things on faith are how we learn about the universe. Far from being an indication of any hollowness to human evolutionary studies or intellectual weakness on the part of science, it shows a robust desire to find out who we are and where we came from. Although the exact course human evolution took or how our ancestors lived may remain elusive, the search as well as the controversies will go on.

# Chronology

| | |
|---|---|
| 800s B.C. | Greeks think fossils are the relics of their ancestors, the heroes and Titans. |
| 1500s | Legends of wild men and monstrous races abound in Europe. Bartolomé de Las Casas writes that the Native Americans are neither degenerate nor intellectual simpletons. |
| 1648 | Thomas Gage speculates that the Native Americans came from Asia. |
| 1658 | Archbishop Ussher calculates the day of creation (4004 B.C.). |
| 1665 | Isaac de La Peyrere publishes *Men before Adam* with its pre-Adamite idea. |
| 1669 | Nicholas Steno argues fossils are the remains of once living creatures. |
| 1677 | Sir William Hale's *Primitive Origination of Mankind* is published. |
| 1686 | Robert Plot discusses archaic stone tools in *Natural History of Stratford-Shire*. |
| 1698 | Edward Tyson creates the first description of a chimpanzee in London. |
| 1709 | Johann Jacob Scheuchzer describes the *Homo diluvinii testis*. |
| 1749 | Count de Buffon publishes the *Histoire Naturelle*. |
| 1758 | Carolus Linnaeus publishes the *Systema Naturae*. |
| 1775 | Johann Friedrich Blumenbach proposes the idea of five races of man. |
| 1789 | Samuel Stanhope Smith publishes *Essays on the Causes of the Variety of Complexion and Figure in the Human Species*. |
| 1790s | Austrian Franz Joseph Gall begins studies that will lead to the introduction of phrenology. |
| 1797 | John Frere finds arrowheads at a quarry in Hoxne, England. |
| 1802 | William Paley publishes *Natural Theology*. Jean-Baptiste Lamarck proposes the law of acquired characters. |
| 1805 | The Guadeloupe skeleton is found. |
| 1813 | James Cowles Prichard publishes *Researches into the Physical Diversity of Man*, championing the monogenetic approach to human development. |
| 1819 | Friedrich Schlegel coins the term *Aryan*. |
| 1820 | Georges Cuvier proposes the ideas of catastrophism and extinction. |
| 1822 | The Reverend William Buckland visits Paviland cave and discovers the Red Lady. Gideon Mantell finds reptile fossils at Sussex, England. |
| 1830 | Charles Lyell publishes *The Principles of Geology* and promotes the uniformitarian view of geology. The Engis skull is found in Belgium. The Devonian controversy rages. Joseph Smith publishes *The Book of Mormon*, detailing the story of the peopling of the Americas. |
| 1831–1836 | Darwin's voyage on HMS *Beagle*. |

| 1833 | William Jardine publishes *Natural History of Monkeys.* |
| 1837 | Josiah Priest publishes *American Antiquities* and argues the native people are descendants of Noah's son Shem. |
| 1838 | William Lawrence publishes *Lectures on Physiology, Zoology, and the Natural History of Man* based on his lectures. |
| 1839 | John Delafield Jr. publishes *An Inquiry into the Origins of the Antiquities of America.* Samuel George Morton publishes *Crania Americana.* |
| 1840s–1850s | Archaeologists and geologists begin combining their data in reference to the age of the earth and the antiquity of man. Jacques Boucher de Crèvecoeur de Perthes finds human artifacts (later known as Acheulian) along the Somme River of France. Swiss naturalists pioneer the concept of the "ice age." First satirical evolution cartoons appear in England. |
| 1841 | Richard Owen names large fossil reptiles dinosaurs. |
| 1844 | Robert Chambers publishes *The Vestiges of the Natural History of Creation.* |
| 1848 | The Gibraltar skull is found. |
| 1850s | In the United States Louis Agassiz supports the polygenesis view of human origins. |
| 1853 | Arthur de Gobineau publishes *The Inequality of the Races.* |
| 1854 | J. C. Nott and George Gliddon publish *Types of Mankind.* Richard Owen states humans and primates are not related. |
| 1856 | The Neanderthal man is found in Germany. |
| 1857 | Hermann Schaaffhausen unveils Neanderthal man at the meeting of the Natural History Society of Prussian Rhineland and Westphalia. |
| 1858 | Alfred Russel Wallace contacts Charles Darwin, asking him to comment on his new explanation of transmutation. Darwin freaks out. |
| 1859 | Charles Darwin publishes *On the Origin of Species.* John Evans sees the similarity of the Hoxne artifacts to those from France. |
| 1860 | The Oxford University debate between T. H. Huxley and the Reverend Wilberforce. |
| 1861 | George Busk translates Hermann Schaaffhausen's papers on the Neanderthal man into English. |
| 1862 | Ernst Haeckel introduces the tree-of-life image and coins the term *phylogeny.* |
| 1863 | T. H. Huxley publishes *Man's Place in Nature.* Charles Lyell publishes *The Antiquity of Man.* James Hunt starts the Anthropological Society of London to promote the polygenetic approach to human diversity. |
| 1865 | John Lubbock publishes *Prehistoric Times* and arranges the first modern scientific names for geologic periods. |
| 1866 | The La Naulette skull is found in Belgium. |
| 1868 | The first Cro-Magnons are found at Les Eyzies, France. |
| 1869 | The Cardiff giant is found in New York. |

| | |
|---|---|
| 1870s | Paul Broca begins his study of brain function and forms the Société d'Anthropologie in Paris. The Volkish movement is born in Germany. |
| 1871 | Charles Darwin publishes *The Descent of Man*. |
| 1876 | St. George Jackson Mivart publishes *Man and Apes*. |
| 1879 | Ernst Haeckel publishes *The History of Creation*. The U.S. government establishes the Bureau of American Ethnology. |
| 1880 | August Wiesmann differentiates between somatic and reproductive cells. Gabriel de Mortillet modifies Lubbock's system, adding Acheulian, Aurignacian, Solutrean, and other ages to the list and forms the group known as the "combat anthropologists." |
| 1888 | Galley Hill man is found along the banks of the Thames River. Madame Blavatsky publishes *The Secret Doctrine*. |
| 1890s | Western naturalists realize China is a trove of possible hominid fossils. |
| 1890–1895 | Eugene Dubois finds Java man. |
| 1899 | The Krapina, Croatia, Neanderthal site is found, with possible evidence of cannibalism. William Zebina Ripley publishes *The Races of Europe*. |
| 1900 | Gregor Mendel's law of heredity is "rediscovered." |
| 1903 | Max Schlosser publishes *Fossil Mammals of China*. |
| 1906 | The first Nebraska man is found outside Omaha. |
| 1908 | George McJunkin finds buffalo fossils outside Folsom, New Mexico. The La Chapelle-aux-Saints Neanderthal skeleton is found. Marcellin Boule calls it "bestial." |
| 1909 | The killer-Neanderthal picture appears in the *Illustrated London News*. The Le Moustier skeleton is found. |
| 1910 | Marcellin Boule establishes the Institut de Paleontologie Humaine. |
| 1912 | Piltdown man is found at Sussex. |
| 1916 | Madison Grant publishes *The Passing of the Great Race*. |
| 1918 | Aleš Hrdlička debunks any notion of fossil humans in the Americas. |
| 1920s | Arthur Keith proposes the "cranial Rubicon" of 750 cubic centimeters for human ancestor brain size. |
| 1921–1930 | Roy Chapman Andrews, sponsored by Henry Fairfield Osborn and the American Museum of Natural History, leads the Central Asiatic Expedition to Mongolia in search of the cradle of man. |
| 1921 | Otto Zadansky finds a hominid tooth at Zhoukoudian, outside Peking. |
| 1922 | The second Nebraska man is found. |
| 1925 | Henry Fairfield Osborn proposes the Dawn Man theory. The Scopes monkey trial is held in Dayton, Tennessee. Raymond Dart announces his discovery of Taung Child (*Australopithecus africanus*) in South Africa. The photo of François de Loys's ape is circulated. |

| | |
|---|---|
| 1926 | Otto Zadansky makes the Peking tooth public. A. W. Grabau dubs it Peking man, and Davidson Black writes the descriptive paper. The Folsom points are verified to show that humans entered the Americas 10,000 years ago. |
| 1927 | The *Buck v. Bell* case is decided. |
| 1930s–1940s | The Nazis begin their eugenic cleansing of evolutionary inferiors, starting World War II and the Holocaust. The Skhul, Tabun, and Qafzeh sites are discovered in Palestine. |
| 1931 | Pei Wenzhong finds the Peking man skullcap. |
| 1933 | Clovis points found in New Mexico push the human entrance to America back to at least 11,500 years ago. |
| 1935 | Jia Lanpo takes charge of the Zhoukoudian site and tries to maintain it in the face of World War II. |
| 1936 | Robert Broom finds more *Australopithecus* fossils at Sterkfontaine and Kromdraai. |
| 1941 | Franz Weidenreich attempts to ship Peking man to the United States for safekeeping, but it is lost in transit. |
| 1950s | Radiometric dating begins. |
| 1953 | Piltdown man is exposed as a fake. James Watson and Francis Crick work out the structure of DNA. |
| 1958 | Bernard Heuvelmans publishes *On the Trail of Unknown Animals*. The film *Teenage Caveman* is released. |
| 1959 | Mary Leakey finds *Zinjanthropus* at Olduvai Gorge, Tanzania. |
| 1964 | Louis Leakey announces his discovery in Africa of *Homo habilis*. |
| 1967 | Alan Wilson begins the genetic study of human evolution. The Patterson-Gimlin "film" of Bigfoot is shot in California. |
| 1968 | The Minnesota Iceman is on display. |
| 1970s | The KBS Tuff controversy rages. Hominid trackways are found at Laetoli. |
| 1972 | Bernard Ngeneo finds skull 1470. Elaine Morgan puts forward the aquatic ape theory. |
| 1973 | James Adovasio unearths the Meadowcroft Rockshelter in Pennsylvania. |
| 1974 | "Lucy" is found in Ethiopia. |
| 1980s | Christopher Stringer proposes the out-of-Africa II population replacement theory. Milford Wolpoff proposes the out-of-Africa I multiregional theory. *Homo ergaster* is described. |
| 1981 | The Arkansas antievolution bill is struck down. |
| 1984 | "Turkana boy" is found in Kenya. |
| 1987 | The "Eve" hypothesis is put forward by Allan Wilson, Rebecca Cann, and Mark Stoneking. |
| 1990s | Solutrean artifacts are found in Virginia. The genetic bottleneck idea is proposed. Ian Tattersall champions hominid diversity. |
| 1991 | Misia Landau publishes *Narratives of Human Evolution*. |
| 1992 | Tim White announces *Ardipithecus ramidus*. |
| 1993 | Nanjing man is found in China. |

| 1995 | Vine Deloria Jr. publishes *Red Earth, White Lies: Native Americans and the Myth of Scientific Fact*, arguing humans first appeared in the Americas. |
| 1996 | Kennewick man is discovered in Washington State. |
| 1999 | The Kansas Board of Education removes references to evolution from state-approved textbooks. |
| 2001 | The Dmanisi skull is found in Russian Georgia. In Chad *Sahelanthropus tchadensis* (Toumai) is found. Also, the discoveries of *Ardipithecus ramadus kadabba, Orrorin tugenensis,* and *Kenyanthropus platyops* are announced. |
| 2002 | More *Homo erectus* material is found at Dakanihyli, Ethiopia. |

# Bibliography

Adamski, George. 1955. *Inside the Space Ships.* New York: Abelard-Shuman.

Adamski, George, and Desmond Leslie. 1953. *Flying Saucers Have Landed.* New York: British Book Centre.

Adovasio, James M., and Jake Page. 2002. *The First Americans: In Pursuit of Archaeology's Greatest Mystery.* New York: Random House.

Agassiz, Louis. 1962. *Essays on Classification.* Ed. Edward Lurie. Cambridge, MA: Belknap Press.

Alexeev, Valerii. 1986. *The Origin of the Human Race.* Moscow: Progress Publishers.

Allen, Don Cameron. 1949. *The Legend of Noah.* Urbana: University of Illinois Press.

Allen, Garland. 1975. *Life Science in the Twentieth Century.* Cambridge: Cambridge University Press.

Ameghino, Florentino. 1900–1901. "L'age des formations sedimentaires de Patagonia." *Anales de la Sociadad Cientific Argentina* 50: 109–130, 145–165, 209–229.

*American Dictionary of Biography.* 1999. New York: Oxford University Press.

*Annual Report of the Board of Regents of the Smithsonian Institution.* 1890. Washington: Government Printing Office.

Ardrey, Robert. 1961. *African Genesis.* New York: Atheneum.

Arsuaga, Juan Luis. 2002. *The Neanderthal's Necklace.* New York: Four Walls Eight Windows.

Asfaw, Berhane, et al. 2002. "Remains of *Homo erectus* from Bouri, Middle Awash, Ethiopia." *Nature* 416, no. 21 (March): 317–319.

Asma, Stephen. 2001. *Stuffed Animals and Pickled Heads: The Culture and Evolution of Natural History Museums.* Oxford: Oxford University Press.

Baldwin, John D. 1872. *Ancient America.* New York: Harper and Bros.

Balter, Michael. 2001. "Paleontological Rift in the Rift Valley." *Science* 292, no. 5515 (April 13): 198.

Barbour, Erwin Hinckley, and Henry Baldwin Ward. 1906. "Preliminary Report on the Primitive Man of Nebraska." *Nebraska Geological Survey* (December 22).

Barkan, Elazar. 1992. *The Retreat of Scientific Racism.* New York: Cambridge University Press.

Bartlett, John Russel. 1847. *The Progress of Ethnology, Archaeological, Philological, and Geographical Researches in Various Parts of the Globe.* New York: Printed for the American Ethnological Society.

Behe, Michael. 1996. *Darwin's Black Box.* New York: Free Press.

Benson, Keith R., Jane Maienschein, and Ronald Rainger, eds. 1991. *The Expansion of American Science.* New Brunswick: Rutgers University Press.

Berman, Judith. 1999. "Bad Hair Days in the Paleolithic: Modern (Re)Constructions of Cave Men." *American Anthropologist* 101:2 (1999): 288–304.

Bird, Roland T. 1985. *Bones for Barnum Brown.* Fort Worth: Texas Christian University Press.

Blanckaert, Claude. 1988. "On the Origins of French Ethnology." In *Bones, Bodies, Behavior,* ed. George W. Stocking. Madison: University of Wisconsin Press.

Blavatsky, Helena Petrovna. 1893. *The Secret Doctrine.* London: Theosophical Publishing Society.

Blinderman, Charles. 1986. *The Piltdown Inquest.* Buffalo: Prometheus Books.

Bloor, David. 1991. *Knowledge and Social Imagery.* Chicago: University of Chicago Press.

Blumenbach, Johann Friedrich. 1865. *The Anthropological Treatises of Johann Friedreich Blumenbach.* London: Longman, Green, Longman, Roberts, and Green.

Boaz, Noel. 1982. "American Research on Australopithecine and Early Homo, 1925–1980." In *A History of American Physical Anthropology,* ed. Frank Spencer, 240–241. New York: Academic Press.

Bollaert, William. 1863–1864. "Contributions to an Introduction to the Anthropology of America." In *Memoirs of the Anthropological Society of London, Vol II.* London: Trübner and Company, 1865–1866, 92–152.

Boule, Marcellin. 1923. *Fossil Men.* Edinburgh: Oliver Oliver and Boyd.

Bovey, Alixe. 2002. *Monsters and Grotesques in Medieval Manuscripts.* London: The British Library.

Bowler, Peter J. 1983a. *Eclipse of Darwinism: Anti-Darwinian Evolutionary Theories in the Decades around 1900.* Baltimore: Johns Hopkins University Press.

———. 1983b. *Evolution: The History of an Idea.* Berkeley and Los Angeles: University of California Press.

———. 1986. *Theories of Human Evolution: A Century of Debates, 1844–1944.* Baltimore: Johns Hopkins University Press.

Boyer, Paul. 1994. *When Time Shall Be No More: Prophecy Belief in Modern American Culture.* Cambridge, MA: Harvard University Press.

Broderick, Alan Houghton. 1963. *The Abbe Breuil, Prehistorian.* London: Hutchinson.

Brodie, Fawn. 1945. *No Man Knows My History.* New York: Alfred A. Knopf.

Brooke, John Hedley. 1993. *Science and Religion.* Cambridge: Cambridge University Press.

Brown, Michael. 1990. *The Search for Eve.* New York: Harper and Row.

Calvin, William. 1996. *Cerebral Code.* Cambridge, MA: MIT Press.

Cann, Rebecca, and Allan Wilson. 2003. "Recent African Genesis of Humans." *Scientific American* 13:2 (August 25): 54–61.

Cann, Rebecca, Mark Stoneking, and Allan Wilson. 1987. "Mitochondrial DNA and Human Evolution." *Nature* 325, no. 6099 (January 1–7): 31–36.

Chambers, Robert. 1994. *Vestiges of the Natural History of Creation and Other Writings.* Ed. James Secord. Chicago: University of Chicago Press.

Chase, Allen. 1977. *The Legacy of Malthus.* New York: Alfred A. Knopf.

Chatters, James. 2001. *Ancient Encounters: Kennewick Man and the First Americans.* New York: Touchstone Books.

Ciochon, Russell, John Olsen, and Jamie James. 1990. *Other Origins: The Search for the Giant Ape in Human Prehistory.* New York: Bantam Books.

Ciochon, Russell, Dolores Piperno, and Robert Thompson. 1990. "*Gigantopithecus blacki:* Implications for Paleodietary Studies." *Proceedings of the National Academy of Science* 87: 8120–8124.

Clark, G. A., and C. M. Willermet, eds. 1997. *Conceptual Issues in Modern Human Origins Research.* New York: Aldine De Gruyter.

Clark, J. D., and W. W. Bishop, eds. 1967. "Recommendations and Appraisal." In *Background to Evolution in Africa,* 890–897. Chicago: University of Chicago Press.

Colbert, Edwin. 1984. *The Great Dinosaur Hunters and Their Discoveries.* New York: Dover Publications.

Collard, Mark, and Bernard Wood. 2000. "How Reliable Are Human Phylogenetic Hypotheses?" *PNAS* 97, no. 9 (April 25): 5003–5006.

Clottes, Jean, and David Lewis-Williams. 1998. *Shamans of Prehistory.* New York: Harry N. Abrams.

Conkin, Paul. 1998. *When All the Gods Trembled: Darwinism, Scopes, and American Intellectuals.* New York: Rowman and Littlefield.

Coon, Carlton. 1962. *Origin of the Races.* New York: Alfred A. Knopf.

Coppens, Yves, F. C. Howell, G. L. Isaac, and R. E. F. Leakey, eds. 1976. *Earliest Man and Environments in the Lake Rudolf Basin.* Chicago: University of Chicago Press.

Corliss, William. 1978. *Ancient Man: A Handbook of Puzzling Artifacts.* Glen Arm, MD: Sourcebook Project.

Cranston. Sylvia. 1993. *H.P.B.: The Extraordinary Life and Influence of Helena Petrovna Blavatsky, Founder of the Modern Theosophical Movement.* New York: Putnam's.

Cravens, Hamilton. 1978. *The Triumph of Evolution: American Scientists and the Heredity-Environment Controversy, 1900–1941.* Philadelphia: University of Pennsylvania Press.

Cremo, Michael, and Richard Thompson. 1994. *The Hidden History of the Human Race.* Badger, CA: Govardhan Hill.

Cromartie, Alan. 2003. *Sir Matthew Hale 1609–1676.* Cambridge: Cambridge University Press.

Cuozzo, Jack. 1998. *Buried Alive.* Green Forest, NY: Master Books.

Czerkas, Sylvia, and Donald F. Glut. 1982. *Dinosaurs, Mammoths, and Cavemen: The Art of Charles R. Knight.* New York: E. P. Dutton.

Daniels, George H. 1968. *American Science in the Age of Jackson.* Tuscaloosa: University of Alabama Press.

Dansie, Amy. 2002. "Review of *Ancient Encounters.*" *Mammoth Trumpet* 17, no. 3.

Dart, Raymond. 1925. "*Australopithecus africanus:* The Man-Ape of South Africa." *Nature* 2884, no. 115 (February 7): 195–199.

Dart, Raymond, and Dennis Craig. 1959. *Adventures with the Missing Link.* New York: Harper and Brothers.

Darwin, Charles. 1859. *The Origin of Species.* London: Murray.

———. 1898. *The Descent of Man and Selection in Relation to Sex.* 2d ed. New York: D. Appleton.

Darwin, Francis, ed. 1903. *The Life and Letters of Charles Darwin.* New York: Appleton's.

Dawkins, Richard. 1996. *Climbing Mount Improbable.* New York: Norton.

Degler, Carl. 1991. *In Search of Human Nature.* New York: Oxford University Press.

Deloria, Vine, Jr. 1969. *Custer Died for Your Sins: An Indian Manifesto.* London: Macmillan.

———. 1995. *Red Earth, White Lies: Native Americans and the Myth of Scientific Fact.* New York: Scribner.

Delson, E. 1985. "Paleobiology and Age of *Homo erectus*." *Nature* 316: 762–763.

Desmond, Adrian. 1984. *Archetypes and Ancestors: Paleontology in Victorian London, 1850–1875.* Chicago: University of Chicago Press.

———. 1997. *Huxley: From Devil's Disciple to Evolution's High Priest.* Reading, MA: Addison-Wesley.

Dillehay, Tom D., and David J. Meltzer, eds. 1991. *The First Americans: Search and Research.* Boca Raton, FL: CRC Press.

Dinsdale, Tim. 1972. *Monster Hunt.* Washington, DC: Acropolis Books Ltd.

Dixon, Ronald B. 1923. *The Racial History of Man.* New York: Scribner's.

Dobzhansky, Theodosius. 1937. *Genetics and the Origin of Species.* New York: Columbia University Press.

Dubois, Eugène. 1896. "The Place of 'Pithecanthropus' in the Genealogical Tree." *Nature* 53, no. 1368 (January 16): 245–247.

Du Chaillu, Paul. 1868. *Stories of the Gorilla Country.* New York: Harper and Brothers.

Dupree, A. Hunter. 1988. *Asa Gray: American Botanist, Friend of Darwin.* Baltimore: Johns Hopkins University Press.

Durant, John. 1985. *Darwinism and Divinity.* New York: Basil Blackwell.

Eldredge, Niles. 2000. *The Triumph of Evolution and the Failure of Creationism.* New York: W. H. Freeman.

Eldredge, Niles, and Ian Tattersall. 1975. "Evolutionary Models, Phylogenetic Reconstructions, and Another Look at Hominid Phylogeny." In *Approaches to Primate Paleobiology,* ed. F. S. Szalay. Basel: Karger, 218–242.

Elliot-Smith, Grafton. 1932. *The Search for Man's Ancestors.* London: Watts.

Elwood, Robert S. 1986. "The American Theosophical Synthesis." In *The Occult in America: New Historical Perspectives,* ed. Kerr and Crow, 115–116. Chicago: University of Illinois.

Ernest, Conrad. 1981. "Tripping over a Trilobite." *Creation/Evolution* 4: 30–33.

Figurier, Louis. 1870. *Primitive Man.* London: Chapman and Hall.

Fitch, J. F., and J. A. Miller. 1970. "Radioisotopic Age Determinations of Lake Rudolf Artifact Site." *Nature* 226 (April 18): 226–228.

Foley, Robert, and Marta Lahr. 1997. "The Antiquity of Man: Mode 3 Technologies and the Evolution of Modern Humans." *Cambridge Archaeological Journal* 7, no. 1 (January): 3–36.

Fort, Charles Foy. 1919. *Book of the Damned.* New York: Boni and Liveright.

———. 1931. *Lo!* New York: Claude Kendall.

———. 1932. *Wild Talents.* New York: Claude Kendall.

Fowler, L. N., and O. S. Fowler. 1868. *New Illustrated Self-Instructor in Phrenology and Physiology.* New York: Samuel R. Wells.

Friedman, John Block. 1981. *The Monstrous Races in Medieval Art and Thought.* Cambridge, MA: Harvard University Press.

Gasman, Daniel. 1971. *The Scientific Origins of National Socialism.* New York and London: Macdonald.

———. 1998. *Haeckel's Monism and the Birth of Fascist Ideology.* New York: Peter Land Publishing.

Gilber, James Burkhart. 1997. *Redeeming Culture: American Religion in an Age of Science*. Chicago: University of Chicago Press.

Gilkey, Langdon. 2001. *Blue Twilight: Nature, Creationism, and American Religion*. Minneapolis: Fortress Press.

Gish, Duane. 1985. *Evolution: The Challenge of the Fossil Record*. El Cajon, CA: Creation-Life Publishers.

Glick, Thomas F., and David Kohn, eds. 1996. *Charles Darwin on Evolution*. Indianapolis: Hackett Publishing.

Gobineau, Arthur de. 1856. *Moral and Intellectual Diversity of Races*. Philadelphia: J. B. Lippincott.

———. 1915. *Inequality of the Races*. New York: H. Fertig.

Godwin, Jocelyn. 1996. *Arktos: The Polar Myth in Science, Symbolism, and Nazi Survival*. Kempton, IL: Adventures Unlimited Press.

Goodman, Jeffrey. 1981. *American Genesis*. New York: Summit Books.

Goodrick-Clarke, Nicholas. 1977. *Ontogeny and Phylogeny*. Cambridge, MA: Belknap Press.

Gordon, Mrs. 1894. *The Life and Correspondence of William Buckland D.D., FRS*. New York: D. Appleton and Company.

Gould, Stephen Jay. 1989. "An Essay on a Pig Roast." *Natural History* (June): 14–25.

———. 1992. *The Occult Roots of Nazism*. New York: New York University Press.

———. 1996. *Mismeasure of Man*. New York: W. W. Norton.

Grant, Madison. 1916. *The Passing of the Great Race*. New York: Charles Scribner's Sons.

Grayson, Donald. 1983. *The Establishment of Human Antiquity*. New York: Academic Press.

Gregory, William K., and Milo Hellman. 1923. "Notes on the Type of Hesperopithecus Harold Cookii Osborn." *American Museum Novitates* 53 (January 6).

Guiley, Rosemary Ellen. 1991. *Harper's Encyclopedia of Mystical and Paranormal Experience*. New York: Harper San Francisco.

Haeckel, Ernst. 1876. *The History of Creation*. New York: Appleton.

———. 1896. *Evolution of Man*. New York: D. Appleton and Company.

Hale, Matthew. 1677. *The Primitive Origination of Mankind Considered and Examined According to the Light of Nature*. London: William Godbid.

Haller, John S., Jr. 1971. *Outcasts from Evolution: Scientific Attitudes to Racial Inferiority, 1859–1900*. Urbana: University of Illinois Press.

Haller, Mark. 1963. *Eugenics: Hereditary Attitudes in American Thought*. New Brunswick: Rutgers University Press.

Hammond, Michael. 1988. "The Shadow Man Paradigm in Paleoanthropology, 1911–1945." In *Bones, Bodies, Behavior: Essays on Biological Anthropology,* ed. George W. Stocking, 117–137. Madison: University of Wisconsin Press.

Haraway, Donna. 1989. *Primate Visions*. New York: Routledge.

Harlan, Richard. 1835. *Medical and Physical Researches*. Philadelphia: Lydia R. Bailey.

Harris, Marvin. 1968. *The Rise of Anthropological Theory*. New York: Crowell.

Heuvelmans, Bernard. 1959. *On the Track of Unknown Animals*. New York: Hill and Wang.

Haynes, C. Vance. 1992. "More on Meadowcroft Rockshelter Radiocarbon Chronology." *Review of Archaeology* 12, no. 1: 8–14.

Herder, J. G. 1803. *Outlines of a Philosophy of the History of Mankind.* Trans. T. Churchill. Vol. 3. London, n.p.

Hodgen, Margaret T. 1971. *Early Anthropology in the Sixteenth and Seventeenth Centuries.* Philadelphia: University of Pennsylvania Press.

Hodgson, Derek. 2000. "Shamanism, Phosphenes, and Early Art: An Alternative Synthesis." *Current Anthropology* 41, no. 5 (December): 866–873.

Howe, Ellic. 1985. *The Magicians of the Golden Dawn: A Documentary History of a Magical Order, 1887–1923.* Wellingtonborough, Northamptonshire, UK: Aquarian Press.

Hrdlička, Aleš. 1907. *Skeletal Remains Suggesting or Attributed to Early Man in North America.* Bureau of American Ethnology Bulletin 33. Washington, DC: Government Printing Office.

———. 1912. *Early Man in South America.* Bureau of American Ethnology Bulletin 52. Washington: Government Printing Office.

———. 1918. *Recent Discoveries Attributed to Early Man in America.* Bureau of American Ethnology Bulletin 66. Washington, DC: Government Printing Office.

Huddelston, L. E. 1967. *The Origins of the American Indians: European Concepts, 1492–1729.* Austin: University of Texas Press.

Hunter, George. 1914. *A Civic Biology.* New York: American Book Company.

Huxley, Leonard, ed. 1901. *The Life and Letters of Thomas H. Huxley.* New York: D. Appleton.

Huxley, Thomas Henry. 1863. *Man's Place in Nature and Other Anthropological Essays.* Westminster Edition. New York: D. Appleton.

Isaac, Glynn, and Elizabeth McCown, eds. 1976. *Human Origins: Louis Leakey and the East African Evidence.* Menlo Park, CA: W. A. Benjamin.

Janus, Christopher G., and William Brashler. 1975. *The Search for Peking Man.* New York: Macmillan.

Jardine, William. 1833. *Natural History of Monkeys, Vol. 1.* Edinburgh: Lizars and Stirling and Kenney.

Jia Lanpo. 1980. *Early Man in China.* Beijing: Foreign Language Press.

Jia Lanpo and Huang Weiwen. 1990. *The Story of Peking Man.* Beijing: Foreign Language Press.

Johanson, Donald. 1996. "Human Origins." *National Forum* 76, no. 1 (winter): 24–28.

Johanson, Donald, and Maitland Edey. 1981. *Lucy: The Beginnings of Humankind.* New York: Simon and Schuster.

Johanson, Donald, and B. Edgar. 1996. *From Lucy to Language.* New York: Simon and Schuster.

Johanson, Donald, and James Shreeve. 1989. *Lucy's Child: The Discovery of Human Ancestry.* New York: William Morrow and Co., Inc.

Johnson, Phillip. 1991. *Darwin on Trial.* Downers Grove, IL: Intervarsity Press.

Keith, Arthur. 1917. Review of *Men of the Old Stone Age: Their Environment, Life, and Art,* by Henry Fairfield Osborn. *Man* (May).

Keith, Arthur, Grafton Elliot Smith, and Arthur Smith Woodward. 1925. "The Fossil Anthropoid Ape of Taung." *Nature* 2885, no. 115 (February 14): 234–236.

Kevles, Daniel J. 1985. *In the Name of Eugenics.* New York: Alfred A. Knopf.

Kindle, E. M. 1935. "American Indian Discoveries of Vertebrate Fossils." *Journal of Paleontology* 9: 449–452.

Knight, Charles R. 1949. *Prehistoric Man: The Great Adventurer.* New York: Appleton-Century-Crofts, Inc.

Knox, Robert. 1850. *The Races of Man: A Fragment.* Philadelphia: Lea and Blanchard.

Kohn, David, ed. 1985. *The Darwinian Heritage.* Princeton: Princeton University Press.

Kossy, Donna. 1994. *Kooks.* Portland, OR: Feral House.

———. 2001. *Strange Creations: Aberrant Ideas of Human Evolution from Extraterrestrials to Aquatic Apes.* Los Angeles: Feral House.

Kottler, Malcolm Jay. 1974. "Alfred Russel Wallace, the Origin of Man, and Spiritualism." *Isis* 65 (June): 145–192.

Krantz, Grover. 1999. *Bigfoot Sasquatch Evidence.* Surrey, BC: Hancock House.

Kuhn, Alan Boyd. 1930. *Theosophy: A Modern Revival of Ancient Wisdom.* New York: Henry Holt .

Kuhn, Thomas. 1970. *Structures of Scientific Revolutions.* Chicago: University of Chicago Press.

Kurtén, Björn. 1972. *Not from the Apes.* New York: Pantheon Books.

Lahr, Marta. 1996. *The Evolution of Modern Human Diversity.* London: Cambridge University Press.

Landau, Misia. 1991. *Narratives of Human Evolution.* New Haven: Yale University Press.

Larson, Edward J. 1998. *Summer for the Gods.* Cambridge, MA: Harvard University Press.

———. 2003. *Trial and Error: The American Controversy over Creation and Evolution.* New York: Oxford University Press.

Lawrence, Jerome, and Robert E. Lee. 1955. *Inherit the Wind.* Toronto: Bantam Publishers.

Lawrence, William. 1828. *Lectures on Physiology, Zoology and the Natural History of Man.* Salem, MA: Foote and Brown.

Leakey, L. S. B. 1953. *Adam's Ancestors.* 4th ed. London: Methven.

———. 1961. "New Finds at Olduvai Gorge." *Nature* 189: 649–650.

———. 1959. "New Fossil Skull from Olduvai." *Nature* 184: 491–493.

———. 1961. *Progress and Evolution of Man in Africa.* London: Oxford University Press.

———. 1967. *Olduvai Gorge, 1951–1961.* Vols. 1, 3. London: Cambridge University Press.

Leakey, L. S. B., P. V. Tobias, and J. R. Napier. 1964. "A New Species of the Genus *Homo* from Olduvai Gorge." *Nature* (April 4): 7–9.

Leakey, Maeve. 2000. "*New Hominid Genus from Eastern Africa.*" *Nature* 410: 433–440.

Leakey, Mary. 1984. *Mary Leakey: Disclosing the Past, an Autobiography.* Garden City, NY: Doubleday.

Leakey, Richard. 1973. "Further Evidence of Lower Pleistocene Hominids from East Rudolf, North Kenya." *Nature* 242: 170–173.

———. 1983. *One Life: An Autobiography.* Salem, NH: Salem House.

Leakey, Richard, and Roger Lewin. 1977. *Origins.* New York: E. P. Dutton.

————. 1978. *People of the Lake.* New York: Anchor Press.

————. 1982. *Human Origins.* New York: E. P. Dutton.

————. 1992. *Origins Reconsidered.* New York: Anchor Press.

Leconte, Joseph. 1884. *Compend of Geology.* New York: D. Appleton.

Lewin, Roger. 1987. *Bones of Contention.* New York: Touchstone.

Lewis-Williams, David. 1990. *Discovering Southern African Rock Art.* Cape Town: David Philips Pub.

————. 2002. *The Mind in the Cave.* New York: Thames and Hudson.

Lewis-Williams, David, and T. A. Dowson. 1994. *Contested Images: Diversity in Southern African Art Research.* Johannesburg: Witwatersrand University Press.

Lightman, Bernard, ed. 1997. *Victorian Science in Context.* Chicago: University of Chicago Press.

Ludmerer, Kenneth M. 1972. *Genetics and American Society: A Historical Appraisal.* Baltimore: Johns Hopkins University Press.

Lull, Richard Swann. 1921. "The Antiquity of Man." In *The Evolution of Man,* ed. George Alfred Baitsell. New Haven: Yale University Press.

Lyell, Charles. 1863. *The Geological Evidence of the Antiquity of Man.* Philadelphia: George Childs.

Maerth, Oscar Kiss. 1974. *The Beginning Was the End.* New York: Praeger Pub.

Maringer, Johannes. 1960. *Gods of Prehistoric Man.* New York: Alfred A. Knopf.

Marlar, R. A., et al. 2000. "Biochemical Evidence of Cannibalism at a Prehistoric Puebloan Site in Southwestern Colorado." *Nature* 407 (September 7): 74–78.

Marsden, George. 1980. *Fundamentalism and American Culture: The Shaping of the Twentieth-Century Evangelicalism, 1870–1925.* New York: Oxford University Press.

Matthew, W. D. 1906. "Hypothetical Outlines of the Continents in Tertiary Times." *Bulletin of the American Museum of Natural History* 22: 353–383.

Matthew, W. D., and Harold Cook. 1909. "Pliocene Fauna from Western Nebraska." *Bulletin of the American Museum of Natural History* 26: 361–414.

Mayor, Adrienne. 2000. *The First Fossil Hunters.* Princeton: Princeton University Press.

Mayr, Ernst. 1942. *Systematics and the Origin of Species.* New York: Columbia University Press.

McCosh, James. 1890. *The Religious Aspects of Evolution.* New York: Charles Scribner's Sons.

McCown, Theodore, and Kenneth Kennedy, eds. 1972. *Climbing Man's Family Tree: A Collection of Writings on Human Phylogeny, 1699 to 1971.* Englewood Cliffs, NJ: Prentice Hall.

M'culloh, J. H. 1817. *Researches in America.*

McCulloh, J. H., Jr. 1829. *Researches Philosophical and Antiquarian, Concerning the Aboriginal History of America.* Baltimore: Fielding Lucas Jr.

McGowan, Christopher. 2001. *The Dragon Seekers.* Cambridge, MA: Perseus Publishing.

McIver, Tom. 1992. *Anti-Evolution: A Reader's Guide to Writings before and after Darwin.* Baltimore: Johns Hopkins University Press.

Meigs, J. Aitken. 1858. *Hints to Craniographers.* Philadelphia: Merrilew and Thompson.

Meltzer, David. 1991. "On 'Paradigms' and 'Paradigm Bias' in Controversies over Human Antiquity in America." In *The First Americans: Search and Research.* Tom Dillehay and David Meltzer, eds. Boca Raton, FL: CRC Press, pp. 13–49.

Meltzer, David, Don Fowler, and Jeremy Sabloff, eds. 1986. *American Archaeology, Past and Future: A Celebration of the Society for American Archaeology, 1935–1985.* Washington, DC: Smithsonian Institution Press.

Mencken, H. L. 1925. "The Hills of Zion." *Baltimore Evening Sun* (July).

Michell, John, and Bob Rickard. 1979. *Phenomena: A Book of Wonders.* New York: Pantheon.

Miller, Hugh. 1859. *Foot-Prints of the Creator.* Boston: Gould and Lincoln.

Mitchell, Michael. 2002. *Monsters: Human Freaks in America's Gilded Age.* Toronto: ECW Press.

Mithen, Steven. 1996. *Prehistory of the Mind.* London: Thames and Hudson.

Moore, James. 1979. *Post-Darwinian Controversies.* New York: Cambridge University Press.

Morgan, Elaine. 1972. *The Descent of Woman.* New York: Stein and Day.

———. 1990. *The Scars of Evolution.* New York: Oxford University Press.

Morgan, Henry Lewis. 1907. *Ancient Society.* New York: Holt and Company.

Morgan, Vincent, and Spencer G. Lucas. 2002. *Walter Granger, 1872–1941, Paleontologist.* Albuquerque: New Mexico Museum of Natural History.

Morton, Samuel George. 1848. "An Account of a Craniological Collection." *Transactions of the American Ethnological Society* 2, 217–222. New York: Bartlett and Welford.

Mosedale, Susan Sleeth. 1978. "Science Corrupted: Victorian Biologists Consider 'The Woman Question.'" *Journal of the History of Biology* 11, no. 1 (spring): 1–55.

Moser, Stephanie. 1998. *Ancestral Images: The Iconography of Human Origins.* Ithaca: Cornell University Press.

Mosse, George. 1964. *The Crisis of German Ideology.* New York: Grosset and Dunlap.

Mulvey, Mina White. 1969. *Digging Up Adam: The Story of L. S. B. Leakey.* New York: Van Ress Press.

Murray, Raymond W. 1943. *Man's Unknown Ancestors.* Milwaukee: Bruce Publishing.

Nelkin, Dorothy. 2000. *The Creation Controversy.* San Jose, CA: toExcel Press.

Newton, Michael. 2002. *Savage Girls and Wild Boys: The History of Feral Children.* New York: St. Martin Press.

Nitecki, M. H., and Doris Nitecki, eds. 1994. *Origins of Anatomically Modern Humans.* New York: Plenum Press.

Numbers, Ronald. 1998. *Darwinism Comes to America.* Cambridge, MA: Harvard University Press.

———. 1993. *The Creationists.* Berkeley and Los Angeles: University of California Press.

———. 1998. *Darwinism Comes to America.* Cambridge, MA: Harvard University Press.

Oakley, Kenneth. 1964. *Frameworks for Dating Fossil Man.* Chicago: Aldine Publishing.

Osborn, Henry Fairfield. 1910. *Age of Mammals.* New York: Macmillan.

———. 1922a. "*Hesperopithecus:* The Anthropoid Primate of Western Nebraska." *Nature* 110, no. 2750 (August 26): 281–283.

———. 1922b. "*Hesperopithecus:* The First Anthropoid Primate Found in America." *American Museum Novitates* 37 (April 25).

———. 1923. *Evolution and Religion.* New York: Charles Scibner's Sons.

———. 1925a. *Hall of the Age of Man.* American Museum of Natural History Guidebook 52. New York: American Museum of Natural History.

———. 1925b. *Men of the Old Stone Age.* New York: Charles Scribner's Sons.

———. 1927. *Man Rises to Parnassus.* Princeton: Princeton University Press.

Pager, Shirley-Ann. 199?. *A Visit to the "White Lady of Brandberg."* Windhoek: Typoprint.

Paul, Diane B. 1995. *Controlling Human Heredity: 1865 to the Present.* New Jersey: Humanities Press.

———. 1998. *The Politics of Heredity.* Albany: State University of New York Press.

Pickford, Martin. 1997. *Louis S. B. Leakey: Beyond the Evidence.* London: Janus.

Pinker, Steven. 1994. "Grammar Puss." *New Republic* 210, no. 5 (January 31): 19–25.

———. 1997. *How the Mind Works.* New York: W. W. Norton.

———. 2000. *The Language Instinct: How the Mind Creates Language.* New York: Perennial.

———. 2002. *The Blank Slate.* New York: Viking Press.

Pozzi, Stefano, and Maurizio Bossi, eds. 1994. *Romanticism in Science: Science in Europe, 1750–1840.* Boston: Kluwer Academic.

Preston, Douglas J. 1986. *Dinosaurs in the Attic.* New York: St. Martin's Press.

Prestwich, Joseph. 1860. "On the Occurrence of Flint Implements, Associated with the Remains of Extinct Mammalia, in Undisturbed Beds of a Late Geological Period." *Proceedings of the Royal Society of London:* 50–59.

Price, George McCready. 1923. *The New Geology.* Mountain View, CA: Pacific Press.

Prichard, James Cowles. 1848. *The Natural History of Man.* London: H. Bailliore.

Priest, Josiah. 1834. *American Antiquities.* Albany, NY: Hoffman and White.

Purcell, Rosamond. 1997. *Special Cases: Natural Anomalies and Historical Monsters.* San Francisco: Chronicle Books.

Quan Yin, Amorah. 1996. *Pleiadian Perspectives on Human Evolution.* Santa Fe: Bean.

Raby, Peter. 1996. *Bright Paradise: Victorian Scientific Travelers.* Princeton: Princeton University Press.

Rainger, Ronald. 1991. *An Agenda for Antiquity: Henry Fairfield Osborn and Vertebrate Paleontology at the American Museum of Natural History, 1890–1935.* Tuscaloosa: University of Alabama Press.

Ratzsch, Del. 1998. "Design, Chance, and Theistic Evolution." In *Mere Creation: Science, Faith, and Intellegent Design,* ed. W. A. Demski. Downers Grove, IL: InterVarsity Press. .

Reader, John. 1981. *Missing Links.* Boston: Little and Brown.

Redfield, Dana, and Jenny Randles. 2001. *The ET-Human Link: We Are the Message.* Hampton Roads Publishing.

Regal, Brian. 2002. *Henry Fairfield Osborn: Race and the Search for the Origins of Man.* London: Ashgate.

Ripley, William Zebina. 1899. *The Races of Europe: A Sociological Study.* New York: Appleton.

Roberts, Jon. 1988. *Darwinism and the Divine: Protestant Intellectuals and Organic Evolution.* Madison: University of Wisconsin Press.

Roede, Machteld, ed. 1991. *Aquatic Ape: Fact or Fiction?* London: Souvenir Press.

Roger, Jacques. 1997. *Buffon: A Life in Natural History.* Trans. Sarah Lucille Bonnefoi. Ithaca, NY: Cornell University Press.

Rogers, Alan. 2001. "Order Emerging from Chaos in Human Evolutionary Genetics." *Proceedings of the National Academy of Science* 98, no. 3 (January 30): 779–780.

Rogers, Spencer L. 1974. *Human Skeleton Found at Del Mar, California.* San Diego, CA: San Diego Museum of Man.

Rudwick, Martin. 1985. *The Great Devonian Controversy.* Chicago: University of Chicago Press.

————. 1992. *Scenes from Deep Time.* Chicago: University of Chicago Press.

Ruse, Michael. 1997. *Monad to Man: The Concept of Progress in Evolutionary Biology.* Cambridge, MA: Harvard University Press.

Sandeen, Ernest. 1970. *The Roots of Fundamentalism: British and American Millenarianism, 1800–1930.* Chicago: University of Chicago Press.

Sanderson, Ivan. 1961. *Abominable Snowmen.* Philadelphia: Chilton Co.

Schaaffhausen, Hermann. 1861. Trans. George Busk. "On the Crania of the Most Ancient Races of Man." *Natural History Review* 1–2 (April): 155–174.

Schienbinger, Londa. 1993. *Nature's Body: Gender in the Making of Modern Science.* Boston: Beacon Press.

Schuchert, Charles, and Clara Maclevene. 1940. *O. C. Marsh: Pioneer in Paleontology.* New Haven: Yale University Press.

Secord, James. 1986. *Controversy in Victorian Geology: The Cambrian-Silurian Dispute.* Princeton: Princeton University Press.

Shapiro, Harry. 1974. *Peking Man.* New York: Simon and Schuster.

Shipman, Pat. 1994. *The Evolution of Racism: Human Differences and the Use and Abuse of Science.* New York: Simon and Schuster.

————. 2001. *The Man Who Found the Missing Link.* New York: Simon and Schuster.

Shreeve, James. 1995. *The Neanderthal Enigma: Solving the Mystery of Modern Human Origins.* New York: William Morrow.

Silverberg, Robert. 1968. *Mound Builders of Ancient America.* Greenwich, CT: New York Graphic Society.

Simpson, George Gaylord. 1943. "The Beginnings of Vertebrate Paleontology in North America." *Proceedings of the American Philosophical Society* 86: 130–188.

————. 1944. *Tempo and the Mode of Evolution.* New York: Columbia University Press.

Singham, Mano. 2000. "The Science and Religion Wars." *Phi Delta Kappan* 81, no. 6 (February): 424–433.

Smith, Ethan. 1825. *View of the Hebrews.* Poultney, VT: Smith and Shute.

Smith, Samuel Stanhope. 1810. *An Essay on the Cause of the Variety of Complexion and Figure in the Human Species.* 2d ed. New Brunswick, NJ: J. Simpson.

Squier, E. G. 1851. *Antiquities of the State of New York.* Buffalo, NY: G. H. Derby and Company.

Stanton, William. 1960. *The Leopard's Spots: Scientific Attitudes towards Race in America, 1815–1859.* Chicago: University of Chicago Press.

Stocking, George W., ed. 1982. *Race, Culture, and Evolution.* Chicago: University of Chicago Press.

———. 1988. *Bones, Bodies, Behavior: Essays on Biological Anthropology.* Madison: University of Wisconsin Press.

Stokes, William Lee. 1986. "Alleged Human Footprint from the Middle Cambrian Strata, Millard County, Utah." *Journal of Geologic Education* 34: 187–190.

Stringer, Christopher. 1990. "The Emergence of Modern Humans." *Scientific American* (December).

———. 2002. "Modern Human Origins: Proposals and Prospects." *Philosophical Transactions of the Royal Society of London* B357: 563–579.

———. 2003. "Out of Ethiopia." *Nature* 423, No. 6941 (June 12): 692–695.

Stringer, Christopher, and Clive Gamble. 1993. *In Search of the Neanderthals.* London: Thames and Hudson.

Stringer, Christopher, and Robin McKie. 1996. *African Exodus.* New York: Henry Holt.

Swisher, Carl, Curtis Garniss, and Roger Lewin. 2000. *Java Man.* Chicago: University of Chicago Press.

Sykes, Bryan. 2001. *The Seven Daughters of Eve.* New York: W. W. Norton.

Taschdjian, Claire. 1977. *Peking Man Is Missing.* New York: Harper and Row.

Tattersall, Ian. 1995. *The Fossil Trail: How We Know What We Think We Know about Human Evolution.* New York: Oxford University Press.

———. 1995. *The Last Neanderthal.* New York: Macmillan.

———. 2002. *Monkey in the Mirror: Essays on the Science of What Makes Us Human.* Oxford: Oxford University Press.

Tattersall, Ian, and Jeffrey Schwartz. 2000. *Extinct Humans.* Boulder: Westview Press.

Thomas, David Hurst. 2000. *Skull Wars.* New York: Basic Books.

Thorne, Allan, and Milford Wolpoff. 1992. "The Multiregional Evolution of Humans." *Scientific American* (April): 76–83.

Tobias, Philip. 1967. *Olduvai Gorge, 1951–1961.* Vol. 2. London: Cambridge University Press.

Trinkaus, Eric, and Pat Shipman. 1993. *The Neanderthals.* New York: Alfred A. Knopf.

Turner, Frank. 1974. *Between Science and Religion.* New Haven: Yale University Press.

Tyson, Edward. 1699. *Anatomy of the Pygmie.* London: Michael Van der Gucht.

Valladas, H., et al. 2001. "Evolution of Prehistoric Cave Art." *Nature* 413 (October 4): 479.

Vaneechoutte, Mario, and John Skoyles. 1998. "The Memetic Origin of Language: Modern Humans as Musical Primates." *Evolutionary Models of Information Transmission* 2.

Van Riper, A. Bowdoin. 1993. *Men among the Mammoths: Victorian Science and the Discovery of Human Prehistory.* Chicago: University of Chicago Press.

Van Wyke, John. "The Authority of Human Nature: The *Schädellehre* of Franz Joseph Gall." *British Journal for the History of Science* 35, No. 124 (March 2002): 17–42.

Walker, Alan, and Pat Shipman. 1996. *The Wisdon of the Bones*. New York: Alfred A. Knopf.

Washington, Peter. 1995. *Madame Blavatsky's Baboon*. New York: Schocken Books.

Waterloo, Stanley. 1923. *The Story of AB: A Tale of the Time of the Caveman*. New York: Doubleday, Page.

Wauchope, Robert. 1963. *Lost Tribes and Sunken Cities*. Chicago: University of Chicago Press.

Weidenreich, Franz. 1945. *Giant Early Man from Java and South China*. Vol. 40, pt. 1. Anthropological Papers of the American Museum of Natural History. New York: American Museum of Natural History.

———. 1949. "Interpretations of the Fossil Material." In *Studies in Physical Anthropology, No. 1: Early Man in the Far East,* ed. W. W. Howells. Detroit: American Association of Physical Anthropology.

White, Tim. 1992. *Prehistoric Cannibalism at Mancos 5Mtum4-2346*. Princeton: Princeton University Press.

———. 2000a. "Cutmarks on the Bodo Cranium: A Case of Prehistoric Defleshing." *American Journal of Physical Anthropology* 69: 503–550.

———. 2000b. "A View on Science." *American Journal of Physical Anthropology* 113: 287–292.

———. 2001. "Once We Were Cannibals." *Scientific American* 285, no. 2 (August): 58–66.

———. 2003. "Early Hominids—Diversity or Distortion?" *Science* 299 (March 28): 1994–1997.

White, Tim, Berhane Asfaw, David De Gusta, Henry Gilbert, Gary D. Richards, Gen Suwa, and F. Clark Howell. 2003. "Pleistocene *Homo sapiens* from Middle Awash, Ethiopia." *Nature* 423, No. 6941 (June 12): 742–747.

White, Tim, Gen Suwa, and Berhane Asfaw. 1995. "*Australopithecus ramidus,* a New Species of Early Hominid from Aramis, Ethipoia." *Nature* 375: 306–312.

Willey, Gordon R., and Jeremy A. Sabloff. 1975. *A History of American Archaeology*. San Francisco: W. H. Freeman.

Wolf, John, and James S. Mellett. 1985. "The Role of 'Nebraska Man' in the Creation/Evolution Debate." *Creation/Evolution* 16: 31–43.

Wolpoff, Milford H., and Rachel Caspari. 1997. *Race and Human Evolution*. New York: Simon and Schuster.

Wright, George Frederick. 1911. *The Ice Age in North America*. Oberlin, OH: Bibliotheca Sacra Co.

———. 1892. *Man and the Glacial Period*. New York: D. Appleton and Company.

Yahya, Harun. 1999. *The Evolution Deceit: The Scientific Collapse of Darwinism and Its Ideological Background*. Istanbul: Okur.

# Excerpts of Primary Sources

*Chapter 1*

*T. H. Huxley*

*This excerpt is taken from* "Note on the Resemblances and Differences in the Structure and the Development of the Brain in Man and Apes," *in* The Descent of Man and Selection in Relation to Sex, *by Charles Darwin (1898).*

The controversy respecting the nature and the extent of the differences in the structure of the brain in man and the apes, which arose some fifteen years ago, has not yet come to an end, though the subject matter of the dispute is, at present, totally different from what it was formerly. It was originally asserted and re-asserted, with singular pertinacity, that the brain of all the apes, even the highest, differs from that of man, in the absence of such conspicuous structures as the posterior lobes of the cerebral hemispheres, with the posterior cornu of the lateral ventricle and the hippocampus minor, contained in those lobes, which are so obvious in man.

But the truth that the three structures in question are as well developed in apes' as in human brains, or even better; and that it is characteristic of all the Primates (if we exclude the Lemurs) to have these parts well developed, stands at present on as secure a basis as any proposition in comparative anatomy. Moreover, it is admitted by every one of the long series of anatomists who, of late years, have paid special attention to the arrangement of the complicated sulci and gyri which appear upon the surface of the cerebral hemispheres in man and the higher apes, that they are disposed after the very same pattern in him, as in them. Every principal gyrus and sulcus of a chimpanzee's brain is clearly represented in that of a man, so that the terminology which applies to the one answers for the other. On this point there is no difference of opinion. Some years since, Professor Bischoff published a memoir on the cerebral convolutions of man and apes; and as the purpose of my learned colleague was certainly not to diminish the value of the differences between apes and men in this respect, I am glad to make a citation from him.

"That the apes, and especially the orang, chimpanzee and gorilla, come very close to man in their organisation, much nearer than to any other animal, is a well known fact, disputed by nobody. Looking at the matter from the point of view of organization alone, no one probably would ever have disputed the view of Linnaeus, that man should be placed, merely as a peculiar species, at the head of the mammalia and of those apes. Both shew, in all their organs, so close an affinity, that the most exact anatomical investigation is needed in order to demonstrate those differences which really exist. So it is with the brains. The brains of man, the orang, the chimpanzee, the gorilla, in spite of all the important differences which they present, come very close to one another."

There remains, then, no dispute as to the resemblance in fundamental characters, between the ape's brain and man's: nor any as to the wonderfully close similarity between the chimpanzee, orang and man, in even the details of the arrangement of the gyri and sulci of the cerebral hemispheres. Nor, turning to the differences between the brains of the highest apes and that of man, is there any serious question as to the nature and extent of these differences. It is admitted that the man's cerebral hemispheres are absolutely and relatively larger than those of the orang and chimpanzee; that his frontal lobes are less excavated by the upward protrusion of the roof of the orbits; that his gyri and sulci are, as a rule, less symmetrically disposed, and present a greater number of secondary publications. And it is admitted that, as a rule, in man, the temporo-occipital or "external perpendicular" fissure, which is usually so strongly marked a feature of the ape's brain is but faintly marked. But it is also clear, that none of these differences constitutes a sharp demarcation between the man's and the ape's brain.

*Joseph Prestwich*

*In this excerpt from "On the Occurrence of Flint Implements, Associated with the Remains of Extinct Mammalia, in Undisturbed Beds of a Late Geological Period" (1860), Prestwich addresses the work of Jacques Boucher de Crèvecoeur de Perthes.*

The Author commences by noticing how comparatively rare are the cases even of the alleged discovery of the remains of man or of his works in the various superficial drifts, notwithstanding the extent to which these deposits are worked; and of these few cases so many have been disproved, that man's nonexistence on the earth until after the latest geological changes, and the extinction of the mammoth, Tichorhine Rhinoceros, and other great mammals, had come to be considered almost in the light of an established fact. Instances, however, have from time to time occurred to throw some doubt on this view, as the well known cases of human bone found by Dr. Schmerling in a cavern near Liege,—the remains of man, instances by M. Marcel de Serres and others in several caverns in France,—the flint implements in Kent's Cave,—and many more. Some uncertainty, however, has always attached to cave evidence, from the circumstance that man has often inhabited such places at a comparatively late period, and may have disturbed the original cave deposit; or, after the period of his residence, the stalagmitic floor may have been broken up by natural causes, and the remains above and below it may have thus become mixed together, and afterwards sealed up by a second floor of stalagmite. Such instances of an imbedded broken stalagmitic floor are in fact known to occur; at the same time the author does not pretend to say that this will explain all cases of intermixture in caves, but that it lessens the value of evidence from such sources.

The subject has however been latterly revived, and the evidence more carefully sifted by Dr. Falconer; and his preliminary reports on the Brixham cave, presented last year to the Royal Society, announcing the carefully determined occurrence of worked flints mixed indiscriminately with the bones of the extinct cave Bear and the Rhinoceros, attracted great and general attention amongst geologists. This remarkable discovery, and a letter written to him by Dr. Falconer on the occasion of his subsequent visit to Abbeville last autumn, instigated the author to turn his attention to other ground, which, from the interest of its later geological phenomena alone, as described by M. Buteux in his "Esquisse Géologique du Department de la Somme," he had long wished and intended to visit.

In 1849 M. Boucher de Perthes, President of the "Société d'Émulation" of Abbeville, published the first volume of a work entitled *Antiquités Celtiques et Antédiluviennes,* in which he announced the important discovery of worked flints in a bed of undisturbed sand and gravel containing the remains of extinct mammalia. Although treated from an antiquarian point of view, still the statement of the geological facts by this gentleman, with good section by M. Raven, is perfectly clear and consistent. Nevertheless, both in France and in England, his conclusions were generally considered erroneous; nor has he since obtained such verification of the phenomena as to cause so unexpected a fact to be accepted by men of science. There have, however, been some few exceptions to the general incredulity. The late Dr. Rigollot, of Amiens, urged by M. Boucher de Perthes, not only satisfied himself of the truth of the fact, but corroborated it, in 1855, by his *Mémoire sur des instruments en silex trouvés à St. Acheul.* Some few geologists suggested further inquiry; whilst Dr. Falconer, himself convinced by M. de Perthes' explanations and specimens, warmly engaged Mr. Prestwich to examine the sections.

*Paul Du Chaillu*

*In* Stories of the Gorilla Country *(1868), Du Chaillu's adventuristic prose comes through as he explains a hunting trip and how the Africans felt about the strange manlike beasts.*

We traveled all day, and about sunset came to a little river. Here we began at once to make a fire and build leafy shelters for the night. Scarcely was the fire-wood gathered, and we were safely bestowed under our shelter, when a storm came up which lasted half an hour. Then all was clear once more. We cooked plantains and smoked some dried fishes.

In the evening the men told stories about gorillas. "I remember," said one, "my father told me he once went out to the forest, when just in his path he met a great gorilla. My father had his spear in his hand. When the gorilla saw the spear he began to roar; then my father was terrified, and dropped the spear. When the gorilla saw that my father had dropped the spear he was pleased. He looked at him, and then left him and went into the thick forest. Then my father was glad, and went on his way."

Here all shouted together, "Yes; so we must do when we meet the gorilla. Drop the spear, that appeases him."

Next Gambo spoke. "Several dry seasons ago a man suddenly disappeared from my village after an angry quarrel. Some time after an Ashira of that village was out in the forest. He met a very large gorilla. That gorilla was the man who had disappeared; he had turned into a gorilla. He jumped on the poor Ashira, and bit a piece out of his arm; then he let him go. Then the man came back with his bleeding arm. He told me this. I hope we shall not meet such a gorilla."

Chorus—"No; we shall not meet such wicked gorillas."

I myself afterward met that man in the Ashira country. I saw his maimed arm, and he repeated the same story.

Then one of the men spoke up: "If we kill a gorilla to-morrow, I should like to have a part of the brain for a fetich. Nothing makes a man so brave as to have a fetich of gorilla's brain. That gives a man a strong heart."

Chorus of those who remained awake—"Yes; that gives a man a strong heart."

Then we all gradually dropped to sleep.

Next morning we cleaned and reloaded our guns, and started off for the hunting ground. There is a particular little berry of which the gorilla is very fond, and where this is found in abundance you are sure to meet the animal.

We had divided. Etia, Gambo, two other men, and I kept together, and we had hardly gone more than an hour when we heard the cry of a young gorilla after his mother. Etia heard it first, and at once pointed out the direction in which it was.

Immediately we began to walk with greater caution than before. Presently Etia and Gambo crept ahead, as they were expert with the net, and were also the best woodsmen. I unwillingly remained behind, but dared not go with them, lest my clumsier movements betray our presence. In a short time we heard two guns fired. Running up, we found the mother gorilla shot, but her little one had escaped; they had not been able to catch it.

The poor mother lay there in her gore, but the little fellow was off in the woods; so we concealed ourselves hard by to wait for its return. Presently it came up, jumped on its mother, and began sucking at her breasts and fondling her. Then Etia, Gambo, and I rushed upon it. Though evidently less than two years old, it proved very strong and escaped from us. But we gave chase, and in a few minutes had it fast, not, however, before one of the men had his arm severely bitten by the savage little beast.

It proved to be a young female. Unhappily, she lived but ten days after capture. She persistently refused to eat any cooked food, or any thing else except the nuts and berries which they eat in the forest. She was not so ferocious as "Fighting Joe," but was quite as treacherous and quite untamable. She permitted no one to approach her without trying to bite. Her eyes seemed somewhat milder than Joe's, but had the same gloomy and treacherous look, and she had the same way as Joe of looking you straight in the eyes when she was meditating an attack. I remarked in her also the same manœuvre practiced by the other when she wished to seize something—my leg, for instance, which, by reason of the chain around her neck, she could not reach with her arm. She would look me straight in the face, then quick as a flash would throw her body on one leg and one arm, and reach out with the other leg. Several times I had narrow escapes from the grip of her strong big toe. I thought sometimes that when she looked at me she appeared cross-eyed, but of this I could not make certain. All her motions were remarkably quick, and her strength was very great, though she was so small.

## Chapter 2

### Hermann Schaaffhausen

*The following excerpt is from "On the Crania of the Most Ancient Races of Man" (1861), originally published in Müller's* Archiv *in 1858. The English translation is George Busk's and appeared in the* Natural History Review. *In it, Schaaffhausen discusses his new fossil.*

In the early part of the year 1857, a human skeleton was discovered in a limestone cave in the Neanderthal, near Hochdal, between Düsseldorf and Elberfeld. Of this, however, I was unable to procure more than a plaster cast of cranium taken at Elberfeld, from which I drew up an account of its remarkable conformation, which was, in the first instance, read on the 4th of February, 1857, at the meeting of the Lower Rhine Medical and Natural History Society, at Bonn (Verhandl. D. Naturhist. Vereins der preuss. Rheinlande und Westphalens, xiv. Bonn, 1857). Subsequently Dr. Fuhlrott, himself gave a full account of the locality, and of the circumstances under which the discovery was made. The bones might be regarded as fossil; and in coming to this conclusion, he laid especial stress upon the existence of dendritic deposits with which their surface was covered, and which were first noticed upon them by Professor Mayer. To this communication I appended a brief report on the results of my anatomical examination of the bones. The conclusion at which I arrived: (1) that the extraordinary form of the skull was due to a natural conformation hitherto not known to exist, even in the most barbarous races; (2) that these remarkable human remains belonged to a period antecedent to the time of the Celts and Germans, and were in all probability derived from one of the wild races of northwestern Europe, spoken of by Latin writers; and which were encountered as autochthones by the German immigrants; and (3) that it was beyond the doubt that these human relics were traceable to a period at which the latest animals of the diluvium still existed; but that no proof in support of this assumption, nor consequently of their so-termed *fossil* condition, was afforded by the circumstances under which the bones were discovered.

As we cannot now look upon the primitive world as representing a wholly different condition of things, from which no transition exists to the organic life of the present time, the designation of *fossil,* as applied to *a bone,* has no longer the sense that it conveyed in the time of Cuvier. Sufficient grounds exist for the assumption that man coexisted with the animals found in the diluvium; and many a barbarous race may, before all historical time, have disappeared, together with the animals of the ancient world, whilst the races whose organization is improved have continued the genus. The bones which form the subject of this paper present characters which, although not decisive as regards a geological epoch, are, nevertheless, such as indicate a very high antiquity. It may also be remarked that, common as is the occurrence of diluvial animal bones in the muddy deposits of caverns, such remains have not hitherto been met with in the caves of the Neanderthal; and that the bones, which were covered by a deposit of mud not more than four or five feet thick, and without any protective covering of stalagmite, have retained the greatest part of their organic substance.

The fragments of crania from Schwaan and Plau, on account both of their anatomical conformation and of the circumstances under which they were found, may probably be assigned to a barbarous, aboriginal people, which inhabited the North of Europe before the *Germani;* and, as is proved by the discovery of similar remains at Minsk in Russia, and in the Neanderthal near Elberfeld, must have been extensively spread—being allied, as may be presumed from the form of the skull, with the aboriginal populations of Britain, Ireland, and Scandinavia. Whilst at Schwaan the bones were deposited in a Germanic grave of stone, and consequently are brought into relation with the historical period; the bones from Plau, on the contrary, were merely laid in the sand, together with implements of bone of the rudest kind. The Minsk skull, in like manner, was found in the sand of an ancient river bed. But the human bones and cranium from the Neanderthal exceed all the rest in those peculiarities of the conformation which lead to the conclusion of their belonging to a barbarous and savage race. Whether the cavern in which they were found, unaccompanied with any trace of human art, were the place of their interment, or whether, like the bones of extinct animals elsewhere, they had been washed into it, they may still be regarded as the most ancient memorial of the early inhabitations of Europe.

## L. N. Fowler and O. S. Fowler

*This excerpt is from the* New Illustrated Self-Instructor in Phrenology and Physiology *(1868). In it, the brothers Fowler discuss the relationship between mind and brain.*

Nature operates always and everywhere by means of *organs,* or instrumentalities—never without them. What one function ever is, has been, or *can* be, carried forward without them? None, ever, anywhere.

And what is more, the organism is in perfect *correspondence* with the function. Thus, whenever Nature would put forth *power* of function, she does so by means of power in the *organ* which puts it forth. And so of quickness, and all other functional conditions. Thus the office of wood is to rear aloft that stupendous tree-top, and hold it there in spite of all the surgings of powerful winds upon its vast canvas of trunk, limbs, leaves, and fruit. Now this requires an immense amount of power, especially considering the great mechanical disadvantage involved. This power Nature supplies, not by bulk, because this, by consuming her material and space, would prevent her making many trees, whereas her entire policy is to form all the trees she can; but by rendering the organic *texture* of wood as solid and powerful as its function is potential. And the more solid its structure, the more powerful its function, as seen in comparing oak with pine, and lignum vitæ with poplar. But, letting this single example suffice to illustrate this law, which obtains throughout the entire vegetable kingdom, let us apply to the animal.

The elephant, one of the very strongest of beasts, is so powerfully knitted together, in dermis, muscle, and bone, that bullet after bullet shot at him, flatten and fall harmless at his feet. The loin, too, is as strong in texture as in function. Only those who know from observation can form an adequate idea of the wiry toughness of those muscles and tendons which binds his head to his body, or of the solidity of his bones—corresponding with the fact that, seizing bullock in his monster jaw, he dashes with him through jungles and over raving as a cat would handle a squirrel. And when he roars, a city trembles. The structures of the white and grizzly bear, of the tiger, hyena, and all powerful animals, and indeed, of all weak ones, in like manner correspond equally with their functions. All quickness of function is put forth by quick-acting organs, all slowness by the slow; and thus of all organs and functions throughout every phase and department of universal life and nature. Indeed, in and by the very nature of things this correspondence *must* exist. For how *could* weak organs possibly put forth powerful functions, or slow organs quick functions? In short, this correspondence between organic conditions and functions is fixed and absolute—is necessary, not incidental—is universal, not partial—is a relation of cause and effect, and governs every organ and function throughout universal life and nature.

Governs, reader, you and I. And in all functions. How can weak muscles put forth strength, or a sluggish brain manifest mental activity? Hence, to become great, one must first become *strong*—and in the special *organs* in whose functions he would excel. Would you become great mentally, then first become strong cerebrally. Or, would you render that darling boy a great man, first make him a *powerful animal*. Not that all powerful animals are great men, but that all great men are, and must needs be, powerful animals. Our animal nature is the basis of all mental and moral function. It so is in the very constitution of things, that the mind can put forth *only* in and by its material organism, and is strong or weak, quick or sluggish, as its organism is either. If, in the plenitude of Divine Wisdom, man had been created a purely mental being, he would have needed no body, and could not have used one; whereas, instead, he has been created a compound being, composed of both body and mind. Nor are those seemingly opposite entities strangers to each other. Instead, they are inter-related by ties of the most perfect reciprocity—so perfect that every conceivable condition of either reciprocally affects the other.

*Hereditary Organism as Affecting Mentality.*
*Hereditary organic quality* is the first, basilar, and all-potent condition of all power of function, all happiness, all everything. This is congenital—is imparted by the parentage along with life itself, of which it is paramount condition and instrumentality. It depends mainly on the original nature of the parents, yet partly also on their existing states of body, mind, and health, their mutual love or want of it, and on other like *primal* life-conditions and causes. It lies behind and below, and is infinitely more potential than education, and all associations and surrounding circumstances—is, in short, what renders the grain cereal, the oak oaken, fish fishy, fox foxy, swine swinish, tiger tigerish, and man human.

Each creature much resembles a galvanic battery, and its life-force depends mainly on how that battery is "got up," and this on those congenital conditions which *establish* the life-conditions—a subject infinitely important, and generally overlooked, but treated elsewhere. This condition can not well be described, hardly engraved, but is easily perceived by a practical eye. It is quite analogous to Temperament, on which little has yet been written, but lies behind and below all temperaments—is, indeed, their determining cause. Some of its signs are coarseness and fineness of hair, skin, color, form, motion, general tone of action and mental operation, etc. A comparison of the following engravings of the artist Carpenter with the idiot Emerson will give some outline idea of this point. A still better is found in comparing man with animal. In fact, the main differences between vegetables and animals, as compared among one another, and all as compared with man, and different men as compared with each other, as well as the style and cast of character and sentiment, everything, is consequent on this condition—in short, is what we call "bottom" in the horse, "the breed" in full-blooded animals, and "blood" in those high and nobly born.

*Eugène Dubois*

*In this article, "The Place of 'Pithecanthropus' in the Genealogical Tree" (1896), Dubois sets a few things straight about his discovery.*

In the report on the scientific meeting of the Royal Dublin Society on November 20, in NATURE of December 5, 1895, it is stated that I placed Pithecanthropus in the genealogical tree, drawn by Prof. Cunningham, below the point of divarication [*sic*] of the Anthropoid apes from the human line. This indeed I did. But this statement could be misleading as to my real views on the genealogy of Pithecanthropus, such as I stated them already on p. 38 of my original memoirs (*"Pithecanthropus erectus,* Eine menschenahnliche Uebergangsform aus Java," Batavia, 1894), and more fully at the last meeting of the Anthropological Institute of Great Britain and Ireland, on November 25.

It may not be superfluous to explain my views here by means of the accompanying diagram, representing the evolution of the Old World apes from a hypothetical common ancestor whom I call Procercopithecus.

In Prof. Cunningham's tree, figured in NATURE of December 5, p. 116, he regards the left branch as all human, the right one as entirely simian, and he placed Pithecanthropus midway between recent man and the point of divarication. Now I could find no place for the fossil Javanese form, which I consider as intermediate between Man and Anthopid apes, in any of the branches of *that* tree, only in the third chief line, the main stem, very near to the point of divarication.

Owing to the same circumstances, which indirectly prevented me from explaining my own views on the matter at Dublin, I did not then reply to two remarks of Prof. Cunningham, which omission I now wish to repair by the following declaration.

(1) I did not exaggerate the relative height and quality of the cranial arch, which Prof. Cunningham had in view (the arch of the glabella-inion part of the calvaria) in Hylobates. The profile outline of the skull of *Hyloblates agilis* figured, directly from the bisected skull, on p. 8 of my memoir, is even somewhat higher than that of Pithecanthropus, of which I have an accurate bisected cast before me. In the latter the height of the said cranial arch is exactly equal to the one-third part of the glabella-inion line, and in the skull of a *Hylobates agilis* it is about 2mm. higher than the third part of the corresponding line. If in the mentioned diagram in my memoir that line in the gibbon skull were drawn equal in length to that of the fossil calvaria, instead of the natural size, this would be more apparent there than it is even now. The said cranial arch of a *Hylobates syndactylus* in the same diagram is much lower than that of the other gibbon species, and the same arch in the chimpanzee would even be lower than in *Hylobates syndactylus*. It is easy to find skulls of Semnopithecus with a higher "cranial arch" than the chimpanzee has. Further, between different individuals of the same ape species and of man, we find great differences in the height of that arch.

All these facts tend to show that there is no reason for regarding the height of the suprainial part of the calvaria as of real importance in our judgment on the place which any human-like being should occupy in the genealogical tree.

(2) In my original memoir (p. 7), I have already pointed out that the occiput of the fossil skull is very ape-like, especially gibbon-like. But, nevertheless, the in-

clination of the planum nuchale on the glabella-inion line is very different from that of all the Old World apes. These accord very nearly with one another in the degree of this inclination, whilst the angle in Pithecanthropus approaches closely human conditions. I not only compared photographs of the median line of the skulls, but also the bisected skulls with the bisected exact cast of the fossil calvaria. The means which I have taken to determine the degree of this declination are therefore, I believe, entirely calculated to yield trustworthy results.

## Chapter 3

### Arthur Keith

*Here British anthropologist and anatomist Arthur Keith takes a look at Henry Fairfield Osborn's best-selling* Men of the Old Stone Age: Their Environment, Life, and Art. *He is critical of Osborn's hypothesis that Asia was the cradle of the human race. The review appeared in May 1917, the height of World War I.*

If this had been a time of peace and we had appealed for an impartial judge to give a verdict on the various and diverse explanations which Europeans have given of the ancient races and cultures of their continent, it is more than probable that our choice would have fallen on the author of this work, Dr. Henry Fairfield Osborn. He has spent a lifetime in resurrecting from broken fragments the fauna of past epochs and buried continents; he is a master in the art of reconstruction of past worlds of living things. It is very evident from this book that he has taken infinite pains to weigh the evidence we have all put forward—the evidence of France, of Italy, of Belgium, of Germany, and of England—and his considered and reasoned verdict is for France—for Boule and for Breuil, with Germany as a bad second—Penck and Brückner being accepted as time-keepers. We do not grudge our colleagues of France their victory; they deserve it; their glorious country provided opportunities—that was their fortune; but they used them—that is their everlasting merit. Out of chaos and welter of artifacts they have organised an orderly sequence of ancient human cultures—a sequence which increasing knowledge leads us to believe holds good for all western and central parts of Europe—and yet I cannot help thinking our judge has been over-persuaded by the clear, definite, logical manner in which our French colleagues have presented their case; the evidence produced by Rutot and Reid Moir of a continuous sequence of human flint cultures from the end of the Pliocene to our modern epoch is brushed aside, which cannot well be done by anyone who has studied and examined their records. Nor do we think that any work which is to deal fully with *Men of the Old Stone Age* can exclude, as Dr. Osborn has, his own continent. Has North America nothing to show of men of the Pleistocene?

Dr. Osborn—as is the case with all who adopt this view, now wearing threadbare—regards Pleistocene Europe as a stage—a stage where human races and human cultures appear, play their part, and then disappear. Behind the "flies" of this European Pleistocene stage is Asia; Asia is the huge dressing room in which all the "making up" is done—ancient Asia, of which we know almost nothing, and therefore can believe it capable of anything. In Asia the cultures are fashioned, and the new races of mankind are evolved to cut transitory figures on the ancient European stage. Why should evolution be a monopoly of Asia? Are we not too apt to solve our difficulties in a childish way, and make Asia a fairy factory of anthropological needs? Does the law of evolution not hold for the soil of Europe? In every one of these ancient European cultures we see evolution at work; from the dawn to the close of every cultural period we see that the fashion is always changing. Did those ancient races, who fashioned flints, undergo no change during the centuries which passed?

The story of *Men of the Old Stone Age* cannot be dissociated from the explanation we must give of how the world has come by its present diverse assemblage of races and cultures. We cannot hope to pierce the darkness of the past except we carry with us the light given by a knowledge of our modern world and its races, and perhaps it is just the lack of that knowledge which has kept Dr. Osborn from appreciating at its worth our British evidence. For him Pithecanthropus is exactly the evolutionary stage one would expect man to have reached in the first interglacial period of the Pleistocene; he sees no more difficulty in adding a few ounces to the brain than to the liver. The problems of the liver and brain are infinitely different, as those who are acquainted with the elaborate structure and organisation of the brain well know; to me nothing less than a biological miracle could turn the brain of Pithecanthropus into the brain of Neanderthal man in the short space of two or three hundred years. Nor, to do Dr. Osborn justice, does he really think this was done; he represents Pithecanthropus, Heidelberg man, Neanderthal man, and Piltdown man as branches which separated from the ancestral stock of modern races at the beginning of the Pleistocene period. For him humanity is a Pleistocene product. That is a bigger burden to throw on the short period of the Pleistocene than Dr. Osborn has fully fathomed.

On the other hand, one cannot but admire the thorough manner in which Dr. Osborn has applied himself to the problems of Ancient Europe, the labour he has taken to examine evidence at first hand and visit sites in person, and the clearness and precision he has stated and illustrated, the evidence and the conclusions he has drawn from that evidence. It is a book to read and to refer to, as good a book on the subject of Ancient Man as has yet appeared in the English language—in many senses it is the best—in spite of the fact that I think he has done less than justice to the work and opinions of his British colleagues.

There are minor details which one might have passed in review, but I shall mention only one of them. Dr. Osborn refers to the classic deposits at Hoxne, and to the arctic beds there. He definitely states that the arctic bed at Hoxne and that discovered in the Lea valley by Mr. Hazzeldine Warren are contemporary deposits—both post-Mousterian and of the fourth period of glaciation. Now, the arctic bed at Hoxne lies deep under the classic brick earth in which the first palaeoliths were discovered by John Frere in the year 1797, and they are palaeoliths of the Acheulean type, they belong to that culture and date. The Lea valley arctic bed belongs to a much later date—late palaeolithic—according to its discoverer, Mr. Hazzeldine Warren. It is quite true that we have much to learn regarding the sequence and approximate dates of our English Pleistocene deposits, and at the present time our geologists and archaeologists are modifying and extending their opinions regarding them, but I am certain that if Dr. Osborn will give them the attention he has given to those in France he will alter some of his conclusions in one of the many new editions into which his book will assuredly pass.

*Jia Lanpo*

*In this excerpt from* Early Man in China *(1980), Jia discusses his belief that the first humans appeared in Asia.*

Probably because of my work, I have often been asked: Where did man first emerge? This is indicative of the widespread interest in this subject. I would like to start off with my own views, which might help the reader to a better understanding of the early man of China.

A simple answer is not enough; evidence is necessary for a fully satisfactory one. Fortunately, in the last 50 years or so, investigators of various countries have collected a fairly substantial amount of specimens which adds immensely to the credibility of paleontological propositions. But the interpretations based on the evidence available so far are not incontrovertible. They are unavoidably inferences. Perhaps in another generation or so sufficient material will have been amassed to upgrade the inferences to firmly grounded concepts.

What answers do we have at present on the question of man's place of origin? Paleontologists still differ. Some hold that it is Africa, others Europe, and many believe it is Asia. For many years contention has been centred on these three continents, while Antarctica, Oceania and the Americas have not been considered at all. Discounting Antarctica the earliest reliable evidence unearthed in North America merely goes back less than 30,000 years and in South America, the sites in Venezuela have yielded specimens of no more than 14,000 years of antiquity. The further down the south of that continent, the shorter the history of the evidence. Human fossil remains at the southern tip is only some 10,000 years old. In Oceania, no cultural objects older than 20,000 years have yet been found.

Europe was once claimed to be the place of man's origin when the first discovery of Paleolithic industry was made there in the 1830s, and a chronology of the Paleolithic Age of Europe was compiled by the end of the 1860s. But, up to now, taking the world as a whole, Europe has yielded much less human fossils and artifacts of great antiquity than Asia and Africa.

Africa is the home of the Gorilla and chimpanzee which are close to the human species. Since the1920s, more anthropoid ape and early man fossils have been found on that continent, giving rise to high popularity of the thesis that man had first evolved in Africa. But Asia is the place that has yielded the greatest number of fossils of simian species that had not known tool making but are most akin to man.

The thesis that Southern Asia is man's birthplace seems more tenable. As Frederick Engels held: "Many hundreds of thousands of years ago, during an epoch not yet definitely determinable of that period of the earth's history which geologists call the tertiary, and most likely towards the end of it, a particularly highly-developed species of anthropoid apes lived somewhere in the tropical zone—probably on a great continent that now has sunk to the bottom of the Indian Ocean." This assertion on the location as well as geological age has been corroborated by later finds consisting of fossil remains of *Ramapithecus* (Rama Ape) of

Upper Miocene and Lower Pliocene, the human fossils of the Lower Pleistocene, and the geographical distribution of cultural sites contemporaneous with the last.

Of all known ape fossils, those of *Ramapithecus* have attracted the most attention. This generic name was first given to the owner of a hominid-simian right upper-jaw fragment found in 1933 by a local resident in the Siwalik Hills in Northern India. Many anthropologists have since then considered this genus as a whole to be the ancestral basis from which modern man evolved, and taxonomically, some scholars have frankly placed it under hominidae.

Fossils of a similar type have been found in Upper Miocene or Lower Pliocene deposits in Kenya, East Africa and were given the generic name *Kenyapithecus* (Kenya Ape) in 1962. The evidence consists of only upper and lower jaw bones of teeth.

In 1957 and 1958, at Xiaolongtan, Kaiyuan County, Yunnan Province, five fossil teeth were unearthed successively in Lower Pliocene coal seams. To these Professor Wu Rukang gave the name *Dryopithecus kaiyuanensis* (Kaiyuan Oak Ape), but further studies resulted in grouping the 1957 Kaiyuan finds with the fossils collected in Kenya and India under one generic name, *Ramapithecus punjapicus* (Punjab Rama Ape). Although the diversity of views on the taxonomical classification of *Kenyapithecus* is not yet resolved, this grouping has provided a more creditable outline of the evolutionary lineage from ape to man.

It is generally believed that *Ramapithecus* lived in tropical or semi-tropical forest and savanna areas. Members of this genus are in general 1.1 to 1.2 meters in height, with a short face, vaulted palate bone, and teeth and upper and lower jawbones similar to that of *Australopithecus* (Southern Ape). As the dentition shows many characters like that of *Homosapiens* in its rudimentary form, the genus can nearly be identified as the precursor to *Homosapiens* who lived 15–10 million years before the present. There is no evidence on hand to show whether *Ramapithecus* walked with an erect gait, as no cranial and pelvic fossils have been found. Nevertheless, since *Australopithecus* has been shown capable of doing so, his lineal precursor *Ramapithecus* may be inferred as being able to walk in a transitional semi-erect gait. No sites have yet yielded any artifacts to show that this genus could make tools.

Among all known ape fossils, *Ramapithecus* is the closest to man, possessing more human characteristics than any other genera. Judging by this fact and the period that he lived, he may be considered as man's simian ancestor who had inherent qualities enabling him to evolve into man. He had crossed the threshold into the stage of hominids.

Increasingly more evidence has been unearthed to show that man's birth place is Asia. Recently, fossils of *Ramapithecus* have been discovered at sites in Pakistan and in Lufeng County (25.7N, 102.7E), Yunnan Province, China. A Pliocene coal seam at the latter site has yielded an almost complete mandible and a few teeth in association with a good collection of mammalian fossils. These specimens are under study. We have only to look at the map of the world to see how *Ramapithecus* fossils and the early Pliocene cultures are distributed. The westernmost site which has yielded *Ramapithecus* remains, if *Kenyapithecus* is included, is Fort Ternan (0.12S, 35.21E), Kenya; the Siwalik Hills (31N, 77E) site in Northern India is in the centre, and the easternmost site is at Xiaolongtan, Kaiyuan County, Yunnan Province, China. Connecting these three points, we get a triangle of unequal sides, with its central area in Southern Asia. This roughly corresponds to what Frederick

Engels had observed. The sites yielding Lower Pleistocene human remains and cultural relics are located around this triangle. These were Sterkfontein (26.03S, 27.42E) and Tuang (27.32S, 24.45E) in South Africa on the southwesternmost side; the Grotte Du Vallonnet at Menton (43.49N, 7.29E), France, on the north-westernmost side; Xihoudu Village, Ruicheng (34.41N, 110.17E), Shanxi Province, China, on the northeasternmost side; and Sangiram (7S, 112E), Java, Indonesia, on the southeasternmost side.

According to available evidence so far, the vast area of southwestern China is within this region where man first appeared. In Yunnan, not only *Ramapithecus* fossils have been found, but teeth and lithic culture of Yuanmou Man dating back to Lower Pleistocene (about 1.7 million years B.P.) have been unearthed as well, which is very revealing evidence.

Neither can the Qinghai-Tibet Plateau be ignored as a possible place of man's origin. In the Teritiary period, the geographical features of this region were quite different from today. Successive explorations in the Qomolangma (Jolmo Lungma) area carried out under the auspices of the Chinese Academy of Sciences have produced abundant scientific data. We know from the flora here that in the Upper Pliocene, the ecological environment in the Mount Xixia Bangma region at that time was marked by sub-tropical climate with a yearly mean temperature of about 10°C and precipitation around 2,000 mm. (See Guo Xudong's paper in *Scientia Sinica,* 1974, No. 1.) In 1975 at a site in the Jilong Basin, which is 4,100–4,300 m. above sea level, on the northern slope of Mt. Xixia Bangma in the middle section of the Himalayas, fossil remains of the Pliocene three-toed horse *(Hipparion)* were found. This species of forest-grassland dweller is at home in a temperate climate. Sporo-pollen analysis has also produced evidence of a flora that included *Loropetalum,* palm, quercitron, goosefoot, cedar, pea and other sub-tropical plants, which tallies with the climatic conditions shown in the composition of local clay minerals. A geological report made on April 16, 1977 by a young geologist Chen Wanyong concluded: "In the Pliocene the Himalayas were about 1,000 metres above sea level and not as pronounced a barrier to the monsoon from the Indian Ocean as it is today, hence both the south and north slopes were benefited by that seasonal, warm, moist wind. It can be safely said that the Himalayas and the Qinghai-Tibet Plateau have since the Pliocene been rising at the rate of approximately 0.025–0.03 mm. per year, with an obvious higher rate of uplift after the Middle Pleistocene. The present-day elevation is at least 3,000 metres higher than in Pliocene times." This information is of great value. It suggests that during the transition from ape to man, the Qinghai-Tibet Plateau was a region still suitable for the evolution of higher Primates, which makes the region a hopeful place for seeking missing links in the evolution of man.

For reasons stated above, I am for the assertion that man's place of origin is in the southern part of East Asia.

*Chapter 4*

*Louis S. B. Leakey*

*In this excerpt from* Progress and Evolution of Man in Africa *(1961; used by permission of Oxford University Press), Leakey discusses who the possible toolmakers from Olduvai Gorge were.*

I do not wish to suggest the Australopithecines were not utilizing natural objects as tools or clubs and cutting tools. I think they were doing so, although I cannot accept the validity of the greater part of what Dart calls the "osteodondtokeratic" culture of his *Australopithecus* species. If Dart's claims are proved to be correct, then *Australopithecus* was making *bone* tools to a set and regular pattern and would rank as a "man" by definition. This possibility cannot be denied, but, at present, I am among those who find Dart's arguments, and his material, unconvincing.

There is, of course, no doubt whatsoever from the study of the teeth, jaws, and skeletal material of the South African Australopithecines that they were members of the family *Hominidae* from the structural and the morphological point of view. They are, indeed, far further removed from the *Pongidae* than many popular writers (and some scientific writers) suggest. That is why I like the term "near men" rather than "ape men" to describe them.

The most probable explanation of the South African evidence would seem to be that the "near men" were considerably advanced as "tool users" but were not yet quite able to make tools to a set and regular pattern (in spite of Dart's claim that they did make some). At the most they made some very simple tools and utilized many natural objects as tools. This is probably beyond question.

That is why I would prefer to abandon the subfamilial designation *Australopithecinae* and *Huminae* and simply retain the family *Hominidae* with *Australopithecus* and *Paranthropus* as specialized side branches within the family.

In my report to "*Nature*" on the discovery of the skull of *Zinjanthropus boisei* at Olduvai Gorge in 1959, I made it clear that I believed that the very close association of quantities of primitive Oldowan stone tools with the skull of *Zinjanthropus*—which while broken into pieces and lacking the lower jaw had not been broken up and scattered over the living floor—suggested that it represented the makers of this culture. I admit that I am no longer quite so certain, but I still think that in all probability *Zinjanthropus* did make the tools on the site and does qualify, from the definition point of view, as a man.

Morphologically, however, *Zinjanthropus* is in many respects close to the South African genera *Australopithecus* and *Paranthropus,* exhibiting indeed some characters of each (as I stressed in my first note) as well as others which occur in neither.

Nevertheless, in many other characters the differences between *Zinjanthropus* and the two South African genera are such that I personally am fully satisfied that the generic rank is justified.

A fact which I would like to stress at this juncture is that I cannot agree with certain of my colleagues, both in Europe and America, who blithely claim that the fact of the close association of *Zinjanthropus* with the Oldowan culture "proves" or "establishes" that the South African genera made such tools. Of course, it proves nothing of the sort, although it may "suggest the possibility."

## Chapter 5

### Steven Pinker

*In this excerpt from "Grammar Puss" (1994; used by permission of the publisher), Pinker discusses language and how we try desperately to make rules about something that is very flexible.*

Language is a human instinct. All societies have complex language, and everywhere the languages use the same kinds of grammatical machinery, such as nouns, verbs, auxiliaries and agreement. Normal children develop language without conscious effort or formal lessons, and by the age of 3 they speak in fluent grammatical sentences. Brain damage or congenital conditions can make a retarded person a linguistic savant or a person of high intelligence unable to speak. All this has led many scientists to conclude that there are specialized circuits in the brain, and perhaps specialized genes, that create the gift of articulate speech.

But when you read about language in the popular press, you get a very different picture. Johnny can't construct a grammatical sentence. As educational standards decline and pop culture disseminates the inarticulate ravings and unintelligible patois of surfers, rock stars and valley girls, we are turning into a nation of functional illiterates: misusing "hopefully," confusing "lie" and "lay," treating "bummer" as a sentence, letting our participles dangle.

What is behind this contradiction? If language is as instinctive to humans as dam-building is to beavers, if the design of syntax is coded in our DNA, why does the average American sound like a gibbering fool every time he opens his mouth or puts pen to paper?

The most benign explanation for this apparent contradiction is that the words "rule" and "grammar" have very different meanings to a scientist and to a layperson. The rules people learn (or, more likely, fail to learn) in school are called "prescriptive" rules, prescribing how one ought to talk. Scientists studying language propose "descriptive" rules, describing how people do talk. Prescriptive and descriptive grammar are simply different things. To a scientist, the fundamental fact of human language is its sheer improbability. Most objects in the universe—rocks, worms, cows, cars—cannot talk. Even in humans, speech comprises an infinitesimal fraction of the noises people's mouths are capable of making. I can arrange a combination of words that explains how octopuses make love or how to build an atom bomb; rearrange the words in even the most minor way, and the result is a sentence with a different meaning or, more likely, word salad. How are we to account for this miracle? What would it take to build a device that could duplicate human language?

Obviously, you would need to build in rules. But prescriptive rules? Imagine trying to build a talking machine by designing it to obey rules such as "Don't split infinitives" or "Never begin a sentence with 'because.'" It would just sit there. Prescriptive rules are useless without the much more fundamental rules that create the sentences to begin with. These rules are never mentioned in style manuals because the authors correctly assume that anyone capable of reading the manuals must already know them. No one, not even a valley girl, has to be told not to say "Apples the eat boy" or "Who did you meet John and?" or the vast, vast majority of the trillions of mathematically possible combinations of words. So when a scientist considers all the high-tech mental machinery needed to order words into everyday sentences, prescriptive rules are, at best, inconsequential decorations.

So there is no contradiction, after all, in saying that every normal person can speak grammatically (in the sense of systematically) and ungrammatically (in the sense of nonprescriptively), just as there is no contradiction in saying that a taxi obeys the laws of physics but breaks the laws of Massachusetts.

So whence the popular anxiety? This is where a less than benign explanation comes in. Someone, somewhere, must be making decisions about "correct English" for the rest of us. Who? There is no English Language Academy. The legislators of "correct English," in fact, are an informal network of copy editors, dictionary usage panelists, style manual writers, English teachers, essayists and pundits. Their authority, they claim, comes from their dedication to carrying out standards that maximize the language's clarity, logic, consistency, precision, stability and expressive range. William Safire, who writes the weekly column "On Language" for the *New York Times Magazine,* calls himself a "language maven," from the Yiddish word meaning expert, and this gives us a convenient label for the entire group.

The foibles of the language mavens, then, can be blamed on two blind spots: a gross underestimation of the linguistic wherewithal of the common person, and an ignorance of the science of language—not just technical linguistics, but basic knowledge of the constructions and idioms of English, and how people use them.

Unlike some academics in the '60s, I am not saying that concern for grammar and composition are tools to perpetuate an oppressive status quo and that The People should be liberated to write however they please. Some aspects of how people express themselves in some settings are worth trying to change. What I am calling for is a more thoughtful discussion of language and how people use it, replacing bubbe-maises (old wives' tales) with the best scientific knowledge available. It is ironic that the Jeremiahs' wailings about how sloppy language leads to sloppy thought are themselves hairballs of loosely associated factoids and tangled non sequiturs. All the examples of verbal behavior that the complainer takes exception to for any reason are packed together and coughed up as proof of The Decline of the Language: teenage slang, sophistry, regional variations in pronunciation and vocabulary, bureaucratic bafflegab, poor spelling and punctuation, pseudo-errors like "hopefully," government euphemism, nonstandard grammar like "ain't," misleading advertising and so on (not to mention occasional witticisms that go over the complainer's head).

I hope to have convinced you of two things. Many prescriptive rules are just plain dumb and should be deleted from the handbooks. And most of standard English is just that, standard, in the sense of standard units of currency or household voltages. It is just common sense that people should be encouraged to learn the dialect that has become the standard in their society. But there is no need to use terms like "bad grammar," "fractured syntax" and "incorrect usage" when referring to rural, black and other nonstandard dialects (even if you dislike "politically correct" euphemisms): the terms are not only insulting, but scientifically inaccurate.

The aspect of language use that is most worth changing is the clarity and style of written prose. The human language faculty was not designed for putting esoteric thoughts on paper for the benefit of strangers, and this makes writing a difficult craft that must be mastered through practice, feedback and intensive exposure to good examples. There are excellent manuals of composition that discuss these skills with great wisdom—but note how their advice concentrates on important practical tips like "omit needless words" and "revise extensively," not on the trivia of split infinitives and slang.

As for slang, I'm all for it! I don't know how I ever did without "to flame," "to dis" and "to blow off," and there are thousands of now unexceptionable English words such as "clever," "fun," "sham," "banter" and "stingy" that began life as slang. It is especially hypocritical to oppose linguistic innovations reflexively and at the same time to decry the loss of distinctions like "lie" versus "lay" on the pretext of preserving expressive power. Vehicles for expressing thought are being created far more quickly than they are being abandoned.

Indeed, appreciating the linguistic genius of your ordinary Joe is the cure for the deepest fear of the mavens: that English is steadily deteriorating. Every component of every language changes over time, and at any moment a language is enduring many losses. But the richness of a language is always being replenished, because the one aspect of language that does not change is the very thing that creates it: the human mind.

## Chapter 6

### William Bollaert

*In "Introduction to the Palæography of America" (1863–1864), Bollaert examines some artifacts thought to indicate the presence of classical civilizations in ancient America.*

The first rather interesting specimen of Indian writing I shall refer to is the *Deighton Rock inscriptions,* met with near Taunton, in Massachusetts. The engravings are on a mass of stone, one of its sides being covered with marks, and lines picked out. In vol. viii, p. 293, *Archoeologia, Soc. of Antiq., London,* are four drawings by Mr. Lort. Numberless copies have been made of the scratchings from 1680 to 1847, and have been by some erroneously supposed to be Phœnician. The Society of Northern Antiquaries, after comparing copies, excepting that of 1847, pronounced them to be Scandinavian! In 1839, drawings were submitted to the Algonkin chief, Chingwauk, when he considered them, in part, to be the work of the New England Indians, which is, I should think, about the truth of the case. The probability is that a portion has been picked out by the Indians of a comparatively early period; fresh markings subsequently added by other Indians (not an uncommon occurrence); then some wag of a white settler has made certain modern marks, which has led to the idea that this is a Scandinavian, Phœnician, or other Old World inscription. Mr. Arnzen, of Massachusetts, sent, in 1863, to the Royal Society of Northern Antiquaries, a "warranty deed," conveying to Rafn and the said society the rock known as the "Writing," or "Deighton Rock," and the lot and parcel of land surrounding it.

As late as 1860, an alleged fac-simile of a Hebrew inscription was presented to the American Ethnological Society, vol. i, p. 14, 1861, taken from a small, polished, wedge-shaped stone, purporting to have been found during the summer of 1869, among ancient earthworks in the vicinity of Newark, Ohio, some sixty miles from the coast of Atlantic. The four inscriptions on the four sides contained ten words, which were interpreted as meaning "Holy of Holies," "King of Earth," "Law of Jehovah," "Word of Jehovah." The manufacture of this spurious object may be placed by the side of the said-to-be-lost (!) gold plates of Joe Smith, the founder of the Mormons, or Latter-day Saints. I may here just state that Joe Smith was born in 1805, at Sharon, Vermont, and killed at Carthage, Illinois, in 1844. He was the vagabond son of a vagabond family. In 1823, he reported that the angel Moroni informed him where he should find the gold plates containing the holy record of how America had been peopled by descendants of Jews; the spot was a hill at Manchester, New York; with the record were two transparent stones, through which the writing on the golden plates would become intelligible.

In January 1861, a communication was made to the American Ethnological Society by Dr. Evans, of New Jersey; it was accompanied by a sculptured stone axe, and the information given that it was found in Rancocas Creek, in Pemberton township; that it was ploughed up on the farm of S. R. Gaskill; some of his family attempted to render the characters more distinct by increasing the original marks, but that portions of the letters, and nearly all the outer edges, had not been disturbed, which afforded evidence, as was said, of its antiquity.

Dr. Dwight observed, in a discussion that ensued, that the axe was of compact sandstone, over six inches long and four broad. The whole neighborhood had been fruitful in Indian relics, such as axes, hammers, arrow-heads, etc. The characters were an inch in length and one-tenth in depth, and smoothly wrought. Some bore a general resemblance to characters on the *Grave Creek Stone* (a hoax),—perhaps they were Numidian (!). Some appeared identical with Phœnician (!), the mark XIII like the Roman for thirteen.

I have but little doubt that the stone axe is an aboriginal relic; but the letters and figures on it are a modern joke of some "smart" Yankee. There are three marks or lines on one side and two on the other, these are *supposed* to have been made with the plough in turning up the land. The next Yankee arrangement purports to come from the *Great Mound* at Grave Creek, and found by the side of a skeleton. The mound, when discovered, contained shell-beads, shells *(marginella),* copper bracelets, slips of mica, and the relic in question (?), which is oval form, two inches in length and one and a half in width, and of compact sandstone. The so-called inscription is arranged in parallel lines, and comprises twenty-four characters, accompanied by a supposed hieroglyph, or ideographic sign. Analyses have been undertaken by various persons, and with different and most amusing results. Mr. Schoolcraft regarded twenty-two of the characters as alphabetic, from which he identifies, as corresponding with ancient Greek, Etruscan, Runic, Gallic, Erse, Phœnician, Old British, and Celtiberic (!).

A notice of this stone appeared in the Cincinnati papers in 1839. Previously, however, a detailed account of the opening of the mound, and of its contents, was communicated to the author of the *Crania Americana,* and published in that contribution to science. This account was written by Dr. Clemens, of Wheeling, Virginia, and contains *no reference* to the inscribed stone. The stone is no longer at the mound in Grave Creek, but supposed be in the possession of a person in Richmond, Virginia, and that the owner of the mound was imposed on. In vol. i, of *Amer. Ethno. Trans.*, there is a paper by Schoolcraft, and a drawing given of a globular stone body, four inches and five-tenths in circumference; one character on it is like the Greek delta. This is also spurious.

Another notable example of fraud is furnished by the six inscribed copper-plates, said to have been found in a mound near Kinderhook, in Illinois; these bear a close resemblance to Chinese. They proved to have been engraved by the village blacksmith, who had, probably, no better suggestion to his antiquarian labours than the lid of a Chinese tea-box. Each plate had an orthodox ideographic sign.

*Aleš Hrdlička*

*In* Recent Discoveries Attributed to Early Man in America *(1918), an excerpt from one of his Bureau of American Ethnology publications, Hrdlička discusses the case of the Florida skeleton known as Vero man.*

The discovery of "fossil human remains" at Vero, on the eastern coast of Florida, was recently announced by Dr. E. H. Sellards, State Geologist. In the early part of October a more extended report on these finds, by the same author, appeared, and other communications on the subject were sent to scientific journals. Meanwhile, generous invitations to visit Vero were extended by Dr. Sellards to a number of scientific men interested in the subject, as a result of which the last few days of October found his camp at Vero filled to capacity. The party included, besides Dr. Sellards and Mr. H. Gunter, his assistant, Dr. Rollin C. Chamberlin, of the University of Chicago, and Dr. T. Wayland Vaughan, of the United States Geological Survey, geologists; Dr. O. F. Hay, of the Carnegie Institution of Washington, vertebrate paleontologist; Prof. George Grant MacCurdy, of the Peabody Museum, Yale University, archeologist and anthropologist; and the writer. A stay of two to five days was made by the several members of the party, and, notwithstanding insects, rain, and finally a partial flood, the locality of the finds, together with the vicinity, was fairly well examined. . . . The reports of the members of the party on the results of their observations, including a preliminary account of similar nature by the writer, will be found in the January–February, 1917, number of *The Journal of Geology,* and are referred to later in this memoir. In this place is presented a more complete account of the subject so far as it relates to the human bones.

*Critical Consideration of the Vero Finds*

In deciding questions of so great importance as the presence of the remains of early man in any part of the American Continent, it would seem only prudent that in any given case final positive conclusions should be deferred until the evidence shall have been submitted to and considered by those who through their training and experience can be assumed to have special qualifications for the interpretation of the phenomena involved, and until all room for serious doubt concerning the age finds shall have been removed. It is particularly regrettable that in the Vero case anthropologists could not have had the opportunity of examining the evidence on the spot while the human remains were still *in situ,* rather than after everything relating to human occupancy had been removed and after far-reaching conclusions concerning the age of the remains had received wide publicity.

It is scarcely safe for the geologist or the paleontologist to assume that the problem of human antiquity is his problem. Although it is only just to acknowledge that geology and especially paleontology can be, on occasion, of the greatest aid to anthropology in determining the age of human remains, yet these branches are not adequate in themselves to deal with the subject. In all cases in which the remains of man are concerned, be they cultural or skeletal, there enters a most important factor into the case which does not exist for the geologist and paleontologist, namely, the *human element,* the element of man's conscious activities.

Like inorganic materials, the remains of plants and animals are passive objects, affected only by the action of living plants and animals and that of the elements. In the main they find their resting places accidentally, and, unless they sink into the soil or are displaced by some agency subsequent to their deposition, they constitute safe evidence of contemporaneity with other similar objects and with the geologic components of the same horizon. Not so, however, with the remains of man. Accidentally or intentionally he introduces cultural objects into the ground, and from the earliest known times has buried his dead at varying depths, thus introducing his remains into deposits and among other remains with which otherwise they had no relation.

There have been accidental deaths in rivers and bogs, and in certain cases human bodies have remained on the surface of the ground unburied, but such instances have been always, as they are to-day, very rare. Still more rare must have been the abandonment of unburied bodies in numbers; this would happen only after a battle, a massacre, or a great pestilence. But what chance would human skeletons left in this way upon the surface have of becoming actually included, in any degree approximating entirety, natural relations of the parts and a good state of preservation, in a slowly forming geological stratum, and so becoming true paleontological specimens, synchronous with the bones of animals and other organic materials in the same deposits? The chance is too slight to deserve serious consideration. The bones, with the exception, perhaps, of those of some compact part, as a hand or a foot, would be broken, scattered, gnawed by animals, weathered, split, moss-eaten, root-eaten, and in nearly all cases wholly or largely destroyed. The same thing happens constantly with the skeletons of the larger animals whose bodies remain on the surface of the ground. What is preserved of them in the geological formations consists usually of individual teeth or bones, or at most of a few related parts, yet animal bones are on the whole more durable than human bones, and there are immeasurably more of them. For every human body abandoned on the surface of the earth there probably millions of carcasses of animals; and this applies even more forcibly to prehistoric times, when men were scarce and animals much more numerous.

## Chapter 7

### Stanley Waterloo

*In* The Story of Ab: A Tale of the Time of the Cave Man *(1923) the protagonist caveman, Ab, finds Lightfoot dead. This prompts him to learn burial techniques and contemplate for the first time death and the afterlife.*

Ab looked towards the forest wherein Lightfoot had fled and then looked upon that which lay at his feet. It was Oak—there were the form and features of his friend—but, somehow, it was not Oak. There was too much silence and the blood upon the leaves seemed far too bright. His rage departed, and he wanted Oak to answer and called to him, but Oak did not answer. Then came slowly to him the idea that Oak was dead and that the wild beasts would that night devour the dead man where he lay. The thought nerved him to desperate, sudden action. He leaped forward, he put his arms about the body and carried it away to a hollow in the wooded slope. He worked madly, doing some things as he seen the cave people do at other buryings. He placed the weapons of Oak beside him. He took from his belt his own knife, because it was better than that of Oak, and laid it close to the dead man's hand, and then, first covering the body with beech leaves, he worked frantically upon the overhanging soil, prying it down with a sharp pointed fragment of limb, and tossing in upon all as heavy stones as he could lift, until a great cairn rose above the hunter who would hunt no more.

Panting with his efforts, Ab sat himself down upon a rock and looked upon the monument he had raised. Again he called to Oak, but there was still no answer. The sun had set, evening shadows thickened around him. Then there came upon the live man a feeling as dreadful as it was new, and, with a yell, which was almost a shriek, he leaped to his feet and bounded away in fearful flight.

He only knew this, that there was something hurt inside his body and soul, but not the inside of him as it had been when once he had eaten poisonous berries or when he had eaten too much of the little deer. It was something different. It was an awful oppression, which seemed to leave his body, in a manner, unfeeling but which had a great dread about it and which made him think and think of the dead man, and made him want to run away and keep running. He had already run far that day, but he was not tired now. His legs seemed to have the hard sinews of the stag in them but up toward the top of him was something for them to carry away as fast and far as possible from somewhere. He raced from the dense woodland down into the broad morass to the west—beyond which was the rock country— and into which he had rarely ventured, so treacherous its ways. What cared he now! He made great leaps and his muscles and sinews responded to the thought of him. To cross that morass safely required a touch on tussocks and an upbounding aside, a zig-zag exhibition of great strength and knowingness and recklessness. But it was unreasoning; it was the instinct begotten of long training and, now, of the absence of all nervousness. Each taut toe touched each point of bearing just as was required above the quagmire, and, all unperceiving and uncaring, he fled over dirty death as easily as he might have run upon some hardened woodland pathway. He did not think nor know nor care about what he was doing. He was only running away from the something he had never known before! Why should he be running now? He had killed things before and not cared and had forgotten. Why should he care now? But there was the something which made him run. And where was Oak? Would Oak meet him again and would they hunt again? No, Oak would not come, and he, this Ab, had made it so! He must run—he knew that—but he must run!

The marsh was passed, night had fallen, but he ran on, pressing into the bear and tiger haunted forest beyond. Anything, anything, to make him forget the strange feeling and the thing which made him run! He plunged into a forest path, utterly reckless, wanting relief, a seeker for whatever might come.

In that age and under such conditions as to locality it was inevitable that the creature, man, running through such a forest path at night, must face some fierce creature of the carnivora seeking his body for food. Ab, blinded of mood, cared not for and avoided not a fight, though it might be with the monster bear or even the great tiger. There was no reason in his madness. He was, though he knew it not, a practical suicide, yet one who would die fighting. What to him were weight and strength to-night? What to him were such encounters as might come with hungry four-footed things? It would but relieve him were some of the beasts to try to gain his life and eat his body. His being seemed valueless, and as for the wild beasts—

and here came out the splendid death-facing quality of the cave man—well, it would be odd if there were not more death than one! But all this was vague and only a minor part of thought.

Sometimes, as to invite death, he yelled as he ran. He yelled whenever in his fleeting visions he saw Oak lying dead again. So ran the man who killed another.

## Chapter 8

### Madison Grant

*Grant was a man who denounced not only the "lower orders" but democracy as well, as he does here in* The Passing of the Great Race *(1916).*

Modern anthropology has demonstrated that racial lines are not only absolutely independent of both national and linguistic groupings, but that in many cases these racial lines cut through them at sharp angles and correspond closely with the divisions of social cleavage. The great lesson of the science of race is the immutability of somatological or bodily characters, with which is closely associated with the immutability of psychical predispositions and impulses. This continuity of inheritance has a most important bearing on the theory of democracy and still more upon that of socialism, and those, engaged in social uplift and in revolutionary movements are consequently usually very intolerant of the limitations imposed by heredity.

Democratic theories of government in their modern form are based on dogmas of equality formulated some hundred and fifty years ago, and rest upon the assumption that environment and not heredity is the controlling factor in human development. Philanthropy and noble purpose dictated the doctrine expressed in the Declaration of Independence, the document which to-day constitutes the actual basis of American institutions. The men who wrote the words, "we hold these truths to be self-evident, that all men are created equal," were themselves the owners of slaves, and despised Indians as something less than human. Equality in their minds meant merely that they were just as good Englishmen as their brothers across the sea. The words "that all men are created equal" have since been subtly falsified by adding the word "free," although no such expression is found in the original document, and the teachings based on these altered words in the American public schools of to-day would startle and amaze the men who formulated the Declaration.

The laws of nature operate with the same relentless and unchanging force in human affairs as in the phenomena of inanimate nature, and the basis of the government of man is now and always has been, and always will be, force and not sentiment, a truth demonstrated anew by the present world conflagration.

It will be necessary for the reader to strip his mind of all preconceptions as to race, since modern anthropology, when applied to history, involves an entire change of definition. We must, first of all, realize that race pure and simple, the physical and psychical structure of man, is something entirely distinct from either nationality or language, and that race lies to-day at the base of all the phenomena of modern society, just as it has done throughout the un-recorded eons of the past.

*Elaine Morgan*

*Here Morgan expounds on her controversial ideas in* The Scars of Evolution *(1990; used by permission of Oxford University Press).*

In the whole history of evolution, the emergence of man is the one episode where the unanswered questions are thickest on the ground, and the challenge is most frequently taken up. At regular intervals, hypotheses are published attempting to account for one or another puzzling feature of human anatomy. These efforts may be criticised or they may be ignored. In either case the hoped-for chorus of "Eureka!" fails to materialise and the theorist goes back to the drawing board. After a time another hypothesis is put forward, with the same result.

The present state of play may be summarised as follows. Four of the most outstanding mysteries about humans are: (1) why do they walk on two legs? (2) why have they lost their fur? (3) why have they developed such large brains? (4) why did they learn to speak?

The Orthodox answers to these questions are: (1) "We do not yet know"; (2) "We do not yet know"; (3) "We do not yet know"; and (4) "We do not yet know." The list of questions could be considerably lengthened without affecting the monotony of the answers.

Scientists do not normally sum up the situation as starkly as that, for several reasons. In the first place, they do not see it like that. They have lived long enough with the conundrums to be no longer surprised by them; they are satisfied that the new data are continually being amassed and steady progress is being made. That is quite true. As in any other form of enquiry, if you can produce solid reasons for discarding a false hypothesis, that represents a significant advance. Over the last thirty years a number of seductive evolutionary scenerios have been successfully demolished.

There is one other reason why they underestimate the extent to which they have been bogged down over this question for more than a century. That is the information explosion. Science has become ever more subdivided, and researchers have become absorbed in their own specialities.

Thus a palaeontoligist on an African dig may be obsessed by the problem of bipedalism and regard it as the last of the great unanswered questions. Crack this one, he feels, and we are home and dry. Meanwhile, in other parts of the world, other specialists are telling themselves that bipedalism must be pretty well understood by this time, and the really baffling characteristic still unexplained is the unusual nature of our skin—larnyx—sex organs—sweat-glands—blood—adipose tissue—brain—tears—vocal communication—extended life span—or whatever is their own particular field of study.

In short, the chief mystery does not lie in any one of these anomalies, not even the wonderful brain or the dexterous hands or the miracle of speech. It lies in the sheer number and variety of the ways in which we differ from our closest relatives in the animal kingdom. Some of these differences are major and some are minor; several appear arbitrary and pointless; others are embarrassing or inconvenient; and it has not proved easy to trace any logical connection between them.

Something happened. Something must have happened to our own ancestors which did not happen to the ancestors of apes and gorillas. In the last analysis no one seriously disputes that. No one, for instance, expresses surprise that the anomalies were not more evenly shared, so that gorillas learned to speak, people walked on two legs, and chimpanzees became naked.

Something changed in the environment, or in the mode of response to the environment, or the genes; that change affected only one particular group among the ancestral anthropoids, and set them on the long road to becoming human.

The key question, then, is: "What happened?" One possible response is: "Who cares what happened? Whatever it was, it was millions of years ago and it can't possibly affect me." But that is not true. Whatever it was, it affects every one of us because it had far-reaching consequences on the way our bodies function—or, frequently, malfunction. Possibly 20 percent of the ills that our flesh is heir to can be traced back to the critical period of transition from non-human to human.

*Franz Weidenreich*

*In this excerpt from* Giant Early Man from Java and South China *(1945; used by permission of the American Museum of Natural History Library, New York), Weidenreich discusses* Gigantopithecus.

Every discovery of early hominids revives the old question as to the relationships between hominids and anthropoid characters which were revealed by *Pithrocan-thropus robustus, Meganthropus,* and *Gigantopithecus* but which, so far, have not been noted in early hominids. We find the list a short one. They are: 1, the persistence of the upper diastema in *Pithrocanthtropus robustus;* 2, the fact that the second upper molar clearly exceeds the first and third in size in the same specimen; 3, the absence of rugosities on the palate of *Pithrocanthtropus robustus;* 4, the great length of the molar in *Gigantopithecus* and the fact that it exhibits no sign of any reduction; 5, the dominance of the trigonid breadth over the talonid in the same specimen. It is interesting to note that the *Meganthropus* mandible, which must certainly be regarded as the most primitive hominid mandible so far discovered, has no specific anthropoid feature except the arrangement of the molar rows in more parallel lines.

Neither gigantism nor the tendency toward its development can be regarded as a specifically anthropoid character. Gorilla apparently has this tendency as does orang-utan, but chimpanzee does not. Nor does the massiveness of the cranial bones fall into this category, for none of the living anthropoids possesses this peculiarity.

On the other hand, certain specific hominid features are common to *Pithro-canthropus robustus, Meganthropus,* and *Gigantopithecus.* Of these, the most prominent are the pattern of the cusps of the molar teeth, the shortness of the jaw, and the character of the canine group in the first two types. In addition to these characters, the *Meganthropus* mandible displays the typical hominid form of the lingual surface of the symphyseal region, a very pronounced incisura submentalis which is never found in anthropoids, and the typical hominid location of the mental foramen.

To these anthropoid and hominid characteristics should be added those that are intermediate and represent an approach from the hominid line toward the general anthropoid stock. In *Meganthropus* the small angle of inclination of the front of the mandible, and the limited remnants of the cingulum belong, among others, to this group of characteristics. They testify to the common origin of the hominid and anthropoid which is already obvious, but they do not present any evidence as to where the diverging branches of this common stock met. *Meganthropus* was certainly already in the human line, as was *Gigantopithecus*. Yet neither of these two hominid types brings the human line closer to any of the three living anthropoids. Nor did analysis of the tooth pattern of *Gigantopithecus* and *Meganthropus* offer a definite clue as to which of the various fossil types of anthropoids—*Dryopithicus, Sivapithicus,* etc.—is the most closely related form. There is no closer approach to any one of these. *Dryopithicus giganteus* is gigantic when its lower molar is compared with the same tooth of other *Dryopithicus* forms, but its size does not exceed that of the recent male gorilla, and its pattern is nearer to that of gorilla or chimpanzee than to that of the *Gigantopithecus molar*. The same is true of other smaller forms, such as *Dryopithicus darwini* which O. Abel considered the most human like primate tooth ever found. *Sivapithecus middlemissi* exhibits a "certain resemblance" to *Gigantopithecus* according to von Koenigswald but the resemblance is no greater than that of the aforementioned forms. The mandible of *Meganthropus* differs from the mandible of *Dryopithicus* and *Sivapithicus; Meganthropus* has hominid and the latter have anthropoid characteristics. All three forms agree in the thickness of the symphysis, but the formation of the entire buccal surface follows the anthropoid pattern in *Dryopithicus and Sivapithicus*. Only a single feature occurring in *Dryopithicus fontani* which A. Smith Woodward described from the Lérida specimen is reminiscent of the condition in the *Meganthropus* mandible. This is the location of the digastric fossa which occupies the buccal side instead of the lower margin of the mandible. However, the formation of a special median recessus, the lateral walls of which are occupied by the digastric fossae of either side, is a unique structure of *Meganthropus* which is not found in any other anthropoid or hominid, recent or fossil. It seems to represent a specific, primitive, hominid peculiarity which disappeared early in the course of human evolution. The same seems to be true, at least to a certain extent, of the incisura submentalis.

Though our search for anthropoid relatives of the newly discovered early hominids seems negative as far as the *Dryopithicus* group and related forms are concerned, it is more promising when the South African Australopithecinae are considered. In contrast to the other group, the Australopithecinae have the short muzzle and the homomorphic canine group in common with the hominids, and, therefore, also with *Meganthropus*.

## Chapter 9

*Ian Tattersall*

*In* The Fossil Trail *(1995; used by permission of Oxford University Press), Tattersall discusses diversity among hominids.*

Given the wealth of interpretations available, it's a tall order to encapsulate the state of play in paleoanthropology today. But if you've read this far, you're already familiar with the most important constituents of the human fossil record and with the principal interpretations of them that have been made. What I can most usefully do by the way of summary is, I think, to follow my own advice and to review the evidence for the past of our species by advancing from the simple to the complex: from a cladogram, to a phylogenetic tree, and finally to a brief scenario of our evolution. But first of all, we need to look at the most basic level of analysis of all: species diversity in the human fossil record. After all, before you can begin to work out the relationships between extinct species in the human family, you have to have a reliable idea of how many such species there are among the hundreds of hominid fossils known.

We've already seen that this has not traditionally been anthropologists' strong suit, and that estimates of the number of extinct hominid species vary widely. There exists no recent minimalist appraisal of the number of australopithecine species, but I would guess that since the demise of the single species hypothesis not many (if any) paleoanthropologists would recognize fewer than three or perhaps four: *A. afarensis, A. africanus, A. robustus,* and (perhaps) *A. boisei.* In the genus *Homo,* by contrast, the minimalists would accept a mere two species: *H. habilis* and *H. sapiens.* In essence, this would reduce the number of species lying between us and our earliest known bipedal ancestors to only two: a ludicrously inadequate figure given what we know about the amounts of bony anatomical difference that are typically found among closely related living species.

A more mainstream assessment would add to the genus *Homo* at least one more species, *erectus,* plus the informal categories of "archaic *Homo sapiens*" and the Neanderthals. My own preference, though—and, I think, that of a growing number of colleagues—would be to recognize at least three genera in the human family, embracing perhaps a dozen species. In this view, the genus *Australopithecus* accommodates only *A. afarensis* and *A. africanus,* the "robust" group being placed in its own genus *Paranthropus.* (I should probably remark at this point that if *afarensis* is truly a "stem" species that gave rise to *africanus* on the one hand and to the species of *Paranthropus* on the other, it would, strictly speaking, require its own separate generic designation. In practice, however, paleoanthropology is not quite ready to contemplate this possibility; and since the reidentification of the growing number of fossils usually allocated to *A. afarensis* promises to be one of the major debating points in the field over the coming years, any concrete suggestion to this effect would anyway be more than a little premature.) Within the genus *Paranthropus,* at least three species are clearly diagnosable as distinct: *P. robustus, P. boisei* and *P. aethiopicus.* Some paleoanthropologists would even squeeze in a fourth, *P. crassidens,* in the probably accurate belief that the robusts from Kromdraai and Swartkrans represent different species. Whether *aethiopicus* is the appropriate name for the species containing the "Black Skull" is a debatable point, but the current conspiracy of silence on that matter is clearly desirable and one hopes that it will be maintained.

The plot thickens further as we approach the genus *Homo,* largely because there is no clearly evident reason why it should include such forms as the gracile fossils from the lower levels of Olduvai. As we've seen, the Olduvai remains were initially allocated to our genus because of presumed stone tool making, a fractional increase in brain size relative to *Australopithecus,* and, perhaps above all, because of Louis Leakey's desire to justify his long-standing belief in the ancientness of *Homo.* In no other group of mammals would such considerations be justification for grouping species as unlike as *habilis* and *sapiens* in the same genus; and even though the taxonomic game seems doomed forever to be played in Hominidae by its own distinctive set of rules, the sheer primitiveness of the postcranial skeleton of the recently discovered Olduvai Hominid 62 should be sufficient to make paleoanthropologists think again about genus-level diversity within Hominidae. Alas, however, they almost certainty won't, so we must continue to live with our curiously inflated concept of the genus Homo. This being the case, how many species of it do we know?

For the moment there is no well-argued alternative to Bernard Wood's conclusion that all of the gracile Olduvai fossils are allocable to the species *Homo habilis,* along with such specimens as the ER 1813 cranium from Koobi Fora and from Sterkfontein. So, provisionally, it's reasonable to accept it. It's even more reasonable to concur with Wood that specimens like the Koobi Fora cranium ER 1470 are quite distinctive and should be placed in the separate species *Homo rudolfensis.* Hard on the heels of these species comes *Homo ergaster,* which, as the "Turkana Boy" attests, is postcranially as well as cranially altogether more modern. Fred Grine has recently reconstructed the Swartkrans SK 847 partial face, long considered to be a close match for the Koobi Fora *Homo ergaster* specimen ER 3733, and has been able to demonstrate that certain differences exist between the two. Whether or not this means that a separate species related to East African *ergaster* lived in South Africa at about the same time, it's a bit early to say for sure. On the other hand, what is very clear, at least to me, is that *H. ergaster* is not the same thing as the classic *Homo erectus* from eastern Asia. A related species, yes; but the African form is more primitive than the Asian one, and it deserves recognition as a distinct species. Later in time, we begin to encounter distinctive early human types that have long been distinguished by informal names, and that are due by now for formal recognition. "Archaic *Homo sapiens,*" as exemplified by such specimens as Bodo and Arago, deserves its own specific epithet, probably *Homo heidelbergensis,* while there can be no doubt at all as to the correct species name for the Neanderthals: *Homo neanderthaleensis.* All humans living today, and all fossil humans who resembled us, are *Homo sapiens.*

*Donald Johanson*

*In this excerpt from "Human Origins" (1996; used by permission of the publisher), Donald Johanson discusses some recently discovered fossils and what he calls the "New Paleoanthropology."*

In 1959, after attention had long been focused on South Africa, Mary and Louis Leakey startled the world with the discovery of a skull from Olduvai Gorge in Tanzania, dated to approximately 1.8 million years ago. This find, initially called *Zinjanthropus* (East Africa Man), and now assigned to *Australopithecus boisei,* dramatically shifted the arena of field exploration from southern to eastern Africa. Expeditions were sent to East Africa in the hope that additional hominid sites would be located in the Great Rift Valley.

The discovery of "Zinj" also heralded the beginnings of the New Paleoanthropology. While exploration and discovery continue to play a pivotal role, the implementation of an integrated, multidisciplinary approach to reconstructing our past characterizes the field today. Paleontologists, archaeologists, anthropologists, geochronologists, palynologists, anatomists, and a cadre of geologists all work very closely together to pursue knowledge about human origins and enhance our understanding of our place in nature.

Through a carefully articulated and targeted approach to paleoanthropology, a number of intriguing discoveries have now, at long last, begun to push back our understanding of hominid origins beyond 4.0 million years. Fossil finds from Ethiopia and Kenya provide possible ancestors for what had been the oldest known species of hominid, *Australopithecus afarensis,* best represented by the 3.2-million-year-old skeleton affectionately called Lucy.

In the 1970s, very successful international expeditions recovered a remarkable storehouse of hominids from the sites of Hadar in Ethiopia and Laetoli in Tanzania. In 1978 my colleagues and I, after careful scientific evaluation of these hominid fossils, dated to between 3 and 3.5 million years ago, described a new species: *A. afarensis.* Most remarkable about this species is the fascinating combination of ape-like and human-like features in their bony anatomy. A small-brained skull bearing ape-like features such as a projecting face, and primitive teeth and jaws, sat atop a post-cranial skeleton that was designed for terrestrial, bipedal locomotion. Bipedalism is a uniquely human feature; because it was documented in a skeleton that still bears the undeniable stamp of ape ancestry in the skull, we can definitively conclude that upright walking preceded changes in the skulls of our ancestors.

There are still traces of an arboreal ancestry in the long arms and slightly curved hand and foot bones of *A. afarensis,* but the overall construction of the foot, ankle, hip, and knee is commensurate with upright walking. Proof of the locomotor abilities of *A. afarensis* came from the stunning hominid footprint trail left at Laetoli in a volcanic ash dated to roughly 3.5 million years ago. Detailed inspection of these footprints confirms that *A. afarensis* did not have a divergent great toe, a climbing adaptation seen in all species of non-hominid primates. These feet were adapted to walking on the ground with evidence of toe-off, strong heel strike, and even a longitudinal arch to the foot.

Until last year, *A. afarensis* was the oldest known hominid species, with fragments from other sites in the Great Rift Valley suggesting that the earliest known occurrence of the taxon is about 3.8 million years ago. In September 1994, however, Dr. Tim White and his team reported 4.4-million-year-old hominid finds from Aramis, a site situated roughly fifty miles south of Hadar. Consisting mostly of teeth, these finds were first assigned to *Australopithecus ramidus,* but more recently they have been allocated to a new genus: *Ardipithecus ramidus.*

Justification for recognizing a new species comes from the host of anatomical features in the teeth that are very ape-like. The first lower milk molar, for example, is virtually impossible to distinguish from that of a modern chimpanzee. The dental enamel is thin, as in chimps and gorillas, as opposed to all other known hominids that have thick enamel, like ourselves.

Whether *ramidus* was a biped is still an open question. Portions of the base of a skull do suggest, however, that the foramen magnum, where the spinal cord exits the skull, opens downward and not backward as in quadrupeds. We will know a great deal more of this species in a few years because a skeleton with bones from the arm, leg, foot, hand, pelvis, backbone, and rib cage has been recovered. The discoverers currently interpret *Ardipithecus ramidus* as the oldest known hominid ancestral to all later hominids, including *A. afarensis*.

Fast on the heels of the *ramidus* announcement, Dr. Meave Leakey and her colleagues in August 1995 reported on hominids from the Lake Turkana region in northern Kenya. These finds, predominantly from the site of Kanapoi, dated to roughly 4.2 million years ago, just slightly younger than those from Aramis.

The hominid finds from Kanapoi, mostly teeth and jaws, show strong similarities with those assigned to *A. afarensis*. The teeth are thick enamelled, and the jaws have parallel-sided tooth rows, as well as many other features seen in *A. afarensis*. However, and perhaps most importantly, the Kanapoi finds are slightly more primitive than those of *A. afarensis*. For example, the mandibular first premolar, the tooth immediately behind the canine, is very asymmetrical and more ape-like than in *afarensis;* the upper molars are wider in front than in back; and the bony shelf in the mandible, just behind the incisors, is long and steeply inclined. These and other anatomical features prompted Dr. Meave Leakey and her co-workers to place these specimens in a new species: *Australopithecus anamensis*.

Portions of a tibia, the shin bone, also were found at Kanapoi, and anatomical features convincingly argue for bipedality. However, the specimen may be closer in age to the Laetoli footprints and therefore does not provide older evidence for bipedalism. The evidence for bipedalism at Laetoli should be taken as the oldest known, realizing that the origins of this hallmark of human behavior extend much further back in time. Postcranial bones are much more difficult to assign to a species, and the tibia from Kanapoi might just belong to *A. afarensis*.

Dr. Meave Leakey considers *A. anamensis* a prime candidate to be a direct ancestor to *A. afarensis*. This is largely because many features in the Kanapoi hominids are similar, yet slightly more primitive, than those seen in *A. afarensis*. The new perspective on early hominid species and relationships offered by the Kanapoi finds has prompted, at least at this time, a reconsideration of the evolutionary position of *ramidus*.

Let me explain. Because *anamensis* is nearly as old as *ramidus* and has anatomical features more similar to those of *afarensis* than to those seen in *ramidus, anamensis* is therefore a better candidate for ancestorship to Lucy. If *ramidus,* with its chimpanzee-like teeth, is too primitive to be an ancestor to later hominids, then where does it fit on the human evolutionary tree?

A suggestion proffered by Meave Leakey places *ramidus* on another lineage, not ancestral to *anamensis* and *afarensis*. Perhaps it belongs to a sister group, a side branch that went extinct. If *ramidus* were an ancestor to *anamensis,* some anatomical changes, such as an increase in enamel thickness, would have had to occur over a relatively short period of 200,000 years, roughly 10,000 generations. This sort of change is not impossible.

At the moment the evolutionary relationship of *ramidus* to later hominids and/or apes is impossible to assess. We know that most of a skeleton of *ramidus* exists, and after careful study of the finds, the position of *ramidus* on the family tree should become clearer.

These are fascinating times in paleoanthropology, and debate about the significance of the new finds from Kanapoi, but especially those from Aramis, is certain to heat up. If any of these early species are found to overlap in time, which at the moment they do not, there is a chance that the human family tree will become more bushy, making decisions about ancestor/descendant relationships even more complex.

Looking back in time, it is clear that as we find more ancient hominids, they resemble, more and more, our ape relatives. Darwin continues to be proven correct with each and every find. Furthermore, it appears that with these new finds we are rapidly getting closer and closer to the common ancestor of African apes and hominids. Nothing could be more exciting! Those who have studied blood proteins and DNA in modern humans and African apes, given their close similarities, suggested nearly thirty years ago that we shared a recent common ancestor with the African apes, one that lived 5 to 8 million years ago rather than 15 to 20 million years ago. They may be correct.

Looking forward from the Kanapoi/Aramis finds, we see *A. afarensis* as the last common ancestor for a number of diverse hominid lineages that appeared in the 2- to 3-million-year time interval. Some of these lineages continued in the *Australopithecus* tradition, giving rise to *A. africanus, A. robustus, A. boisei,* and probably other species. But another, hitherto poorly represented lineage gave rise to a new genus, *Homo,* which probably first appeared around 2.5 million years ago. Rather than adapting to specific diets by developing large crushing and grinding teeth, massive jaws, and powerful chewing muscles, *Homo* appears to signal a new evolutionary adaptation. This adaption was characterized by increasing brain size and complexity that may have left its first signature in the fossil record with the first stone tools at 2.5 million years ago.

It is hard to think of a more exciting time to be involved with the pursuit of the past. Paleoanthropology is maturing quickly, and it is certain that as we move into the next millennium our view of human origins will be substantially enhanced.

Knowing our origins teaches us about our place in nature. This enlightenment about our place in nature we hope will enhance our sense of responsibility to the world around us. Let us also hope that we can use the knowledge left behind in the fossilized remains of our ancestors to develop a more mature perspective on our role in preparing a successful future for all life on this planet.

## Chapter 10

*Scopes Trial transcript, 1925*

*Early in the trial the two sides set up their respective positions. The first two selections are from the defense and prosecution respectively. It is followed by a brief cross-examination of young Howard Morgan by a prosecutor and by Clarence Darrow.*

Darrow's co-council Dudley Malone states the theory of the Defense:

The purpose of the defense will be to set before you all available facts and information from every branch of science to aid you in forming an opinion of what evolution is, and of what value to progress and comfort is the theory of evolution, for you are the judge of the law and the facts, and the defense wishes to aid you in every way to intelligent opinion. The defense denies that it is part of any movement or conspiracy on the part of scientists to destroy the authority of Christianity or the Bible. The defense denies that any such conspiracy exists except in the mind and purpose of the evangelical leader of the prosecution. The defense maintains that the book of Genesis is in part a hymn, in part an allegory and work of religious interpretations written by men who believe that the earth was flat and whose authority cannot be accepted to control the teachings of science in our schools. The narrow purpose of the defense is to establish the innocence of the defendant Scopes. The broad purpose of the defense will be to prove that the Bible is a work of religious aspiration and rules of conduct which must be kept in the field of theology. The defense maintains that there is no more justification for imposing the conflicting views of the Bible on courses of biology than there would be for imposing the views of biologists on courses of comparative religion. We maintain that science and religion embrace two separate and distinct fields of thought and learning. We remember that Jesus said: "Render unto Ceasar the things that are Caesar's and unto God the things that are God's."

Mr. McKenzie, for the Prosecution, attacks the defense's theory:

This is wholly improper, argumentative. It is not a statement as to what the issues are. Your honor has already held that this act is constitutional, it being the law of the land, there is but one issue before this court and jury, and that is, did the defendant violate the statute. That statute interprets itself, and says that whenever a man teaches that man descended from a lower order of animals as contradistinguished from the record of the creation of man as given by the word of God, that he is guilty. Does the proof show that he did that, that is the only issue, if it please the honorable court, before this jury. My friend is talking about a theory of evolution that it took him two years to write, that speech (laughter). That is not proper, if your honor please, if it is proper, it would be like a couple of gentlemen over in my country, where they were engaged and were trying a lawsuit before a justice of the peace, and they had a large number of witnesses. Finally one lawyer said, "let us have a conference," and they went out to confer, and they came back in and said, "if your honor please, the witnesses in this case, some of them are not very well, others are awfully ignorant, and we have just agreed among ourselves to dispense with the evidence and argue the case." That is what my good friend Malone wants to do. (Loud laughter and officer rapping for order.)

Testimony of a student of Scopes:

Direct examination by General Stewart: Q—Your name is Howard Morgan? A—Yes, sir. Q—You are Mr. Luke Morgan's son? A—Yes, Sir. . . . Q—Your Father is in the bank here, Dayton Bank and Trust company? A—Yes, sir. Q—How old are you? A—14 years. Q—Did you attend school here at Dayton last year? A—Yes, sir. Q—What school? A—High School. Q—Central High School? A—Yes, sir. Q—Did you study anything under Prof. Scopes? A—Yes sir. Q—Did you study this book, General Science? A—Yes, sir. . . . Q—Were you studying that book in April of this year, Howard? A—Yes, sir. Q—Did Prof. Scopes teach it to you? A—Yes, sir. Q—When did you complete the book? A—Latter part of April. Q—When was school out? A—First or second of May. Q—You studied it then up to a week or so before school was out? A—Yes, sir. Q—Now, you say you were studying this book in April; how did Prof. Scopes teach that book to you? I mean by that did he ask you questions and you answered them or did he give you lectures, or both? Just explain to the jury here now, these gentleman here in front of you, how he taught the books to you. A—Well, sometimes he would ask us questions and then he would lecture to us on different subjects in the book. Q—Sometimes he asked you questions and sometimes lectured to you on different subjects in the book? A—Yes, sir. Q—Did he ever undertake to teach you anything about evolution? A—Yes, sir. . . . Q—Just state in your own words, Howard, what he taught you and when it was. A—It was along about the 2d of April. Q—Of this year? A—Yes, sir; of this year. He said that the earth was once a hot molten mass too hot for plant or animal life to exist upon it; in the sea the earth cooled off; there was a little germ of one cell organism formed, and this organism kept evolving until it got to be a pretty good-sized animal, and then came on to be a land animal and it kept on evolving, and from this was man. Q—Let me repeat that; perhaps a little stronger than you. If I don't get it right, you correct me. Hays—Go to the head of the class. . . . Stewart—I ask you further, Howard, how did he classify man with reference to other animals; what did he say about them? A—Well, the book and he both classified man along with cats and dogs, cows, horses, monkeys, lions, horses and all that. Q—What did he say they were? A—Mammals. Q—Classified them along with dogs, cats, horses, monkeys and cows? A—Yes, sir.

Cross examination by Mr. Darrow: Q—Let's see, your name is what? A—Howard Morgan. Q—Now, Howard, what do you mean by classify? A—Well, it means classify these animals we mentioned, that men were just the same as them, in other words. Q—He didn't say a cat was the same as a man? A—No, sir: he said man had a reasoning power; that these animals did not. Q—There is some doubt about that, but that is what he said, is it? (Laughter in the courtroom.) The Court—Order. Stewart—With some men. Darrow—A great many. Q—Now, Howard, he said they were all mammals, didn't he? A—Yes, sir. Q—Did he tell you what a mammal was, or don't you remember? A—Well, he just said these animals were mammals and man was a mammal. Q—No; but did he tell you what distinguished mammals from other animals? A—I don't remember. Q—If he did, you have forgotten it? Didn't he say that mammals were those beings which suckled their young? A—I don't remember about that. Q—You don't remember? A—No. Q—Do you remember what he said that made any animal a mammal, what it was or don't you remember? A—I don't remember. Q—But he said that all of them were mammals? A—All what? Q—Dogs and horses, monkeys, cows, man, whales, I cannot state all of them, but he said all of those were mammals? A—Yes, sir; but I don't know about the whales; he said all those other ones. (Laughter in the courtroom.) The Court—Order. . . . Q—Well, did he tell you anything else that was wicked? A—No, not that I remember. . . . Q—Now, he said the earth was once a molten mass of liquid, didn't he? A—Yes. Q—By molten, you understand melted? A—Yes, sir. Q—After that, it got cooled enough and the soil came, that plants grew; is that right? A—Yes, sir, yes, sir. Q—And that the first life was in the sea. Q—And that it developed into life on the land? A—Yes, sir. Q—And finally into the highest organism which is known to man? A—Yes, sir. Q—Now, that is about what he taught you? It has not hurt you any, has it? A—No, sir. Darrow—That's all.

*Harun Yahya*

*In* The Evolution Deceit: The Scientific Collapse of Darwinism and Its Ideological Background *(1999; used with permission of the author), Yahya takes on the age-old creationist target of the protobird* Archaeopteryx.

All of these bring another question to the mind: even if we suppose this impossible story to be true, then why are the evolutionists unable to find any "half-winged" or "single-winged" fossils to back up their story?

*Another Alleged Transitional Form: Archæopteryx*

Evolutionists pronounce the name of one single creature in response. This is the fossil of a bird called Archæopteryx, one of the most widely-known so-called transitional forms among the very few that evolutionists still defend. Archæopteryx, the so-called ancestor of modern birds according to evolutionists, lived approximately 150 million years ago. The theory holds that some small dinosaurs, such as Velociraptors or Dromeosaurs, evolved by acquiring wings and then starting to fly. Thus, Archæopteryx is assumed to be a transitional form that branched off from its dinosaur ancestors and started to fly for the first time.

However, the latest studies of Archæopteryx fossils indicate that this creature is absolutely not a transitional form, but an extinct species of bird, having some insignificant differences from modern birds.

The thesis that Archæopteryx was a "half-bird" that could not fly perfectly was popular among evolutionist circles until not long ago. The absence of a sternum (breastbone) in this creature was held up as the most important evidence that this bird could not fly properly. (The sternum is a bone found under the thorax to which the muscles required for flight are attached. In our day, this breastbone is observed in all flying and non-flying birds, and even in bats, a flying mammal which belongs to a very different family.)

However, the seventh Archæopteryx fossil, which was found in 1992, caused great astonishment among evolutionists. The reason was that in this recently discovered fossil, the breastbone that was long assumed by evolutionists to be missing was discovered to have existed after all. This fossil was described in Nature magazine as follows:

The recently discovered seventh specimen of the Archaeopteryx preserves a partial, rectangular sternum, long suspected but never previously documented. This attests to its strong flight muscles.

This discovery invalidated the mainstay of the claims that Archæopteryx was a half-bird that could not fly properly.

Moreover, the structure of the bird's feathers became one of the most important pieces of evidence confirming that Archæopteryx was a flying bird in the real sense. The asymmetric feather structure of Archæopteryx is indistinguishable from that of modern birds, and indicates that it could fly perfectly well. As the eminent paleontologist Carl O. Dunbar states, "because of its feathers [Archæopteryx is] distinctly to be classed as a bird."

Another fact that was revealed by the structure of Archæopteryx's feathers was its warm-blooded metabolism. As was discussed above, reptiles and dinosaurs are cold-blooded animals whose body heat fluctuates with the temperature of their environment, rather than being homeostatically regulated. A very important function of the feathers on birds is the maintenance of a constant body temperature. The fact that Archæopteryx had feathers showed that it was a real, warm-blooded bird that needed to regulate its body heat, in contrast to dinosaurs.

*Speculations of Evolutionists: The Teeth and Claws of Archæopteryx*

Two important points evolutionist biologists rely on when claiming Archæopteryx was a transitional form, are the claws on its wings and its teeth.

It is true that Archæopteryx had claws on its wings and teeth in its mouth, but these traits do not imply that the creature bore any kind of relationship to reptiles. Besides, two bird species living today, Taouraco and Hoatzin, have claws which allow them to hold onto branches. These creatures are fully birds, with no reptilian characteristics. That is why it is completely groundless to assert that Archæopteryx is a transitional form just because of the claws on its wings.

Neither do the teeth in Archæopteryx's beak imply that it is a transitional form. Evolutionists make a purposeful trickery by saying that these teeth are reptile characteristics, since teeth are not a typical feature of reptiles. Today, some reptiles have teeth while others do not. Moreover, Archæopteryx is not the only bird species to possess teeth. It is true that there are no toothed birds in existence today, but when we look at the fossil record, we see that both during the time of Archæopteryx and afterwards, and even until fairly recently, a distinct bird genus existed that could be categorised as "birds with teeth."

The most important point is that the tooth structure of Archæopteryx and other birds with teeth is totally different from that of their alleged ancestors, the dinosaurs. The well-known ornithologists L. D. Martin, J. D. Steward, and K. N. Whetstone observed that Archæopteryx and other similar birds have teeth with flat-topped surfaces and large roots. Yet the teeth of theropod dinosaurs, the alleged ancestors of these birds, are protuberant like saws and have narrow roots.

These researchers also compared the wrist bones of Archæopteryx and their alleged ancestors, the dinosaurs, and observed no similarity between them.

Studies by anatomists like S. Tarsitano, M. K. Hecht, and A. D. Walker have revealed that some of the similarities that John Ostrom and others have seen between Archæopteryx and dinosaurs were in reality misinterpretations.

All these findings indicate that Archæopteryx was not a transitional link but only a bird that fell into a category that can be called "toothed birds."

# Index